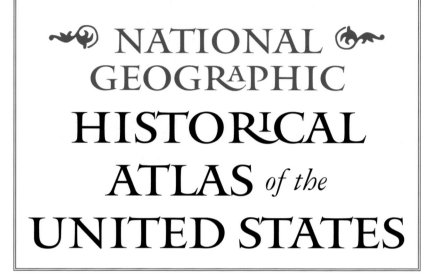

NATIONAL GEOGRAPHIC

HISTORICAL
ATLAS *of the*
UNITED STATES

# NATIONAL GEOGRAPHIC
# HISTORICAL
# ATLAS *of the*
# UNITED STATES

TEXT ADAPTED BY RON FISHER

NATIONAL GEOGRAPHIC

WASHINGTON, DC

# CONTENTS

INTRODUCTION BY JOHN CARLIN, ARCHIVIST OF THE UNITED STATES 6

## *An Age of Rediscovery* 8
## 1400-1749

*The First Americans 12 • The Vikings 14 • The First Arrivals 16 •
Native Claims on the Soil 18 • The First Settlers 20 • The Missionaries 22*

## *New People in a New World* 24
## 1750-1799

*The Dispersal of Slaves 28 • The First Colonies 30 • The Revolutionary War 32 •
Declaration of Independence 36 • Development of the Political Parties 38 • The Cotton Gin 40*

## *Forming a More Perfect Union* 42
## 1800-1849

*The American Press 46 • The Louisiana Purchase 48 • Lewis and Clark 50 • Steam and the Mississippi 54 •
The Industrial Revolution 58 • Westward Expansion 60 • The Trail of Tears 62 • The Texas Revolution 64 •
Remembering the Alamo 66 • Parceling Out the Land 68 • Manifest Destiny 70 • The Spread of Religion 72 • The Rush for Gold 74*

## *A Nation Comes of Age* 76
## 1850-1899

*The Underground Railroad 80 • A Standard Education 82 • The Pony Express 84 • The Civil War 86 •
Emancipation Proclamation 90 • Oil and Oilmen 92 • Capturing America on Film 94 • The Reconstruction 96 •
The Railroads 98 • Home on the Range 100 • Forging the Future 102 • Organizing the Workers 104 • The Lawless Land 106 •
National Parks 108 • The Telegraph and Telephone 110 • Manufacturing and Marketing 112 • Putting the Rivers to Work 114*

## *A Nation at War* 116
## 1900-1949

*The Pioneers of Aviation 120 • Social Reform 124 • The Automobile 126 • Henry Ford and Co. 130 • The Revolution in Mexico 132 •
World War One 134 • Women Go to the Polls 138 • Going Dry 140 • Life in Menlo Park 142 • Pictures That Talk 144 •
Waves of New Americans 146 • Riding the Airwaves 150 • Bigger, Taller, Longer 152 • The Stock Market Crash 154 •
The New Deal 156 • On the Reservation 158 • The Superheroes 160 • Feeding the Nation 162 • Spending the Resources 164 •
World War Two 166 • The Manhattan Project 170 • Integrating Sports 172*

## *Decades of Change* 174
## 1950-PRESENT

*The Small Screen 178 • The Major Leagues 180 • Stemming the Communist Tide 182 • The Fight for Civil Rights 184 •
Tragedy and Loss 188 • The War in Southeast Asia 190 • The First Small Steps 194 • Commonplace Miracles 198 •
The New Global Tensions 200 • The American Hostages 202 • Natural Disasters 204 • Misbehaving in America 206 •
The Gulf War 208 • The Internet Takes Off 210 • The 2000 Presidential Election 212 • Fanatics and Zealots 214 •
A Second War in the Gulf 216 • Higher, Deeper, Farther 218*

THE AMERICAN PRESIDENTS 220
THE ELECTORAL COLLEGE: STATES' VOTES 221
STATE FLAGS AND FACTS 222
MAP APPENDIX 224
INDEX, PHOTO CREDITS, AND COPYRIGHT 238

# INTRODUCTION

## *John Carlin,*
### *Archivist of the United States*

The National Archives and Records Administration is our nation's record keeper, and as Archivist of the United States, I have the great honor to oversee a collection of the documents, photographs, video and audiotapes, and other records that have been witness to American history as it was made. These billions of records tell the first-hand stories of our both our triumphs and tragedies as a nation and illustrate the passion, genius, and spirit that have shaped America since its beginning.

At the National Archives we work to preserve and provide access to the records of the federal government for the American people. For without these records, we would not know or be able to understand our past. We would not be able to hold our elected officials accountable for their actions. We would not be able to claim our rights and entitlements. Without these records, we would no longer live in a democracy.

Among the most famous records we care for are the Declaration of Independence, the Constitution, and the Bill of Rights—collectively known as the Charters of Freedom. Other documents, such as Eli Whitney's patent for the cotton gin, the Homestead Act, the Emancipation Proclamation, and the Civil Rights Act of 1964, to name a few, have helped mold our national character and reflect our changing culture. Still other records such as the papers of Presidential administrations, World War II battle plans, or routine files from the State Department capture glimpses of history in the making and chronicle the actions of our government.

However, our history is not only found in constitutional amendments, Presidential proclamations, and well-known historical documents. It is also found in the veteran's records of the brave men and women who have fought for our country; in the immigration records of the people whose dreams have shaped our country; and the census records that enumerate each individual, family, and community that made up our country at a given point in time.

Each record that we hold tells a story. Some of these stories changed history, while some quietly resonated in the lives of individuals. But each story is significant as they all weave together to form the ever-growing tapestry that is our national history. To remember the stories and details of our history is honorable work, and this atlas does such work.

The pages of this book represent more than five hundred years of the history of our nation. Each page unfolds a new event, a new piece of the masterwork that is the United States as we know it today. As a collection it captures all of our country's pivotal moments of decision. It shows a nation at war, unfortunately several times including once with itself, a nation struggling to have its existence recognized, and after this hard-won recognition, a nation struggling with growing pains as it inches across the continent. In its later pages, this book bears evidence of a maturing nation measuring its place in a world order. Having satisfactorily set itself a course, it begins to test how this course will be received.

There is no doubt that we can see the journey of the United States illustrated as

Americans declare their independence, rally for their rights, walk on the moon, and cast their votes in Presidential elections. But we also find America in the simplicity in which people live out their lives. We see it in the pages of comic books, the sounds of radio performers, the once unheard of inventions we now use everyday, and of course on baseball diamonds and playing fields across the country.

In the history of America, there are Abraham Lincolns, Martin Luther Kings, Thomas Edisons, Neil Armstrongs, and Babe Ruths—these are the Americans we all know. But there are even more Americans whose names we can't recall— the colonists, homesteaders, immigrants, farmers, shopkeepers, riveters, and veterans who pieced together the seams of the story of the United States.

Like the records held in the National Archives, this book tells the collective history of the people of the United States. Each chapter of history builds upon those before it, as each generation of Americans learns from the sacrifices, successes, and lessons of those that came before. This

atlas brings to life the events that solidify history and perpetuate its telling.

Every day we make history, as our government does the work of a powerful democracy, and we each live our individual lives. Each day brings changes that will shape the path of the United States for generations to come. And in the future, the days we live now will be as rich in history as the book you now hold in your hands.

PAGES 2–3: *A wagon train of homesteaders, ca 1885, migrates westward.*

PAGE 4: *Somber Lady Liberty marches hopefully into the future in this Currier & Ives lithograph, produced around 1860.*

OPPOSITE: *General Philip Sheridan, far left, and George Custer, far right, played pivotal roles in both the Civil War and the Indian wars. Lt. Col. Custer would famously be killed at the Battle of Little Bighorn.* (© HULTON/GETTY)

ABOVE: *Teddy Roosevelt, later the 26th President of the U.S., stands proudly with his troops—"Teddy's Colts"—atop San Juan Hill in Cuba. Their successful charge captured a blockhouse and opened the route to Santiago, assuring American victory in the Spanish-American War.*

## An Age of
## Rediscovery

*North America in 1698, two centuries after
Columbus made landfall.*

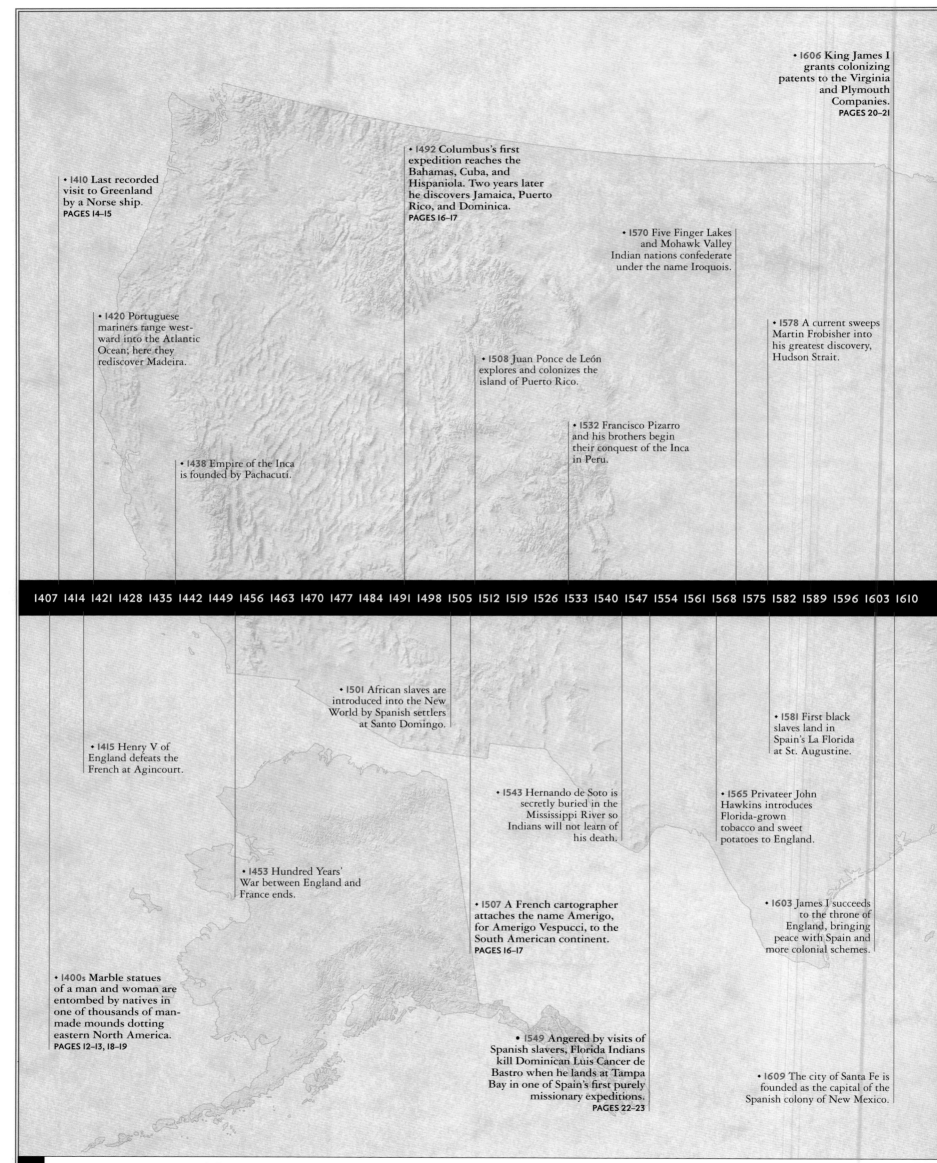

- **1606** King James I grants colonizing patents to the Virginia and Plymouth Companies. **PAGES 20–21**

- **1492** Columbus's first expedition reaches the Bahamas, Cuba, and Hispaniola. Two years later he discovers Jamaica, Puerto Rico, and Dominica. **PAGES 16–17**

- **1410** Last recorded visit to Greenland by a Norse ship. **PAGES 14–15**

- **1570** Five Finger Lakes and Mohawk Valley Indian nations confederate under the name Iroquois.

- **1420** Portuguese mariners range westward into the Atlantic Ocean; here they rediscover Madeira.

- **1578** A current sweeps Martin Frobisher into his greatest discovery, Hudson Strait.

- **1508** Juan Ponce de León explores and colonizes the island of Puerto Rico.

- **1532** Francisco Pizarro and his brothers begin their conquest of the Inca in Peru.

- **1438** Empire of the Inca is founded by Pachacuti.

1407 1414 1421 1428 1435 1442 1449 1456 1463 1470 1477 1484 1491 1498 1505 1512 1519 1526 1533 1540 1547 1554 1561 1568 1575 1582 1589 1596 1603 1610

- **1501** African slaves are introduced into the New World by Spanish settlers at Santo Domingo.

- **1581** First black slaves land in Spain's La Florida at St. Augustine.

- **1415** Henry V of England defeats the French at Agincourt.

- **1543** Hernando de Soto is secretly buried in the Mississippi River so Indians will not learn of his death.

- **1565** Privateer John Hawkins introduces Florida-grown tobacco and sweet potatoes to England.

- **1453** Hundred Years' War between England and France ends.

- **1507** A French cartographer attaches the name Amerigo, for Amerigo Vespucci, to the South American continent. **PAGES 16–17**

- **1603** James I succeeds to the throne of England, bringing peace with Spain and more colonial schemes.

- **1400s** Marble statues of a man and woman are entombed by natives in one of thousands of man-made mounds dotting eastern North America. **PAGES 12–13, 18–19**

- **1549** Angered by visits of Spanish slavers, Florida Indians kill Dominican Luis Cancer de Bastro when he lands at Tampa Bay in one of Spain's first purely missionary expeditions. **PAGES 22–23**

- **1609** The city of Santa Fe is founded as the capital of the Spanish colony of New Mexico.

• 1732 Benjamin Franklin begins publication of *Poor Richard's Almanack,* a collection of moral maxims and practical advice.

• 1620 English settlers disembark at Plymouth, Massachusetts.
PAGES 20–21

• 1718 New Orleans is founded by France as a commercial gateway to the Mississippi River.

• 1692 Witch trials that sentenced 20 New Englanders to death are defended by Cotton Mather in *The Wonders of the Invisible World.*

• 1656 Quakers arrive in Boston, only to be imprisoned, beaten, and deported by the Puritan authorities.

• 1718 Blackbeard, Edward Teach, infamous for piracy on the Carolina coast is hunted down by a British naval force.

• 1622 Public whippings are used to discourage Virginia settlers from picking corn before it is ripened.

1617 1624 1631 1638 1645 1652 1659 1666 1673 1680 1687 1694 1701 1708 1715 1722 1729 1736 1743 1749

• 1679 Fire-ravaged Boston requires houses to be made of stone or brick, with slate or tile roofs.

• 1635 Boston Latin School is the colonies' first public secondary school.

• 1713 Tea is introduced to the American Colonies, where hot chocolate reigned as the most popular nonalcoholic drink.

• 1649 Maryland legislates religious freedom for Roman Catholics and most other Christians.

• 1743 The American Philosophical Society is founded by Benjamin Franklin and others.

• 1613 The Dutch erect a permanent trading post on Manhattan Island.

"THE UNITED STATES THEMSELVES are essentially the greatest poem," wrote Walt Whitman. Its stanzas are expressed in its climate, its people, and its land. The physical continent of North America is enormously varied. East Coast bedrock gives way to Appalachian highlands, which recall the ancient collision of North America, Africa, and Eurasia. Farther inland are the folded, faulted, and metamorphically wrenched rocks of the Superior upland, once scoured by glaciers. The central lowlands give way to the Great Plains. The Rocky Mountains, part of the Americas' spinal cordillera, and the Colorado Plateau, home to grand canyons and towering buttes and mesas, melt into basins and ranges and the Columbia Plateau. The Sierra Nevada and the Cascades edge the western ocean.

It was not an empty continent. The greatest Native American population densities were on the coast of California, around Lake Michigan, and along the Eastern seaboard and in central Florida.

Boundaries between tribal groups were elastic and shifted over the years. European immigration, especially along the East Coast, caused major shifts in the Native American population. Different European nations adopted different policies toward the Indians: The Spaniards tried to convert them to Christianity and relocate them to designated areas; the French were more interested in establishing trade with them; early English legislation prohibited unauthorized confiscation of Indian land, and the Proclamation of 1763 even designated the entire area west of the Appalachians as land belonging to Native Americans.

In 1830 the Indian Removal Act began the long process of coercive relocation and the confiscation of Indian lands. Long before this, however, it was clear that the European settlers had come to stay, and this was their New World—a world ordered and based on European accession of American lands.

**1400–1749** *Saw the addition of no states, but witnessed the influx of the first Europeans to the New World to explore and claim lands.*

# The FIRST AMERICANS

⋙

## Early Native Civilizations

The very first Americans were the paleo-Indians—or the "ancestral" Indians. Several million strong, they populated nearly every corner of the continent, developing societies based on hunting and gathering, farming, fishing, and the nomadic roaming after herds of game.

Their world began to change 10,000 years ago, when the earth warmed and the ice began to retreat. Deserts and plains took over much of the West, grasslands spread across the prairies, and forests blanketed the East. The farming revolution—knowledge of planting and harvesting, especially three important crops: squash, corn, and beans—began in Mexico to the south. It spread eastward, freeing people to develop a more settled existence. This in turn led to the development of new skills and the eventual emergence of the continent's great early civilizations.

Indians of the Northwest Coast were fortunate in their environment: cool coastal rain forest adjacent to food-rich rivers and the ocean. With food not a problem, they developed structured societies with a profound spiritual life rich in artwork and complex rituals.

The first of the true Native American civilizations was apparently the Hohokam, an agricultural community that grew up along the Gila and Salt Rivers in the deserts of the Southwest. The Hohokam began to emerge about 300 B.C., and their men built America's first known irrigation canal and their women produced some of North America's first pottery. They lived in pit houses near their fields and raised two crops a year. Through contact with natives in Mexico they learned to build oval ball courts for their games.

Another culture, the Mogollon, emerged to the east of the Hohokam. They

built pit houses on mesas and grew crops in river valleys. Around A.D. 1000 they began building their houses in apartment-like complexes, hinting at pueblos to come.

Perhaps the most impressive civilization was that of the Anasazi, who came later. They built multifamily pueblos. They devised elaborate irrigation systems and studied the stars from observatories. They

---

## The HAWAIIAN ISLANDS

When Capt. James Cook made landfall on the islands of Hawaii in 1778 the population was perhaps 300,000, descendants of those who had sailed from the Marquises Islands some 1,500 years before. Food was plentiful, the climate was sublime—but they were ruled by a religion that included taboos. It was forbidden for men and women to eat together or for the shadow of a commoner to fall on a chief.

After gaining control of Hawaii, King Kamehameha in 1790 launched a conquest of islands to the west. Within 20 years all were under his rule. "Endless is the good that I have given you to enjoy," he told his people from his deathbed in 1819.

Within six months his successors had overturned traditions and abolished most taboos.

---

never learned to use the wheel, nor did they have beasts of burden, yet they constructed hundreds of miles of roads across the sun-blasted Southwest. Men performed ceremonies, in underground chambers called kivas, to keep track of the seasons and to wheedle rain from the infrequent clouds.

In present-day New Mexico the Anasazi built their most impressive city—Pueblo Bonito, in Chaco Canyon. Most of the people lived in the scores of villages outside the

12-14 Great Houses. The effort required for building such a city was tremendous: Some 200,000 timbers, some weighing 600 pounds and all transported from pine forests 40 miles away, were needed. An average room in Pueblo Bonito took about 100,000 pounds of stone, 33,000 pounds of clay, and 1,000 gallons of water.

In the eastern part of the country, people were settling into villages and being ruled by chiefs by A.D. 500. Two waves rolled across the East: the Aden way of life, which flourished from about 500 to 1 B.C., and the more complex Hopewell culture, which peaked between A.D. 1 and 300. Both cultures crossed linguistic and geographic barriers. Communities learned about each other's crops, pottery, and burial-mound building in trading expeditions. Traders may have been chosen by their tribes or were individual adventurers. Woodland Indians lived in villages of 50 to 70 and sustained themselves by hunting and foraging and cultivating edible seeds and squash.

The mound-building tradition evidently began along the coasts of Georgia and South Carolina and in Florida, where the precursors of earthen burial and temple mounds began to appear after 1000 B.C.

Eventually, thousands of mounds would be built throughout the eastern United States. Hundreds of workers were needed to carry loads of dirt for the platform mounds of the Southeast. They supported temples or rulers' houses and served as focal points of religious and civic life. Cahokia was the largest of the Mississippian settlements, which were named for the Indian farms then beginning to found along the Mississippi River. The largest mound there, Monks Mound, covered 14 acres and was 100 feet tall and 1,000 feet long. It took 22 million cubic feet of soil to build it, an effort comprising 14 different phases over three hundred years. The residence of a great chief stood on its summit: As brother of the sun, he lived as near his sibling as possible. All this building probably contributed to the eventual collapse of Cahokia, as the Indians became exhausted by the effort.

The Mississippian people were accomplished artisans, crafting ceramic bottles, plates, and pans, and sculpting portraits of themselves. Most impressive was their trade network, which reached people all over North America: Trading partners included the nomadic tribes on the Great Plains, the woodland Indians of the Northeast, and other Mississippian tribes up and down the river. They acquired copper from the upper Great Lakes, mica from southern Appalachia, and seashells from tribes on the Gulf of Mexico.

Cahokia was located near the confluence of the Mississippi, Missouri, and Illinois Rivers. At its apex, the city was home to 10,000 residents, but on festival days the population probably grew to 40,000—a population greater than London's at that time.

A hallmark of the Mississippian culture was reliance, for the first time in the East, on farming as the main food source. Corn, beans, and squash were staples. Ritual life reflected the need for abundant crops. One great festival was the annual Green Corn Ceremony, which celebrated the first harvest. Mississippian peoples were keenly territorial and wrested land from one another and dispatched warriors to carry on tribal feuds. By the time

Europeans found the Mississippian centers, they were fatally weakened by drought and intertribal warfare.

The last of the First Americans to arrive on the continent evidently were the Inuit, who reached Alaska thousands of years ago. As they arrived, the climate was improving, and they slowly moved eastward, reaching Greenland. They developed the Thule culture—harpoons, stone lamps, fishhooks, bows and arrows. They domesticated dogs to help carry belongings.

The Thule Inuit were part of a vast but gradual migration of peoples into North America from out of Siberia between 10,000 and 40,000 years ago. With much of the oceans' waters tied up in glaciers, a thousand-mile-wide land bridge linked Siberia with the Alaskan tip of North America. Over the centuries, migrants—who had no notion that they were crossing a bridge—flowed across the North American continent, some to the south to reach, by 9000 B.C., the southernmost tip of South America; others eastward across the top of North America to father the Skraelings who confronted the Vikings. They followed game. Those moving across northern Alaska and Canada were

probably pursuing bowhead whales, creatures expanding their range as the seas warmed. Southern migrants moved across broad grasslands, preying on mammoths, caribou, and giant bison. Sometimes they left archaeological evidence by killing animals mired in mud and swamps.

Archaeologists trace the routes of these paleo-Indians through their artifacts—especially their projectile points. Chipped Clovis points tipped spears throughout the continent by 9200 B.C.; later Folsom points had long flutes along their faces; by 2500 B.C. some Eskimos were using abrasives such as sand in water to grind points from slate; between 3000 and 1200 B.C. hammered copper points appeared.

Over thousands of years, with the Earth warming, some of the migrants' prey died out or migrated, and they stopped their nomadic wanderings and settled into communities that developed farming and trade.

---

BELOW: *Cliff Palace, largest of the Anasazi pueblos, clings to a shelf in Mesa Verde National Park. Built between A.D. 1190 and 1280, it housed perhaps a hundred "ancient ones."*

# The
# VIKINGS

## New Founders Reach the Shores

Only the buzzing of mosquitoes, the perky chirping of birds, and the gentle hiss of surf against the shore broke the silence one day in the year A.D. 1000. Here in the upper right-hand corner of North America the Labrador Current flows along the coast of what would one day be Newfoundland. Icebergs can often be seen, bobbing in the swells, especially in early summer. Inland from the coast is a landscape of bogs, barrens, and stunted forests.

People have lived here for 7,000 years, but today a ship unlike any they've ever seen is approaching. From it a crew of some 30 pale, sinewy men with golden hair peer shoreward. Their leader is Leif Eriksson. We know something of what happened from the ancient Norse sagas, stories that were passed down by word of mouth for centuries, then, beginning in the 1100s, written. The sagas chronicling the journeys of Erik the Red and Bjarni Herjolfsson tell of the landing of the Vikings in North America.

They sailed from Scandinavia, ocean-going pirates who raped and pillaged and colonized large sections of Europe between the 8th and the 11th centuries. Their very name—*vikingr* in Old Norse—meant far-traveler. They may have been urged seaward by overpopulation at home, where they worked largely as peaceful farmers. Once they learned how easily they could dominate their foes, they may have come to love conquest for its own sake. They planted colonies over much of the known world: from England and Ireland to the Seine; from the Orkneys, the Faroes, the Shetlands, the Hebrides to the Iberian Peninsula; even eastward from the Baltic into Russia.

In the 9th century they made landfall on Iceland and in the 10th Greenland. Erik the Red named the frigid island Greenland in an early public relations campaign so that "men would be drawn to go there."

Near their Newfoundland site, one of their number, Tyrkir the German, out exploring, found wild grapes growing in the forest so they called the newly discovered land Vinland. The sagas report, "Nature was so generous here that...no cattle would need any winter fodder, but could graze outdoors." The climate was mild—grass stayed green even in winter—and salmon were plentiful in the streams. Leif and his men

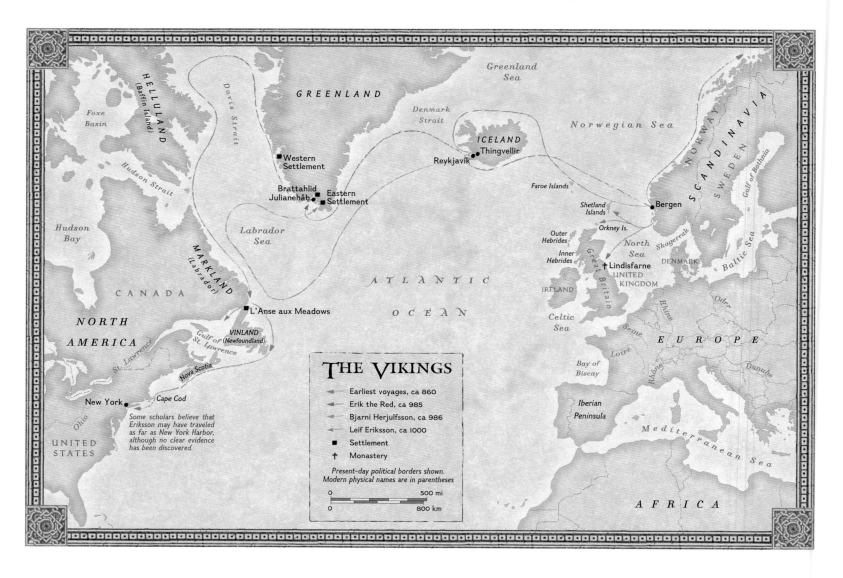

### THE VIKINGS

- Earliest voyages, ca 860
- Erik the Red, ca 985
- Bjarni Herjulfsson, ca 986
- Leif Eriksson, ca 1000
- ■ Settlement
- † Monastery

*Present-day political borders shown. Modern physical names are in parentheses*

0 — 500 mi
0 — 800 km

*Some scholars believe that Eriksson may have traveled as far as New York Harbor, although no clear evidence has been discovered.*

hauled a cargo of lumber home to Greenland—it was valuable in the nearly treeless country—and grapes, probably as raisins or wine. They talked enthusiastically of the new landfall, prompting more expeditions. Thorfinn Thorsdarsson Karlsefni led one that consisted of perhaps 135 men and 15 women, along with livestock in at least three ships. They used Leif's camp as a base and lived there for several years, shipping cargoes of lumber, pelts, and other local goods home. One of the expeditions settled for a time at the head of Newfoundland's Great Northern Peninsula at a place now called L'Anse aux Meadows.

The question of Viking settlements in the New World was long debated by scholars—some doubting they ever existed, others persuaded by the sagas that they had. In 1960 a Norwegian explorer, writer, and archaeologist named Helge Ingstad, searching for Norse landing places, came to L'Anse aux Meadows. A local showed him a group of overgrown hillocks and ridges that turned out to be the remains of structures. Ingstad and his wife, archaeologist Anne Stine Ingstad, directed a dig at the site, and from underneath the hills emerged Viking houses, workshops, and even a blacksmith shop. Here iron had for the first time been smelted in the New World.

The Vikings had built their houses of turf with sod roofs. Skylights let light in and smoke out. Long fireplaces were laid in the middle of the floors, providing

## ERIK *the* RED

While still a child, young Erik left his native Norway for Iceland with his father, who had been exiled for manslaughter. When Erik was also exiled, about 980, he set off to explore the land to the west, which was visible from the mountaintops of western Iceland. We know it now as Greenland. Erik's party, complete with livestock, rounded the southern tip of Greenland and settled near present-day Julianehåb. Erik returned to Iceland in 986 with fabulous tales of the territory; encouraged by his reports, 350 colonists in 14 ships sailed to Greenland, whose population by 1000 was about 1,000 Scandinavians.

Erik's son, Leif Eriksson, established the settlement at L'Anse aux Meadows.

heat, light, and fire for cooking. Remains from the blacksmith shop included iron boat nails. A knitting needle proved that women had been among the colony. And one small find seemed to prove conclusively that these had been Vikings: a bronze, ring-headed pin that the hardy explorers used to fasten their cloaks.

In the mid-1970s archeologists with Parks Canada, the Canadian Park Service, continued digging at L'Anse aux Meadows, primarily in a peat bog. Diggers found some 2,000 pieces of worked wood, much of it shavings and scraps from work Norsemen had done on trees before shipping timber home.

Another site evidenced where dwellings and workshops had been con-structed. Ironworkers had lived in one structure near a stream and smelted iron in a furnace in another. Because the furnace was primitive—just a pit lined with clay and topped with large stones—the quality of the iron produced was poor: Barely a fifth of the iron in the ore was extracted.

After the dig was completed and documented, Parks Canada, to protect the site for future study, buried the entire area under a layer of white sand and covered it again with fresh turf.

L'Anse aux Meadows is the only confirmed Viking site in North America.

ABOVE: *Fearsome Viking raiders prepare to invade France in an illustration from a ninth-century manuscript.*

# The
# FIRST ARRIVALS

❦

## *Europeans and the New World*

Amerigo Vespucci lost the race but won the banner: History books are full of "Columbus, Discoverer of America," but Amerigo's is the name attached to our country—the United States of America. His voyages brought him to the New World—another name he bequeathed—at least twice and maybe as many as four times. An accomplished merchant and explorer, he was for a while the influential "master navigator" of Seville.

His duties included fitting out ships, including the vessels used by Columbus in later trips. The two were acquainted, probably having met when Columbus returned from his first voyage.

Vespucci's expeditions to the New World occurred between 1497 and 1504. One kept him at sea from May 1499 to June 1500 and took him to the coast of Guyana. From there he headed south and became the first European to reach the

mouth of the Amazon River. Like Columbus, he thought he was off the coast of Asia. In May 1501 he set off on another voyage, which took him to the coast of Brazil; he may have gone as far south as Patagonia. The more trips he made the less certain he became that he had reached the Orient, and finally became convinced that he was sailing in previously unknown territories. Within a few years a German cartographer was suggesting that these new lands should be named in his honor: "…from Amerigo the discoverer…as if it were the land of Americus or America." At first the name was attached only to South America but eventually included both continents of the New World.

Amerigo's colleague Christopher Columbus—or, in Italian, Cristoforo Colombo—made four journeys across the Atlantic, in the service of Spain, between the years of 1492 and 1504. Contemporaries say he was tall and red-haired. His discoveries set off the era of European exploration, exploitation, and colonization of the Americas.

His original goal was to find a westerly route to the Orient but, like his peers, he expected the Orient to be significantly closer to Europe than it actually was. When he made landfall at Cuba, Haiti, and San Salvador, he thought the islands were off the coast of China and Japan. He called the native peoples he met Indians, a misnomer that has lasted for more than 500 years.

To Europeans, his discoveries were a triumph, bringing profit to Spain and other countries and opening vast new territories to expansion and settlement; to the peoples who were indigenous to the New World, his landfall was anything but a triumph. For them there followed centuries of exploitation, slavery, and countless deaths from diseases against which they had no resistance.

Of those on San Salvador, Columbus wrote, "They are so ingenuous and free with all they have that no one would believe it who has not seen it; of anything that they possess, if it be asked of them, they never say no; on the contrary, they invite you to share it…." Coming centuries would make them see things very differently.

Vespucci and Columbus were not the only early explorers to cross the broad oceans.

In 1497 Venetian John Cabot reached the coast of Newfoundland, and a year later Vasco da Gama sailed to India via the Cape of Good Hope. In 1500 Portuguese explorer Gaspar Côrte-Real spotted Greenland and explored the coast of Newfoundland. His sailors reported "men of the forest and white bears." That same year Pedro Alvares Cabral claimed Brazil for Portugal. In 1513 Vasco Núñez de Balboa sighted the Pacific Ocean after crossing the Isthmus of Panama from the Caribbean. In 1508 Juan Ponce de León explored and colonized Puerto Rico. Nine

to find a water route through or around America that would take them to Asia.

The Spaniards often claimed to be exploring in order to find more souls for God, but they had other motives, too. Bernal Díaz wrote that they came to the New World "to serve God...to give light to those in darkness and also to get rich." Tales of fabulous mines and jeweled cities lured the Spaniards on; the Indians, soon learning tricks of their own, told their conquerors tales of riches to be found in more distant lands. A few found the wealth they were

was destroyed as Spanish culture was spread across the New World.

Spain, France, England, and Holland planted their flags on huge territories in the Americas. They laid claim first to coastal lands or sites on the big rivers—the Rio Grande, Hudson, Mississippi—where trading ships could navigate.

As nations of Europe competed for New World colonies and settlements, geographic knowledge of the discoveries spread quickly. Cartography kept pace, and maps began to reflect actual coastlines

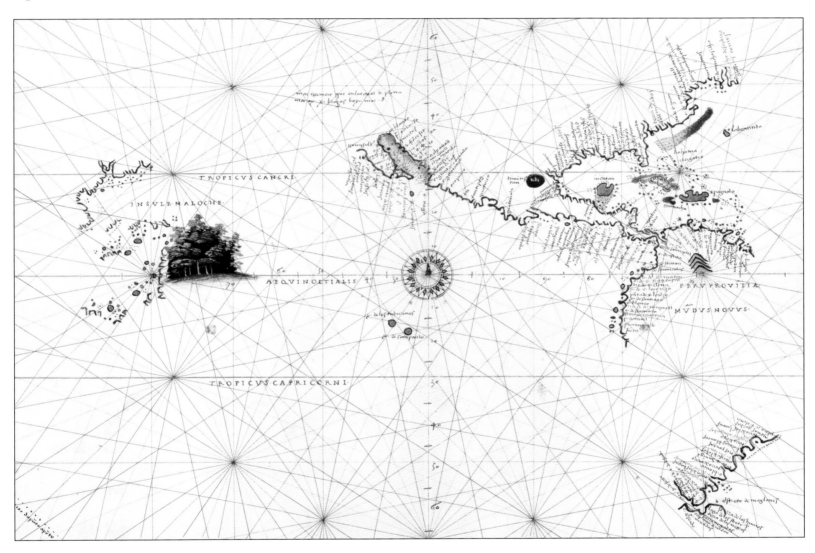

years later Francisco Fernández de Córdoba discovered the Yucatán Peninsula and battled the Maya, and just two years after that Magellan set out to achieve Columbus's goal—to reach the Orient by sailing west. He was killed in the Philippines, but one of his five ships made the first world circumnavigation in 1522. Of Magellan, one of his men wrote, "No other had so much natural wit, boldness, or knowledge to sail...."

Many were motivated to come to the New World in hopes of finding the silks and spices of the Orient that would make them fortunes at home. Later, others hoped

looking for: Cortés in Mexico and Pizarro in Peru amassed great riches.

Those who found no gold found slave labor instead. *Encomiendas*, feudal-like land grants, gave some Spaniards vast holdings; the native populations were distributed with the land. While missionaries converted the Indians, working to save their souls, most Spaniards enslaved them, forcing them to march in baggage trains and to fight in their armies. Assaulted by their masters and by the diseases the Europeans had brought with them, millions of Indians died. Much of their art and architecture also

and islands, not suppositions and theories. Some leaders of the time hungered for knowledge. Prince Henry the Navigator of Portugal sent ships along the west coast of Africa because he wanted "to know the land that lay beyond."

OPPOSITE: *A triumphant Columbus contemplates a new world in 19th-century artist Cesare Dell'Acqua's "Christopher Columbus and the Discovery of America."*
ABOVE: *Columbus's discoveries are reflected in a chart of the Americas created by cartographer Battista Agnese for his 1544 atlas.*

# NATIVE CLAIMS on the SOIL

## Indian Civilizations at Contact

When European explorers first arrived in the New World, their claims to have "discovered" it must have baffled the indigenous population, people who had lived on the American continents for millennia. Scattered across North America at contact were two million or more Native Americans, whom the Europeans lumped together as Indians. All hunted and gathered for sustenance, but the settled people of the East, Southwest, and Great Plains cultivated corn, squash, and beans as well. Continent-wide, these diverse peoples spoke perhaps 200 languages, representing 17 language families.

In the arid Southwest, the Hopi built adobe cities and farmed nearby fields. Pueblos built of sandstone blocks mortared and plastered with adobe sometimes reached five stories. Their thick walls helped keep the rooms cool during the day and warm at night. Wooden ladders gave access from one level to another.

Lake Pomo Indians of central California built small dwellings of bulrushes, sometimes large enough for several families. Their boats also were made of bulrushes. California's large population was already diverse. Some 70 languages were spoken there. California's Indians gathered plant foods, primarily acorns for meal, and made fine woven basketry.

Nootka Indians of the Northwest Coast made dwellings of overlapping cedar planks lashed to a timber frame. They, like many other coastal tribes, lived largely by fishing. Food was so plentiful they had the leisure to create a complex society. They carved elaborate totem poles to chronicle their family histories, as well as canoes and tools.

Inland, the Flathead and Shuswap often lived in pit houses whose floors were as deep as three feet, providing earth-sheltered insulation. They lived largely by hunting deer, fishing, and digging for roots. Their three great rivers—the Columbia, the Snake, and the Fraser—were avenues of travel and trade.

Brush huts sheltered such Great Basin nomads as the Southern Paiute, who lived largely on game and wild plants, as well as seeds, roots, and small animals.

On the Great Plains, before the arrival of the horse, the Indians lived in sod-covered lodges shored up by heavy cottonwood frames. The Mandan built permanent villages near their gardens on the Missouri floodplain; during buffalo-hunting season, when they followed the immense herds across the landscape, they lived in portable tepees. The Spaniards introduced horses in the Southwest in the 1500s, and by the mid-1700s the animals were reaching the Plains tribes through trade. They transformed the Cheyenne and others from farmers settled along river bottoms into mounted buffalo hunters.

The Cherokee and Chickasaw in the Southeast built wattle-and-daub houses of split saplings and canes woven around poles. Gaps were packed with mud-and-moss mixtures, then plastered with clay. Thatched grasses provided a roof. The people survived largely on cultivated plants. The Muskogee were skilled at crafts and devising herbal medicines.

In a vast territory surrounding the Great Lakes and stretching east through New England, the Ojibwa, the Illinois, and the Micmac supplemented the game they hunted with some cultivated plants. Their wigwams were small, domelike structures framed with saplings and covered with bark and reed mats. A fire pit was vented through a central roof hole. The Mohawk and other farmers lived in permanent villages.

North of them, along a broad stretch of Canada that reached up to the farther distances of Alaska, subarctic tribes of the spruce and fir forests, who averaged as few as three people per 100 square miles, lived in tents made of hide or bark, banked with turf and snow for winter insulation. The Northern Ojibwa and Cree fashioned toboggans and snowshoes they used in tracking caribou, moose, and elk.

A thin band of Arctic peoples rimmed the northern edge of the continent, a mixture of Eastern Aleuts, Eskimos, and Inuit. They built kayaks and harpoons to hunt seals and other sea mammals. Communal hunts rounded up caribou and drove them into stockades to be slaughtered. Their houses varied greatly in materials but had a common purpose—to keep out the cold and wind. Wood-framed, sod-covered huts, for instance, had a typically long, sunken entryway that prevented heat from escaping. Domed snow-block igloos used a similar entrance.

ABOVE: *Bird's-eye view of a Secotan Indian village on Roanoke Island finds natives engaged in ceremonial dancing and trading. Sturdy houses edge corn fields, shown here in three states: "newly sprong, greene, and rype."*

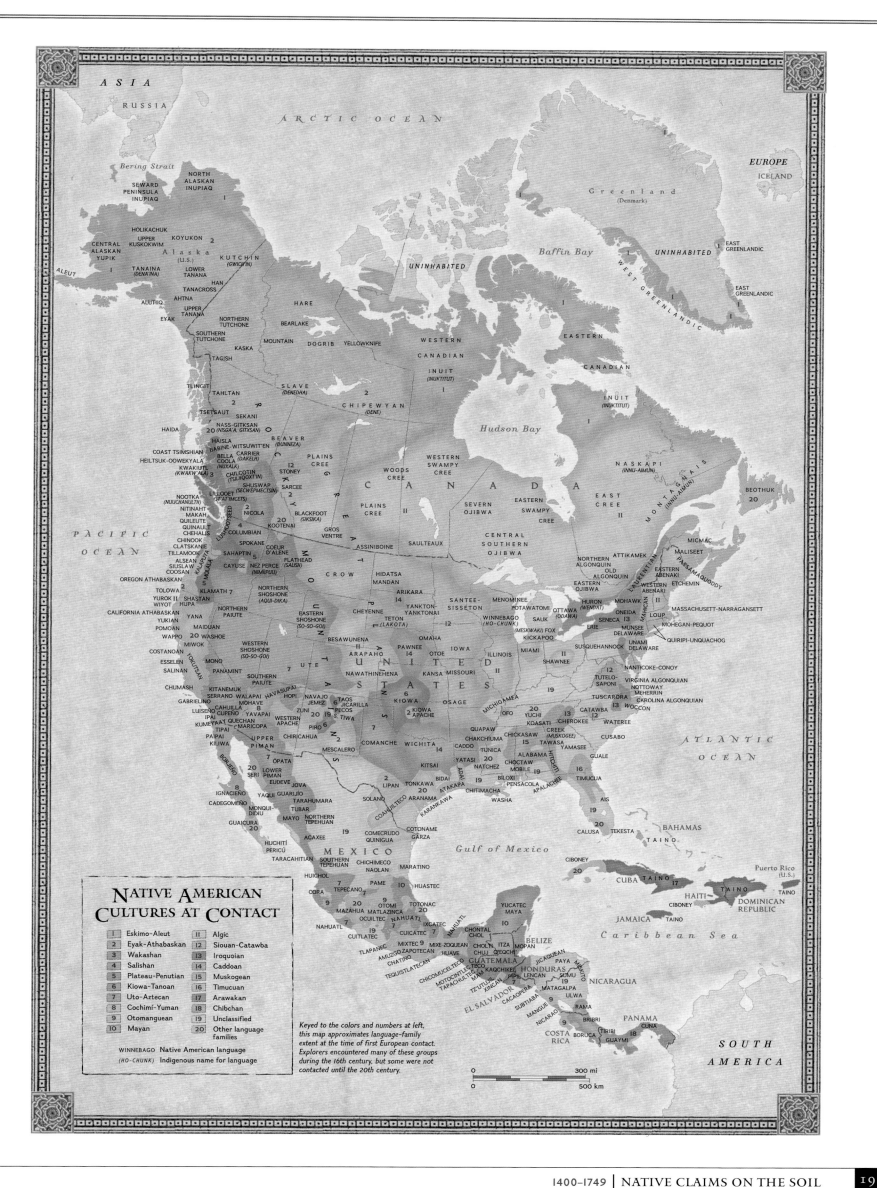

# NATIVE AMERICAN CULTURES AT CONTACT

| | | | |
|---|---|---|---|
| 1 | Eskimo-Aleut | 11 | Algic |
| 2 | Eyak-Athabaskan | 12 | Siouan-Catawba |
| 3 | Wakashan | 13 | Iroquoian |
| 4 | Salishan | 14 | Caddoan |
| 5 | Plateau-Penutian | 15 | Muskogean |
| 6 | Kiowa-Tanoan | 16 | Timucuan |
| 7 | Uto-Aztecan | 17 | Arawakan |
| 8 | Cochimí-Yuman | 18 | Chibchan |
| 9 | Otomanguean | 19 | Unclassified |
| 10 | Mayan | 20 | Other language families |

WINNEBAGO  Native American language
(HO-CHUNK)  Indigenous name for language

Keyed to the colors and numbers at left, this map approximates language-family extent at the time of first European contact. Explorers encountered many of these groups during the 16th century, but some were not contacted until the 20th century.

0    300 mi
0    500 km

# The
# FIRST SETTLERS

## European Claims and Exploration

Between 1492, when Columbus first made landfall, and the early 1600s, a long and distinguished list of explorers crossed the ocean: They included Cabot, Balboa, Ponce de León, Cortes, Verrazano, Cartier, de Soto, Coronado, Champlain, and Hudson, among others.

As soon as the explorers' reports were received at home in Europe, the great powers began claiming chunks of the New World for themselves.

Cabot, an Italian sea captain sailing for the English, reached the North American continent first, rediscovering Newfoundland, where the Vikings had landed, but Spaniards led its exploration. Ponce de León sailed from his colony on Puerto Rico to the mainland in 1513 and named it Florida, Spanish for "flowery." De Soto, who was "fond of this sport of killing Indians," and Coronado explored inland. Both were searching for gold, de Soto from Florida to the Mississippi and Coronado farther west. Coronado didn't find any but did discover the Grand Canyon. Verrazano, searching for a passage to Asia, didn't get beyond the harbor of New York. Cartier, a French captain, made three trips across the Atlantic and sailed up the St. Lawrence to the site of present-day Montreal. Alongside the great river, wild grapes and corn grew, as well as berries and "flowers of sweet smell." But natives turned unfriendly and many of the Cartier colonists died, stricken with scurvy and weakened by winter cold. The gold they found turned out to be worthless fool's gold.

The Spaniards had better luck in South America. Their treasure-laden galleons skirted the coast of La Florida as far north as Chesapeake Bay. French and English privateers wanted coastal bases, and their governments wanted Spain's treasure pipeline siphoned. In the 1560s France built forts in La Florida. Spain eradicated each and built forts of its own.

The European powers—the Spanish, French, English, and Dutch, especially—tried to establish permanent settlements in America.

In 1598 the Spaniards forged up the Rio Grande to San Gabriel, where they founded a settlement. In the north, French sea captain Samuel del Champlain established the first French colony at Quebec.

Sir Walter Raleigh, Queen Elizabeth I's favorite explorer and privateer, put together the first expeditions to the New World. Elizabeth was hopeful of the things other European monarchs wanted: a passage to Asia, the fabled gold mines of the Americas, and another way to challenge Spain. She chartered Raleigh to explore the eastern coast of North America and the "remote, heathen and barbarous lands" inland.

Such charters gave explorers wide leeway: they could claim lands in the name

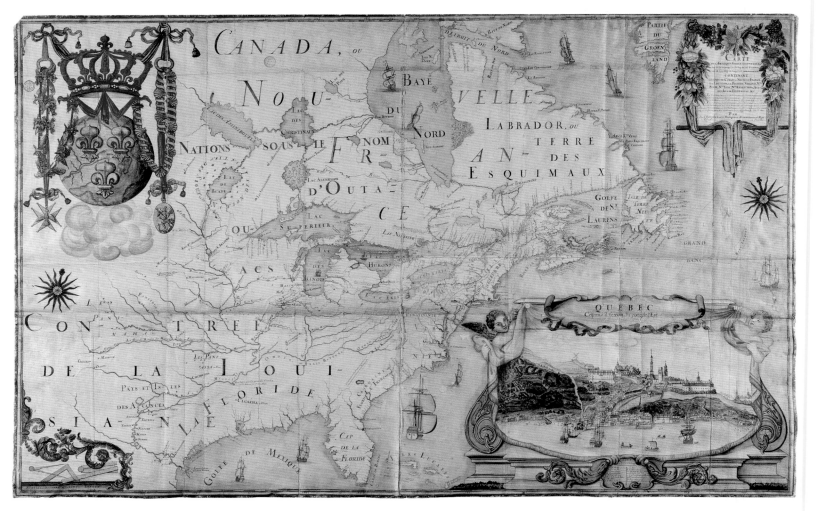

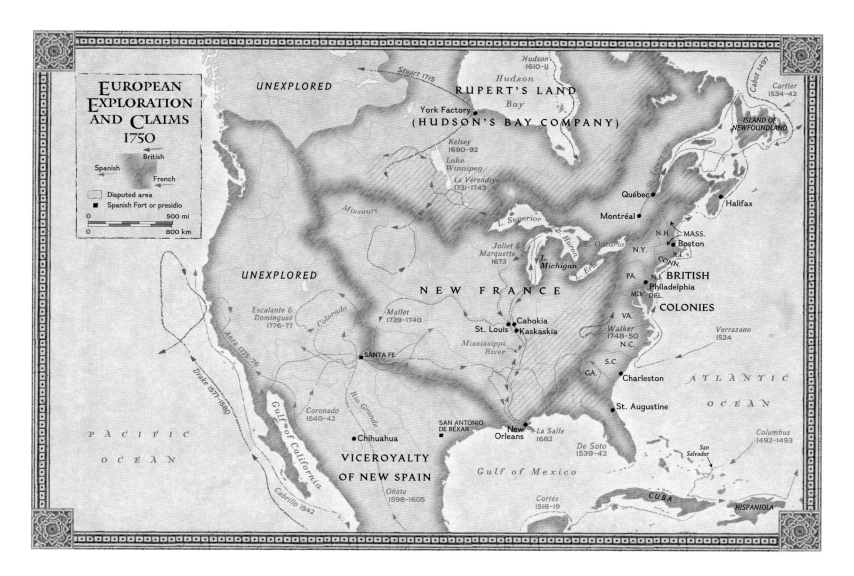

UNEXPLORED

Hudson 1610-11

Hudson Bay

RUPERT'S LAND

York Factory

(HUDSON'S BAY COMPANY)

Cabot 1497

Cartier 1534-42

ISLAND OF NEWFOUNDLAND

Stuart 1715

Kelsey 1690-92

Lake Winnipeg

La Vérendrye 1731-1743

Missouri

L. Superior

Québec

Montréal

Halifax

N.H. MASS.
N.Y. ■ Boston
CONN. R.I.

Joliet & Marquette 1673

L. Huron

L. Michigan

L. Ontario

L. Erie

PA.
N.J.
MD. DEL.

Philadelphia

BRITISH

UNEXPLORED

NEW FRANCE

COLONIES

Escalante & Dominguez 1776-77

Colorado

Mallet 1739-1740

St. Louis  Cahokia
Kaskaskia

VA.

Walker 1748-50

N.C.

Verrazano 1524

Anza 1775-76

Rio Grande

Mississippi River

S.C.

GA.

Charleston

ATLANTIC

OCEAN

Drake 1577-1580

SANTA FE

St. Augustine

Coronado 1540-42

PACIFIC

OCEAN

Gulf of California

Chihuahua

SAN ANTONIO DE BÉXAR

New Orleans

La Salle 1682

De Soto 1539-42

San Salvador

Columbus 1492-1493

Cabrillo 1542

VICEROYALTY OF NEW SPAIN

Oñate 1598-1605

Gulf of Mexico

Cortés 1518-19

CUBA

HISPANIOLA

of their sovereign; they could organize settlers and ship them across the ocean; they could establish and rule the settlements. The charters of England gave colonists the same rights and privileges of Englishmen at home: to own property, to be tried by juries of their peers, and to be ruled by a representative government.

Off North Carolina, in Roanoke Island's Pamlico Sound, two of Raleigh's captains found seashores that were "sandy and low toward the water's side, but so full of grapes that the very beating and surge of the sea overflowed the fruit." They also found Indians farming, fishing, and hunting and thought them "most gentle, loving and faithful, void of all guile and treason...."

Raleigh, remembering his virgin Queen, called the place Virginia, and the first child born here, the first English child to be born in the New World, was Virginia Dare, also named for the Queen. But the settlement on Roanoke Island was in trouble from the beginning. There was no anchorage deep enough to service privateers. The colonists, busy looking for gold, neglected to plant crops, so Roanoke failed as a commercial

colony, too. In a few years, all evidence of the colony and its colonists was gone.

The Virginia Company made the next English attempt at a colony in the New World 17 years later. They raised money and their first three ships carried 108 settlers, all men. They came ashore on the James River and founded Jamestown. The Virginia Company advertised for more settlers, promising paradise, where the oranges, apples, lemons were "so delicious that whoever tastes them will despise the insipid watery taste of those we have in England."

But the swamps bred malarial mosquitoes, and contaminated water caused dysentery. Indians were a constant menace, and by 1609 most of the settlers had died.

It was tobacco that saved the day. Indians had long been growing the crop, but Londoners found the American strain too harsh. Farmer John Rolfe found a milder variety that pleased, and it swept across Europe. Soon successful tobacco farms lined the James, and between 1619 and 1624, 5,000 English settlers came to Virginia.

In the meantime, Henry Hudson, another explorer seeking the elusive north-

west passage, had found his way 150 miles up the river that would one day bear his name. It was beautiful country, where Indians were clothed in the skins of fur-bearing animals—beaver, otter, mink, bear. Henry's employer, the Dutch East India Company, launched successful settlements in the Hudson Valley to export furs. They built forts on the tip of Manhattan Island and near present-day Albany to service the fur trade. From the forts, European settlers moved steadily inland.

On December 21, 1620, English settlers came ashore at Plymouth, on Cape Cod. They fancied themselves a stronger breed than the English who had preceded them. One wrote, "It is not with us as with other men, whom small things can discourage."

OPPOSITE: *Cartographer to the French court in Quebec, Jean-Baptiste-Louis Franquelin's 1688 map of eastern North America reflected the latest geographical thinking. His greatest error: sending the Mississippi River flowing west into Texas before turning it east toward the Gulf of Mexico.*

# The MISSIONARIES

## Settling the Land, Spreading The Word

**C**hristian soldiers spreading The Word, missionaries found fertile ground in the pagan New World, and emigrants fleeing organized religions in Europe found tolerance and acceptance.

Spain, having agreed by treaty with Portugal to divide the non-Christian world into exclusive spheres of influence, won the right to the New World, and few Spanish explorers embarked without representatives of the church aboard their ships. They were not always welcomed warmly: In 1549, angered by visits of Spanish slavers, Florida Indians killed Dominican Luis Cancer de Bastro when he landed at Tampa Bay in one of Spain's first purely missionary expeditions.

Large areas of the West and Southwest claimed by Spain were largely empty of Spaniards. A thin line of military presidios and missions held their territory. In 1718 a Franciscan mission was built in the Spanish outpost of San Antonio de Valero, and by 1770 Franciscan missionaries had introduced draft animals and European farming methods to Indians living near Monterey and San Diego. To combat damage done to crops by seasonal flooding and dry seasons, the friars experimented successfully with dams and aqueducts.

Franciscan Fathers built 21 missions in California, beginning in 1769, when they founded Misíon San Diego de Alcala. Their most renowned mission was San Juan Capistrano, built between Los Angeles and San Diego. It is still famous for the legendary return each year in March of its resident swallows.

To solidify Spanish control—and also to stop other powers from staking claims in the territory—the Fathers built their missions about a day's ride apart. But their primary impulse was Christian—to encourage literacy among the Indians and to convert their souls. Spanish settlements grew up around the missions, each with a military garrison, or presidio,

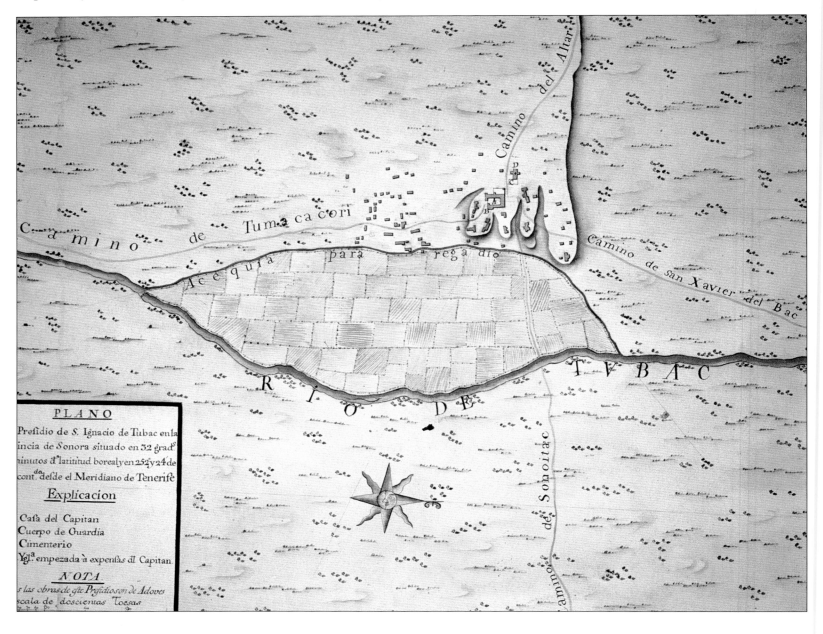

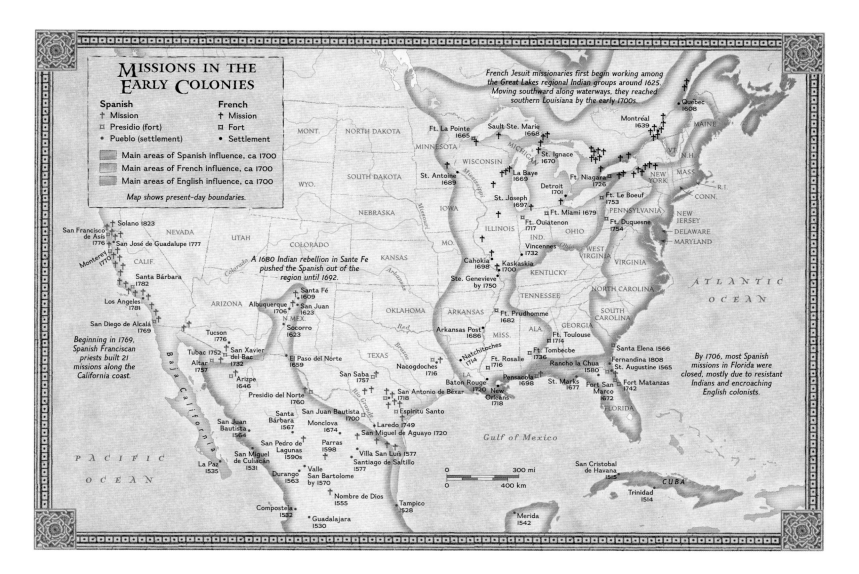

## MISSIONS IN THE EARLY COLONIES

**Spanish**
† Mission
⊡ Presidio (fort)
• Pueblo (settlement)

**French**
† Mission
⊡ Fort
• Settlement

Main areas of Spanish influence, ca 1700
Main areas of French influence, ca 1700
Main areas of English influence, ca 1700

*Map shows present-day boundaries.*

French Jesuit missionaries first begin working among the Great Lakes regional Indian groups around 1625. Moving southward along waterways, they reached southern Louisiana by the early 1700s.

A 1680 Indian rebellion in Sante Fe pushed the Spanish out of the region until 1692.

Beginning in 1769, Spanish Franciscan priests built 21 missions along the California coast.

By 1706, most Spanish missions in Florida were closed, mostly due to resistant Indians and encroaching English colonists.

which served to protect the missions and the colonists. The economy of California would one day benefit from the introduction by the friars of the state's first domestic grapes and oranges.

But the effect on the Indians was not benign. The Spaniards felt themselves to be superior to their charges and didn't hesitate to treat the Indians as less than human. And as elsewhere in the world, the missionaries, in their zeal, destroyed the pillars of the Indians' society, which collapsed under missionary rule.

Elsewhere, other faiths took root. In 1701 William III chartered a society to support Anglican missionary efforts in the colonies, and in 1709 a Quaker meetinghouse was built in Boston, confirming growing tolerance in Massachusetts.

Pious Roger Williams was banished in 1635 from the Massachusetts Bay Colony for challenging the church and championing Indian rights. He reminded the Puritan elders that "forced worship stinks in God's nostrils." In Rhode Island, which detractors called "Rogue's Island," he made a refuge for Quakers, Jews, Baptists,

and others, where church and state were kept separate.

By the 1720s diversity had spread. Except for Maryland's Roman Catholics, Christians generally shared Martin Luther's vision: The Bible—not church tradition—was the sole authority and gave believers immediate access to God. Yet fervor had declined. So preachers began revivals that flared in the 1740s into the Great Awakening. Colonists suddenly felt united in a crusade. Institutions of learning arose to train ministers; two such colleges later grew into Princeton and Brown.

By 1750 a religious impulse, largely Protestant and reform-minded, had taken root in Britain's New World settlements. Churches "of the Congregational Way" dominated New England. Baptist dissenters moved to Rhode Island and then spread south. Reformed churches followed ethnic settlement patterns. Pennsylvania, home to Quakers, Moravians, and Mennonites, had a predominantly Presbyterian frontier. Pluralism was also the rule in southern colonies, though the num-

ber of parishes lagged behind "well-churched" New England. Anglicans were in the majority in southern areas, even in Maryland, which was begun as a Roman Catholic colony. Slaves at first clung to Islam and tribal religions. By 1750 these and many other religions made a diversity of devotions uniquely tolerated in the New World. In 1791 the colonists, having won independence, enshrined Williams's doctrine in the Bill of Rights, making freedom of conscience a matter of law.

Missionaries came to the Oregon country in 1834, looking for Indian souls to convert to Christianity. They sent back word of the farming and lumbering potential, and by 1846 some 8,000 emigrants had responded. In 1870, Illinois-born Mormons followed Brigham Young to Utah.

OPPOSITE: *Quiltlike patchwork of fields hugs the Tubac River in present-day Arizona. Structures of the Spanish presidio cluster around a crossroads of several* caminos. *Juan Bautista de Anza, the garrison's second commander, blazed the first trail from Mexico to San Francisco.*

# 1750
## THROUGH
# 1799

❧

## New People in
## a New World

*British forces surrender to the Americans at
Yorktown, October 19, 1781.*

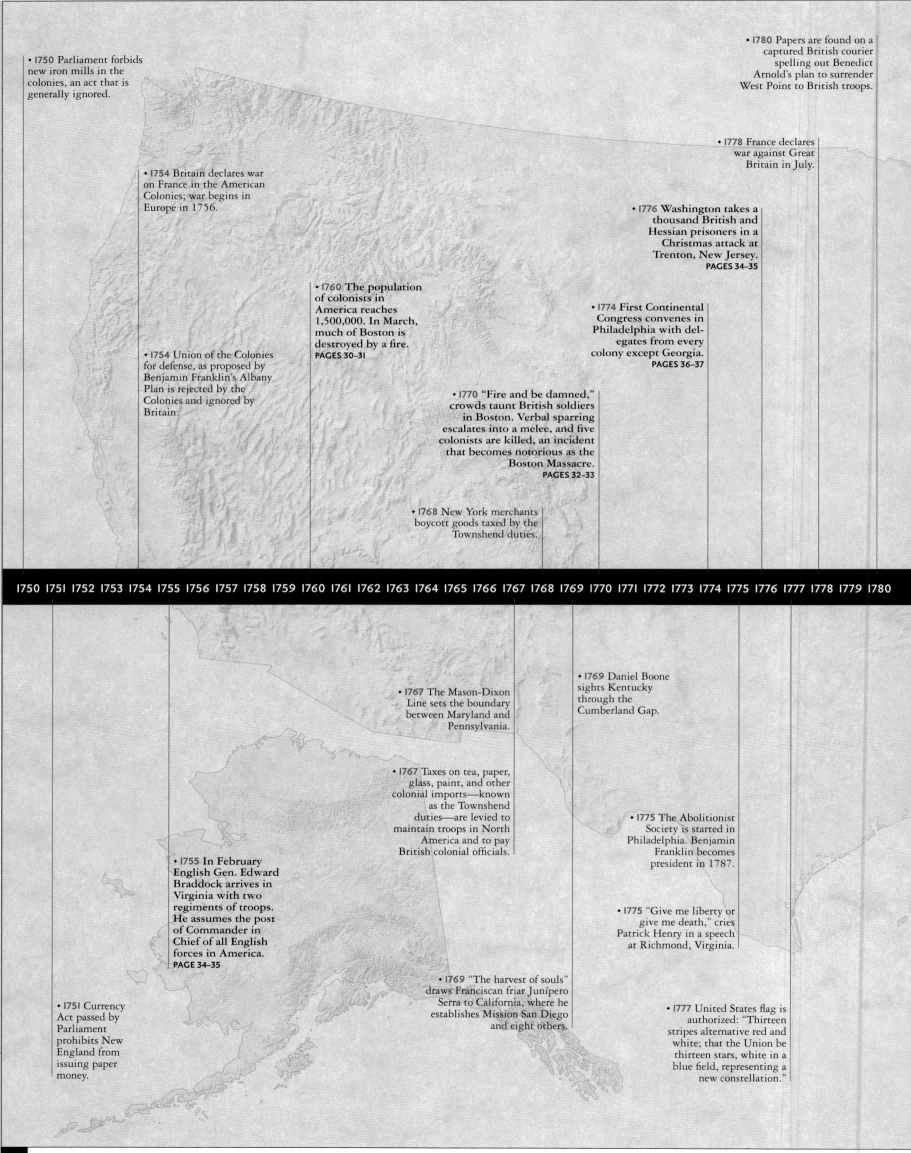

• 1780 Papers are found on a captured British courier spelling out Benedict Arnold's plan to surrender West Point to British troops.

• 1750 Parliament forbids new iron mills in the colonies, an act that is generally ignored.

• 1778 France declares war against Great Britain in July.

• 1754 Britain declares war on France in the American Colonies; war begins in Europe in 1756.

• 1776 Washington takes a thousand British and Hessian prisoners in a Christmas attack at Trenton, New Jersey.
PAGES 34–35

• 1760 The population of colonists in America reaches 1,500,000. In March, much of Boston is destroyed by a fire.
PAGES 30–31

• 1774 First Continental Congress convenes in Philadelphia with delegates from every colony except Georgia.
PAGES 36–37

• 1754 Union of the Colonies for defense, as proposed by Benjamin Franklin's Albany Plan is rejected by the Colonies and ignored by Britain.

• 1770 "Fire and be damned," crowds taunt British soldiers in Boston. Verbal sparring escalates into a melee, and five colonists are killed, an incident that becomes notorious as the Boston Massacre.
PAGES 32–33

• 1768 New York merchants boycott goods taxed by the Townshend duties.

1750 1751 1752 1753 1754 1755 1756 1757 1758 1759 1760 1761 1762 1763 1764 1765 1766 1767 1768 1769 1770 1771 1772 1773 1774 1775 1776 1777 1778 1779 1780

• 1769 Daniel Boone sights Kentucky through the Cumberland Gap.

• 1767 The Mason-Dixon Line sets the boundary between Maryland and Pennsylvania.

• 1767 Taxes on tea, paper, glass, paint, and other colonial imports—known as the Townshend duties—are levied to maintain troops in North America and to pay British colonial officials.

• 1775 The Abolitionist Society is started in Philadelphia. Benjamin Franklin becomes president in 1787.

• 1755 In February English Gen. Edward Braddock arrives in Virginia with two regiments of troops. He assumes the post of Commander in Chief of all English forces in America.
PAGE 34–35

• 1775 "Give me liberty or give me death," cries Patrick Henry in a speech at Richmond, Virginia.

• 1751 Currency Act passed by Parliament prohibits New England from issuing paper money.

• 1769 "The harvest of souls" draws Franciscan friar Junípero Serra to California, where he establishes Mission San Diego and eight others.

• 1777 United States flag is authorized: "Thirteen stripes alternative red and white; that the Union be thirteen stars, white in a blue field, representing a new constellation."

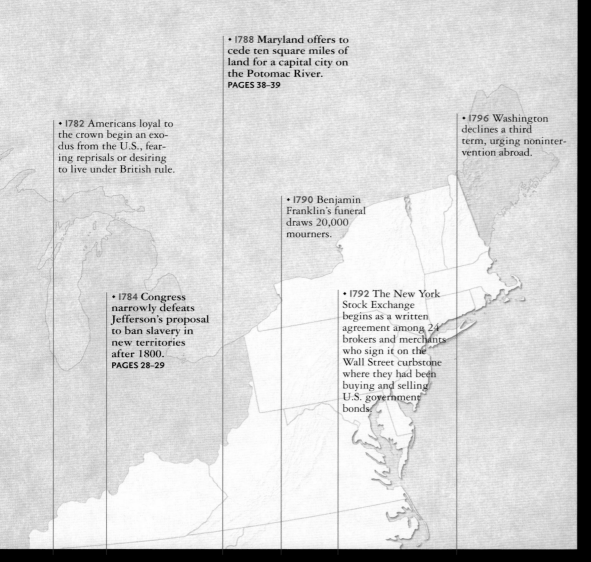

• **1788** Maryland offers to cede ten square miles of land for a capital city on the Potomac River.
**PAGES 38–39**

• **1782** Americans loyal to the crown begin an exodus from the U.S., fearing reprisals or desiring to live under British rule.

• **1796** Washington declines a third term, urging nonintervention abroad.

• **1790** Benjamin Franklin's funeral draws 20,000 mourners.

• **1784** Congress narrowly defeats Jefferson's proposal to ban slavery in new territories after 1800.
**PAGES 28–29**

• **1792** The New York Stock Exchange begins as a written agreement among 24 brokers and merchants who sign it on the Wall Street curbstone where they had been buying and selling U.S. government bonds.

1781 1782 1783 1784 1785 1786 1787 1788 1789 1790 1791 1792 1793 1794 1795 1796 1797 1798 1799

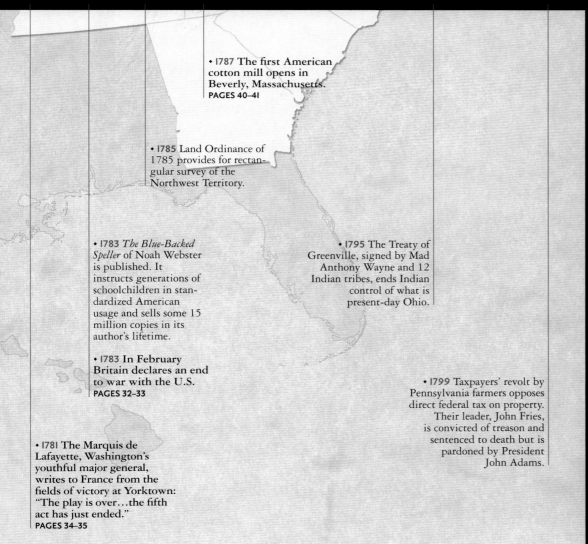

• **1787** The first American cotton mill opens in Beverly, Massachusetts.
**PAGES 40–41**

• **1785** Land Ordinance of 1785 provides for rectangular survey of the Northwest Territory.

• **1783** *The Blue-Backed Speller* of Noah Webster is published. It instructs generations of schoolchildren in standardized American usage and sells some 15 million copies in its author's lifetime.

• **1795** The Treaty of Greenville, signed by Mad Anthony Wayne and 12 Indian tribes, ends Indian control of what is present-day Ohio.

• **1783** In February Britain declares an end to war with the U.S.
**PAGES 32–33**

• **1799** Taxpayers' revolt by Pennsylvania farmers opposes direct federal tax on property. Their leader, John Fries, is convicted of treason and sentenced to death but is pardoned by President John Adams.

• **1781** The Marquis de Lafayette, Washington's youthful major general, writes to France from the fields of victory at Yorktown: "The play is over...the fifth act has just ended."
**PAGES 34–35**

I N THE SECOND HALF OF the 18th century, with Britain's attention often diverted by war with France, the American Colonies thrived during long stretches of virtual independence. When Britain demanded help with staggering war debts, the Americans saw the virtue of common cause. Each British attempt to collect taxes forced the Colonies closer and broke another link to the mother country.

During these years, the Colonies' population grew, and borders were drawn; a flag was designed, and a capital city laid out on ten square miles of marshy land on the Potomac River in Maryland; George Washington evolved from being a tenacious and successful general to a higher status as Father of His Country; slaves were plentiful, and the colonists gradually began thinking of the Native Americans—the Indians—as the intruders and unlawful barriers to *their* plans and desires.

"The Revolution was effected before the war commenced. The Revolution was in the minds and hearts of the people," John Adams recalled. But minds and hearts couldn't govern a nation. Several years of loose confederation taught the need for a stronger central government. By 1788 adoption of the new Constitution seemed to fulfill Samuel Adams's optimism of a decade earlier: "Our union is now complete; our constitution composed, established and approved. You are now the guardians of your own liberties."

The people's representatives grappled with issues that would survive into the 21st century: how to collect taxes, enforce laws, and get reelected.

"In the beginning all the world was America," wrote English philosopher John Locke in 1690, remembering the innocent time before life in the New World began to get complicated.

*1750–1799 Saw the addition of Delaware, Pennsylvania, New Jersey, Georgia, Connecticut, Massachusetts, Maryland, South Carolina, New Hampshire, Virginia, New York, North Carolina, Rhode Island, Vermont, Kentucky, and Tennessee to the Union.*

# The DISPERSAL of SLAVES

## The Spread of Human Bondage

About the last of August came in a dutch man of warre that sold us twenty Negers," wrote John Rolfe of Jamestown, Virginia, in his record of 1619. These were the first blacks known to have entered a mainland English colony. They probably were actually indentured servants, in which case they would have been freed after a fixed period of service.

The term "Negro slave" first appeared in legislation in Virginia in 1659, and in 1662 it was decreed that the child of a black woman "shall be bond or free according to the condition of the mother," which effectively made slavery hereditary. A 1705 Virginia law broadened and codified the rights of white servants, but it also defined the role of black slaves as "real estate [which] shall descend unto heirs and widows." If slaves escaped, anyone might legally "kill and destroy" them.

Colonists soon found that slaves were cheaper labor than indentured servants. Between 1670 and 1700 the white population of the English colonies doubled, while in the same period the number of blacks increased fivefold.

Americans joined in the enterprise, trading with African kings for what became more than nine million slaves. Some tried to rebel. In September 1739 about 75 slaves of Stono River country, near Charleston, stole weapons and with shouts of "Liberty!" set off for St. Augustine and a promise of freedom in Spanish territory. Before militia suppressed the rebellion, 40 blacks and 20 whites died.

Shipping routes connected Britain with trading bases around the world. In a notorious link, British merchants sold iron and silver, finished goods, and textiles from British India to African kings and traders, who paid with slaves.

Between 1532 and 1870, 5.5 million slaves were imported into the Americas from Africa. Nearly 40 percent came from Angola, with large numbers coming from the Bights of Benin and Biafra and Gold

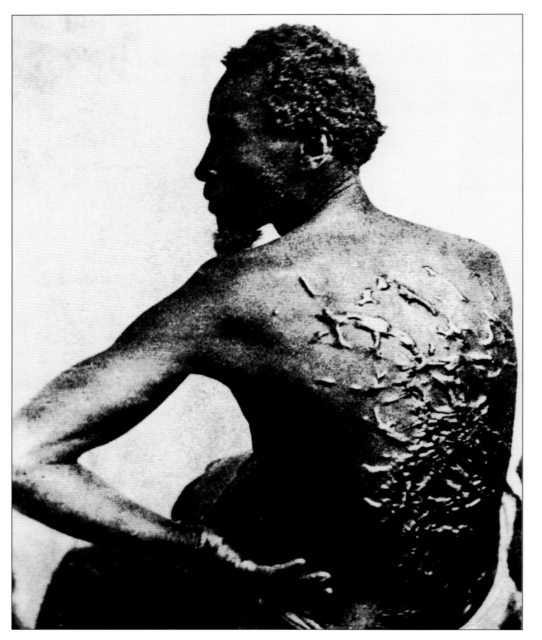

### APRIL 21, 1807
### *from the* CHARLESTON COURIER

A Jury of Inquest was held on Sunday afternoon, on the body of an Africa negro woman, found floating near the Market dock—it appeared to the jurors, from its having on the usual dress, of a blue flannel frock, to have belonged to one of the slave ships in the harbour, and thrown into the river, to save the expense of burial; a custom too prevalent in this port with the officers of slave ships, and in itself shocking to humanity. The jury brought in a verdict, that she came to her death by the visitation of God. And the coroner begs leave to remind the seamen and petty officers of those ships, that the City Council have passed an Ordinance, prohibiting so inhuman and brutal a custom,...The Coroner has received information that there are at this time, the bodies of three or more of these poor wretches floating about Hot-Island, and the marshes opposite the city—the effluvia arrising from which, must be very prejudicial to the health of passengers in boats, passing and repassing them daily.

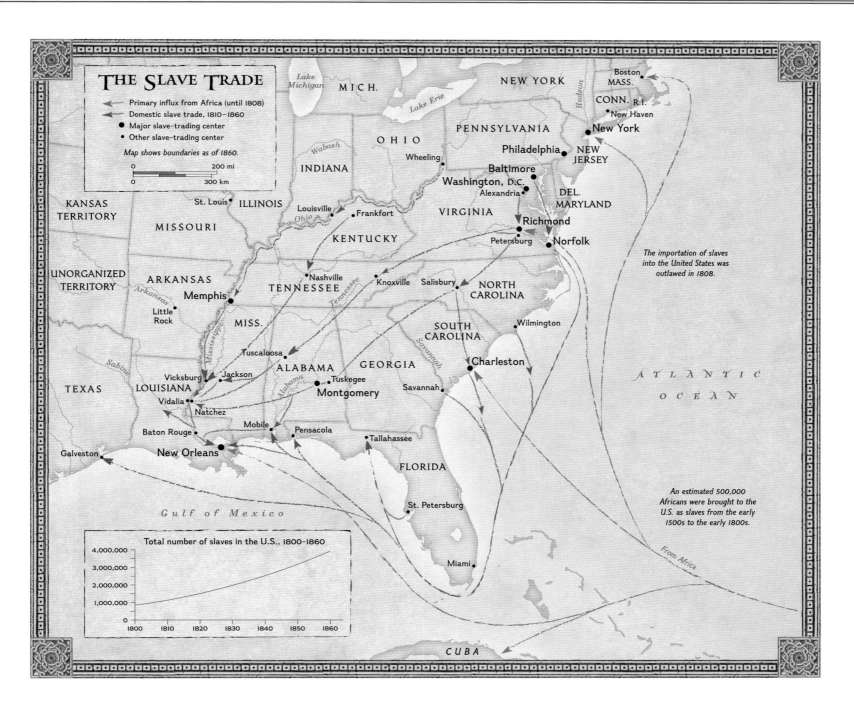

**THE SLAVE TRADE**

→ Primary influx from Africa (until 1808)
→ Domestic slave trade, 1810–1860
● Major slave-trading center
• Other slave-trading center

Map shows boundaries as of 1860.

0 — 200 mi
0 — 300 km

*The importation of slaves into the United States was outlawed in 1808.*

*An estimated 500,000 Africans were brought to the U.S. as slaves from the early 1500s to the early 1800s.*

*From Africa*

**Total number of slaves in the U.S., 1800-1860**

Coast. Of the 5.5 million, 3.6 million were shipped to Portuguese Brazil, 1.6 million to the British Caribbean, 1.5 million to Spanish America, and some 400,000—about 6 percent—to British Colonial America. About two million African captives died at sea.

Farms that needed many workers—tobacco, rice, indigo—came to depend on slaves. By 1790 the slave population of the colonies was nearly 700,000, with 75 percent in the southern Atlantic states. By 1810, though all northern states had abolished slavery or provided for its end, 30,000 slaves worked there in fields, homes, and factories. The largest number, 15,017, labored in New York state under the harshest codes in the North. Twenty years later, Virginia still had the most slaves, but the spread of cotton into Alabama and Mississippi required massive increases in slaves. The nation's slave population had grown to two million, and

in the South more stringent codes were introduced to control and confine.

Josiah Henson was a slave until 1830, when he escaped to Canada. He described field-hand life: "The principal food of those upon my master's plantation consisted of corn-meal, and salt herrings; to which was added in summer a little buttermilk, and the few vegetables which each might raise for himself and his family.…In ordinary times we had two regular meals in a day:— breakfast at twelve o'clock, after laboring from daylight, and supper when the work of the remainder of the day was over. In harvest season we had three.…We lodged in log huts, and on the bare ground. Wooden floors were an unknown luxury. In a single room were huddled, like cattle, ten or a dozen persons, men, women and children.…Our beds were collections of straw and old rages, thrown down in the corners

and boxed in with boards;…In these wretched hovels were we penned at night, and fed by day; here were the children born and the sick—neglected."

Nearly 40 percent of slaves that reached the British mainland colonies between 1700 and 1775 disembarked at Sullivan's Island, Charleston. It was later described as the "Ellis Island of black Americans."

When the legal U.S. slave trade with Africa ended in 1808, domestic trading became big business in the South, where demand was growing as fast as the cotton. Finding less profit in owning slaves than in selling them, eastern farmers shipped slaves to the Gulf states. Most were auctioned at centers such as New Orleans, where a slave sold for a third more than in Virginia.

OPPOSITE: *A slave's scarred back gives visceral evidence of the brutality of the institution.*

# *The* FIRST COLONIES

## *Predecessors to the States*

During the colonial period in North America, the British settlements grew so fast that by 1750, 13 separate colonies stretched in a bumpy line between Maine and Georgia.

Farmers, fishermen, and craftsmen, mostly Puritans, came to New England. "The air of the country is sharp," said a Massachusetts woman, "the rocks many, the trees innumerable, the grass little, the winter cold." It wouldn't be long before many of the New Englanders realized the area was not suitable for farming and turned to fishing, ship-building, or trade.

"There is so great an increase of grain," one boasted, "that within three years, some plantations have got 20 acres of corn, some 40, some 50....There are also peaches, in great quantities." Small farms and large manor houses grew alongside one another in the rich river valleys, and the bigger landowners imported servants and slaves to work their land and manage their houses.

Connecticut's first three permanent settlements—Hartford, Windsor, and Wethersfield, founded in 1635 and 1636—were established by colonists from Massachusetts Bay. In 1639 they

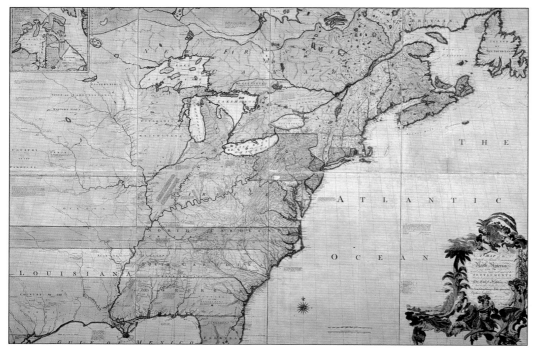

The temperate climate and richer soils of the middle colonies in the mid-Atlantic region were better suited to farming. Charles II made his brother James, Duke of York, proprietor of everything between the St. Croix and Delaware Rivers. James named the region after himself: New York. Some of the proprietors there in turn offered to sell parts of their holdings, publishing enticing advertisements.

adopted a constitution they called "Fundamental Orders," the first in the nation to be based on the consent of the governed; it later served as a model for the U.S. Constitution.

Delaware was, famously, the first state to ratify the Constitution. Its first settlement by the Dutch was destroyed by Indians, and it became English in 1664.

Georgia, the last colony to be settled, was named for King George II and granted in 1732 to one of his generals, James Oglethorpe. It was hoped Georgia would slow the encroachment of Spanish and French settlers from the south.

Leonard Calvert, son of Lord Baltimore, led the first group of settlers to Maryland in 1633. The colony was named for England's Queen Henrietta Maria, and its first capital was St. Marys.

The Pilgrims were the first English colonists to permanently settle in what is now Massachusetts. Their ship *Mayflower* set off from Plymouth, England, in 1620, with 102 passengers. The Mayflower Compact, written and signed aboard the ship, set rules to guide the settlers in establishing a new community. It served as the official constitution of the Plymouth Colony for many years.

New Hampshire, aggressively explored by both the British and the French, was first settled by the English near Portsmouth in 1623 and named for Hampshire County in England. It shared a governor with Massachusetts until 1741.

More than 90 Revolutionary War battles were fought in the colony of New Jersey, which was named for the Isle of Jersey in the English Channel, birthplace of one of its early land grantees.

By 1624 the Dutch West India Company was exploring and settling in the New York region. Dutch settlers—one of them was Peter Minuit—bought Manhattan Island from local Indians and called it New Amsterdam. It became English in 1664.

By 1653 Virginia colonists were moving south to settle around Albemarle Sound, strengthening the colony's southern frontier. The name North Carolina first appeared in 1691, when the English crown officially recognized the region.

Pennsylvania might have been called just Sylvania, Quaker William Penn's first choice. He was granted a charter to the region in 1681. Its location in the middle of the arc of the 13 original colonies earned it a nickname: the Keystone State.

# CURRENCY
## of the COLONIES

The metal money of the 18th century in America was largely silver, not gold. The chief coin was the Spanish milled dollar—the piece of eight. There were some gold coins in circulation, however, especially the Johannes of Portugal, which circulated after 1722, and the Spanish Pistole, which had a substantial circulation in Virginia prior to the French and Indian War. The silver came largely through trade with the West Indies and the gold from trade with southern Europe. The colonies retained the British monetary units: pounds, shillings, and pence. Values were placed upon the coins by the colonial legislatures.

Paper currency was generally called "bills of credit" and was issued on two bases: on the credit of the colony supported by tax funds, and on loan, which meant a legislature printed a sum in bills and made them legal tender; these were then loaned, usually to landowners in the form of a mortgage on their property. Such currency gave individuals credit necessary for acquiring and improving land, and the interest they paid went into the public treasury. And the bills, while outstanding, supplied a medium of exchange.

Rhode Island, never an island, was the smallest colony and is the smallest state. It was the first colony to declare independence but, worried that because of its small size it wouldn't be equitably represented, was the last to ratify the Constitution.

The Spanish reached the South Carolina region as early as 1514 and the French attempted settlement in 1562. It was the first state to secede from the Union in 1860, one of the triggers that launched the Civil War.

Virginia was the site of the first permanent English settlement in the New World—Jamestown—as well as the first popular assembly in America, convened in 1619. As a state it was home to four of the first five Presidents of the U.S.

OPPOSITE: *The finest depiction of the colonies in 1755, John Mitchell's map was drafted for the Lords Commissioners for Trade and Plantations.*

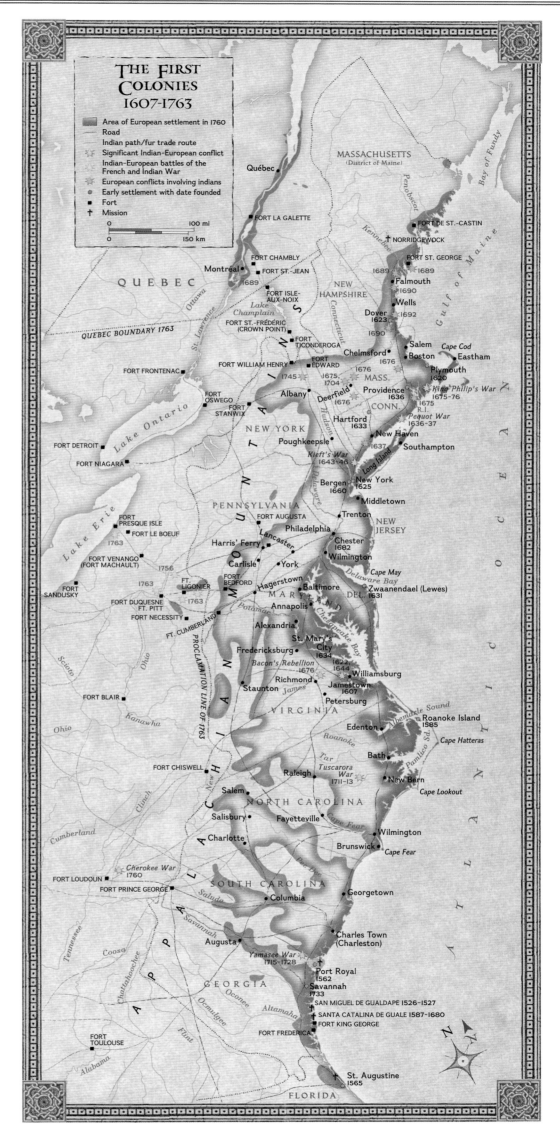

**THE FIRST COLONIES 1607-1763**

- Area of European settlement in 1760
- Road
- Indian path/fur trade route
- Significant Indian-European conflict
- Indian-European battles of the French and Indian War
- European conflicts involving indians
- Early settlement with date founded
- Fort
- Mission

0      100 mi
0      150 km

# The REVOLUTIONARY WAR

## Seeds of Unrest

**B**y 1700, while France and Spain held her New World possessions with nothing more than a string of missions and presidios, and the French were more interested in furs than permanent settlements, England's mainland colonies had grown to 250,000 people. The citizens were a varied lot, ranging from religious zealots and pioneering merchants to eccentric aristocrats. After struggling, Jamestown eventually grew, as did other English colonies. Free land and political and religious asylum lured

officials. And with Britain's attention often diverted by war with France, the colonies thrived during long stretches of virtual independence. When war broke out once again with France in the 1750s, Britain demanded the colonies help with the huge war debts. But each demand for more taxes forced the colonies closer to one another and broke another thread to England.

In the early 1700s, prosperity in the colonies grew. From southern planters, dependent on slave labor, to Pennsylvania

Ships from New England carried produce to the British West Indies. Colonists were required by Parliament to ship some commodities—including tobacco—to Britain, which sold them in Europe for nice profits. By 1750 American products accounted for a third of Britain's export trade. But American merchants were finding ways to evade British laws. The British policy of "salutary neglect" regulated only defense and trade, so elected assemblies in each colony assumed the powers to make laws and levy taxes. Royal governors retained veto powers, but assemblies had the authority to withhold their pay.

Between 1700 and 1750 colonial population multiplied fivefold to more than a million, and pressure grew to occupy lands west of the Appalachians. This expansion threatened the Indians, the French, and the Spanish. Militiamen from the populous British colonies and Indians allied to the French engaged in sporadic frontier fighting that flared and waned without conclusion. In the French and Indian War, early British losses in a series of scattered engagements eventually turned to victory in

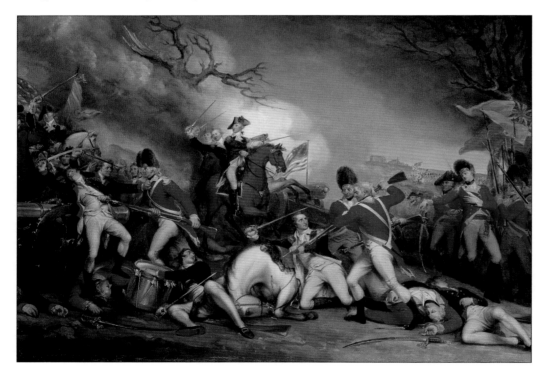

English emigrants to the New World. They paid or worked their way to land from Nova Scotia to the West Indies. Among them were younger sons seeking the holdings and status denied them by law in England.

The colonies set up advisory assemblies with the authority to levy taxes and pay

wheat farmers in spacious houses, wealth based on agriculture was expanding. In New England, yeomen owned their land. Land ownership was "what chiefly induces people into America," said a New York official. English ships bound for world markets were filled with tobacco from Virginia and Maryland and rice from the Carolinas.

### The FIRST SUBMARINE

**A**n unlikely craft saw service in the American Revolution. The *Turtle*, a watertight oak submarine designed and built by David Bushnell, was the first submarine used during warfare. The barrel-shaped craft held one person and was propelled by a handcrank. It could descend or rise by admitting and releasing water into ballast tanks. It had enough air to last half an hour. Its mission was to submerge beneath a British ship and force a long screw into the ship's hull. A watertight cask filled with gunpowder would then be attached to the screw and a fuse ignited.

The *Turtle* launched itself against a British warship anchored in the New York Harbor on September 6, 1776. Army sergeant Ezra Lee was at the controls. But the submarine's screw hit an iron plate and was unable to penetrate the hull. *Turtle* made two more unsuccessful attempts before being retired. But it won fame as the first submarine to be used in a military operation.

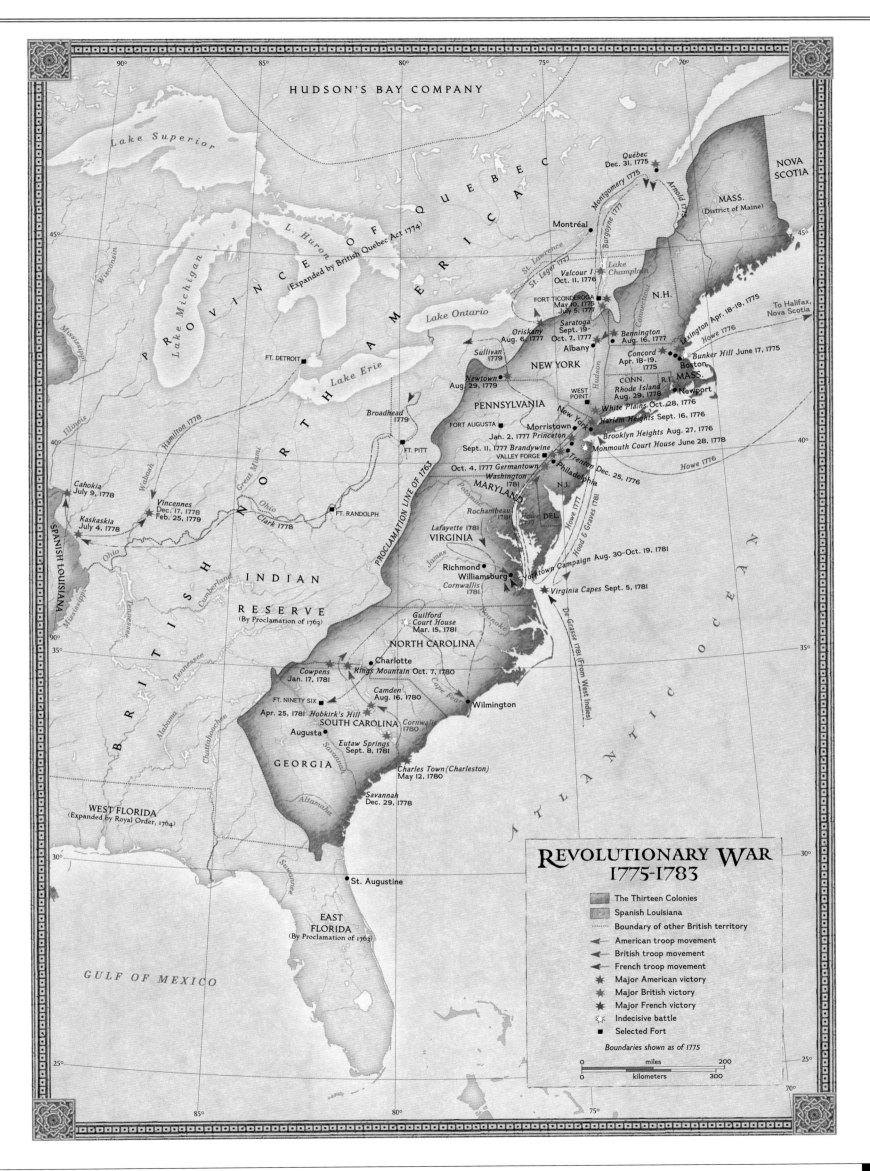

HUDSON'S BAY COMPANY

Lake Superior

L. Huron

Lake Michigan

PROVINCE OF QUEBEC

(Expanded by British Quebec Act 1774)

Lake Ontario

Lake Erie

NORTH AMERICA

FT. DETROIT

Montréal

Québec
Dec. 31, 1775

Montgomery 1777

Burgoyne 1777

Arnold 1775

NOVA
SCOTIA

MASS.
(District of Maine)

St. Lawrence

St. Leger 1777

Valcour I.
Oct. 11, 1776

Lake
Champlain

FORT TICONDEROGA
May 10, 1775
July 5, 1777

N.H.

Oriskany
Aug. 6, 1777

Saratoga
Sept. 19–
Oct. 7, 1777

Bennington
Aug. 16, 1777

Lexington Apr. 18-19, 1775

Howe 1776

To Halifax,
Nova Scotia

Sullivan
1779

Albany

NEW YORK

Connecticut

Concord
Apr. 18-19,
1775

Bunker Hill June 17, 1775

Boston

Newtown
Aug. 29, 1779

Broadhead
1779

PENNSYLVANIA

WEST
POINT

CONN.
Rhode Island
Aug. 29, 1778

R.I.
MASS.

Newport

Hudson

White Plains Oct. 28, 1776

Harlem Heights Sept. 16, 1776

FORT AUGUSTA

Morristown

New York

Brooklyn Heights Aug. 27, 1776

FT. PITT

Princeton
Jan. 2, 1777

Sept. 11, 1777 Brandywine

VALLEY FORGE

Oct. 4, 1777 Germantown

Monmouth Court House June 28, 1778

Trenton Dec. 25, 1776

N.J.

Howe 1776

FT. RANDOLPH

Washington
1781

Philadelphia

Cahokia
July 9, 1778

Vincennes
Dec. 17, 1778
Feb. 25, 1779

Clark 1778

Hamilton 1778

Great Miami

Ohio

MARYLAND

Rochambeau
1781

Howe 1777

DEL.

Kaskaskia
July 4, 1778

SPANISH LOUISIANA

Ohio

Wabash

BRITISH

PROCLAMATION LINE OF 1763

Lafayette 1781

VIRGINIA

Potomac

Richmond

Williamsburg

Cornwallis
1781

Yorktown Campaign Aug. 30-Oct. 19, 1781

Virginia Capes Sept. 5, 1781

De Grasse 1781 (From West Indies)

James

Illinois

Wisconsin

Mississippi

Tennessee

Cumberland

Tennessee

INDIAN

RESERVE
(By Proclamation of 1763)

Roanoke

Guilford
Court House
Mar. 15, 1781

NORTH CAROLINA

Cowpens
Jan. 17, 1781

Charlotte

Kings Mountain Oct. 7, 1780

FT. NINETY SIX

Camden
Aug. 16, 1780

Apr. 25, 1781 Hobkirk's Hill

SOUTH CAROLINA

Cornwallis
1780

Cape Fear

Wilmington

Alabama

Chattahoochee

Augusta

Savannah

Eutaw Springs
Sept. 8, 1781

GEORGIA

Charles Town (Charleston)
May 12, 1780

Altamaha

Savannah
Dec. 29, 1778

WEST FLORIDA
(Expanded by Royal Order, 1764)

Suwannee

St. Augustine

EAST
FLORIDA
(By Proclamation of 1763)

GULF OF MEXICO

ATLANTIC OCEAN

## REVOLUTIONARY WAR
## 1775-1783

▨ The Thirteen Colonies
▨ Spanish Louisiana
⋯ Boundary of other British territory
← American troop movement
← British troop movement
← French troop movement
✦ Major American victory
✦ Major British victory
✦ Major French victory
✷ Indecisive battle
■ Selected Fort

*Boundaries shown as of 1775*

0          miles          200
0                         300
       kilometers

1763. The war demonstrated how independent the colonists had become. Virginia's governor Robert Dinwiddie said it took "great Persuasions, many Argum'ts and much difficulty" to get the assembly to raise money and troops. With the French routed from North America, Britain secured control east of the Mississippi River and gained enormous territory: Canada from France and Florida from Spain.

At the same time, American merchants were trading illegally with French Caribbean sugar islands. The British resolved to reassert control. Customs agents were ordered to crack down and courts to try smugglers. For the first time, Britain posted a large peacetime army in her American colonies.

"The cause of Boston," said George Washington, "the despotick measures in respect to it, I mean, now is and ever will be considered as the cause of America." Boston had won the other colonies' sup-

port in 1774 when the British Parliament closed Boston Harbor after colonial agitators called the Sons of Liberty dumped British-owned tea into the harbor. Britain was attempting to make the colonies shoulder part of the tremendous debts and expenses of maintaining troops in the new territories, but Americans, accustomed by now to governing and taxing themselves, saw no reason to pay the mother country's bills. Various money-raising acts—the Sugar Act of 1764, the Stamp Act of 1765, the Townshend duties of 1767—spurred American defiance.

Colonists sent delegates to congresses in 1765, 1774, and 1775; committees of correspondence traded news.

John Adams and other colonial lawyers argued that Parliament could not pass laws that violated Americans' "essential rights as British subjects," such as trial by jury and taxation only if accompanied by representation. Positions on both sides hardened, and rhetoric grew inflammatory.

In 1775, George III and his ministers vowed to master the "unhappy and deluded multitude" of Americans, an end easier announced than accomplished.

## Into the Fray

Force "should be repelled by force," the British government commanded Gen. Thomas Gage when New England began raising troops. On April 18, 1775, Gage sent troops from Boston to Concord, Massachusetts, to capture colonial leaders and shot, powder, and other military stores. Warned by Paul Revere, 70 militiamen met 180 British soldiers at Lexington on April 19. The forces exchanged shots, and the redcoats marched on to Concord, where 450 Americans faced 700 British. Americans lined the roads to Boston, firing continually from behind houses, barns, trees, and stone walls. By day's end, 49 Americans and

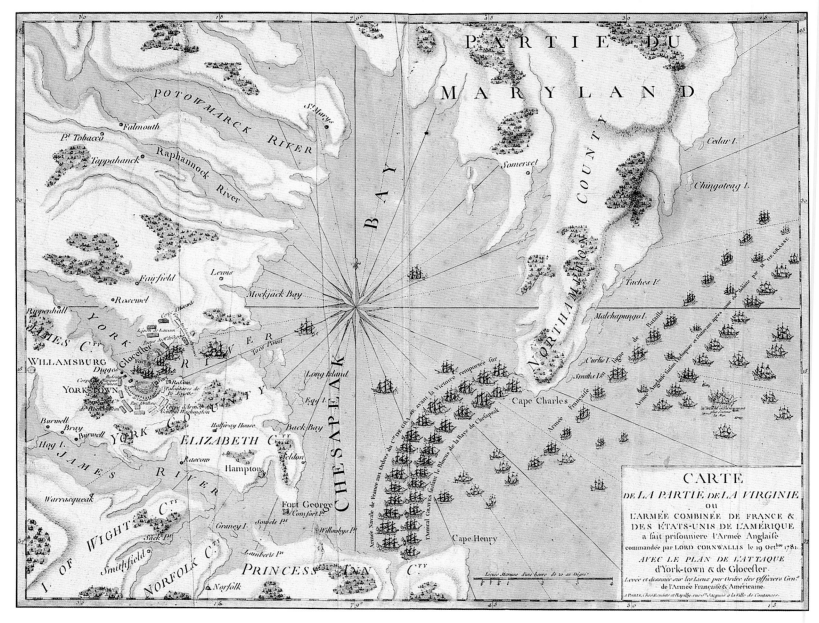

73 British had been killed, and the march to Boston was a new and bitter experience for British soldiers, who were accustomed to battling in orderly ranks and squares. The retreat established guerrilla warfare as the Americans' best defense strategy against the more traditional British troops.

Early battles raged around Boston. British Maj. John Pitcairn, who had said the "peasants" fired first at Lexington, was killed at Breed's Hill in Charlestown. There some 3,000 colonists amassed to loosen the British grip on Boston. Gen. William Howe, the new British commander, ordered a traditional frontal attack on June 17, 1775. The Americans succeeded in repelling the 2,300 redcoats twice but retreated after running out of ammunition. Technically a British victory, the battle—misnamed for nearby Bunker Hill—killed 226 redcoats and boosted American morale.

Thomas Paine's fiery tract, *Common Sense,* inflamed passions. "Everything that is right or reasonable pleads for separation. The blood of the slain, the weeping voice of nature cries, *'Tis time to part.*" The pamphlet sold 120,000 copies in 1776 and, according to George Washington, worked "a powerful change in the minds of men."

John Adams was skeptical of ever making "thirteen clocks strike at the same time," but it happened on July 4, 1776, when delegates from each of the 13 Colonies approved the Declaration of Independence. Author Thomas Jefferson had "turned to neither book nor pamphlet" in preparing the landmark document. But Adams brooded about the "bloody conflict we are destined to endure." American spirits were buoyed by news that at Christmas time, 1776, Washington took a thousand British and Hessian prisoners at Trenton, New Jersey. Upon meeting Washington, French officer Claude Blanchard described his countenance as "grave and serious, but it is never stern, and, on the contrary, becomes softened by the most gracious and amiable smile."

Britain brought to the conflict the world's largest navy, but its small professional army was no match for the colonials in the hinterland of America. They lost an entire army at Saratoga, New York, in 1777, which showed the dangers of marching into a countryside up in arms.

After the failed British offensive in Massachusetts and disastrous American forays into Canada, the war shifted to the mid-Atlantic region. Defeats did not discourage Washington, who by 1778

## PAUL REVERE'S RIDE *by* HENRY LONGFELLOW

Listen my children and you shall hear
Of the midnight ride of Paul Revere
On the eighteenth of April, in Seventy-five;...
He said to his friend, "If the British march
By land or sea from the town to-night,
Hang a lantern aloft in the belfry arch
Of the North Church tower as a signal light,—
One if by land, and two if by sea;
And I on the opposite shore will be,...
Now he patted his horse's side,
Now he gazed at the landscape far and near,
Then, impetuous, stamped the earth,
And turned and tightened his saddle girth;...
And lo! as he looks, on the belfry's height
A glimmer, then a gleam of light!
He springs to the saddle,...
A hurry of hoofs in a village street,
A shape in the moonlight, a bulk in the dark,
And beneath, from the pebbles,
in passing, a spark
Struck out by a steed flying fearless and fleet;...
It was two by the village clock,
When he came to the bridge in Concord town.
He heard the bleating of the flock,
And the twitter of birds among the trees,
You know the rest. In the books you have read
How the British Regulars fired and fled,—
A cry of defiance, and not of fear,
A voice in the darkness, a knock at the door,
And a word that shall echo for evermore!
For, borne on the night-wind of the Past,
Through all our history, to the last,
In the hour of darkness and peril and need,
The people will waken and listen to hear
The hurrying hoof-beats of that steed,
And the midnight message of Paul Revere.

acknowledged a standoff: "Both armies are brought back to the very point they set out from." Also in 1778, seven states signed the Articles of Confederation, and France declared war against Great Britain.

But a joint campaign of American troops under Gen. John Sullivan and the French fleet of Count Jean Baptiste d'Estaing failed to force the surrender of British-held Newport, Rhode Island.

The American situation was not helped by the dithering of colonial politicians. The Continental Congress hesitated to exercise its power. Instead of raising funds through taxation, it printed paper dollars until they inflated to worthlessness. Much of the burden of managing the war fell on Washington. The longer he managed to keep his ragged troops in the field, the more war weariness grew in Britain. French alliance with the colonists in 1778 and loans from European bankers further helped the revolutionary cause.

Late in 1778 Britain looked to the South to find "good Americans to subdue the bad ones." A British army led by Lord Cornwallis instead found guerrilla war and mounting casualties. Harried by Gen. Nathanael Greene, Cornwallis turned north to Virginia, which he considered pivotal in training and supplying American troops. His surrender at Yorktown ended Britain's southern strategy—and effectively ended the war.

In August 1782, Britain and the colonial army clashed in South Carolina, their last battle in the East, and the next year the Continental Army disbanded, though a contingent stayed on duty until all British troops had withdrawn.

The end of the war did not usher in unanimity among the Americans. When the British Army departed, so did much of the Americans' sense of common cause. "The rage of civil discord hath advanced among us with an astounding rapidity," wrote New York farmer and essayist J. Hector St. John de Crèvecour. "The laws are no longer respected and all the social bonds are loosened."

PAGE 32: *On horseback, General Washington surveys the carnage at the Battle of Princeton; John Trumbull painted this version.*

LEFT: *French generals ordered this map of Yorktown, Virginia, drawn on-site at the Battle of Yorktown. Complex waterways of Chesapeake Bay made escape nearly impossible for British General Cornwallis.*

# DECLARATION *of* INDEPENDENCE

## *First Steps to Freedom*

On a day sacred to Americans—July 4, 1776—the Continental Congress, gathered in Philadelphia, declared to the world that the Colonies were separating, officially and permanently, from their mother country, Great Britain. They issued a document—"unanimously"—that set out the arguments why "these United Colonies" should be free and independent. It was called the Declaration of Independence, and its impact reverberates to this day.

Professor Stephen E. Lucas, writing for the U.S. National Archives, has called the Declaration "perhaps the most masterfully written state paper of Western civilization."

Before the fighting against Britain's forces began on April 19, 1775, most colonists favored continued union with the mother country. But as the fighting continued month after month, and as Britain's forces in North America grew ever larger and more intrusive, most people came to favor separation. At the Continental Congress, Thomas Jefferson, John Adams, Benjamin Franklin, Roger Sherman, and Robert R. Livingston were named to a committee to draft a statement, setting out the reasons for independence. The committee in turn chose Jefferson to write the first draft. They "unanimously pressed on myself alone to undertake the draught. I consented; I drew it...." Franklin and Adams read the document and made a few changes. It was presented to the full congress, which passed it.

The American Declaration of Independence is formally structured and classically argued. It has a clear beginning, middle, and end—introduction, body, and conclusion. The "causes" that make disunion necessary are stated first, among them the principles already considered "self-evident" by most thoughtful 18th-century Englishmen.

What the colonists considered a "long train of abuses and usurpations" that they had endured at the hands of King George III began the heart of the document. Then followed a complaint that their "British brethren" had ignored their appeals for a greater measure of freedom. Having argued its position, the Declaration ends with ringing prose: "...these United colonies are, and of Right ought to be Free and Independent States; that they are Absolved from All Allegiance to the British Crown, and that all political connection between them and the State of Great Britain, is and ought to be totally dissolved."

John Dunlap, official printer to the Congress, worked through the night and on the morning of July 5, copies were dispatched by members of Congress to various assemblies, conventions, and committees, as well as to the commanders of Continental troops. There are 24 copies known to exist today.

But the Declaration had not yet become the image so familiar today. On July 19, Congress ordered that Declaration be "fairly engrossed on parchment, with the title and stile of 'The

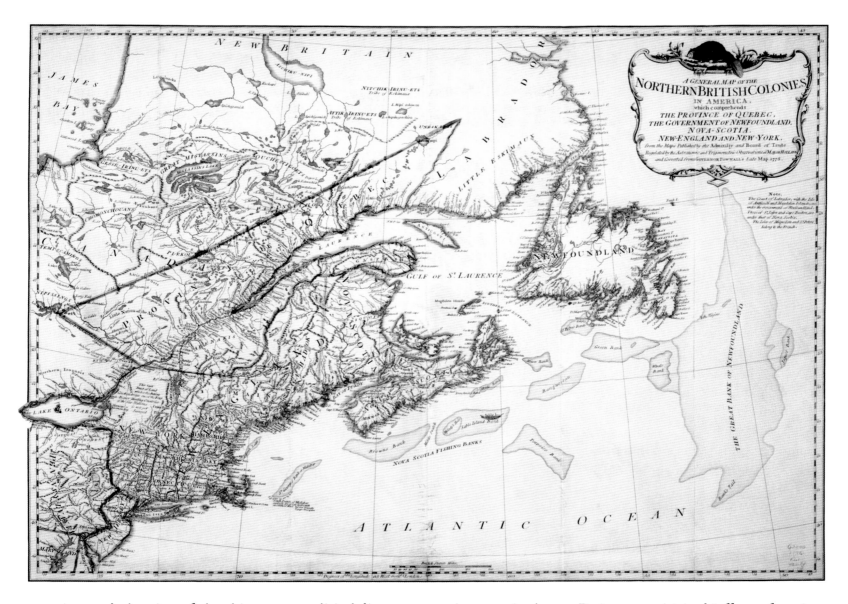

unanimous declaration of the thirteen United States of America,' and that the same, when engrossed, be signed by every member of Congress." An embosser, perhaps Timothy Matlack, though no one is quite certain, created the handsome document, with its flowing calligraphy, that is so familiar today. On August 2 the document was ready for signing. John Hancock went first, with a flourish; the other delegates followed. As was standard procedure in the day, their signatures are spaced on the document according to the geographic location of their states: New Hampshire appears at the top of the list and Georgia at the bottom. Though 56 delegates signed, several demurred: John Dickinson, still hopeful of reconciliation with Britain, and Robert R. Livingston, who thought it too soon for such a declaration, refused.

Thomas Jefferson employed all the tricks of 18th-century rhetoric in writing the Declaration. The first long sentence, with its magisterial language, elevates the quarrel with England from a petty political dispute to a major event in the grand sweep of history. Also, it labels the Americans "one people" and the British "another," and because two alien peoples cannot be made one, it reinforced the notion that breaking the political bands with England was a necessary step. And importantly, once it had been established that the Americans and English are two distinct peoples, the conflict could not be seen as a civil war. This was crucial in opening the way for aid from other countries, for, as Samuel Adams explained, "no foreign Power can consistently yield Comfort to Rebels, or enter into any kind of Treaty with these Colonies till they declare themselves free and independent."

Highly literate and well read, Jefferson was a careful student of the written prose of the 18th century, with all its rhetorical flourishes and classical formality. In 1786 he even wrote a 28-page essay, "Thoughts on English Prosody," in order "to find out the real circumstance which gives harmony to English prose and laws to those who make it." The *Edinburgh Review* once criticized Jefferson for using newly coined American words and corrupting the purity of the traditional English language. Jefferson responded: "[H]ad the preposterous idea of fixing the language been adopted by our Saxon ancestors, of Peirce Plowman, of Chaucer, of Spenser, the progress of ideas must have stopped with that of the language…what do we not owe to Shakespeare for the enrichment of the language, by his free and magical creation of words?"

In the Declaration of Independence, ideas and words came together in a lasting and dramatic union.

---

OPPOSITE: *Thomas Jefferson (standing) submits his draft of the Declaration of Independence to Benjamin Franklin and John Adams, soliciting their "judgments and amendments."* ABOVE: *Little more than a month after the Declaration was signed in Philadelphia, this English map, subtitled "The Seat of War in the Northern Colonies," was printed in London.*

# DEVELOPMENT
## *of the* POLITICAL PARTIES

❧

## *Whigs, Tories, and War Hawks*

With the Revolution won, and Americans independent, with a President and a Congress installed, early patriots got down to the business of running the country. Almost at once, two distinct philosophies of governing began to emerge, philosophies whose basic ideas survive today, though the names have changed.

In 1790, after the war, the administration of President Washington instituted brilliant but severe fiscal measures devised by Alexander Hamilton, the 35-year-old Treasury secretary from the West Indies. His followers spoke of themselves as Federalists and were in favor of Britain, industry, and a strong central government.

Thomas Jefferson had his own supporters, anti-Federalist Americans who were known as Jeffersonian Republicans or Democratic-Republicans. They favored an agrarian society of farmers and merchants and a minimal federal government. They took much of their inspiration from the French Revolution. They elected Jefferson as their first president.

As political parties sorted themselves out, shifting from left to right and back again to the center, a mechanism for selecting a party's candidates for office evolved along with them—the party convention. The first were held in 1832.

In 1840, at their third national nominating convention, the Democratic-Republicans adopted "Democratic party" as their official name. A group focused attention on the frontier. Led by Henry Clay, they called themselves the "War Hawks" and promoted increasing the size of the American territories by acquiring Florida and Texas from Spain and Canada from Britain. They favored improving transportation to tie the frontier, where they felt isolated and vulnerable, more closely to the rest of the country. As part of that program,

---

### AARON BURR

Grandson of the theologian Jonathan Edwards, Aaron Burr came from a prominent New Jersey family, studied law, and served on the staff of General Washington during the Revolution. Tied with Jefferson for electoral votes in the election of 1800, Burr was finally anointed vice president; he blamed Alexander Hamilton for lobbying against him. In 1804 he was nominated for the governorship of New York, but once again Hamilton contributed to his defeat by disseminating letters containing derogatory comments about him. On July 11, 1804, the two fought a duel in Weehawken, New Jersey. Hamilton had won the right to choose the weapons and right to say when to fire, but Burr may have fired before the signal was given. Witnesses disagreed. Charged with murder, and with a warrant out for his arrest, he fled to Philadelphia, then tried to escape to Spanish territory. He was arrested and returned for trial in the Circuit Court in Richmond, Virginia, before Chief Justice John Marshall.

Acquitted, he journeyed to Europe, where he lived for four years before returning to New York in 1812. He married a wealthy widow in 1833, frittered away much of her fortune, and died on the day a divorce decree—charging adultery—was granted in 1836.

---

they favored a strong western army to protect settlers from Indians. They thought the country's defense in general should be in the hands of a strong federal army and navy, rather than in state militias.

Another group of Democrats in the North urged tariff protection against foreign competitors, and both groups favored state banks instead of a strong, central bank. President Andrew Jackson promoted these positions, and with his support and encouragement, today's Democratic party was born.

In the meantime, the modern Republican party grew from different impulses. The Federalists had been powerful under presidents Washington and John Adams, but began to lose influence when Jefferson came to power. They were reborn a couple of decades later as National Republicans, which in turn became the Whig party in the years between 1834 and 1856.

The Whigs traced their ancestry to two revolutions against monarchies—their own American Revolution and the 17th-century English revolution—in which opponents of the King had been known as Whigs. But this time they were in opposition to Andrew Jackson, whom they regarded as a tyrant as dangerous as King George. Henry Clay of Virginia and Daniel Webster of New Hampshire were strong Whig leaders, but when they both died in 1852 the party began to fade away.

By 1854 the two-party system had collapsed, destroyed by the disappearance of the Whigs and the breaking up of the Democratic party into noisy factions. From the ashes grew the Republican party, organized in 1854 to oppose the Kansas-Nebraska Bill, which provided that the question of slavery in the proposed territories of Kansas and Nebraska be left to the residents of each territory.

In the presidential campaign of 1856 they promoted their candidate, John C. Frémont, with the slogan, "Free Soil, Free Labor, Free Speech, Free Men, Frémont." A four-way presidential race in 1860 brought Abraham Lincoln to the White House and the stage was set for the Civil War.

Before the conventions came along, candidates for office had generally been chosen in informal caucuses of the states' congressional delegations. But the caucuses were closed to the public, and the secrecy bred abuses and corruption. Leaders hoped that the conventions would open the process to the public. But in fact most decisions were made in the notorious "smoke-filled rooms" out of sight of the public and often corrupted by a network of local Good Ol' Boys. Today most states hold primary elections to choose delegates to the conventions, who in turn select the candidates.

The growth of these presidential primaries has lessened the importance of conventions; generally, today they simply ratify the candidate already selected by the voters. A candidate who has won enough delegates in the primaries can be pretty certain of winning the nomination on the first ballot.

For some years in mid-century, televised political conventions were spectacles that riveted the attention of the nation. Several ballots might be needed to select a candidate, as delegates wheeled and dealed, and the conventions received nearly gavel-to-gavel coverage. But with the increasing importance of the primary system, along with polling, which now tells party leaders which candidate is most popular among the electorate, television coverage has decreased.

Critics accuse party conventions of being undemocratic spectacles, but defenders argue that they not only promoted party unity and enthusiasm but also allowed for compromises. Too, they tended to produce nominees and platforms that represented the political center rather than the extremes of either right or left.

BELOW: *As envisioned by its architect, the new capital city of Washington was a checkerboard crisscrossed by broad avenues. This version from 1792 of the city plan appeared on a souvenir handkerchief.*

# The
# COTON GIN

<figure style="text-align:center">⤬</figure>

## *Machine of Slavery*

"Wanted: lands…in the climate of middle Georgia, on rivers flowing smoothly to the sea, under laws favorable to the holding Negroes in bondage." Such notices in the early 19th century announced many a southern farmer's intention to move west and to take slavery with him.

By 1820 the cotton frontier had pushed west into parts of Tennessee, Alabama, Mississippi, and Louisiana. Tobacco growers broke new ground in Tennessee and Kentucky. Rice and sugarcane remained confined to coastal regions in the Carolinas, Georgia, and Louisiana.

The spread of cotton throughout the South was in significant part due to the invention of one man.

The plantations along the coast grew a long-fibered cotton that could be easily separated from the seed. But this long-fibered cotton could be grown only in a small coastal area of the South, so the planters could not produce enough to meet demand.

They turned to a green-seeded, or short-staple, cotton, a variety hardy enough to survive inland winters, but, to an 18th-century grower, it was "so full of Seeds, that it cannot be cleansed by the ordinary Way of a Gin, or by any other Means than picking out with Fingers."

Most of the cotton was grown on plantations, cultivated and picked by slaves. But even with slave labor the job of seeding cotton by hand was enormously time-consuming. A young Yale graduate named Eli Whitney solved the problem, and his invention helped to spread cotton plantations throughout the South.

"The artist of his Country," a contemporary called Whitney in 1801, adding, "all Men of all parties agree that his talents are of immense importance…."Whitney was the first child of Eli Whitney, Sr., and Elizabeth Fay, born on December 8, 1765, on a farm near Westborough, Massachusetts, just 12 miles from Concord, where the shot heard round the world had been fired. His mother died when he was 12, and two years later he acquired a stepmother and two stepsisters.

Yearning for an education, Whitney when nearly 18 became a schoolteacher. At the time, anyone who could satisfy town authorities could have the job, and it gave Whitney valuable training: In order to teach, he had first to learn, studying to stay ahead of his pupils. He taught for nearly five years.

At 23 he departed for New Haven and Yale.

College broadened Whitney's outlook, stimulated his already active mind, and smoothed his country manners. It also introduced him to contacts who would be important to him as a businessman throughout his life. While in school he worked to help support himself, but still wrote to his father: "I have succeeded very well in my studies, & meet with no other difficulties but the want of money, which indeed is very great."

Nearly 27 years old, penniless, and without prospects, Whitney graduated intending to study law and engaged himself as a tutor to a South Carolina planter's family. The tutoring job fell

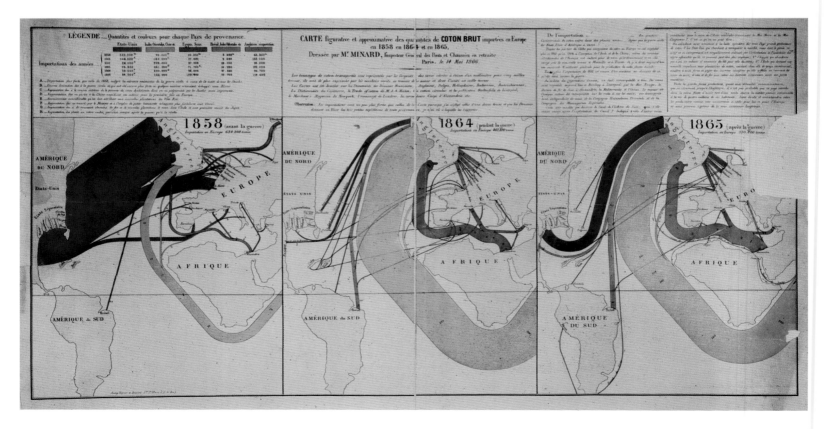

COOVERT, MEMPHIS, TENN. № 307

through, but while journeying south Whitney had met Catherine Greene, widow of the late Gen. Nathanael Greene, her children, and her estate manager. Their friendship blossomed and Mrs. Green—a vivacious and generous person—invited Whitney to stay at her plantation as her guest. Within two weeks of his arrival in 1793 he had invented the machine that made his fame.

It was simplicity itself. Slender wire fingers, picking up cotton fed into a curved hopper, carried the fibers through a grid at the top that was too fine for seeds, which fell away. "The cotton is put into the Hopper," he wrote, "carried thro' the Breastwork by the teeth, brushed off from the teeth by the Clearer and flies off from the Clearer with the assistance of the air, by its own centrifugal force. The machine is turned by water, horses or in any other way as is most convenient. It was so simple that farmers found they could make their own, and Whitney spent years fighting to protect his patent and for a share of the

wealth from cotton. He managed to persuade several states to pay him a flat fee for the right to use his machine, but he barely covered expenses before his patent expired in 1807.

By 1811 he was a bitter man. He wrote to fellow inventor Robert Fulton: "this Machine being immensely profitable to almost every individual in the Country all were interested in trespassing, & each justified & kept the other in countenance."

Cotton farming mushroomed. In 1795 planters grew eight million pounds; 12 years later the crop had increased to 80 million pounds, thanks largely to Whitney's gin. Cotton was king. But its rapid spread also led to an explosion of slavery: from fewer than 700,000 slaves in 1790 to more than two million 40 years later.

By early in the 18th century, growing waves of immigrants were arriving on America's shores. Many poor Irish, especially, turned hopefully toward America. During the 1820s some 50,000 Irish crossed the Atlantic and in the 1830s more than three times that number. Then,

beginning in 1845, a famine hit Ireland, caused by a potato blight. During those famine years, a million Irish people died, but a million and a half came to America. Many found work in mills that made thread and cloth. Such mills used up enormous quantities of raw cotton, which by 1850 became firmly established as America's most valuable crop.

At about the same time that the Whitney gin was catching on, the newly mechanized British textile industry was increasing its demand for U.S. cotton. Two million pounds were sent to Europe in 1794; 62 million were sent in 1811. Southern cotton growers could meet the demand largely because of Whitney's cotton gin.

OPPOSITE: *Civil War's effect on the cotton trade is graphically illustrated. In 1858 England imported nearly all of its cotton from America; but during and after the war, the U.S. was replaced as chief source.*
ABOVE: *Huge demand for cotton had to be met by slaves and sharecroppers alike. Here, black sharecroppers work a Tennessee cotton field.*

## Forming a More Perfect Union

*Heart of New Orleans: the Vieux Carré and its bustling waterfront ca 1885.*

• 1802 E. I. DuPont de Nemours and Company begin building a gunpowder factory on the Brandywine River near Wilmington, Delaware.
PAGES 58–59

• 1806 Frederick Tudor ships ice to the Caribbean, the start of New England's world-wide ice trade.

• 1808 Congressional ban on importing slaves from Africa is enacted after the expiration of a 20-year moratorium on such action written into the Constitution. Illegal importing continues.

• 1826 Thomas Jefferson's death, followed hours later by John Adams's, strikes many Americans as a sign of divine approval for the nation. The former Presidents died on July 4, the 50th anniversary of the Declaration of Independence.

• 1824 Fur trapper and scout Jim Bridger discovers Great Salt Lake.

• 1814 Francis Scott Key writes "The Star-Spangled Banner" after the shelling of Fort McHenry.

• 1814 The White House, the Capitol, and other buildings in Washington are burned by British forces in retaliation for the burning of Toronto by the U.S.

1800 1801 1802 1803 1804 1805 1806 1807 1808 1809 1810 1811 1812 1813 1814 1815 1816 1817 1818 1819 1820 1821 1822 1823 1824 1825 1826 1827 1828 1829 1830

• 1817 American Colonization Society is founded to buy land in West Africa for the resettlement of free blacks. There, Liberia's capital, Monrovia, is named for U.S. President James Monroe.

• 1807 Steamboat era begins with a New York City to Albany round-trip (five days with stops) made by Robert Fulton's paddle wheeler. Top speed: five miles an hour.
PAGES 54–55

• 1819 Washington Irving publishes "Rip Van Winkle" and "The Legend of Sleepy Hollow."

• 1823 James Fenimore Cooper publishes The Pioneers, a detailed account of frontier life and the first of the Leatherstocking tales.
PAGES 70–71

• 1803 The Supreme Court rules an act of Congress null and void in Marbury v. Madison, establishing itself as the ultimate interpreter of the Constitution.

• 1811 Construction begins on the National Road—from Cumberland, Maryland, to the Ohio River.
PAGES 60–61

• 1821 Sequoyah works 12 years to invent a written version of the Cherokee language. Thousands of his people learn to read and write the language, calling their Cherokee newspaper and books "talking leaves."
PAGES 62–63

• 1811 First Mississippi steamboat, S.S. New Orleans, leaves Pittsburgh for a four-month trip to the Gulf.
PAGES 54–55

• 1801 Mastodon fossils unearthed on two New York farms give the world its first skeletons of the extinct mammal.

• 1829 The first commercial railroad, the Baltimore & Ohio, carries passengers in a horse-drawn excursion train.

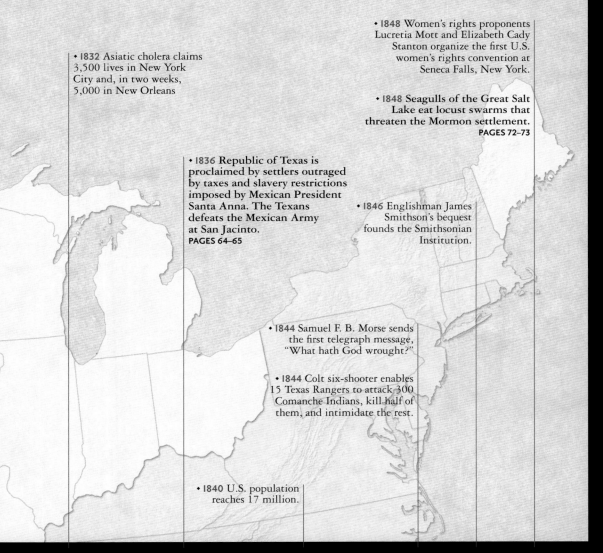

• **1832** Asiatic cholera claims 3,500 lives in New York City and, in two weeks, 5,000 in New Orleans

• **1848** Women's rights proponents Lucretia Mott and Elizabeth Cady Stanton organize the first U.S. women's rights convention at Seneca Falls, New York.

• **1848** Seagulls of the Great Salt Lake eat locust swarms that threaten the Mormon settlement. **PAGES 72–73**

• **1836** Republic of Texas is proclaimed by settlers outraged by taxes and slavery restrictions imposed by Mexican President Santa Anna. The Texans defeats the Mexican Army at San Jacinto. **PAGES 64–65**

• **1846** Englishman James Smithson's bequest founds the Smithsonian Institution.

• **1844** Samuel F. B. Morse sends the first telegraph message, "What hath God wrought?"

• **1844** Colt six-shooter enables 15 Texas Rangers to attack 300 Comanche Indians, kill half of them, and intimidate the rest.

• **1840** U.S. population reaches 17 million.

**1831 1832 1833 1834 1835 1836 1837 1838 1839 1840 1841 1842 1843 1844 1845 1846 1847 1848 1849**

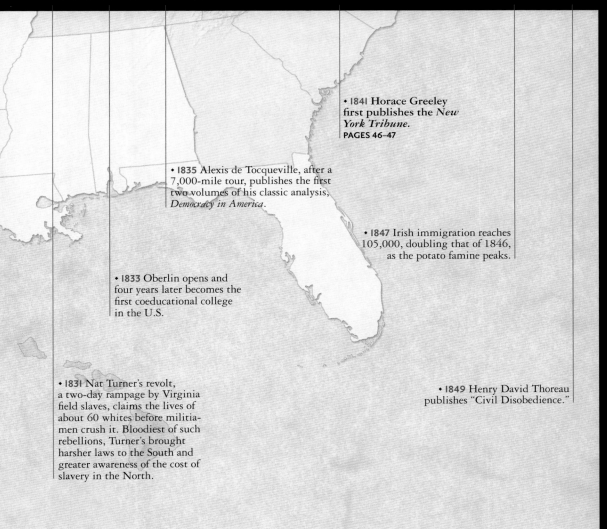

• **1841** Horace Greeley first publishes the *New York Tribune*. **PAGES 46–47**

• **1835** Alexis de Tocqueville, after a 7,000-mile tour, publishes the first two volumes of his classic analysis, *Democracy in America*.

• **1847** Irish immigration reaches 105,000, doubling that of 1846, as the potato famine peaks.

• **1833** Oberlin opens and four years later becomes the first coeducational college in the U.S.

• **1831** Nat Turner's revolt, a two-day rampage by Virginia field slaves, claims the lives of about 60 whites before militiamen crush it. Bloodiest of such rebellions, Turner's brought harsher laws to the South and greater awareness of the cost of slavery in the North.

• **1849** Henry David Thoreau publishes "Civil Disobedience."

ICTORY IN THE REVOLU-tionary War brought the United States a vast western domain, as Virginia, New York, and Connecticut abandoned claims to land northwest of the Ohio River. But Indian strength impeded settlement. After settling land disputes with New York, Vermont became the first state added to the original 13. Virginia's western district of Kentucky gained statehood a year later.

After victory at Yorktown, the young United States found themselves with an enormous national debt, millions of dollars owed to France and to private citizens. With no authorization to levy taxes, the Confederation Congress looked to land sales for revenues. Land it had in abundance—the public domain, swaths of land stretching to the Mississippi River. This land could be disposed of for money, and as the country grew westward more vast stretches of public domain became available.

A grid of geometric square-mile sections would pattern the growing United States. Surveying had its beginnings in the Land Ordinance of 1785, which empowered a national geographer to direct the survey of lands purchased from the Indians northwest of the Ohio River. By 1796 the grid system was standard, though it seemed to contradict the actual shape of the land. However, it simplified the buying and selling of land in the West. Abraham Lincoln's parents settled on the Indiana frontier in 1816 on "S. W. 1/4 of sect. 32, T. 4 S., R., 5 W." This was the legal description of its location (four townships south and five ranges west of the second principal meridian), its shape (square), and its size (160 acres).

The survey also fixed the arrow-straight courses of Main Streets and Elm Streets of thousands of new towns.

**1800–1849** *Saw the addition of Ohio. Louisiana. Indiana. Mississippi. Illinois. Alabama. Maine. Missouri. Arkansas. Michigan. Florida. Texas. Iowa. and Wisconsin to the Union.*

# The
# AMERICAN PRESS

### ❧

## Newspaper Presses Get Rolling

In 1799, Aaron Oliver, a post rider, carried the news by horseback through nearby Massachusetts cities. He advertised his service with a bit of doggerel: *O'er ruggid hills, and vallies wide,/He never yet has fail'd to trudge it;/As steady as the flowing tide,/He hands about the* Northern Budget.

In colonial times there were but three ways of relaying information: in person, by post, and by private messenger. News— whether spoken, written in letters, or printed—traveled only as quickly as those who carried it. Travelers and couriers put up at coffeehouses where they swapped tales, read broadsides, and exchanged newspapers that had been brought by ship from overseas. Just one issue of Benjamin Harris's 1690 *Publick Occurrences, Both Forreign and Domestick* appeared. "Therein," proclaimed the governor and council of Massachusetts, "is contained Reflections of a very high nature...also sundry doubtful and uncertain Reports."

The *Boston News-Letter*, founded by John Campbell in 1704, became the colonies' first successful newspaper. It was published "by Authority," which meant it was censored, but carried European reports from foreign journals and brief local bulletins. In 1721 James Franklin's *New-England Courant* began offering Boston readers more stimulating fare, including essays by "Silence Dogood," the pen name of Franklin's teenage brother Benjamin. Ben later had a press and paper of his own in Philadelphia. The infamous Stamp Act of 1765 taxed documents, including newspapers, throughout the colonies. The act was soon repealed but not before infuriating publishers and readers.

In 1775 roughly 20 cities along the Eastern Seaboard had weekly newspapers, some of them, like Philadelphia with seven and Boston with five, several of them. Trading vessels brought news to fill the journals in the commercial towns. Merchants, keen for news of commodity prices and naval doings, paid hefty subscription fees. Rivalries developed: "Its sheets smell stronger of beer than of midnight oil. It is not reading fit for people!"

one Boston paper claimed of another. Only the most successful papers turned a profit.

Printers trailed pioneers west, setting up shop in all major cities. A single office might churn out newspapers and stationery, church bulletins and business forms. Scholarly tomes and journals issued from university presses. Literature, pulp fiction, and, since the 1930s, comic books flourished.

With independence life's pace quickened in the cities, and informal coffeehouse newsbooks gave way to daily newspapers as sources of the best intelligence. New York City printers between them gave readers a paper on six days of the week in 1779. By 1800 editors in seven cities were publishing daily papers. In fact, Philadelphia had eight and even Charleston boasted three. Before long there was even a newspaper west of the Mississippi, the *Missouri Gazette,* established in St. Louis in 1808.

By 1820 Quaker Elihu Embree of Tennessee had established the *Manumission Intelligencer* and the *Emancipator,* the first U.S. papers to deal exclusively with abolition. Tempers ran high: In 1837 the Reverend Elijah Lovejoy was shot to death by a mob in Alton, Illinois, while trying to safeguard the press on which he printed his weekly antislavery newspaper.

In 1833, the New York *Sun,* priced to sell for just a penny—"It shines for all," ran its motto—put the six-cent competition to rout as it promptly matched, then doubled, the circulation of its closest rival. Dailies in New York, Boston, Baltimore, and Philadelphia joined in the price war, luring readers with low prices and lively stories, trusting high advertising revenues to cover costs. Cultured people, like James Fenimore Cooper, dismissed the papers as "vulgar," but the "penny press" had come to stay, spreading news every American could afford.

Benjamin Day, who founded the *Sun,* came to New York as a young man from the *Springfield Republican.* His innovative ideas made up for lack of funds, and within just six months of starting the paper he had increased its circulation to eight thousand, the largest circulation of any paper in New York. It covered crime with impudence and scandals with as much explicitness as he could get away with. Day was evidently the first newsman to hire boys to hawk single copies of his paper in the streets.

A serious rival came along two years later when James Gordon Bennett began publishing the *Morning Herald.* The two papers vied to see which could be the more irreverent. Though the *Sun* carried more foreign news and its reports on the doings on Wall Street were more reliable, both reported extensively on sensational crimes—murder and mayhem filled the pages. By 1860 Bennett's *New York Herald* was printing 77,000 copies a day.

A serious rival to both papers came along in 1841, when Horace Greeley began publishing the *Tribune,* a paper that reflected the Whig point of view. He used a combination of borrowed money and savings to

launch the paper, which was immediately successful; in two months it had a circulation of 11,000, which by the time of the Civil War had climbed to 65,000. It was a strong proponent of abolition.

The *New York Times* began life as the *New York Daily Times* in 1851. From the beginning it was more serious, aiming at a more intellectual and cultured reader than its rivals. It tried to cover "all the news"—generating the famous motto, "All the News That's Fit to Print." But it was losing $1,000 a day by 1896, when Adolph Ochs bought it and transformed it into the universally respected paper it is today.

Merchants and manufacturers quickly came to rely on newspapers to get word of their products and services to citizens. Advertisements are "the religion of the people," wrote one New York editor in 1873. "What a picture of the metropolis one day's advertisements in the *Herald* presents to mankind!"

Truly vulgar—and popular—were the brash yellow journals of the 1890s. Two New York papers, William Randolph Hearst's *Journal* and Joseph Pulitzer's *World,* led the pack, serving up scandal to an eager public and even inciting war with Spain. "A better place in which to prepare a young man for eternal damnation than a yellow journal office does not exist," declared E. L. Godkin, editor of the city's reserved *Evening Post.* Crusades against wealthy slumlords, garment-district sweatshops, and politicians on the take did much to redeem the sensational dailies "dedicated," in Joseph Pulitzer's words, "to the cause of the people."

Even as yellow journalism flooded American streets, Adolph Ochs's *New York Times* showed that careful, comprehensive reporting could also sell. Ochs aimed "to produce a highbrow newspaper for the intellectuals"—or so wrote one of his editors. Shunning excess, the *Times* accrued readers, intellectual and otherwise.

An 1894 handbook invited sensationalism from would-be journalists: "This trick of drawing upon the imagination for the non-essential parts of an article is certainly one of the most valuable secrets of the profession." The number of dailies peaked in 1909 as yellow papers ebbed.

By the 1840s New York supported a host of publishers and was becoming the center of American printing. Its magazines were read nationwide. Sales of paperbacks, pirated British novels, and sanctioned volumes (such as *Moby Dick* and an abridged Webster's dictionary) made Manhattan publisher Harper & Brothers the world's largest by 1853.

OPPOSITE: *Typographers and printers in an 1882 shop in Socorro, New Mexico, work to publish one of the many journals that helped keep sparsely settled communities in the West informed.*

# The LOUISIANA PURCHASE

❦

## Bargain of the Century

In 1801, when people spoke of Louisiana they meant, roughly, the mid part of North America encompassed by the drainage systems of the Missouri River and the southwestern tributaries of the Mississippi River. It was an enormous territory, claimed by Spain though, except for a handful of garrisons on the Mississippi, in St. Louis, and in New Orleans, there

Thomas Jefferson had long cast a covetous eye on the West, envisioning a day when the U.S. would be populated by citizens "speaking the same language, governed in similar forms, and by similar laws." He was worried by news from Europe in 1801.

Napoleon Bonaparte, determined to rebuild a French colonial empire in

In a bold move, Jefferson set out to buy Louisiana from France. His minister there, Robert R. Livingston, was directed to open negotiations—but only for New Orleans, through whose port most of the nation's produce passed, and for the colonies of eastern and western Florida.

Jefferson received another piece of bad news in 1802: Spanish officials in New Orleans had withdrawn the United States' "right of deposit," which meant American merchants could no longer store goods waiting to be shipped in the city. They wanted action.

Coincidentally, Napoleon was having troubles of his own. His island colony on Santo Domingo was in open rebel-

The PRAIRIE DOG sickened at the sting of the HORNET or a Diplomatic Puppet exhibiting his Deceptions!

were few Spaniards there to hold onto it. The Spaniards also claimed the whole of the Pacific Coast, though Russians had settled around the mouth of the Columbia River. And the Oregon country west of the Rocky Mountains, sprinkled with British fur traders, was claimed by England. The French, especially the trappers, had seen more of Louisiana than anyone else, and they seemed to be the only Europeans with much interest in it.

North America, had, through the Treaty of San Ildefonso in 1800, persuaded the Spanish to "retrocede" the port of New Orleans and all the territory of Louisiana west of the Mississippi to France. Jefferson knew very well what this meant: Instead of a weak Spanish government in America's West there would be a French one. And the French were, at the time, the most powerful military force in the world.

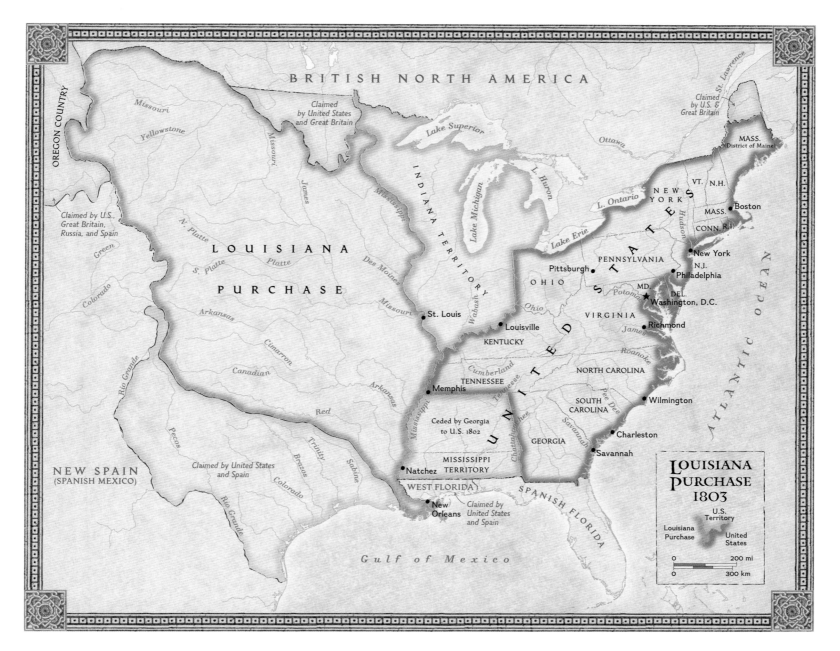

Map legend:

**LOUISIANA PURCHASE 1803**

U.S. Territory

Louisiana Purchase — United States

0 — 200 mi
0 — 300 km

lion. The French force there, the force that would be used to occupy Louisiana, had been routed from the island by a combination of yellow fever and guerrilla warfare.

Jefferson moved on two fronts. He sent James Monroe to France to assist Livingston with the negotiations. And he quietly sent a message to Congress proposing an expedition into the West. He knew the Federalists would object, so he called it a "literary pursuit." He emphasized the commercial advantages, noting the "great supplies of furs & pelty" that could be trapped in the region. He sought and was granted $2,500 "for the purpose of extending the external commerce of the U.S."

Meanwhile, in France, Napoleon was losing interest in Louisiana. He had lost 50,000 French lives in Santo Domingo and had concluded that Louisiana wasn't worth the trouble or the money. "I renounce Louisiana," he said. But he didn't want the territory to fall into the hands of his hated enemies, the British. To have it under U.S. control would be "more useful to the policy and even to the commerce of France." He would sell the Americans the entire territory.

His foreign minister, Charles Maurice de Talleyrand-Périgord had been meeting with Livingston for months in casual negotiations. When he requested another meeting, Livingston assumed it would be more of the same—routine discussions. He was astonished when Talleyrand inquired, "What would you give for the whole?"

Neither Monroe, who arrived in Paris the next day, nor Livingston had the authority for such a purchase. To buy territory that would in effect double the size of the U.S. far exceeded their warrant. But there was no time to send to America for instructions. With breathtaking audacity, they accepted the challenge. Henry Adams would later call the 1803 purchase "an event so portentous as to defy measurement."

Napoleon, too, was delighted with the deal. He knew he was permanently denying the land to the British. "The sale assures forever the power of the United States," he said, "and I have given England a rival who, sooner or later, will humble her pride."

Under the American flag now came more than 830,000 square miles of new territory—for 15 million dollars, less than three cents an acre. And with Louisiana in American hands, Jefferson was more determined than ever to have the new territory explored. He immediately turned his attention to organizing an expedition.

---

OPPOSITE: *Jefferson's purchase of the Louisiana Territory evokes scorn from an early cartoonist. Napoleon, a hornet, stings Jefferson, a prairie dog, causing him to cough up two million dollars; a French diplomat dances in glee.*

# LEWIS and CLARK

## Exploring the West

President Thomas Jefferson, a product of the Age of Enlightenment, was a man of enormous curiosity and learning. He had long hungered for knowledge about that part of the North American continent that lay beyond the Alleghenies, and when he got Congress to agree to finance an exploratory expedition there, he immediately set to work on it. To lead it he chose someone whom he had come to trust, his personal secretary Meriwether Lewis; Lewis, in turn, called upon an old friend and colleague, William Clark, to be his co-captain.

Their instructions from Jefferson were lengthy and precise: to collect information both scientific and practical about the land, soil, geology, flora and fauna, even what he called "useful" plants and animals. They were to explore the possibility of engaging in friendly relations with the western Indian tribes.

The two leaders decided between themselves to share command as well as the title "Captain" and devoted some months to putting together a party of about 25 frontiersmen, soldiers, and French trappers who had some knowledge of the West. They drew supplies from the army depot at Harpers Ferry. For food they packed flour, pork, a hundred gallons of whiskey, salt, and corn. They took 14 bales of beads and tobacco and ribbon and fishhooks for trading with the Indians. To help them map the countryside, they carried a sextant and chronometer, telescope and quadrant. Their gunpowder was packed in lead canisters that could be melted down and made into bullets as the powder was used up.

They pushed off up the muddy Missouri River in May 1804. They would traverse a total of 8,000 miles between St. Louis and the Pacific Ocean. They would impress many of the Indian tribes they met with the inevitable growth of the United States, an entity of which the Indians had never heard. They would fight biting winds and clouds of "musquitrs and knats" but would persevere.

They called themselves the Corps of Discovery. Included in the party were a Newfoundland retriever named Seaman and Clark's African American slave, York. In the first winter, the Corps would grow to include a young Indian girl. Her name—Sacagawea—translates as Bird Woman. For many years legend gave her more credit than she actually deserved,

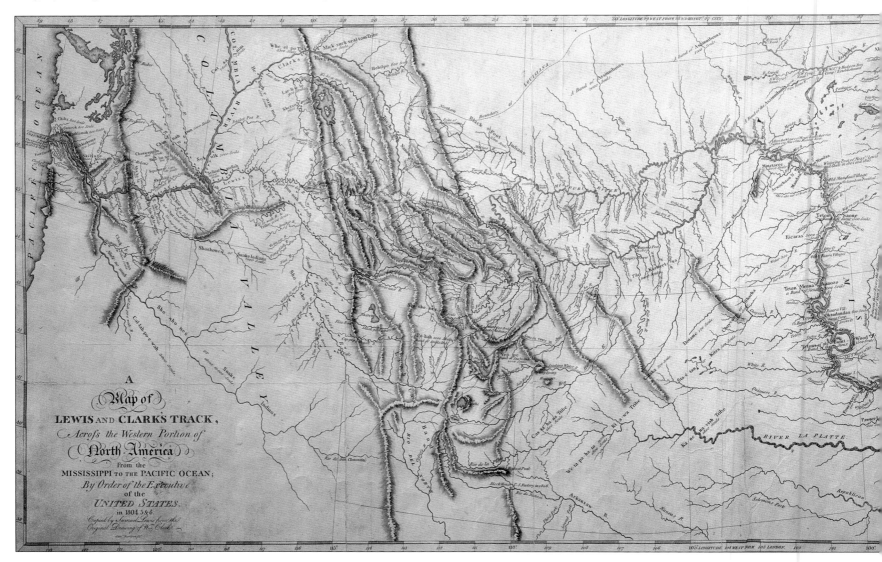

A Map of LEWIS AND CLARK'S TRACK, Across the Western Portion of North America From the MISSISSIPPI TO THE PACIFIC OCEAN; By Order of the Executive of the UNITED STATES in 1804, 5 & 6. Copied by Samuel Lewis from the Original Drawing of Wm. Clark.

calling her the expedition's guide and describing her as pointing the way West. She didn't do those things, but she did add measurably to the success of the expedition. She served as interpreter with her people, the Shoshone, during crucial negotiations for horses and guides to cross the mountains. And one day on the river a boating mishap nearly destroyed essential medicines and supplies. While some about her flailed about in panic, Sacagawea calmly retrieved the items. Lewis praised her "fortitude and resolution." Perhaps most important, she reassured potentially hostile tribes of Indians by her mere presence: No war party, they knew, would be accompanied by a woman.

Both captains and several of the other men kept journals of the journey. Clark was the worse speller but the more conscientious diarist; long gaps exist in Lewis's journals.

During the hot summer of 1804 they battled the strong Missouri current across present-day Missouri and along the border between Iowa and Nebraska. The heat and the mosquitoes bothered them greatly: "Muskuitors verry trou-

blesom," Clark wrote. One man got "snakebit," but recovered.

As an Army unit, military discipline was maintained. One man was lashed for drinking on duty and another for sleeping on watch. The countryside provided the hunters with more game than the Corps could eat: "Cat fish is cought in any part of the river. Turkeys Geese & a Beaver Killed & Cought every thing in prime order...."

Jefferson's instructions to them had included orders to observe "the face of the country, it's growth & vegetable productions...the animals of the country generally, & especially those not known in the U.S." They logged careful observations of plants and animals that were new to them into their journals, and by the end of the journey they had described hundreds of species previously unknown to science. They were first to describe the grizzly bear, whose ferocity they soon learned to respect; first to record the presence of the black-tailed prairie dog, the white-tailed jackrabbit, the Missouri beaver, the sage grouse, the western rattler and western tanager, the cottonwood, and the mountain goat. They lost many of their plant specimens when water seeped into a cache but still managed to bring back 200 gathered between Great Falls and the Pacific coast.

It took them two and a half months to reach the vicinity of present-day Council Bluffs, where they met with some Otoe and Missouri Indians. Nearby, on August 20, Sergeant Charles Floyd died. Incredibly he was the only casualty the party would suffer during the entire journey.

They encountered a band of Sioux who were seemingly spoiling for a fight, an episode that broke the routine and provided some excitement. The Sioux were long accustomed to charging a sort of toll on the fur traders who ascended the river. When Lewis and Clark refused to pay it tempers flared, arms were displayed, and a round of shoving and tugging took place.

The captains had invited the chiefs onto the keelboat and given them whiskey. One pretended to be drunk—to cloak his "rascally intentions," Clark thought, and the captains quickly sent their guests back ashore. There three young warriors seized the boat's cable,

and a chief bumped Clark, complaining that he had not received enough presents. Clark drew his sword and Lewis ordered the men to aim their weapons at the Indians. The Sioux had never seen such resistance from whites and backed down. It ended peacefully and the Corps

## SEAMAN

"Very active strong and docile," Lewis wrote of his Newfoundland dog Seaman. He would prove himself to be all those things during the trip to the Pacific and back. Lewis bought him for $20 somewhere in the East and, even before the expedition set out, he was catching squirrels on the river and retrieving them to Lewis, who found fried squirrel a "pleasant food."

During the trip up the Missouri, Seaman retrieved a goose, finished off a deer a hunter had wounded, and caught beaver—the men considered their tails a delicacy—even diving into their lodges. Near the mouth of the Yellowstone he caught an antelope in midstream and brought it ashore. One night while the camp slept, Seaman barked to turn aside a buffalo bull lurching toward camp and the sleeping men.

With his heavy coat, Seaman suffered from the summer heat, and a wounded beaver bit his leg, severing an artery and nearly killing him. The bugs and prickly pear cactus that tormented the men also tormented him.

They named a creek after him—Seaman Creek, now Monture Creek—a swift stream that flows into the Blackfoot River.

Lewis, the more contemplative of the captains, enjoyed walking along the shore as they ascended the river, and presumably Seaman was always with him.

Seaman makes his last appearance in the Journals when the party again neared Great Falls on the return journey. Mosquitoes were so bad that "my dog even howls with the torture he experiences." There is no further mention of him, so presumably he made as remarkable a trek as the men of the Corps—boating and walking thousands of miles to the Pacific Ocean and back again.

LEFT: *Using compass readings taken on the outward trek, Clark drew an amazingly accurate map of Western topography.*

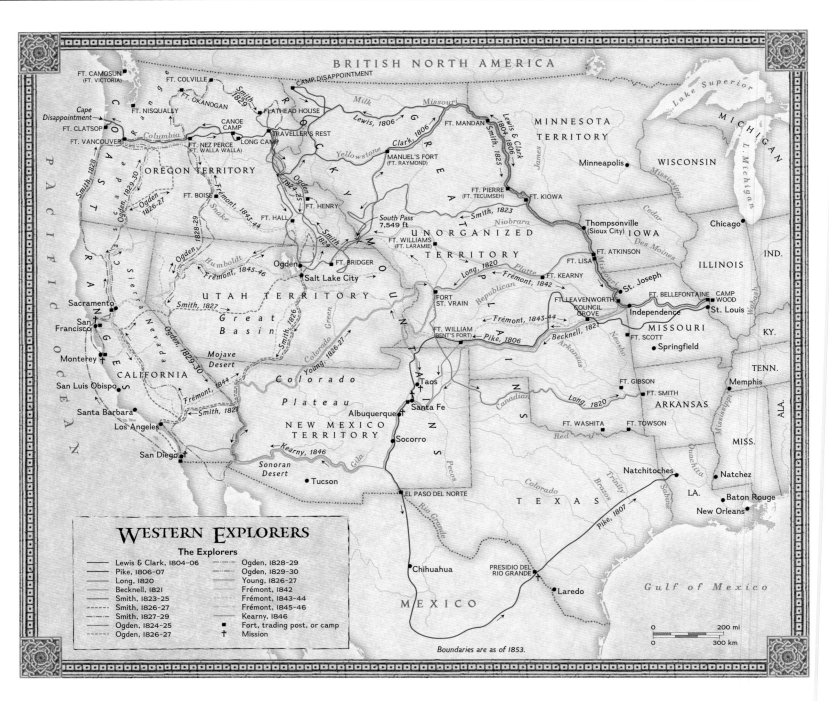

# A New Spring

had no more serious trouble with Indians until they reached the Pacific coast, where tribes had been corrupted by contact with white sailors.

They spent their first winter among the Mandan Indians near present-day Bismarck, North Dakota. They built Fort Mandan, a wooden stockade, and settled in. During the long dark winter the captains prepared an interim report for Jefferson, and packed Indian artifacts and scientific specimens to send back to him in the spring.

When spring arrived they set off up the river once more, in two pirogues—a sort of flat-bottomed dugout—and six canoes that the men had made during the winter. Lewis wrote, "We were now about to penetrate a country at least two thousand miles in width…the good or evil it had in store for us was for experiment yet to determine…."

In the great western plains of America, the Corps of Discovery encountered "emence" herds of bison and numerous deer, elk, and beaver. They had been warned about grizzly bears, and here they began coming upon them. At first they doubted the animals could be as fierce as they had been told: "…[T]he Indians may well fear this anamal," wrote Lewis, "with their bows and arrows…but in the hands of skillful riflemen, they are by no means as formidable or dangerous as they have been represented." He would soon eat those words. The bears proved to be ferocious, unpredictable, fearless, and extremely difficult to kill. A wounded one even chased Lewis into the river.

Everything they saw, they named, sprinkling names across the land with enthusiasm. Every river, creek, and island was named, often for family, friends, or colleagues. The farther they went, the shallower and more rapid the river became; sometimes the men were forced into the river to manhandle the heavy boats upstream, "even to their armpits."

They devoted several weeks to portaging around the Great Falls of the Missouri—five cataracts within twelve miles, now largely lost behind dams. It was a hot 16-mile portage, across endless stretches of prickly-pear cactus whose spines penetrated their moccasins. The falls, "hising flashing and sparkling" in their path, were one of the greatest obstacles they would face.

It had been reported to them that a portage of just 20 miles separated the headwaters of the Missouri from those of the Columbia. If only! Instead they found

220 miles of "high mountain countrey thickley covered with pine." By early summer they could see the glitter of snow on distant mountains to the north and west, mountains they would have to cross. They were discouraged to find that "the adjacent mountains commonly rise so high as to concel the more distant…from our view." Here were the massive ranges of the American Rocky Mountains.

They pressed on. They reached a place where the river forked into three branches. They named them for Gallatin, Madison, and Jefferson and correctly chose the Jefferson as the route that would take them to the Missouri's headwaters. But now they needed guides and horses to cross the mountains. And they must cross before another winter set in. They were counting on Sacagawea, who had been born nearby—she had been kidnapped by a rival tribe as a child—to help in negotiating for horses and guides. And when they finally found some Indians, an amazing coincidence was revealed. Sacagawea, called to interpret, "came into the tent, sat down, and was beginning to interpret, when in the person of [the chief] she recognized her brother: She instantly jumped up, and ran and embraced him, throwing over him her blanket and weeping profusely." The Corps of Discovery had stumbled upon the very band from which she had been stolen.

Now mounted and accompanied by friendly guides, the Corps set off across the Bitterroot Mountains. It was a difficult crossing, as difficult as anything they faced. The autumn snows began. They passed "up & Down Steep hills, where Several horses fell, Some turned over, and others Sliped down…one horse Crippeled & 2 gave out." Fallen trees and deep snows blocked their way. They melted snow for water and, as food supplies ran lower and lower, subsisted on dehydrated soup and bear's oil. "I have been wet and as cold in every part as I ever was in my life," wrote Clark.

But on September 19, Clark looked westward from a peak and saw an "emence Plain and leavel Countrey." They were across the worst of the mountains.

They gave up their horses and built more canoes, this time from huge pine

trees, and took to the water once again, this time traveling with the current. They replenished their food from friendly Nez Percé Indians. Plentiful salmon meant they were on a river that led to the ocean.

They floated the Clearwater to the Snake, the Snake to the Columbia, the Columbia to the ocean. On October 21, they met an Indian wearing a "Salors Jacket" and a week later "Great numbers of Sea Otters."

At the mouth of the Columbia, as fall progressed, they began building another

fort where they would spend their second winter. They called it Fort Clatsop after a local tribe of Indians and spent a miserable winter in it. It rained virtually every day and food once again was in short supply. They traded for fish with the Indians, and the hunters could only drag home skinny elk. Their Christmas meal consisted of "pore Elk, so much Spoiled that we eate it thro' mear necessity, Some Spoiled pounded fish and a fiew roots."

By early spring they were eager to start for home. The two captains split the party temporarily, Lewis to explore up the Marias River and Clark the Yellowstone. With only a couple of men with him, Lewis had a run-in with some Blackfeet and killed two of them when they tried to steal his guns and horses. They were the only Indians killed by the expedition during two tense years among them. Lewis was himself nearly killed later when one of the hunters mistook him for an elk and shot and wounded him. But in September 1806, they came floating down to a tumultuous welcome in St. Louis.

"Never did a similar event excite more joy thro' the United States," wrote a relieved Jefferson on their return. He was delighted with the information they brought him on natural history and the Indians. Their diaries catalogued 122 new species and subspecies of birds, fish, amphibians, mammals, and reptiles; and nearly 200 plants, many of them edible or medicinal.

Jefferson was disappointed with two pieces of information: There was no "practicable water communication across this continent for the purposes of commerce," as he had hoped. And there was no evidence of an ice-free Northwest Passage.

Still, the explorers brought back information about the American West that would lure more explorers and finally settlers. And their successful trip would give the U.S. a strong advantage as it laid claim to the Pacific Northwest.

ABOVE: *Meticulous in their thirst for knowledge of the natural world, Lewis and Clark made extensive notes and drawings of the flora and fauna of the new West. From the Columbia River came a eulachon, or candlefish (top); nearby grew the salmonberry (bottom).*

# STEAM *and the* MISSISSIPPI

## *Arteries of Trade*

Before steamboats and railroads, canals successfully provided transport in the U.S. At their height, a score of canals veined the East with 4,000 miles of waterways. Settlers could travel for a penny and a half a mile on the Erie Canal in 1825, while moving a ton of freight from Albany to Buffalo dropped from $100 by wagon to $20 by barge and the time from 20 days to 8 days. Settlers in the Midwest could ship a hundred times more coal or wheat on a canal boat than on a wagon, and the load could be hauled twice as far in a day with the same number of horses it took to pull the wagon.

Treasury Secretary Albert Gallatin had proposed a national plan of canals and roads as early as 1808. Construction began at Rome, New York, on the Fourth of July, 1817, on the Erie Canal, a mammoth project designed to connect the Atlantic seaboard with the Great Lakes.

The canal—dismissively referred to as "Clinton's Ditch, for its chief proponent New York governor DeWitt Clinton— was 40 feet wide, 4 feet deep, and 363 miles long. In October 1825, the last link was dug and the buoyant governor, aboard the canalboat *Seneca Chief,* led a ceremonial flotilla from Lake Erie to New York Harbor. Fireworks exploded from canalside towns as the boats passed.

Many of the laborers on the canal were Irish immigrants who were met at the New York docks and hired to work on the promise of "roast beef guaranteed twice a day, regular whiskey rations, and wages eighty cents." For their eighty cents a day, they worked from dawn to sunset, year round, in cold and wet.

MISSISSIPPI RIVER BOAT WITH COTTON, BATON ROUGE, LA.

New York used a combination of techniques for financing the canal: sale of canal stocks, tolls, and taxes on salt and auctions. It was so successful that a frenzy of canal building began throughout the states that produced 3,326 miles of canals by 1840. By 1861 state and local governments had raised 137 million dollars to finance the building of canals. All hoped to match the success of the Erie Canal. Maine, Massachusetts, and Connecticut built canals. The Delaware and Hudson Canal stitched together Pennsylvania and New York. There were the Lehigh, Morris, Union, Susquehanna, and Tidewater. The 395-mile-long Main Line passed through Pennsylvania and crossed the Allegheny Mountains; a cable railroad carried the canalboats over the mountains. The longest of the canals, the Wabash and Erie, stretched for 468 miles but it was a financial failure. Canals were useful to the public for shipping goods, but less successful investments for stockholders. The coming of the railroad spelled their doom, marking the beginning of the end of their usefulness.

Nonetheless, by 1852 canals were hauling nine million tons of freight, and just before the Civil War 188 million dollars had been invested in canals.

Beyond the reach of eastern canals, rivers were the main arteries for exploration and trade. First proved commercially feasible in 1807 by Robert Fulton, steamboats fanned out on the Ohio, Mississippi, Missouri, Red, and Arkansas Rivers.

With serviceable roads few and far between, the West was blessed with a network of long, navigable rivers. The Mississippi and Missouri—along with their hundreds of miles of navigable tributaries—served the same purpose as roads, though usually one way: downstream. At their destination, flatboats were frequently sold for their lumber; it was far easier to dispose of them than to urge the awkward craft back upstream. Crews returned home overland. Keelboats were more maneuverable than the flatboats and could be sailed, poled, or towed upriver, but it was a difficult job that often took months. While a Pennsylvania boat, for instance, could float down the Ohio and Mississippi Rivers to New Orleans in a few weeks, it could take

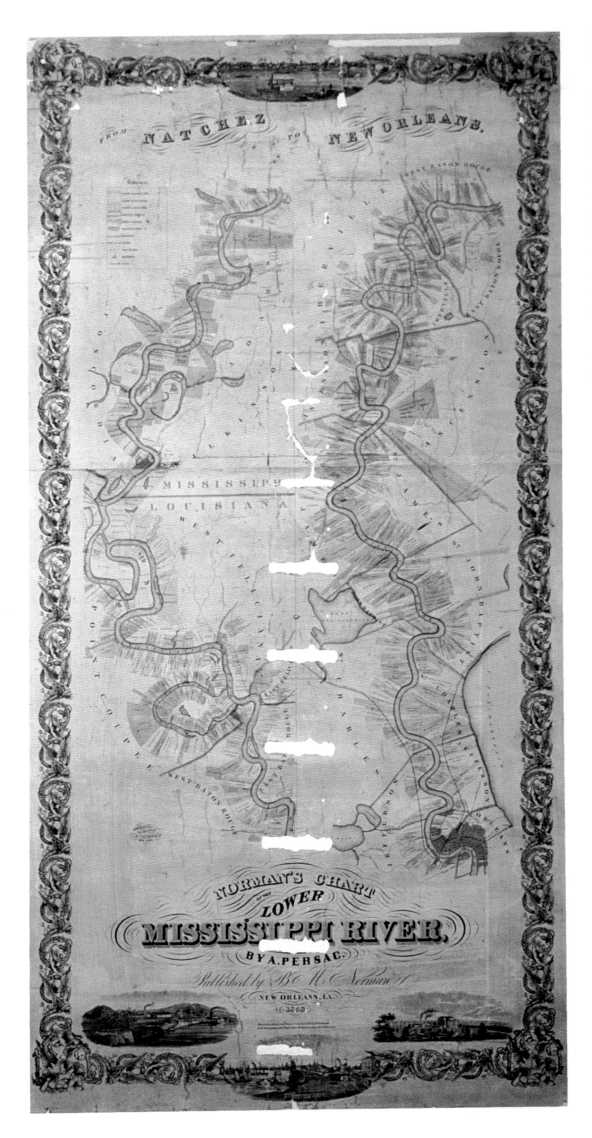

NORMAN'S CHART OF THE LOWER MISSISSIPPI RIVER,

BY A. PERSAC.

Published by B. M. Norman

NEW ORLEANS, LA.

months to get it back again, even with crews of tough and brawny crewmen.

In 1805 F. A. Michaux wrote, in *Travels to the West of the Alleghany Mountains,* "The amazing rapidity of the Ohio has an influence on the shape of the boats that navigate upon it, and that shape is not calculated to accelerate their progress; but to stem the current of the stream. All…whether those in the Kentucky or Mississippi trade, or those that convey the families that go into the eastern or western states, are built in the same manner. They are of a square form, some longer than others; their sides are raised four feet and a half above the water; their length is from fifteen to fifty feet; the two extremities are square, upon one of which is a kind of awning, under which the passengers shelter themselves when it rains…. I perceived in these barges several families, carrying with them their horses, cows, poultry, waggons, ploughs, harness, beds, instruments of agriculture, in fine, every thing necessary to cultivate the land, and also for domestic use. These people were abandoning themselves to the mercy of the stream, without knowing the place where they should stop…."

## Life on the River

I loved the profession far better than any I have followed since," wrote Mark Twain of his years as a steamboat pilot, "and I took a measureless pride in it. The reason is plain: a pilot, in those days, was the only unfettered and entirely independent human being that lived in the earth."

The arrival of steamboats on the Mississippi River in 1811 revolutionized trade and communications over an area almost as large as Europe. Freight and passengers now could be carried upriver almost as easily as down—and at far less cost than by road. River ports became boomtowns. By 1851 a visitor to the St. Louis waterfront

OPPOSITE: *Stacked cotton bales leave little room for crewmen on the steamship* William Carig, *docked on the Mississippi River near Baton Rouge, Louisiana.*

LEFT: *To assure every planter river frontage, plantations were laid out in narrow strips, as shown on an 1858 map of the lower Mississippi.*

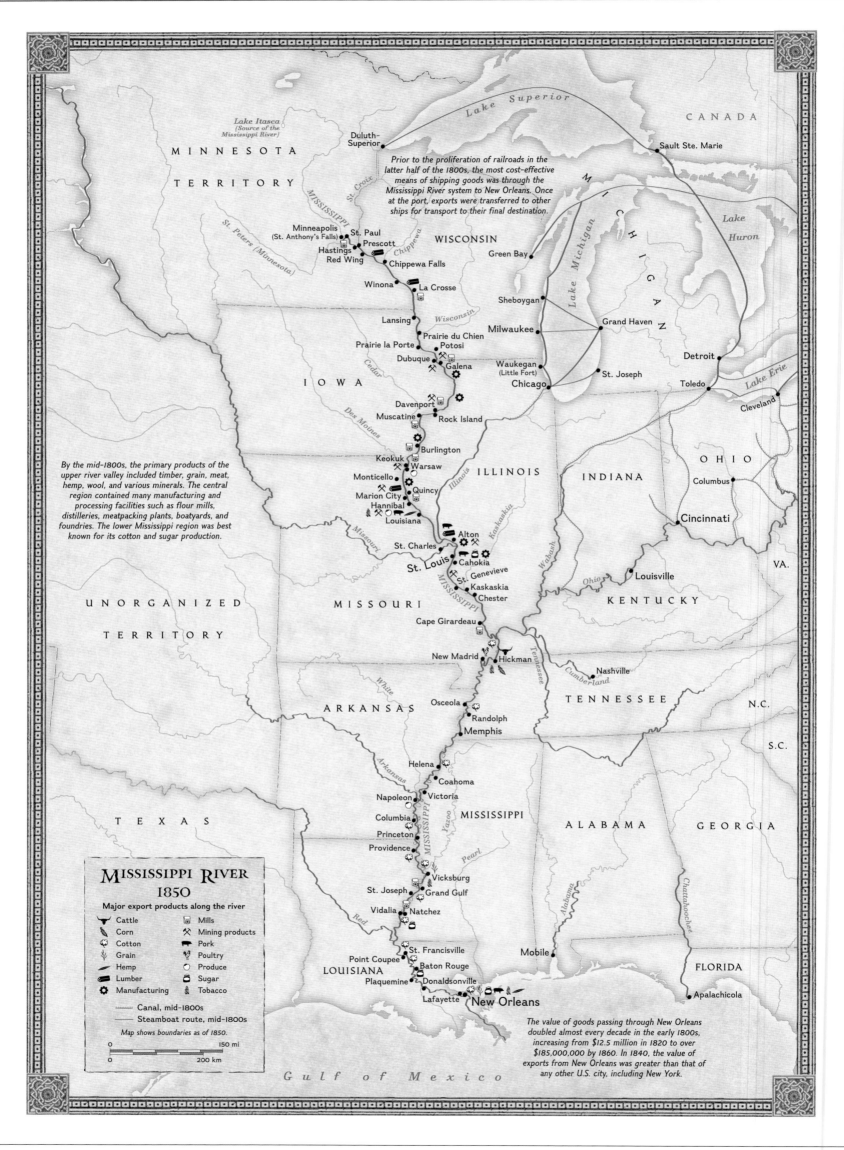

Prior to the proliferation of railroads in the latter half of the 1800s, the most cost-effective means of shipping goods was through the Mississippi River system to New Orleans. Once at the port, exports were transferred to other ships for transport to their final destination.

By the mid-1800s, the primary products of the upper river valley included timber, grain, meat, hemp, wool, and various minerals. The central region contained many manufacturing and processing facilities such as flour mills, distilleries, meatpacking plants, boatyards, and foundries. The lower Mississippi region was best known for its cotton and sugar production.

## MISSISSIPPI RIVER
### 1850

Major export products along the river

- Cattle
- Corn
- Cotton
- Grain
- Hemp
- Lumber
- Manufacturing
- Mills
- Mining products
- Pork
- Poultry
- Produce
- Sugar
- Tobacco

— Canal, mid-1800s
— Steamboat route, mid-1800s

Map shows boundaries as of 1850.

0    150 mi
0    200 km

The value of goods passing through New Orleans doubled almost every decade in the early 1800s, increasing from $12.5 million in 1820 to over $185,000,000 by 1860. In 1840, the value of exports from New Orleans was greater than that of any other U.S. city, including New York.

could describe it as a "forest of smoke stacks." By now America's western waterways were carrying more freight than Britain's entire merchant fleet.

The chief inventor, Robert Fulton, was born the son of Irish immigrants in 1765. He studied at a Quaker school and later was an apprentice in a jewelry shop in Philadelphia. There he painted miniature portraits on ivory for lockets and rings. He journeyed to London to study painting and heard there of new inventions for propelling boats, inventions that intrigued him. One used a water jet ejected by a steam pump for propulsion.

He lost interest in painting and returned to America, where he became fascinated by the new science of canal building. He wrote a "Treatise on the Improvement of Canal Navigation" in 1796. In it he solved various engineering problems associated with canals: the design of bridges, plans for inclined planes to raise and lower boats, aqueducts for crossing valleys, even boats designed to carry specialized cargo.

The Age of Steam on the western rivers began when he and his partner Robert Livingston procured the monopoly rights to the lower Mississippi River. In the autumn of 1811 their steamboat *New Orleans* made the first successful voyage by steam from Pittsburgh to New Orleans. Oddly, an earthquake occurred while the ship was making its voyage, seemingly heralding a new day. At night, passengers brushed away sparks from the smokestack that floated down around them.

In 1814, 20 steamboats pulled up to the docks at New Orleans; within 20 years their number had climbed to nearly 1,200. They mostly carried passengers, cotton, and sugar. By 1830 they ruled the waves on navigable western waters.

Steam opened the hinterlands to world trade, hauling barreled meats from Cincinnati, iron and coal from Pittsburgh, and cotton from Tennessee and Arkansas. Boats chugged up the Missouri River, helping to settle the country and to transport hides, timber, and grain to market. By 1860 stern-wheelers steamed the 2,200 miles up the Missouri to Fort Benton, Montana.

The average lifespan of a river steamboat was only four to five years. Many were poorly constructed and maintained, many more were sunk by snags and other obstructions in the river, and some had their huge boilers explode.

Mississippi steamboats varied widely in quality. Timothy Flint recalled in 1826 his journey. "A stranger to this mode of travelling, would find it difficult to describe his impression upon first descending the Mississippi in one of the better steamboats. He contemplates the prodigious establishment, with all its fitting of deck, common, and ladies' cabin

---

### From *LIFE on the MISSISSIPPI*

Then there's your pitch-dark night; the river is a very different shape on a pitch-dark night from what it is on a starlight night. All shores seem to be straight lines, then, and mighty dim ones, too; and you'd *run* them for straight lines only know better. You boldly drive your boat right into what seems to be a solid, straight wall (you knowing very well that in reality there is a curve there) and that wall falls back and makes way for you. Then there's your gray mist. You take a night when there's one of these grisly, drizzly, gray mists, and then there isn't *any* particular shape to a shore. A gray mist would tangle the head of the oldest man that ever lived....You only learn the shape of the river; and you learn it with such absolute certainty that you can always steer by the shape that's *in your head* and never mind the one that's before your eyes.

–Mark Twain/Samuel L. Clemens

---

apartments. Overhead, about him and below him, all is life and movement. He sees its splendid cabin, richly carpeted, its finishing of mahogany, its mirror and fine furniture, its bar-room, and sliding tables, to which eighty passengers can sit down with comfort. The fare is sumptuous, and everything in a style of splendour, order, quiet, and regularity....You read, you converse, you walk, you sleep, as you choose..."

John James Audubon traveled down the river in 1843 and had a very different experience. "The weather has been bad ever since we left Baltimore....And such a steamer as we have come in from Louisville here!—the very filthiest of all filthy old rat-traps I ever travelled in; and the fare worse, certainly much worse, and so scanty withal that our worthy commander could not have given us another meal had we been detained a night longer....as she struck a sawyer one night we all ran like mad to make ready to leap overboard; but as God would have it, our lives and the "Gallant"— were spared—she from sinking, and we from swimming amid rolling and crashing hard ice. The Ladies screamed, the babies squalled, the dogs yelled, the steam roared, the captain...swore—not like an angel, but like the very devil—and all was confusion and uproar.... Our *compagnons de voyage*, about one hundred and fifty, were composed of Buckeyes, Wolverines, Suckers, Hoosiers, and gamblers, with drunkards of each and every denomination, their ladies and babies of the same nature, and specifically the dirtiest of the dirty....When it rained outside, it rained also within."

Mark Twain, whose real name was Samuel Clemens, earned his license to pilot steamboats on the Mississippi between St. Louis and New Orleans when he was 24 years old. He had spent more than a year of apprenticeship on what he called the most "villainous" and "crookedest" of rivers. He was tutored by veteran pilot Horace Bixby, who once complained that he didn't know "enough to pilot a cow down a lane" and admonished him to keep notes "to get this entire river by heart."

Years later, in *Life on the Mississippi,* Clemens explained the basic technique of pushing upriver: Avoid currents by hugging the shores, and cross over only when necessary. When going downriver, a pilot had to "stay well out" to take advantage of the current. The worst part of piloting was that the river constantly changed, with banks caving in, sandbars shifting, channels "dodging and shirking," and snags "always hunting up new quarters."

All of that drove Clemens to complain that to be a pilot a man had to learn "more than any one man ought to be allowed to know" and "learn it all over again in a different way every twenty-four hours." Besides memory he must have "good and quick judgment...and a cool, calm courage that no peril can shake." Clemens's own career on the river ended abruptly in 1861, when the Civil War closed the Mississippi to commercial traffic.

# The INDUSTRIAL REVOLUTION

## American Ingenuity

If thou wilt come and do it, thou shalt have…. the *credit* as well as the advantage of perfecting the first water-mill in America," wrote retired Quaker merchant Moses Brown. He needed a hand getting his cotton mill to work, and was soliciting the help of Samuel Slater, who had apprenticed under the Arkwright system of water-powered cotton spinning in England.

Slater passed outbound through British customs in 1789 with precise knowledge of the system. He was disguised, and he carried no plans; their export was as illegal as his exit.

Thus did industry begin in the U.S., with bootleg technology based on the illegal transfer of trade secrets. Slater later immigrated to Rhode Island and, in 1793, built America's first successful mill in Pawtucket. To attract workers, he also built housing for the laborers' families, forming a village around the mill. Early manufacturing communities were often built in rural settings and were utopias when compared with the choked and grimy warrens of Britain's factories.

"I well recollect the state of admiration and satisfaction with which we sat by the hour, watching the beautiful movement of this new and wonderful machine," wrote Boston merchant Nathan Appleton of his 1814 meeting with inventor Francis Lowell. The mechanized loom was not a new invention—Lowell had studied looms in English factories before creating his own design—but it was worthy of awe. Crafted mostly of wood and powered by water, Lowell's rhythmic power loom soon had New England workers weaving cloth for the country's rapidly growing population.

In the early factories, young women were housed, regulated, and exhorted to work hard. Late in her life, Harriet Robinson remembered her experiences as a mill worker from 1832 to 1848 in Lowell, Massachusetts. The youngest girls, some not over ten, were called "doffers," she wrote, because they doffed, or took off, the full bobbins from the spinning frames. They worked just 15 minutes of each hour and were allowed to read, knit, or go outside the mill yard to play the rest of the time. They were

---

### NORTH and HALL

In 1813 a Connecticut armorer, Simeon North, did what Eli Whitney took public credit for but failed to do: produce guns with interchangeable parts. The first hundred or so of North's horse pistols were completely interchangeable and thus capable of quick repair on the battlefield. The government, however, added new demands to the specifications. Production slipped and quality suffered.

North's advances inspired others, including John H. Hall, manufacturer of a breechloading rifle at an armory in Harpers Ferry, Virginia. The U.S. Army in 1828 ordered 5,000 of the weapons. Hall used precision machines, files, gauges, and hard-nosed inspectors to create a process later adopted for mass-producing sewing machines, watches, and bicycles—the so-called "American system." But workers disliked the new rules; at Harpers Ferry a superintendent was shot for enforcing them.

---

paid two dollars a week and were expected to put in nearly 14 hours a day. These oppressive labor conditions would only grow worse as the Industrial Revolution grew apace.

Most of the girls were between 16 and 25 and worked from eight to ten months a year; some taught school during the summer months. "The most prevailing incentive to labor was to secure the means of education for some male member of the family…to give him a college education…I have known more than one to give every cent of her wages, month after month, to her brother, that he might get the education necessary to enter some profession…." Having a job meant substantial changes in the status of women. "Hitherto woman had always been a money saving rather than a money earning, member of the community."

By the 1840s workers feared immigrants who might take their jobs. The *Voice of Industry* in Fitchburg, Massachusetts, complained: "Isolated capital everywhere and in all ages protects itself by the poverty, ignorance, and servility of a surplus population who will submit to its base requirements."

Heavily capitalized by wealthy Bostonians, Lowell's system flowered in the city named for him, harnessing Pawtucket Falls on the Merrimack River. Boston merchants bought up the headwaters of the Merrimack and developed textile complexes that controlled much of the nation's cotton industry along its length. Upstream from Lowell, Manchester was laid out near the "hideous rapids" of Amoskeag Falls. It developed into one of New England's largest textile companies. Downstream from Manchester was Nashua, the first site to follow Lowell, though Nashua was hampered by high dams downstream that backed water up against its mill wheels. Eleven miles downstream from Lowell at Lawrence, the Great Stone Dam—a 32-foot-high wall of granite—turned a mere five-foot drop into the power source for the nation's largest woolen-textile center.

The city of Lowell had no need to advertise its first mills: U.S. presidents, foreign dignitaries, and the "mill girls" themselves gave endless testimonials. The city began in 1822 as a paternalistic community of young Yankee women living in company-owned boardinghouses.

In the mills themselves, millwrights of the 1830s began installing laced

cowhide belts and pulleys instead of the common cast-iron gear drive systems. Heavy shafts and poorly cast parts had made gear systems noisy, slow, and unreliable. But the new belts, when they became worn, could often be repaired in a day, rather than the week it took to replace a broken gear part.

In early textile mills, the weight of water flowing into buckets turned the water wheels. Gears on their perimeters meshed with smaller pinion gears to drive the main drum, transmitting power to horizontal main shafts on alternate floors. These in turn drove overhead shafts whose belts also reached up through the ceiling. Shaft speed increased as drum sizes grew smaller. Belts from these shafts drove carding machines on the first floor, spinning frames on the second, looms on the third, and dressers on the fourth. Even after electric power became available, some Lowell mills were still using the multiple-belt drive system as late as the 1920s.

Technical advances changed other industries as well; interchangeable parts spurred the manufacture of firearms and clocks and, later, agricultural tools, sewing machines, and other consumer goods. Steam engines began to expand production in the 1830s. These innovations brought a new standard of living to many Americans. Affordable cotton meant a change of sheets and, for some, their first undergarments. Others paid dearly, losing a sense of control and self-worth. One mill girl wrote in 1841: "I object to the constant hurry of every thing. We cannot have time to eat, drink, or sleep…. Up before day, at the clang of the bell—and out of the mill by the clang of the bell—into the mill, and at work, in obedience to that ding-dong of a bell—just as though we were so many living machines."

Between 1820 and 1850 manufacturing was the fastest growing segment of the economy. With the canals, roads, and regional railroads extending navigable rivers into a transportation system, factories spread out to forge tools and produce the cloth, clocks, and furniture sought by a growing urban population. Steam now powered boats, trains, and factories themselves.

As industrial processes changed, so too did the products they manufactured. By 1820 processors had learned to preserve seafood, which became available on the market. After 1840 vegetables and fruits could be found canned in glass jars or tins. Gail Borden's condensed and canned milk soon became available. The workplace changed, too. Factories replaced small shops and handicraft industries. Carpet weaving was a hand industry before 1845, but by 1860 it was being done largely on power looms. Blast furnaces and rolling mills sprang up. Coal replaced charcoal in smelting, and all over America smokestacks began belching the smoke that would darken industrial cities.

ABOVE: *More and faster looms meant more work for Yankee women, such as these in a small New England mill in the 1850s. They tended looms by replacing bobbins of starched and wound yarn and watching for broken warp threads as the rolls of cloth emerged.*

# WESTWARD EXPANSION

*The Spread of the Settlers*

Fur trappers were among the first to see much of the West. By the early 1820s they were ranging the Plains and Rockies for beaver and trading at company posts along major rivers. In 1825 entrepreneur William Ashley and trapper Andrew Henry introduced the summer trading rendezvous in the mountains, a system of trade that quickly caught on.

Other mountain men, including Kit Carson and Joseph Walker, began breaking trails.

In 1826 fur trapper and trader Jedediah Smith led an expedition southwest from the Great Salt Lake to the Pacific Ocean—the first such passage to California. He wrote: "In taking the charge of our Southwestern Expedition I followed the bent of my strong inclination to visit this unexplored country and unfold those hidden resources of wealth and bring to light those wonders which I readily imagined a country so extensive might contain. I must confess that I had at that time a full share of that ambition (and perhaps foolish ambition) which is common in a greater or lesser degree to all the active world. I wanted to be the first to view a country on which the eyes of a white man had never gazed and to follow the course of rivers that run through a new land."

By 1840 trappers, their quarry scarce and their markets drying up, were concentrated in central Colorado. Their new calling was guiding settlers along the old trails. Since 1785 land surveyors had advanced the frontier, measuring out plots for the nation to grow into. Their legacy: a grid of survey lines that divides the nation neatly into one-square-mile chunks.

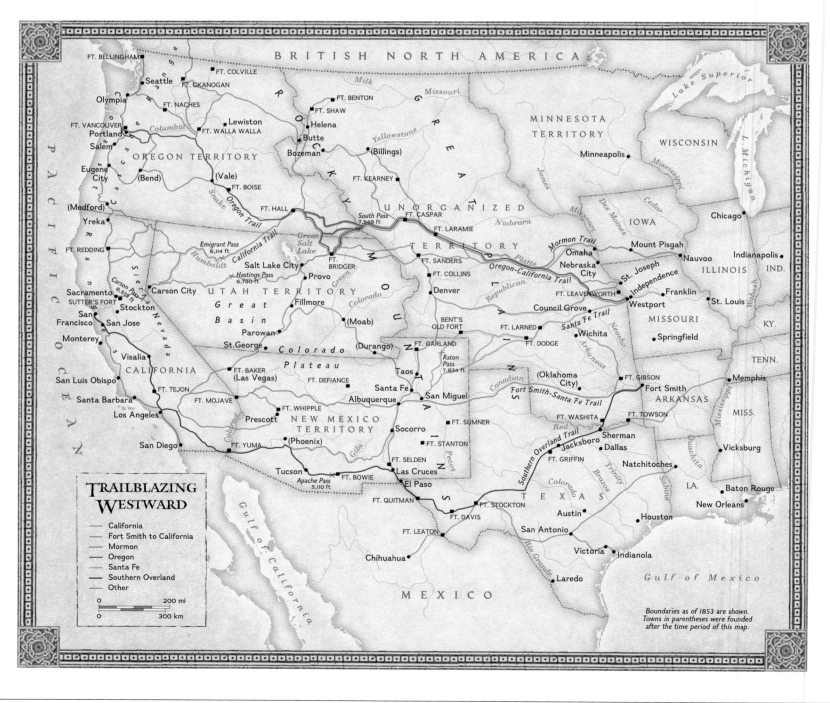

**TRAILBLAZING WESTWARD**

— California
— Fort Smith to California
— Mormon
— Oregon
— Santa Fe
— Southern Overland
— Other

0          200 mi
0          300 km

*Boundaries as of 1853 are shown. Towns in parentheses were founded after the time period of this map.*

After 150 years of colonialism, only a hardy few thousand souls had ventured west of the Appalachians. But after fewer than 80 years of U.S. independence 100,000 settlers had come to California, and the continent had been spanned.

The migration was facilitated by generous government land policies wedded to the survey system. In 1794, the governor of Spanish Louisiana had warned of a "new and vigorous people" to the east whose "method of spreading themselves and their policy are so much to be feared by Spain as are their arms." After the Louisiana Purchase in 1803, American emigration would go on to overwhelm Mexican military garrisons in Texas and California, British claim to much of the Oregon Country, and the immemorial domain of the Indians.

Morris Birkbeck came from England in 1817 to settle in Illinois, and was impressed by the large number of emigrants moving toward Pittsburgh, jumping-off place for the frontier. "We have now fairly turned our backs on the old world, and find ourselves in the very stream of emigration. Old America seems to be breaking up, and moving westward. We are seldom out of sight, as we travel on this grand track towards the Ohio, of family groups.... A small waggon...with two small horses; sometimes a cow or two, comprises their all, excepting a little store of hard-earned cash for the land office of the district;...the wagon has a tilt, or cover, made of a sheet, or perhaps a blanket. The family are seen before, behind, or within the vehicle, according to the road or weather, or perhaps the spirits of the party....The New Englanders, they say, may be known by the cheerful air of the women advancing in front of the vehicle; the Jersey people by their being fixed steadily within it; whilst the Pennsylvanians creep lingering behind, as through regretting the homes they have left."

Many wagon trains were outfitted in Independence, Missouri. The Santa Fe Trail, pioneered in 1822, took pioneers to New Mexico. It was the first major wagon road to the Far West. By 1843 Independence was the starting point of the Great Migration: wagons loaded with emigrants who were heading for Oregon Country. Many thought their chances of making it poor. In New York City Horace Greeley wrote, "This migration of more

than a thousand persons in one body to Oregon wears an aspect of insanity."

Oregon lay 2,000 miles away. Getting there might take six months. "Travel, *travel*, TRAVEL," Dr. Marcus Whitman told the

## JAMES FENIMORE COOPER

An unlikely novelist, Cooper began writing suddenly and without premeditation. One evening he casually remarked to his wife that even he could write a better book than the English novel he had been reading. She immediately challenged him to do so. His first book, a novel of manners, was *Precaution*, published in 1820 when he was 31 years old. Within a year he had written *The Spy,* which was a huge success. In 1822 he moved to New York and completed more than 30 novels in quick succession. His fame was worldwide.

But Mark Twain was not impressed. "Cooper's art has some defects," he wrote. "In one place in *Deerslayer,* and in the restricted space of two-thirds of a page, Cooper has scored 114 offenses against literary art out of a possible 115. It breaks the record."

Franz Schubert was a huge fan. In 1828 he pleaded from his deathbed for another Cooper novel to read while he lay dying. "I have read [his] *Last of the Mohicans, The Spy, The Pilot,* and *The Pioneers,*" he wrote a friend. "If by any chance you have anything else of his, do please leave it for me...." But within a week he was dead.

emigrants. "Nothing else will take you to the end of your journey; nothing is wise that does not help you along; nothing is good for you that causes a moment's delay."

Travel settled into routines along the monotonous Platte River, jolting over the "black hills" of the Laramie Mountains, soaking their heat-cracked wheels in the Sweetwater River, axing a rough route through the Blue Mountains, rafting down the Columbia. When they reached the Willamette Valley in late October they had left a road marked for all comers.

Land, gold, religious refuge—these had brought Europeans to the New World, and they lured Americans west. Within the decade Oregon-bound farmers traveled with boisterous, bickering forty-niners and devout, organized Mormons. Indian attacks claimed lives, accidents claimed more, cholera more still. An average of ten graves would line each mile of the Oregon Trail by 1859.

A northern editor named John O'Sullivan was one of many Americans who saw the nation stretching from sea to sea, a country that would "overspread the continent allotted by Providence for the free development of our yearly multiplying millions." He called it the nation's Manifest Destiny. It became a catchphrase that gave license to further Westward expansion.

ABOVE: *Weary from trekking westward, women and children rest near Colorado Springs. Some of the wagon trains were three miles long.*

# The TRAIL of TEARS

## Displacing American Natives

Of all the sufferings and betrayals visited upon Native Americans, few are more wrenching than that of the Cherokees, Iroquoian Indians who lived in the mountains of eastern Tennessee and the western Carolinas and Georgia. Their population in 1650 was an estimated 22,500; they were spread over 40,000 square miles of the Appalachians. As they grew to know and admire the white settlers moving into their areas, they quietly began adopting their ways. Their government was modeled on that

The Cherokee Legislative Council issued a statement in July 1830: "…Inclination to remove from this land has no abiding place in our hearts, and when we move we shall move by the course of nature to sleep under this ground which the Great Spirit gave to our ancestors and which now covers them in their undisturbed peace."

But a small group of Cherokee, motivated perhaps by greed, in December 1835, acquiesced. The Treaty of New Echota ceded all of their lands east of the Mississippi to

the Creek, was determined that the Cherokee lands would pass into the hands of the whites. "John Marshall has made his decision," he said, "now let him enforce it."

Of course Marshall couldn't, and under the Indian Removal Act of 1830, the Cherokee were ordered transported to Indian Territory in the West.

The Army began rounding them up and housing them in 30 temporary stockades in North Carolina, Georgia, Alabama, and Tennessee. From there they were moved to 11 internment camps, mostly in Tennessee. By the end of July 1838 some 15,000 Cherokee, virtually all of the tribe in the East, were imprisoned in the camps. Seven camps in and around Charleston, Tennessee, alone held nearly 5,000 Indians.

A few escaped. The Oconaluftee Cherokee produced an 1819 treaty that made them American citizens on lands that did not belong to the Cherokee Nation. They refused to join the roundup,

of the U.S., and under their chief, Junaluska, they fought alongside the whites against the Creek. Their farms, textiles, and houses were patterned after those of their white neighbors. One of their chiefs, Sequoyah, dazzled by books whites read, invented a system for writing Cherokee. They soon had a written constitution and a Cherokee Bible.

But when gold was discovered in the hills of Georgia, it brought a tidal wave of white intruders that demanded their land.

the state of Georgia for five million dollars. Most of the Indians hated the treaty and vowed to fight it. They managed to get their case before the U.S. Supreme Court, then under Chief Justice John Marshall. The Court sided with the Indians, ruling that the state had no jurisdiction over the Cherokee and no valid claim to their lands.

But President Andrew Jackson, conveniently forgetting the Cherokee who had fought alongside him in the war with

---

### SEQUOYAH

The Cherokee scholar Sequoyah was born of a British trader named Nathaniel Gist and a Cherokee mother in the Tennessee country sometime between 1760 and 1770. He never learned to speak, read, or write English but was an accomplished silversmith, painter, and warrior. He served with the U.S. Army in the Creek War in 1813-14.

As an adult he became convinced that the secret of the white people's superior power was their written language. It enabled the whites to accumulate and transmit more knowledge than was possible for a people dependent on memory and word-of-mouth. Around 1809, helped by his daughter, he began working to develop a system of writing for the Cherokees. He experimented with pictographs and with symbols that represented the syllables of spoken Cherokee. By 1821 he had a syllabary of 86 symbols that represented all the syllables of the Cherokee language. It was a simple system that soon spread throughout the nation and resulted in books and newspapers in Cherokee and schoolchildren studying their language in written form in their schools. Yet Sequoyah's great accomplishment would not be enough to save his people.

---

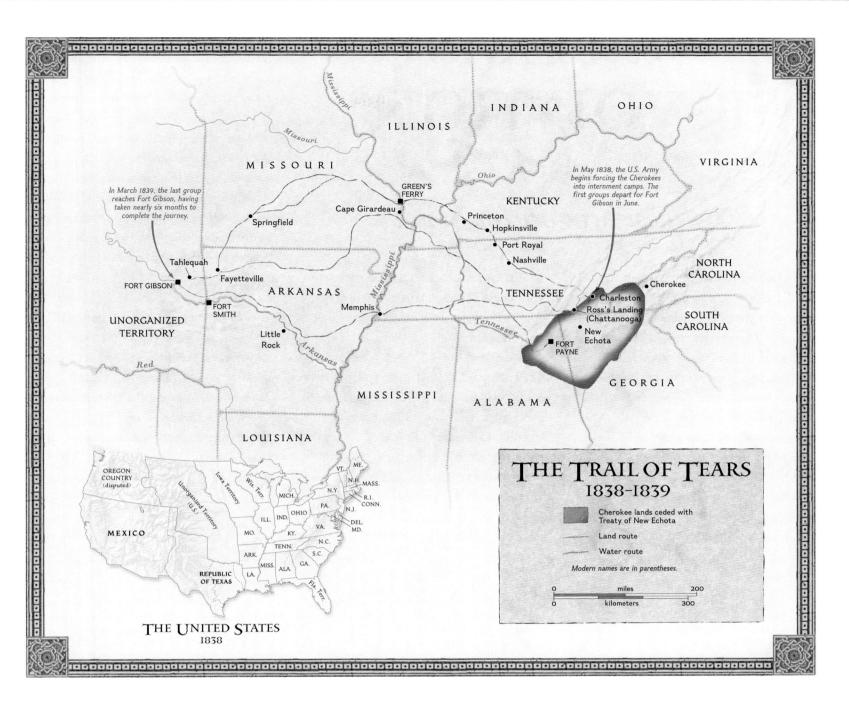

In March 1839, the last group reaches Fort Gibson, having taken nearly six months to complete the journey.

In May 1838, the U.S. Army begins forcing the Cherokees into internment camps. The first groups depart for Fort Gibson in June.

**THE TRAIL OF TEARS**
**1838–1839**

Cherokee lands ceded with Treaty of New Echota

Land route

Water route

*Modern names are in parentheses.*

miles 200

kilometers 300

**THE UNITED STATES**
**1838**

and North Carolina ultimately recognized their rights. Other raggedy bands simply took to the hills as the roundup began, hiding out in the thickets and hollows of the Great Smoky Mountains. They eventually joined up with the Oconaluftee Band to become the Eastern Band of the Cherokees, and they live today in the beautiful hills and valleys surrounding Great Smoky Mountains National Park.

During the fall and winter of 1838 and 1839 the awful eviction of the Cherokee began. Three detachments made up of 2,800 Indians were put aboard boats and made the journey west by river. Most traveled overland on existing roads in groups of 700 to 1,600. A detachment usually was accompanied by a physician and sometimes a clergyman, but there was little they could do. The movement was badly organized. Food ran short and winter arrived. The food they

did manage to find was often of poor quality. Draft animals hauled possessions but had to forage for their feed; drought reduced the available supply. The people walked alongside their animals, carrying what they could. It was a forced march and came to be called the Trail of Tears. More than 4,000 Indians died en route.

An Army private named John G. Burnett wrote, "I saw the helpless Cherokees arrested and dragged from their homes, and driven at the bayonet point into the stockades. And in the chill of a drizzling rain on an October morning I saw them loaded like cattle or sheep into six hundred and forty-five wagons and started toward the west…. On the morning of November the 17th we encountered a terrific sleet and snow storm with freezing temperatures and from that day until we reached the end of the fateful journey on March the 26th 1839, the sufferings of the

Cherokees were awful. The trail of the exiles was a trail of death. They had to sleep in the wagons and on the ground without fires. And I have known as many as twenty-two of them to die in one night of pneumonia due to ill treatment, cold and exposure…."

One historian lamented, "The Cherokee are probably the most tragic instance of what could have succeeded in American Indian policy and didn't…they may be Christian, they may be literate, they may have a government like ours, but ultimately they are Indian. And in the end, being Indian is what kills them."

OPPOSITE: *Members of the Cherokee tribe of the Southeastern United States undertake a midwinter trek to new homes in a harsh and unfamiliar land called "Indian Territory"— later Oklahoma. More than 4,000 died, most of diseases and lack of adequate supplies.*

# The TEXAS REVOLUTION

## An Uprising in the South

A blank slate in 1528, when the first Europeans entered its interior, the territory that would become Texas might have been sparsely settled, but the culture and habitations of the Indians who lived there exerted considerable influence on the later history of the region. The Spaniards in the New World were intrigued with Texas, and by the 1730s had sent more than 30 expeditions into the large borderland that nearly bumped against the United States. San Antonio, with a military post and a mission, had by 1718 become its administrative center. When the Louisiana Territory was bought in 1803 it included lands as far west as the Rio Grande River, and the attention of Americans turned westward. Colonization in Texas increased.

Mexico became a sovereign nation in 1821, when it gained independence from Spain, and during its first years was happy to accept settlers into its Texas region, with its mild winters and lush valleys. But more and more came. The Mexican government was forced to begin limiting immigration. Worse, some of the new settlers were defying the laws of Mexico by bringing their slaves with them. Colonists began lobbying to govern themselves and resisted the Catholic religion, which was nearly universal among Mexicans. Finally they went too far, setting up their own rules of governance, and Mexican president Gen. Antonio Lopez de Santa Anna was forced to act.

One of the Texas settlers, Stephen F. Austin, had received a grant of 200,000 acres along the lower Brazos and Colorado Rivers. By 1834 he had induced 8,000 to 9,000 settlers to live there. Other colonies in the region brought the total of the Anglo-American population to 20,000. They were aggrieved by restrictive governmental measures emanating from Mexico City, and Austin set out to have them redressed. He expected a friendly hearing from Santa Anna's government, but was instead imprisoned in Mexico City and charged with encouraging insurrection. When released in 1835, he returned home and found that fighting between the colonists and Mexican troops had already begun. Santa Anna, he heard, was sending reinforcements.

The Texans responded with determination and resolve. Following the example of the American colonists, they declared independence at the village of

Washington-on-Brazos in March 1836. They wrote a constitution that declared slavery in Texas lawful. In April, commanded by Sam Houston, they clashed with Santa Anna's army at the Battle of San Jacinto. The battle lasted just 20 minutes, and Houston fought much of it with a boot full of blood from a wound to his leg. Texas won the battle.

From a state famous for its outsized characters, Sam Houston was one of the most colorful. He grew up on a Tennessee farm with five brothers and three sisters. At 16 he ran away from home and joined a band of Cherokee Indians. Its chief, Oolooteka, took him under his wing and gave him a new name, The Raven. He left the Indians to fight in the War of 1812, then studied law. Tennessee twice sent him to Congress as a representative. In 1827 he ran for governor—and won. After a marriage to Eliza Allen ended after three short months, Sam gave up the governorship and returned to his beloved Cherokees. But he was restless. He migrated to Texas while it was still under Mexican rule, and when the Texans wrote their Declaration of Independence he enthusiastically signed. He later became president of the Republic, and when Texas won statehood, he served first as a senator and finally as its governor.

Neither President Andrew Jackson nor his successor, Martin Van Buren, was eager to accept Texas into the Union. Its enormous western areas could one day be made into slave states. Further, to admit it would cause trouble among Northerners, who were becoming more insistent that the westward expansion of slavery be stopped. Complicating the issue even more, Mexico naturally did not recognize Texas as an independent nation, so admitting it into the Union might very well lead to further conflict with Mexico.

As their presidential candidate in 1844, the Democrats chose James K. Polk of Tennessee. They were hoping to win northern approval of new slave territories in the South by promising an equal amount of free territory in the North. So the Democrat Polk ran for office promising "all of Texas, and all of Oregon." When Polk won, it made war with Mexico nearly a certainty; a victory would give the U.S. not only Texas but California, a rich territory with valuable

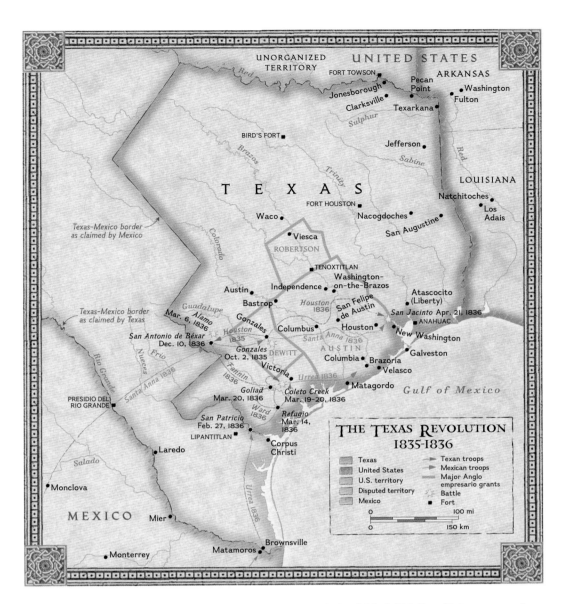

coastal ports. Many Americans agreed with newspaperman John O'Sullivan that it was the nation's destiny "to overspread the continent allotted by Providence."

As he prepared for war, Polk turned his attention to Oregon. England and the U.S. agreed to split the territory along the 49th parallel, the current boundary with Canada. Land north of the parallel went to Great Britain, land to the south to the U.S. In the spring of 1846 Mexican troops clashed with U.S. cavalry patrols on the northern bank of the Rio Grande River, and Polk had the excuse he needed for a war.

Henry Clay, the old War Hawk of 1812, objected: "This is no war of defense, but one of unnecessary and of offensive aggression. It is Mexico that is defending her firesides, her castles and altars, not we."

The American invasion of Mexico took place in 1846 and 1847, and the result was total defeat for Mexico. On September 13, 1847, the last major battle of the war was fought on the heights of Chapultepec. There stood the governor's palace and a training school for young cadets, where had once

stood the fabled "Halls of Moctezuma," an Aztec palace. In 1847 it guarded the western approaches to Mexico City.

General Winfield Scott led assaults by U.S. troops, and Chapultepec was taken. Among the battle's heroes: teenage Mexican cadets, *Los Niños,* the Boys, who fought and died defending their hill. Another hero: a young American lieutenant, Thomas Jonathan Jackson, the future "Stonewall."

In February 1848 the U.S. imposed a treaty of peace at the town of Guadeloupe Hidalgo. Mexico surrendered Texas, New Mexico, and California—an enormous area that stretched from the Gulf of Mexico to the Pacific Ocean. Yet the valuable land was territory into which many northerners feared slaveholders would take their slaves, further troubling the uneasy peace between North and South.

---

OPPOSITE: *Badly wounded, with a boot full of blood, commander of American forces Sam Houston accepts the surrender of Mexican President Gen. Antonio Lopez de Santa Anna, at the Battle of San Jacinto, April 22, 1836.*

# REMEMBERING
## *the* ALAMO

❦

## A Battle of Legend

A quiet 18th-century Franciscan mission in San Antonio, Texas, founded to bring education and Christianity to the local Indians, gained lasting fame as the site of a historic battle. It pitched a small group of determined fighters for the independence of Texas against the forces of Mexico. Its participants became legendary as stalwart defenders of a lost cause; the suspense of its outcome caught the attention of the whole country.

The mission itself was founded in 1718 by Franciscans. By the end of the 18th century, however, it was abandoned and its buildings were crumbling. Now and then, after 1801, its chapel was occupied by Spanish troops, who named the place Alamo, Spanish for "cottonwood." A grove of the beautiful trees stood nearby.

In December 1835 a band of Texans attacked Mexican troops stationed there, forced them out of the city, and took up residence at the Alamo. Two months later, the Mexican army of Santa Anna arrived. The Texans were caught by surprise but prepared to defend themselves and the Alamo.

To Texans today, Antonio Lopez de Santa Anna is perhaps the chief villain of their state's history. He was born in Mexico on February 21, 1794, supported emperor Agustin de Iturbide while a young officer, and even, perhaps, at one time courted the emperor's sister. By 1833 he had been democratically elected president of Mexico. But, in the way of despots everywhere, he thought Mexico not quite ready for democracy, so pronounced himself dictator. His army of somewhere between 2,000 and 6,000 men surrounded the Alamo in February 1836.

Among the defenders were famous names that reverberate today. Davy Crockett and Colonel James "Jim" Bowie, of Bowie knife fame, were there. Bowie had been born in Georgia in 1796 but had come to Texas in search of the silver and gold that legend held was hidden in the interior of Texas. He made friends of the Tejanos, unusual for his time, and was in command of a group of Texas volunteers in San Antonio when William Travis arrived. Travis was leading regular army troops, and he and Bowie shared an uneasy command during much of the siege. But at the time of the attack, Bowie was evidently confined to his cot, laid low by a lung infection.

Davy Crockett was born in Tennessee on August 17, 1786. He served as a scout for a militia in 1813, and in 1815 he explored Alabama, looking for a suitable spot to settle. He encouraged his reputation as a hunter, a crack shot, and a teller of tall tales, and by 1831 he had a national reputation. He was even the model for Nimrod Wildfire, the hero of a play called *The Lion of the West,* which ran in New York in 1831. In 1835, accompanied by several companions, he set out for Texas, expecting "to explore the Texes well before I return." He was impressed with the ter-

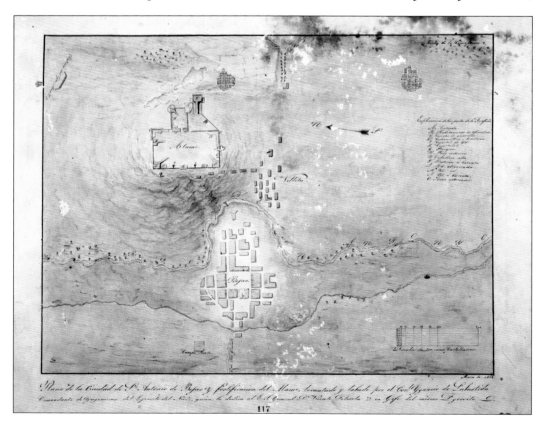

Plano de la Ciudad de S. Antonio de Bejar y fortificacion del Alamo, levantado y kabado por el Cap.n Ygnacio de Labastida Comandante de Yngenieros del Exercito del Norte, quien la dedica al Exc.l General S.r Presid.e Gral.mo &c.a en Gefe del mismo Exercito 🞔
117

ritory. He wrote home, "I must say as to what I have seen of Texas it is the garden spot of the world. The best land and the best prospects for health I ever saw, and I do believe it is a fortune to any man to come here." But as a member of the Texas volunteers, he found himself at the Alamo in February 1836.

Many of the volunteers were fighting with a deep sense of patriotism. North Carolinian Micajah Autry wrote home, "I may or may not receive promotion as there are many very meritorious men seeking the same. I have become one of the most thorough going men you ever hear of. I go

dren, were spared. There is no accurate count of Mexican casualties, but historians estimate them at between 600 and 1,600.

As Santa Anna dictated a message announcing his victory, his aide, Col. Juan Almonte, remembering all the casualties, noted: "One more such glorious victory and we are finished." The loss of the Alamo roused the Texans, who defeated the Mexicans at the Battle of San Jacinto on April 21, capturing Santa Anna himself.

The Mexican army maintained control of the garrison. They pulled down some of the outer walls, including one called Crockett's Palisade, making it more dif-

of deeds of chivalry, and perused with ardor the annals of war; we have contemplated, with the highest emotion of sublimity, the loud-roaring thunder, the desolating tornado, and the withering {storm} of the desert; but neither of these, nor all, inspired us with emotions like those felt on this occasion! The officers and men seemed to be actuated by a like enthusiasm. There was a general cry which pervaded the ranks— 'Remember the Alamo!'"

For years after 1845 the Alamo was used by the U.S. Army for quartering troops and storing supplies. In 1905 the state of Texas had acquired title to every-

whole hog in the cause of Texas. I expect to help them gain their independence and also to form their civil government, for it is worth risking many lives for."

The defenders of the Alamo numbered perhaps as few as 184 men. They resisted the Mexican siege for 13 days, but on the morning of March 6 the Mexicans stormed through a breach in the outer courtyard wall and overwhelmed them. Santa Anna had ordered his troops to take no prisoners, so 183 of the defenders were put to death. Some 15 people, mostly women and chil-

ficult for the Americans, should they wish, to refortify it. When Texas forces entered San Antonio on June 4, 1836, they found just 18 Mexican soldiers holding the fort. Both sides acted peaceably and withdrew, the Mexicans on June 6 and the Texans a few weeks later.

Shocked to hear that the Alamo had fallen, Texans quickly adopted the site as a battle motto. A month later, at the Battle of San Jacinto, according to historian John H. Jenkins's *Papers of the Texas Revolution,* the Texans were in full cry. "We have read

thing that remained of the mission and its grounds. Today they have all been restored and are maintained as a historic site.

ABOVE: *Chaos envelops the Alamo on March 6, 1836, as Mexican troops storm the embattled garrison. "The tumult was great," wrote a Mexican officer, "the disorder frightful...it seemed as if the furies had descended upon us."*

OPPOSITE: *This map was prepared for Mexican leader Santa Anna by his engineer Col. Ygnacio de Labastida before the attack.*

# PARCELING OUT the LAND

## *The Pre-emption and Homestead Acts*

Since the War of 1812 western lands had been much sought after, and the land-office business had boomed. Land revenues poured into the Treasury, only to return west to finance canals, roads, and additional land surveys. But in 1833 President Andrew Jackson reported a skewed balance of payments: The 38 million dollars received from land sales since 1789 did not equal the 49 million invested in western lands.

Settlers and speculators had operated in uneasy partnership since the earliest days of the frontier. Settlers wanted land; speculators wanted money. When land sales were booming, it seemed that everyone was a speculator. "I never saw a busier place than Chicago," wrote a woman visiting from England in 1836. "As the gentlemen of our party walked the streets, store-keepers hailed them from their doors, with offers of farms, and all manner of land-lots, advising them to speculate before the price of land rose higher."

The "fever for speculation" was periodically broken by financial panics that kept the land market chaotic throughout the 19th century. Unsound currency touched off depressions in 1819 and 1837.

During the late 1850s deadlocks over railroad locations stemmed western growth as the country slid into civil war. Later, beginning in the 1880s, free homesteads, European investment, and massive land grants to railroads and states all propelled a series of land booms.

The depression of 1837 soured speculation, as prices plummeted. A hundred midwestern towns never made it off their grandly inscribed rectangular plats.

Another major bar to speculation was the Pre-emption Act of 1841. Previously, first settlers—or "squatters"—on public lands could purchase the property if they had improved it. But they could never acquire a secure title to the land. When it was surveyed and put up for auction, speculators could buy it out from under them. With little money and no title, the existence of squatters was precarious. They were even in danger from claim jumpers who might resort to force to evict a family of squatters.

They urged their congressmen to pass legislation that would allow them to get title to their land without having to bid for it at an auction. Temporary preemption laws in the 1830s helped somewhat but angered Eastern businessmen, who feared their cheap labor would move west if land was too easy to acquire.

Henry Clay in 1841 devised the compromise: an act to provide squatters the right to buy 160 acres of surveyed public land at a minimum price of $1.25 per acre before the land was sold at auction. The act remained in effect for 50 years but led to enormous corruption as nonsettlers acquired great tracts of land illegally. Its failure led in part to passage of the Homestead Act of 1862 which, by giving squatters a legal system for acquiring their 160 acres of land, in effect legalized preemption.

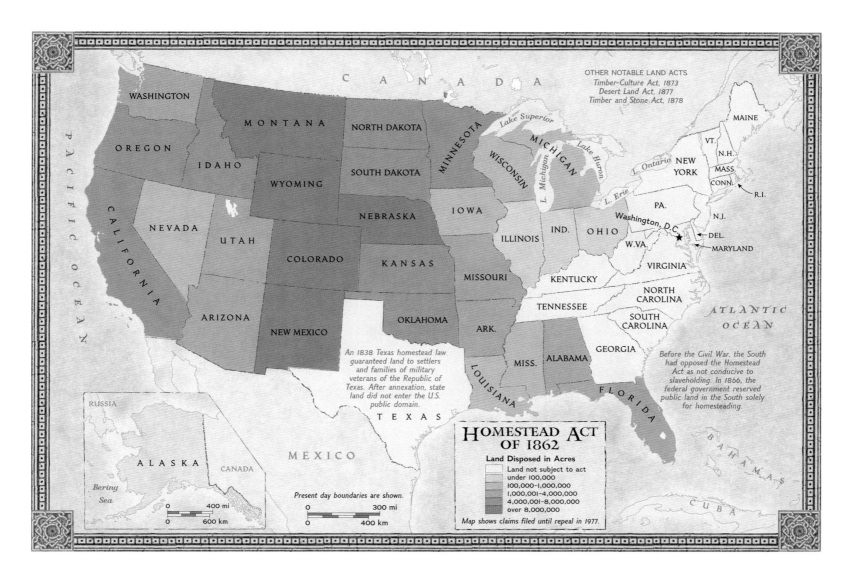

On the map:

OTHER NOTABLE LAND ACTS
Timber-Culture Act, 1873
Desert Land Act, 1877
Timber and Stone Act, 1878

An 1838 Texas homestead law guaranteed land to settlers and families of military veterans of the Republic of Texas. After annexation, state land did not enter the U.S. public domain.

Before the Civil War, the South had opposed the Homestead Act as not conducive to slaveholding. In 1866, the federal government reserved public land in the South solely for homesteading.

Present day boundaries are shown.

**HOMESTEAD ACT OF 1862**
Land Disposed in Acres
- Land not subject to act
- under 100,000
- 100,000–1,000,000
- 1,000,001–4,000,000
- 4,000,001–8,000,000
- over 8,000,000

Map shows claims filed until repeal in 1977.

## From *A LOST LADY*

The Old West had been settled by dreamers, great-hearted adventurers who were unpractical to the point of magnificence; a courteous brotherhood strong in attack but weak in defense, who would conquer but not hold. Now all the vast territory they had won was to be at the mercy of men like Ivy Peters who had never dared anything, never risked anything. They would drink up the mirage, dispel the morning freshness, root out the great brooding spirit of freedom, the generous, easy life of the great landholders. The space, the colour, the princely carelessness of the pioneer they would destroy and cut up into profitable bits, as the match factory splinters up the primeval forest. All the way from the Missouri to the mountains this generation of shrewd young men, trained to petty economies by hard times, would do exactly what Ivy Peters had done when he drained the Forrester marsh.

—Willa Cather

Homesteading failed in its attempt to settle the Great Plains. The act offered 160 acres free to anyone who wanted it, and optimistic "sodbusters," as the farmers were called because of the sod houses they built, eagerly took up the challenge. They used three-foot-long strips of topsoil like bricks to construct their homes, which stayed cool in summer and warm in winter but were messy when it rained. And all the creatures of the soil—worms, bugs, snakes, and mice—lived in the ceiling and walls.

Officials doubted the region could be successfully cultivated, though Mormons had proved otherwise even farther west. The Army's commanding officer on the plains, Gen. William Tecumseh Sherman, reported that the land west of Iowa was "fit only for Nomadic tribes of Indians, Tartars, or Buffaloes." Settlers came anyway. A report in an eastern newspaper described Kansas as an ocean of "luxuriant grass and flowers. Day after day a man may travel, and still one word will characterize all he sees—Beautiful!" By 1910 many states had doubled the size of a homestead to 320 acres; Nebraska allowed 640. The larger size suited drier conditions west of the 100th meridian.

One item the homesteaders brought with them—barbed wire—led to conflict with cattle ranchers. Invented by an Illinois farmer in 1874, it was both blessed and cursed by cowboys. It kept cattle from straying vast distances and enabled choice herds to be kept apart for selective breeding. But it also brought homesteaders swarming onto the plains—and allowed them to fence off pastures and water holes the cattlemen regarded as rightfully theirs. Such conflict led to years of bitterness and bloodshed across the plains.

By 1900, more than 80 million acres had been claimed by 600,000 homestead farmers.

OPPOSITE: *Humble but home, a shack rises in the Oklahoma Territory; two million acres of Indian Territory were opened to settlement on April 22, 1889. For some black families, perhaps this one, an Oklahoma homestead was their first chance to own property. By 1910 black Oklahomans numbered 138,000.*

# MANIFEST DESTINY

---

## A Call from the Land

The "Open Sesame" that gave the United States theoretical license to expand its empire from the Atlantic Ocean to the Pacific—and even beyond, to Alaska, Hawaii, and the Philippines—was called Manifest Destiny. Journalist John L. O'Sullivan coined the phrase in his *United States Magazine and Democratic Review* in the issue of July 1845. He prophesied "the fulfillment of our manifest destiny to overspread the continent allotted by Providence..." When Congress took up the issue of westward expansion, three specific areas concerned them: the Mexican-American War, the question of the Oregon Territory, claimed both by the U.S. and England, and the annexation of the huge Texas territory.

Earlier, in 1839, O'Sullivan's prose had become impassioned as he argued his case. "...So far as regards the entire development of the natural rights of man, in moral, political, and national life, we may confidently assume that our country is destined to be the great nation of futurity....What friend of human liberty, civilization, and refinement, can cast his view over the past history of the monarchies and aristocracies of antiquity, and not deplore that they ever existed?... America is destined for better deeds. It is our unparalleled glory that we have no reminiscences of battle fields, but in defence of humanity, of the oppressed of all nations, of the rights of conscience, the rights of personal enfranchisement....The expansive future is our arena, and for our history. We are entering on its untrodden space, with the truths of God in our minds.... We are the nation of human progress, and who will, what can, set limits to our onward march?...The far-reaching, the boundless future will be the era of American greatness. In its magnificent domain of space and time, the nation of many nations is destined to manifest to mankind the excellence of divine principles; to establish on earth the noblest temple ever dedicated to the worship of the Most High—the Sacred and the True. Its floor shall be a hemisphere—its roof the firmament of the star-studded heavens.... For this blessed mission to the nations of the world, which are shut out from the life-giving light of truth, has America been chosen."

Several forces in the U.S. coincided to encourage the concept of Manifest Destiny. A high birth rate coupled with increased

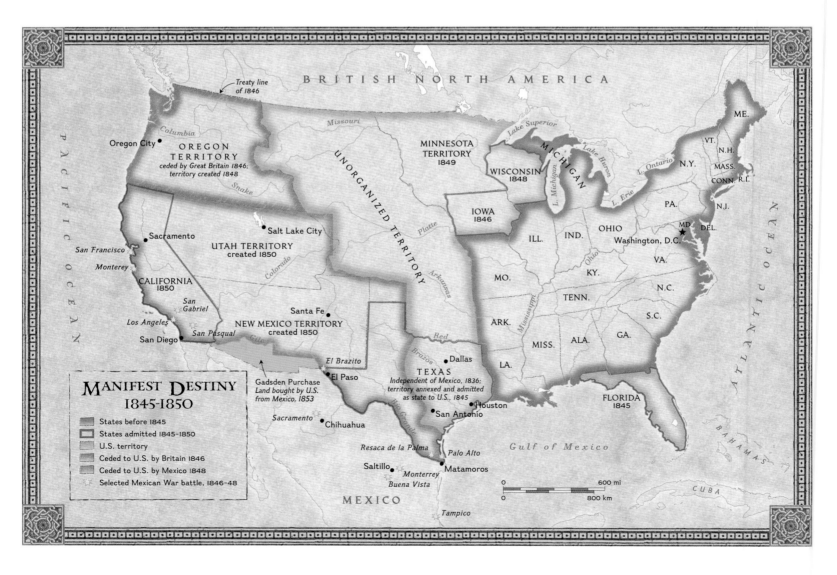

**MANIFEST DESTINY 1845-1850**

- States before 1845
- States admitted 1845-1850
- U.S. territory
- Ceded to U.S. by Britain 1846
- Ceded to U.S. by Mexico 1848
- Selected Mexican War battle, 1846-48

immigration was contributing to a growing population. As most families were farmers, the more children they had, the more labor to plant, sow, and harvest—so a large family was a plus to a farmer. Between 1800 and 1850, the U.S. population increased from more than 5 million to more than 23 million. The new Americans needed land, and new territories were beckoning them.

Also, an economic depression in 1818 and another in 1837 tended to move people toward the frontier, where they could acquire land that was cheap, or, in some cases, free. To own land was highly desirable: It hinted at wealth, self-sufficiency, and political power. And last, merchants looked hungrily at the long western coast where ports could be built and goods imported and exported.

To people in favor of expansion, the issue was clear: To prosper and grow, the country had to enlarge. They invoked Thomas Jefferson's views, that yeoman farmers were the backbone of the country. Then, too, some Americans worried that Great Britain had her eyes on the Pacific Coast and bore watching.

At least two peoples were not as enthusiastic about Manifest Destiny: the Mexicans and the American Indians.

Mexican historian Miguel Angel González Quiroga has said that Manifest Destiny "has an immense fascination for

many of us in Mexico….It is dangerous to underestimate the power of an idea. Especially one which captures the imagination of a people. Manifest Destiny was such an idea. To extend American democ-

## JOHN JAMES AUDUBON

From a tangled childhood—he was born in Haiti in 1785, adopted by a Frenchman and a Creole woman in Nantes, France, in 1794, moved to America in 1803—came the painter who most perceptively and spiritedly caught the natural likenesses of America's birds.

He arrived in the U.S. with two passions: dancing and drawing birds. His innate talent was evidently rudimentary, but by constant practice and determination he developed a rare degree of refinement in his bird portraits. When his work was shown abroad in the late 1820s it caused a stir: "Who would have expected such things from the woods of America?" asked Parisian artist François Gérard.

He was nearing 60 when he made his last sortie into the wilderness, a journey to Fort Union at the mouth of the Yellowstone River. He was gathering material for a book on mammals, but died before it could be completed.

His monumental *The Birds of America*, with 432 original water color drawings, appeared between 1827 and 1838.

racy to the rest of the continent was to place a mantle of legitimacy on what was essentially an insatiable ambition for land."

He noted the denigration of Mexico by proponents of Manifest Destiny and quotes Walt Whitman: "What has miserable, inefficient Mexico—with her superstition, her burlesque upon freedom, her actual tyranny by the few over the many— what has she to do with the great mission of peopling the new world with a noble race? Be it ours, to achieve that mission!"

Quiroga concludes, "Manifest Destiny was a graceful way to justify something unjustifiable."

The Indians, considered by most Americans of the time as an inferior people who would never fit into the life of the East, were unceremoniously shifted to regions beyond the frontier where they could maintain their "uncivilized" ways. Some saw the hypocrisy in this: Many of the Indians who were removed were as sophisticated as whites. The literacy rate of the Cherokee Nation was higher than that of the white South up through the Civil War. Yet Manifest Destiny insisted they be moved out of the way of America's expansion.

Texas, the enormous and thinly populated region of Mexico, was irresistible to the expansionists, not least because it held the future California, portal to trade with the East.

"Broadly stated," American historian David M. Pletcher at Indiana University has said, "Manifest Destiny was a conviction that God intended North America to be under the control of Americans. It's a kind of early projection of Anglo-Saxon supremacy, and there was a racist element to it. But there was also an idealistic element. It is very hard to measure the two. If you asked a person to define Manifest Destiny, he might tell you it is an ideal, or he might say, 'Well, we want the land and this is the easiest way to justify our taking it.'"

ABOVE: *The spirit of Manifest Destiny floats westward in an 1873 painting by John Gast. She carries a schoolbook in one arm and strings telegraph wire behind her with the other. On the ground below, Native Americans and bison retreat before her, and the signs of western expansion—trains, ships, covered wagons, and settlers—follow.*

# The SPREAD of RELIGION

## Movements Across the Land

With religious freedom a beacon, many Europeans gravitated to the newly United States to escape the rigid dogmas of their homelands. Their faiths took root in the broad continent and flourished, watered by the Bill of Rights, which made freedom of conscience a matter of law. The founding fathers' determination to keep state and religion separate echoes through American courtrooms and churches even into the 21st century.

Many early thinkers in the U.S., having escaped the heavy religious dogmas of Europe, were deeply suspicious of organized religions. Thomas Paine published a carefully reasoned attack on orthodox religious beliefs and on the Bible in *The Age of Reason.* In its first year it sold out eight editions.

Probably most of the men who signed the Declaration of Independence would gave agreed with Paine's deism: that God worked solely through the laws of nature. Intellectuals gravitated toward Unitarianism, the amalgam of deism and Congregationalism that stressed reason and individual freedom of belief.

But ordinary men and women often felt a need for a more personal and comforting god. They were drawn to the more theatrical evangelism of the Baptists and Methodists. Horseback preachers carried the Word to distant frontiers beyond the Appalachians. At camp meetings they prayed and sang gospel hymns and shouted their message of sin and repentance. Some rolled on the ground in paroxysms of religious fervor.

The Puritanism of New England was a rigid system that took some visitors by surprise before it mellowed. A traveler in Boston in 1783 wrote, "A Frenchman that lodged with me took it into his head to play on the flute on Sundays for his amusement; the people upon hearing it were greatly enraged, collected in crowds round the house and would have carried matters to extremity in a short time with the musician, had not the landlord given him warning of his danger, and forced him to desist."

But while the Puritans were mellowing, worshippers in the South moved toward a revival of Calvinist theology, which allowed no deviations from its tenets. Southerners knew that liberalism

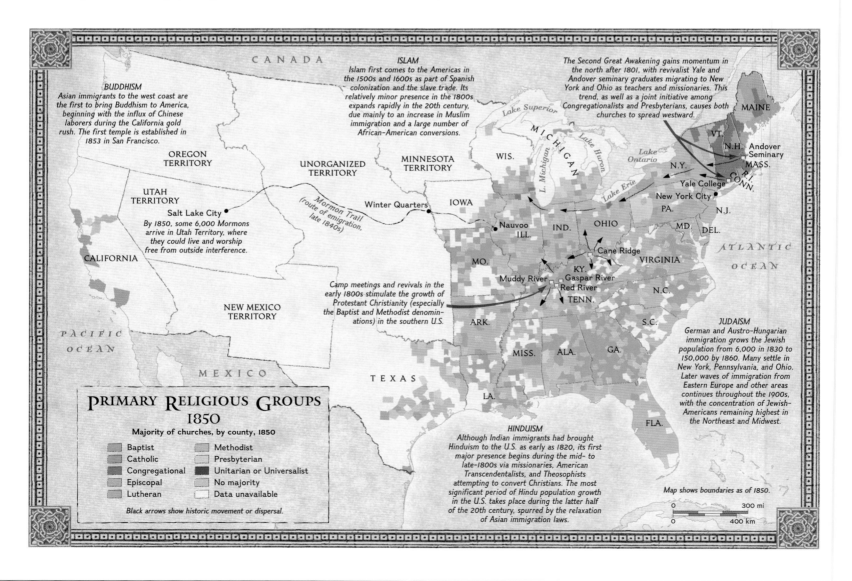

**PRIMARY RELIGIOUS GROUPS 1850**

Majority of churches, by county, 1850

- Baptist
- Catholic
- Congregational
- Episcopal
- Lutheran
- Methodist
- Presbyterian
- Unitarian or Universalist
- No majority
- Data unavailable

*Black arrows show historic movement or dispersal.*

**BUDDHISM**
Asian immigrants to the west coast are the first to bring Buddhism to America, beginning with the influx of Chinese laborers during the California gold rush. The first temple is established in 1853 in San Francisco.

**ISLAM**
Islam first comes to the Americas in the 1500s and 1600s as part of Spanish colonization and the slave trade. Its relatively minor presence in the 1800s expands rapidly in the 20th century, due mainly to an increase in Muslim immigration and a large number of African-American conversions.

The Second Great Awakening gains momentum in the north after 1801, with revivalist Yale and Andover seminary graduates migrating to New York and Ohio as teachers and missionaries. This trend, as well as a joint initiative among Congregationalists and Presbyterians, causes both churches to spread westward.

By 1850, some 6,000 Mormons arrive in Utah Territory, where they could live and worship free from outside interference.

Camp meetings and revivals in the early 1800s stimulate the growth of Protestant Christianity (especially the Baptist and Methodist denominations) in the southern U.S.

**JUDAISM**
German and Austro-Hungarian immigration grows the Jewish population from 6,000 in 1830 to 150,000 by 1860. Many settle in New York, Pennsylvania, and Ohio. Later waves of immigration from Eastern Europe and other areas continues throughout the 1900s, with the concentration of Jewish-Americans remaining highest in the Northeast and Midwest.

**HINDUISM**
Although Indian immigrants had brought Hinduism to the U.S. as early as 1820, its first major presence begins during the mid- to late-1800s via missionaries, American Transcendentalists, and Theosophists attempting to convert Christians. The most significant period of Hindu population growth in the U.S. takes place during the latter half of the 20th century, spurred by the relaxation of Asian immigration laws.

*Map shows boundaries as of 1850.*

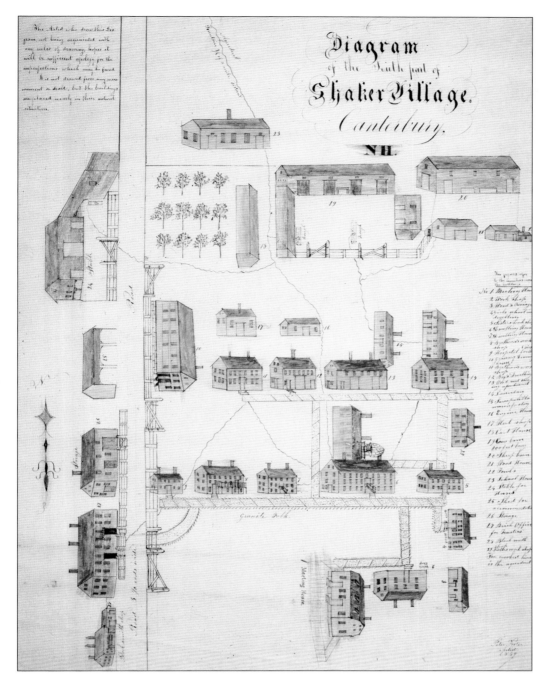

When Lt. John C. Frémont praised the "bucholic" Salt Lake Valley, he helped to inspire Brigham Young's Mormons to immigrate. "This is the place," proclaimed Young in 1847 when he first came upon the Great Basin valley where his Mormons would build Salt Lake City. In 1846, in a well-planned migration, more than 5,000 Mormons trekked from Illinois to the Great Salt Lake area of Utah. Their goal was not that of the expansionists: They didn't want to enlarge the Union, they wanted to flee the persecution they suffered from it. A mob had lynched their founder, Joseph Smith, and forced them to flee Nauvoo, Illinois. They sought a place beyond the laws of the U.S. where they could live in peace and practice their own brand of religion and teach their unique beliefs.

Brigham Young organized the trek west with care. The Mormons spent the winter just across the Mississippi River from Council Bluffs, Iowa, then set up stations where the trekkers could rest, repair their wagons, and let their animals graze. Groups were run like military units and were large enough to discourage the Indians from pestering them. Young brooked no foolery: "Joking, nonsense, profane language, trifling conversation and loud laughter do not belong to us," he informed some noisy youngsters.

In Utah, they set up communities that were self-contained where they could worship untroubled by outside interference.

With them they brought the original system of community planning that their founder, Joseph Smith, had established in 1833. Under a strict grid of wide streets, the alignment of each block of lots was rotated 90 degrees from each facing block so that houses fronted yards rather than other houses.

By 1850, 6,000 Mormons had arrived in Utah.

in theology could lead to unanswerable questions about slavery.

Sensing this danger, the South closed theological ranks. Black slaves had long since begun to develop churches of their own with messages of misery and longing. Many formed their own Baptist and Methodist branches, where most remain.

A second Great Awakening swept the frontier between 1790 and 1850, helping to double church attendance. Farm families at camp meetings were inspired and entertained for days. Like the first Great Awakening of the 1740s, the revival stressed personal commitment and piety over church doctrine. Despite Protestant opposition and ethnic tensions, Roman Catholics emerged by 1850 as the nation's largest denomination.

As for the Jews, immigrating from Germany and, after 1880, from Eastern Europe, they shared little beyond their essential Judaism and a desire for religious freedom. German Jews scattered widely and sought to reform their religious services, with sermons in English, organ music, choirs, and mixed seating. Jews from Eastern Europe clung to orthodoxy, to the Yiddish language, and to seaports like New York City. By the end of the 20th century, New York was home to the world's largest Jewish population. Millions of Jews in the U.S. claim no affiliation with a congregation, be it Reform, Orthodox, or the compromise, Conservative. For them, Jewishness is affirmed through friends, family traditions, membership in community organizations, and, for many, a bond with the state of Israel.

ABOVE: *A Shaker village, part of Canterbury, New Hampshire, appears in an 1849 sketch by Peter Foster. An apology for its quality appears in the upper left, a legend down its right side. The Shakers were a celibate Protestant sect that established communal settlements in the U.S. in the 18th century but declined to the point of extinction in the 20th.*

# The
# RUSH for GOLD

## Miners and Boomtowns

The fabled California gold rush began on January 24, 1848. A carpenter named James Marshall and crew were constructing a water-powered sawmill on the American River for trader John Sutter. Marshall saw a glittering at the bottom of a waterway. "I reached my hand down and picked it up; it made my heart thump, for I was certain it was gold. The piece was about the size and shape of a pea. Then I saw another." The rush was on.

In Washington, President James Polk confirmed the news from California. "The accounts of the abundance of gold in that territory are of such extraordinary character as would scarcely command belief were they not corroborated by authentic reports of officers in the public service."

In the *New York Tribune,* Horace Greeley wrote, "Fortune lies upon the surface of the earth as plentiful as the mud in our streets."

Gold seekers—who came to be called Forty-Niners—made their way to California by any means possible. Some made the long trek overland, but those with money bought tickets on steamships or clipper ships. From the east coast, the ships would sail all the way down the coast of South America, round Cape Horn, and put the potential prospectors ashore in San Francisco. The journey required at least three months at sea.

A San Franciscan named Sam Brannan was first to recognize where the real money was to be made. He quickly bought up the variety of tools the gold seekers would need—pickaxes, pans, shovels—then hawked them through the streets. "Gold!" he would shout. "Gold on the American River." A metal pan he had bought for twenty cents a few days earlier he was now willing to part with for fifteen dollars. In nine weeks he made $36,000.

According to one historian, "The people who went to California by the tens of thou-

sands were greenhorns. They didn't have a callus on their hands, had never fired a rifle, had never followed a plow, had never rode a horse, didn't know up from down in the wilderness world, the frontier life."

By the end of 1849 as many as 80,000 had left friends, families, and fields to pan for

California gold. Some mining towns survived the boom; most did not. "In no other land…have towns so absolutely died and disappeared," Mark Twain observed in 1871.

It was a wild and bizarre world, where a miner who might have been paid a dol-

lar a day back home could now make $25 a day mining but pay about that for dinner. It was a freewheeling world with little or no government, no military, no taxes to be paid or tax collectors to collect them, no judicial system. To extract the tiny flakes from streams, prospectors swirled pans of silt or shoveled dirt into strainers. "I tell you this mining among the mountains is a dog's life," one wrote home. A few of the early miners struck it rich, but the days when fortunes could be obtained by simply bending down and picking them up quickly passed.

Poor John Sutter clung to his vision of building an agricultural empire, ignored mining, and made nothing. Forty-Niners invaded his land, trampled his crops, and tore down his fort for the lumber and

nails. He eventually left California, a dejected and disillusioned man.

Towns with colorful names sprang up: Hangtown, Gouge Eye, Rough and Ready, Whiskeytown. It was largely a classless society, and even women could profit. Many

MINING & BOOMTOWNS

■ Major gold, silver or copper lode
1850 Date city or mining camp was founded

Boundaries are as of 1880.

were prostitutes, but others ran boarding houses, cooked, did laundry for the miners.

To clothe them, Levi Strauss began manufacturing heavy canvas trousers, which the miners liked. New York butcher Philip Armour walked all the way to California where he opened a meat market in Placerville. With the money he made he built a meat processing plant in Milwaukee. John Studebaker, also in Placerville, sold wheelbarrows; he took his profits home to Indiana and the family's wagon-making business. Henry Wells and William Fargo offered a badly needed service: secure and honest banking, transportation, even delivery of the mail.

San Francisco boomed. In the 1840s only a few hundred people lived there but it was soon building 30 new houses a day. It also averaged two murders a day. In 18 months a parcel of land that cost $16 in 1847 was going for $45,000. In less than two years, the city burned to the ground six times. In the 1850s perhaps half a billion dollars' worth of gold passed through the city. Soon it had

its own opera, theaters, and more newspapers than any city except London.

By mid-1849, the quick and easy gold had all been mined, but the Forty-Niners still arrived in droves. Towns were virtually lawless. Forty-Niner John Bucroft wrote home: "I take this opportunity of writing these few lines to you hoping to find you in good health. Me and Charley is sentenced to be hung at five o'clock for a robbery. Give my best to Frank and Sam."

"They were rough in those times!" wrote Sam Clemens. "They fairly reveled in gold, whiskey, fights, and fandangoes, and were unspeakably happy."

Mining companies brought in heavy ore-processing machinery, which replaced the shovel-and-pan prospectors. Many simply went home, but some pushed into Nevada and Colorado in the late 1850s, into Montana and Idaho in the 60s, and into the Black Hills of the Dakota Territory in the 70s.

Foreigners as well as Americans became Forty-Niners. A Norwegian in the gold fields wrote home: "Fine order and peace pre-

vail here…[since] an insult will usually be paid back with a piece of lead." Chinese, Chileans, Mexicans, Irish, Germans, French, Turks—all came to join the gold rush. Most intended to get rich, then return home.

The gentle and persecuted Chinese, easy prey to robbers, took the gold they found to San Francisco where they melted it down into woks, frying pans, and other utensils, which they then carried home to China.

To profit from the foreign miners, the California legislature passed the Foreign Miners Tax in 1850, which collected $20 a month from every foreigner in the gold fields. California's Native Americans, in the path of the rush, were nearly annihilated.

When gold was discovered near present-day Denver, thousands of miners headed for there, declaring "Pike's Peak or bust!"

ABOVE: *Forty-Niners man a sluice box in the gold fields of California around mid-century. The rush began when flakes of the precious metal were found in the tailrace of John Sutter's mill in 1848.*

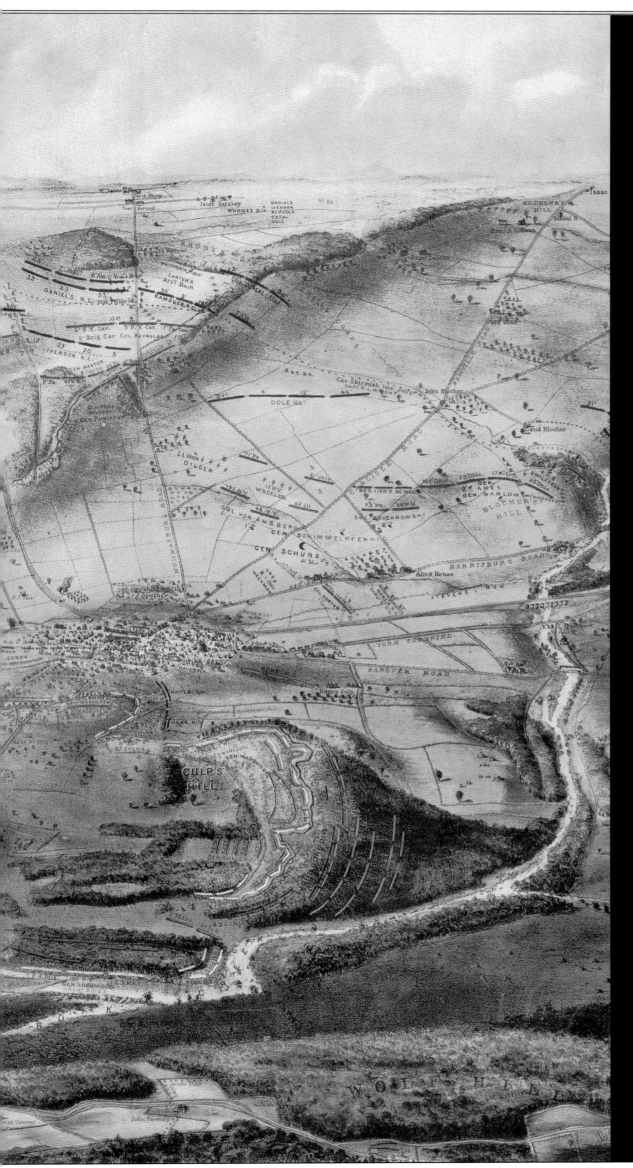

# A Nation Comes of Age

Gettysburg, Pennsylvania, the Confederacy's northernmost Civil War battlefield.

• 1852 *Uncle Tom's Cabin* sells 300,000 copies in its first year, earning fame for author Harriet Beecher Stowe and stoking northern hatred of slavery. **PAGES 80–81**

• 1852 James Ives joins famed Nathaniel Currier in producing lithographs.

• 1854 Henry David Thoreau publishes *Walden,* a mix of natural history and social criticism, and Walt Whitman produces the first edition of *Leaves of Grass,* a volume on love and democracy.

• 1856 On the Senate floor South Carolina Congressman Preston Brooks beats Massachusetts Senator Charles Sumner senseless with a cane for criticizing slavery and insulting his uncle, also a senator.

• 1858 Cabinetmaker George Pullman designs sleeping cars for the Chicago & Alton Railroad. **PAGES 98–99**

• 1862 One hundred sixty acres, free, are offered under the new Homestead Act.

• 1864 On September 2, Sherman wires Lincoln: "Atlanta is ours, and fairly won." **PAGES 88–89**

• 1870 Fifteenth Amendment grants suffrage to black males 21 years and older.

• 1878 John Wesley Powell's *Report on the Lands of the Arid Regions of the United States* is submitted to Congress. It creates heated debate over new policies of damming western rivers for irrigation in the water-shy West. **PAGES 114–115**

• 1876 The Centennial Exposition opens in Philadelphia amid great fanfare. It features recent American innovations such as the telephone, sewing machine, power loom, and the Corliss engine. **PAGES 112–113**

• 1876 Lt. Col. George Custer's Seventh Cavalry is wiped out by Indian forces at the Little Bighorn.

1850 1851 1852 1853 1854 1855 1856 1857 1858 1859 1860 1861 1862 1863 1864 1865 1866 1867 1868 1869 1870 1871 1872 1873 1874 1875 1876 1877 1878 1879 1880

• 1857 Dred Scott, a slave who had been taken temporarily into free territory, has his suit for freedom heard by the Supreme Court. The justices decide, seven to two, that Scott is still a slave and even if free he could not—as a black—claim U.S. citizenship and sue in federal court. **PAGES 90–91**

• 1861 In February, six Deep South states join South Carolina in secession. The Stars and Bars of the South's first flag wave over Montgomery, Alabama, on March 4, the same day as Abraham Lincoln's inauguration. **PAGES 86–87**

• 1851 *The Flying Cloud,* a clipper ship, sails from New York to San Francisco in 89 days, 8 hours.

• 1865 The Thirteenth Amendment to the Constitution abolishes slavery.

• 1865 Capture of Jefferson Davis on May 10 in Georgia ends a month-long flight, during which he urged Southerners to wage guerrilla warfare until Union forces, "baffled and exhausted," depart. **PAGES 88–89**

• 1871 U.S. government arrests Mormon Bringham Young on charges of polygamy.

• 1871 The Chicago fire kills 250 and leaves another 100,000 homeless. Lincoln's original draft of the Emancipation Proclamation is lost.

• 1867 Ridiculed by the press and public as "Seward's icebox," Alaska is purchased from Russia for 7.2 million dollars.

• 1875 A small chestnut colt named Aristides wins the first Kentucky Derby.

• 1877 Last federal troops patrolling the South are withdrawn from Louisiana and South Carolina. The policy of Reconstruction, shy of its major goals, is effectively terminated. **PAGES 96–97**

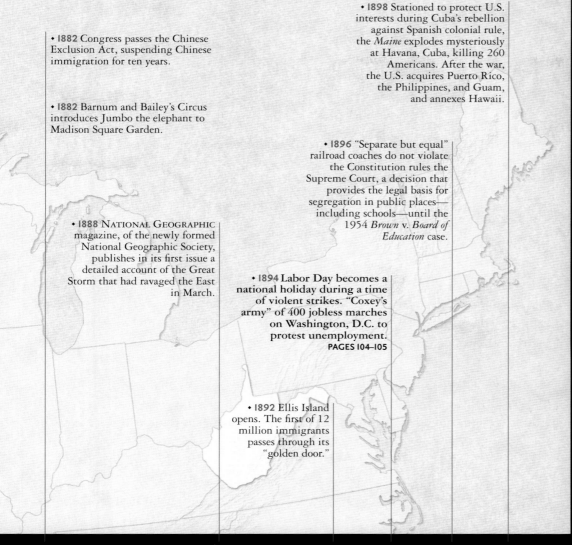

• 1882 Congress passes the Chinese Exclusion Act, suspending Chinese immigration for ten years.

• 1882 Barnum and Bailey's Circus introduces Jumbo the elephant to Madison Square Garden.

• 1888 NATIONAL GEOGRAPHIC magazine, of the newly formed National Geographic Society, publishes in its first issue a detailed account of the Great Storm that had ravaged the East in March.

• 1898 Stationed to protect U.S. interests during Cuba's rebellion against Spanish colonial rule, the *Maine* explodes mysteriously at Havana, Cuba, killing 260 Americans. After the war, the U.S. acquires Puerto Rico, the Philippines, and Guam, and annexes Hawaii.

• 1896 "Separate but equal" railroad coaches do not violate the Constitution rules the Supreme Court, a decision that provides the legal basis for segregation in public places—including schools—until the 1954 *Brown* v. *Board of Education* case.

• 1894 Labor Day becomes a national holiday during a time of violent strikes. "Coxey's army" of 400 jobless marches on Washington, D.C. to protest unemployment.
**PAGES 104–105**

• 1892 Ellis Island opens. The first of 12 million immigrants passes through its "golden door."

1881 1882 1883 1884 1885 1886 1887 1888 1889 1890 1891 1892 1893 1894 1895 1896 1897 1898 1899

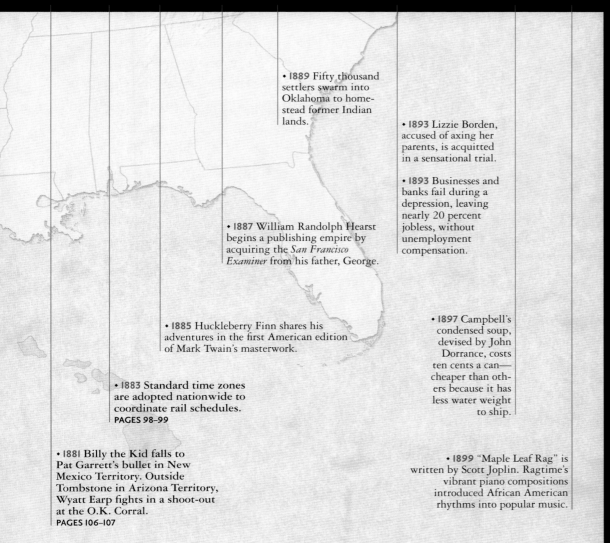

• 1889 Fifty thousand settlers swarm into Oklahoma to homestead former Indian lands.

• 1893 Lizzie Borden, accused of axing her parents, is acquitted in a sensational trial.

• 1893 Businesses and banks fail during a depression, leaving nearly 20 percent jobless, without unemployment compensation.

• 1887 William Randolph Hearst begins a publishing empire by acquiring the *San Francisco Examiner* from his father, George.

• 1885 Huckleberry Finn shares his adventures in the first American edition of Mark Twain's masterwork.

• 1897 Campbell's condensed soup, devised by John Dorrance, costs ten cents a can—cheaper than others because it has less water weight to ship.

• 1883 Standard time zones are adopted nationwide to coordinate rail schedules.
**PAGES 98–99**

• 1881 Billy the Kid falls to Pat Garrett's bullet in New Mexico Territory. Outside Tombstone in Arizona Territory, Wyatt Earp fights in a shoot-out at the O.K. Corral.
**PAGES 106–107**

• 1899 "Maple Leaf Rag" is written by Scott Joplin. Ragtime's vibrant piano compositions introduced African American rhythms into popular music.

"LANDING ON THIS GREAT continent is like going to sea," wrote Hector St. John de Crèvecoeur of a visit to America in 1782. By the second half of the 19th century, the waters of the sea were troubled, and the ship of state was being tossed by rising tempests.

Forces set in motion early in the country's history were about to meet at bloody battlefields across much of the new nation. Slavery, North vs. South, manufacturer vs. farmer, urbanization vs. the rural life: All served to drive sections of the country apart.

It was also a period of movement and growth. In 1833 Samuel Taylor Coleridge had written, "The possible destiny of the United States of America—as a nation of a hundred million of freemen—stretching from the Atlantic to the Pacific, living under the laws of Alfred, and speaking the language of Shakespeare and Milton, is an august conception."

With a dream called Manifest Destiny to guide them Americans built railroads and newspapers, mined gold and petroleum, forged steel and factories, dammed rivers, and even began to set aside portions of land in parks for future enjoyment. Homesteads and ranches carpeted the far-flung West; a flood tide of immigrants turned the wheels of northern industry. An American might work a 12-hour day at one machine and give his vote to politicians who ran another. Workers made themselves heard through growing labor unions.

Alexis de Tocqueville spotted a force that would flower in the next century: "If I were asked…to what the singular prosperity and growing strength of that people [the Americans] ought mainly to be attributed, I should reply: To the superiority of their women."

1850–1899 *Saw the addition of California, Minnesota, Oregon, Kansas, West Virginia, Nevada, Nebraska, Colorado, North Dakota, South Dakota, Montana, Washington, Idaho, Wyoming, and Utah to the Union.*

# The UNDERGROUND RAILROAD

## Escape to Liberty

The secret routes and daring operators of the Underground Railroad helped thousands of slaves find freedom in the North and Canada. The Railroad's people, places, and events have become legendary.

Benjamin Pearson built his house in Iowa with a trapdoor and a secret basement where he hid runaway slaves. Bold John Indian Territory to Canada. Called Moses by her people, Harriet Tubman escaped to the North and then made many perilous trips back to the South to escort other slaves to freedom. Fugitives set up colonies in Canada, but after the Civil War more than half returned. Fiery orator Frederick Douglass, born a slave, devoted his life to the fight for

As the system for helping slaves escape to the North from the South developed, some of the terms of railroading came to be used: routes were lines, safe places to rest were stations, the men and women assisting along the way were conductors, the slaves themselves were often called freight or packages. Hence the term Underground Railroad, even though the system was neither underground nor an actual railroad. But its branches extended throughout 14 of the northern states and into Canada, a country where slavery was forbidden and into which the fugitive-slave hunters could not pursue the fleeing slaves.

The Fugitive Slave Act of 1850, passed as part of a compromise to pacify Southerners, made it possible for a black fugitive in the North, even one who had lived there 15 or 20 years, to be seized on the presentation of an affidavit of a Southern slaveholder. The fugitive could not testify or summon witnesses or have a jury trial. A federal commissioner would decide his fate, and there was no appeal. Federal marshals enforced the act. The marshals themselves could be fined a thousand dollars if they refused to apprehend a fugitive. Anyone concealing or helping a fugitive was subject to a similar fine, plus civil damages, plus a possible six months in jail.

Few northerners actually participated in the work of the Underground Railroad, but they knew of it and many were sympathetic

Brown liberated slaves in Missouri and led them across ice and snow to Canada. Master of disguise John Fairfield posed 28 slaves as a funeral procession in Kentucky and marched them to freedom. Slave Henry "Box" Brown had himself shipped from Richmond to Philadelphia in a wooden crate. Many slaves stowed away on ships or paid profiteering boatmen high fees to take them north. Jane Lewis, a black woman, regularly rowed fugitives across the Ohio River. Escaping on a stolen horse, Henry Bibb coolly passed as a free man all the way from

black rights. Pennsylvania abolitionist Lucretia Mott helped black Union Army veterans buy land for a community they named La Mott in her honor.

Runaways usually braved the hazards of the South alone, walking and getting food from blacks along the way. In border and free states abolitionists sheltered fugitives, calling their network of way stations the Underground Railroad. Ingenuity supplied a few escape routes; runaways rode trains disguised as whites in mourning or hid in shipping crates.

### HARRIET BEECHER STOWE

"So you're the little woman who wrote the book that made this great war," President Lincoln is reported to have said when he was introduced to Harriet Beecher Stowe. Her book, *Uncle Tom's Cabin,* was a heartrending story of the cruelty of slavery. First published during 1851-52 as a serial in an abolitionist newspaper, then in 1852 as a book, *Uncle Tom's Cabin* strengthened and spread antislavery sentiment among Northerners, already angered by the Fugitive Slave Act of 1850. More than 300,000 copies of the book were sold within a year. Southerners claimed that the book was not true to life. They called Mrs. Stowe a "vile wretch in petticoats."

Along the map:

UNORGANIZED TERRITORY

MINNESOTA

St. Paul

*Lake Superior*

CANADA

MAINE

Augusta

Lake Placid

Montpelier

VT. N.H.

Concord

Brunswick

NEBRASKA TERRITORY

WISCONSIN

Madison

*L. Huron*

*L. Ontario*

Rochester

Albany

Concord

Manchester

Boston

MASS.

Milton

Lansing

Buffalo

Auburn

Hartford

Providence

New Bedford

IOWA

Beloit

Battle Creek

Detroit

*Lake Erie*

Erie

NEW YORK

CONN. R.I.

Des Moines

Cleveland

Oberlin

Pittsburgh

PENNSYLVANIA

N.J. New York

Trenton

ILLINOIS

INDIANA

OHIO

Wheeling

Norristown

Philadelphia

Wilmington

KANSAS TERRITORY

Lawrence

Springfield

Indianapolis

Columbus

Cincinnati

Harrisburg

Baltimore

Osawatomie

Jefferson City

St. Louis

Louisville

Frankfort

Harpers Ferry

MD.

Washington, D.C.

Dover DEL.

Annapolis

MISSOURI

KENTUCKY

VIRGINIA

Richmond

UNORGANIZED TERRITORY

ARKANSAS

TENNESSEE

Nashville

Jonesboro

New Garden

Raleigh

NORTH CAROLINA

New Bern

Little Rock

Tuscumbia

SOUTH CAROLINA

Columbia

Wilmington

Atlanta

MISSISSIPPI

ALABAMA

Macon

Milledgeville

Charleston

LOUISIANA

Montgomery

GEORGIA

Jackson

TEXAS

Natchitoches

Austin

Natchez

Savannah

San Antonio

Houston

Baton Rouge

Mobile

Pensacola

Tallahassee

St. Augustine

Wallace

New Orleans

Galveston

FLORIDA

*Gulf of Mexico*

MEXICO

*ATLANTIC OCEAN*

**UNDERGROUND RAILROAD**

U.S. territory (open to slavery)

Free state

Slave state

Arrows show major avenues of escape. Widths indicate relative numbers.

0        200 mi

0        300 km

*Boundaries as of 1860.*

---

to its purpose. Southerners knew of it, too, and many were convinced that it was evidence that the North would fight to see slavery abolished once and for all.

Along intricate and shifting routes, northerners who hated slavery felt it their duty to help runaway slaves to the safety of Canada. Famous for her novel *Uncle Tom's Cabin,* Harriet Beecher Stowe was among them. She gathered information of fugitive slaves through her contact with the Underground Railroad in Cincinnati, Ohio.

Another, the Reverend John Rankin, who lived in Ohio, helped many slaves. He was the prototype of the man who aided the fleeing Eliza and her baby in *Uncle Tom's Cabin.* Of the Underground Railroad, he said, "There was no secret society organized. There were no secret oaths taken, nor promises of secrecy

extorted. And yet there were no betrayals."

Nicknamed "President of the Underground Railroad," Levi Coffin assisted more than 3,000 runaway slaves. He was born in 1789 on a North Carolina farm. With only a rudimentary education he became a schoolteacher and in 1821 established a Sunday school where the region's slaves could learn Bible stories and Christian hymns. A devout Quaker, he hated slavery. He moved north to Newport, Indiana— today's Fountain City—where he discovered that he had accidentally stumbled upon one of the way stations of the Underground Railroad. He devoted his life—as well as much of the money he was acquiring as a successful merchant—to helping fugitives on their way. His home became a well-known

depot, and his neighbors were called upon and persuaded to contribute food, clothing, and supplies for the runaways.

With the outbreak of the Civil War, Coffin devoted himself to helping the newly liberated slaves. He journeyed to England in 1864 to raise money for the freed slaves and to Paris in 1867 to attend, as a delegate, the International Anti-Slavery Conference. By the time of his death on September 16, 1877, in Cincinnati, he had seen the end of slavery but not the misery that it had caused.

OPPOSITE: *Harriet Tubman, standing at far left, poses with fellow African Americans, some of them former slaves she helped flee along the Underground Railroad. She escaped from slavery to the North but returned to the South many times to assist other runaways.*

# A STANDARD EDUCATION

## Compulsory Schooling for Boys and Girls

Census takers in 1890 asked, "Can you read and write?" Even though that definition of literacy was crude, the question reflected a persistent interest in the value of public schooling in a nation whose literacy was high by world standards.

Laws requiring the establishment of schools dated from 17th-century New England, and compulsory school attendance was first enacted in the 1850s. By then free public schooling had reached the Midwest and, to a lesser degree, the South, though formal schooling for slaves there was prohibited. Across the nation compulsory public education was increasingly regarded as a means to personal fulfillment and economic success as well as a national necessity.

Free, compulsory public schooling came at the end of an ever branching road that began in a Puritan New England determined to stanch temptations of the wilderness: "degeneracy, Barbarism, Ignorance and irreligion." At first most schooling was done at home with parents as teachers. The means might include a hornbook of ABC's, a primer, and a catechism, with the pupil learning to read familiar biblical passages.

The one-room colonial schools were not the idyllic places nostalgia would like them to be. Many were overcrowded and gloomy, the benches splinter-filled rough planks, and heating rudimentary. Those near the stove were too warm while those in far corners endured "blue noses, chattering jaws, and aching toes," one student complained. One-room schools were disappearing by 1850, when women were rapidly filling teaching positions; ungraded classrooms might house 40 to 60 boys and girls. Many teachers had little schooling, but normal schools for teacher training were expanding.

Generations used the readers of the McGuffey brothers and the *New England Primer*. The primer was devised in the 1680s to teach reading with appropriate biblical examples and other injunctions: "He who ne'er learns his ABC, forever will a blockhead be." From 1836 pupils copied or recited examples of "good literature" from McGuffey's graded readers. With emphasis on moral and intellectual values, the readers had enough appeal in the 1980s to reenter the curriculum of some states.

Family schooling was even more dominant in the scattered farmsteads of Chesapeake country, Tidewater Virginia, and farther south. At the end of the 1600s dozens of schools had been established, most in New England, often with a faculty of one. If the schoolmaster decamped, so did the school. By the late 1700s schools were growing faster than the population and fell, roughly, into one of three categories. Elementary "common schools" taught the three R's; Latin grammar schools (college preparatory) added classical languages and literature; academies might teach all those subjects and others, even at the college level.

First by necessity, later by national temperament, American learning tended to be practical. Many schooled themselves in books and expanded their learning by observation and experience. That was Benjamin Franklin's method—printer's devil turned almanac writer turned philosopher and scientist. Franklin's route became a well-beaten path for making one's way in the world.

The Revolution established—it was broadly thought—a republic dependent on well-informed citizens, though even Thomas Jefferson could not persuade Virginia to establish a system of public primary schools. Still, by 1830 about a third of all white children ages five to nineteen were enrolled in some sort of school; many had public support, especially in the expanding West.

---

## HORACE MANN

Education for the common people was advocated by Horace Mann, who became Massachusetts' education secretary in 1837. Though he believed in then popular phrenology and reviled "vices" such as ballet, Mann's central ideas on public education have persisted: schooling as a necessity in a democratic nation and local control of schools in a state system.

He pressed for humane teaching methods and motivated communities to lengthen the school term, increase teachers' salaries, and establish high and normal schools. Mann's influence spread nationwide by the 1850s.

He was born poor in Franklin, Massachusetts, on May 4, 1796. Taking advantage of the Franklin town library and some tutoring by a traveling schoolmaster, he was able to acquire the rudiments of an education. Enough, in fact, to be admitted to the sophomore class of Brown University at age 20. He succeeded brilliantly as a student, and upon graduation gave the valedictory address. His subject: the gradual advancement of the human race in dignity and happiness.

By the end of his life in 1859 he was president of Antioch College in Yellow Springs, Ohio. He helped to continue the school's commitment to coeducation, nonsectarianism, and equal opportunity for "Negroes." Just two months before dying, he told the graduating class, "I beseech you to treasure up in your hearts these my parting words: Be ashamed to die until you have won some victory for humanity."

Indian and African American children were schooled irregularly, if at all.

Advocates of common schools, most notably Horace Mann of Massachusetts, aimed to create, enlarge, and regularize publicly funded school systems open to all. By 1870 more than 60 percent of school-age children were enrolled. By 1900 the broad goals of public education were in place. If a school, academy, or college did not serve, education might still be had. Americans learned from books, colleagues, and their own experience.

Most colonial colleges were founded to produce clerics, though graduates often chose other careers. To answer new needs, natural science and practical courses were added, and, with westward expansion, many new liberal arts institutions were created after 1800. Civic pride planted academies and colleges to draw settlers, and churches established others.

A number of state universities and public colleges had already been founded before Justin Morrill's 1862 Land-Grant College Act. Under it land was ceded at the rate of 30,000 acres per member of

Congress to fund "agriculture and the mechanic arts" colleges. At first few realized the value of such education, but later enrollments were huge.

In the late 1800s standardization of professions, notably law and medicine, increased formal training, though the tradition of "reading" law continued. To prepare for teaching, women entered low-cost normal schools. They also trained in private "business" schools for clerical jobs. Yet, for one significant group of Americans, education was still a distant dream.

In the late 1930s a former slave recalled the collapse of hope after Reconstruction: "It seems like the white people can't get over us being free, and they do everything to hold us down all the time...They had us down and they kept us down."

Disfranchisement and segregation at every level spread across the South. Southern legalization of segregation came in the 1880s through a series of Jim Crow laws. In 1875 Congress passed a Civil Rights Act banning segregation—the practice of keeping blacks apart simply because of the color of their skin—and some Reconstruction

governments had passed similar laws between 1867 and 1870. But in 1896 the Supreme Court upheld the constitutionality of legal segregation. By the 1920s laws authorized complete separation of white and blacks in public facilities.

Schooling grew like a vine in the late 19th and throughout the 20th century—quickly and in every direction. While apprenticeships in skilled crafts were dissolving in the face of 19th-century industrialization, public education pointed the way to other opportunities. The percentage of adolescents in high schools doubled from 1890 to 1910 and doubled again to 32 percent by 1920. The system reached outward, though slowly, to those not male and not white.

ABOVE: *Reading, writing, 'rithmetic—and recess—became 20th-century standards for children like these playing in a Cleveland, Ohio, school yard about 1910. Free, compulsory public education for boys and girls (universal in the U.S. by 1918) meant that elementary school at least was legally guaranteed to all Americans.*

# The
# PONY EXPRESS

## Delivering the Mail

The famous advertisement— "Wanted. Young, skinny, wiry fellows. Not over 18. Must be expert riders. Willing to risk death daily. Orphans preferred"—called attention to an exciting new enterprise: the Pony Express. During its brief life it provided mail service between St. Joseph, Missouri, and Sacramento, California. Men on horseback rode night and day, summer and winter, 1,800 miles back and forth. Riders changed horses at 157 stations along the way, then hurried on. It took an average of 10 days for a rider to make the entire trip.

Some 400 horses, including Morgans, mustangs, pintos, and thoroughbreds, were bought for the riders. At least 183 men rode for the Pony Express; they were paid $100 a month. At first, it cost a customer $5 to send a half-ounce letter, but by the time the service ended, that price was down to $1.

The service caught the imagination of Americans—a flood of books and movies would follow—but it was a disastrous financial failure for its backers, who put up $700,000 and lost it all. The completion of the transcontinental telegraph system, on October 24, 1861,

put a quick end to the Pony Express, which had operated only from April 3, 1860, to late October 1861.

In the early 1800s, the mail came by pouch, if at all. Postage was due on delivery and cost as much as 25 cents a sheet, so some correspondents wrote from top to bottom, turned the page 90 degrees, and wrote top to bottom again. Sent without envelopes, letters were subject to prying eyes. Even so, frontier constituents petitioned Congress to extend the mails. In 1800, 903 post offices served territo-

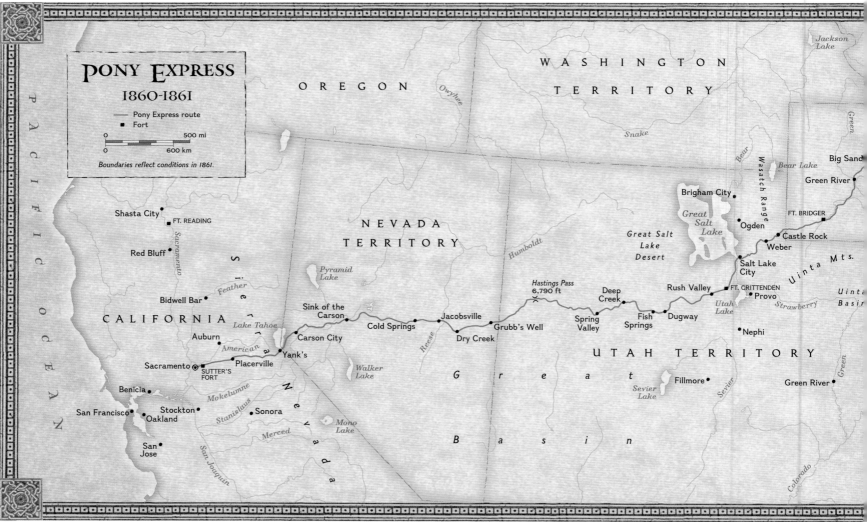

ries as distant as Indiana and Mississippi. Not until 1855 did prepayment of postage become mandatory; free home delivery in major cities began in 1863.

By the mid-1800s the California gold rush extended the demand for mail to the Pacific Coast, first by clipper ship and steamer to San Francisco, later by overland stagecoach lines and the Pony Express. These methods were soon eclipsed—for speed by the telegraph, for carrying capacity by the railroad. The exchange of information accelerated enormously.

Samuel F. B. Morse had begun his struggle to develop and win acceptance for a practical electromagnetic telegraph in 1832. Congress awarded him a $30,000 grant in 1843 to construct a line between the District of Columbia and Baltimore, the country's first. The rhythmic clicking of Morse code soon spread across the land. Only after World War II would cheap long-distance telephone service send telegrams into decline.

Rail and telegraph, "Siamese twins of Commerce," followed the central route of the Pony Express. Telegraph companies won exclusive contracts along railroad rights-of-way and reciprocated by wiring messages to prevent accidents and to dispatch trains.

Newspapers were quick to use the "lightning line" and carried "flashes" about the Mexican War in 1846. Telegraph news columns and news agencies followed. The first transcontinental telegraph message was sent in 1861— word of California's loyalty to the Union. By 1866 nearly 100,000 miles of wire connected every sizable town, and the lightning line had become indispensable to government, commerce, and the press.

Mail volume grew despite competition from the telegraph and the telephone. In 1886, 3.7 billion pieces of mail were processed; by 1985 the volume had climbed to 140 billion, the only interim dip coming in the Great Depression. Seventy-five post offices in 1790 became 76,945 in 1901, a steady rise except after the Civil War.

The first mail to move by train came as early as 1832, on a route from Philadelphia to Lancaster, Pennsylvania. Railroads connected the coasts in 1869 and soon moved the most mail; by 1930 more than 10,000 trains were employed. Service to the countryside lagged, however, and farmers had to agitate until 1902 for rural free delivery, which laid groundwork for the 1913 advent of parcel post.

For airlines carrying the U.S. mail in 1940, routes from California to New York were the highest in volume and profit. Although mail contracts initially provided the lifeblood for the fledgling airlines, by 1940 revenues from passengers were more than double those from mail. Telegrams too had taken to the air. Satellites and microwave towers were relaying good news and bad, congratulations and sympathies, expressions of political approval and outrage.

Under the weight of political pressure postal rates dropped as low as two cents a letter, guaranteeing postal deficits well into the 20th century. In 1971 the Post Office Department—and generations of political patronage— gave way to the U.S. Postal Service, an independent federal agency.

OPPOSITE: *Saddlebags bulging with mail, rider Frank E. Webner sits on his horse ca 1861.*

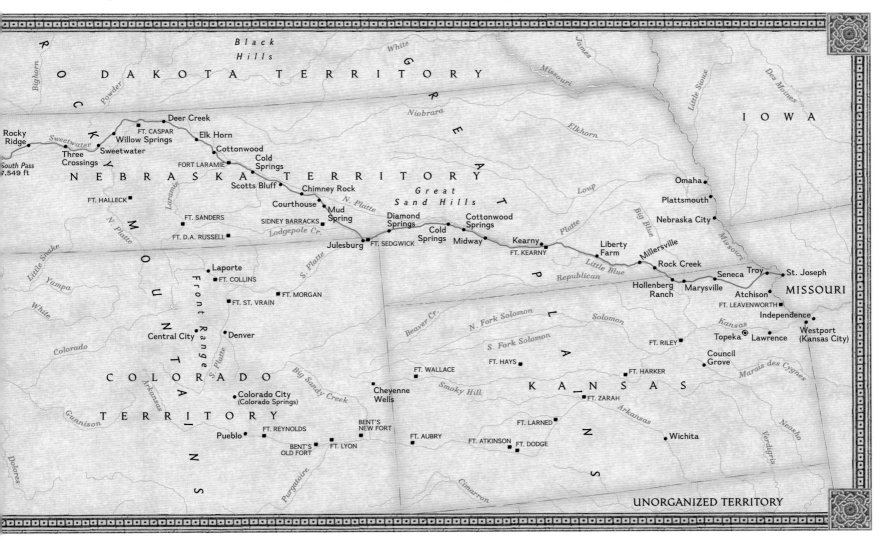

# The
# CIVIL WAR

## The Failure of Compromise

When Congress finally resolved the impasse over slavery's place in the lands just wrested from Mexico by enacting five bills later called the Compromise of 1850, the public's relief was palpable. Southern leaders, who had opposed admitting California as a free state, acquiesced in exchange for a tougher Fugitive Slave Act. But, relief or no, the heart of the dispute remained. The South needed more states to support slave-tended cotton and to keep pace with the North in Senate representation. Northern abolitionists demanded immediate freedom for slaves. Southern fire-eaters demanded immediate secession.

This followed another compromise that had failed: the Missouri Compromise of 1830, which had barred slavery north of 36°30'. In 1853 Secretary of War Jefferson Davis convinced Congress to buy land from Mexico for a southern route for a transcontinental railroad. Stephen Douglas countered with a rail scheme dependent on organizing Kansas and Nebraska as territories. To get southern votes, Douglas proposed erasing the Missouri Compromise line that had stood for 34 years. Douglas expected resistance in the North; he spurred blind rage.

Slaveholders were intent on spreading slavery everywhere, a notion made more threatening to the North when the Supreme Court ruled in the 1857 Dred Scott case that Congress could not forbid slavery in any territory and that African Americans could never be citizens.

Illinois attorney Abraham Lincoln captured the presidency with a promise to contain slavery. To the South the worst had happened. Its enemies were united; the President-elect was a puppet of the North. The South sensed its choices narrow to two: Abolish slavery and invite mayhem, or leave the Union. In December 1860 South Carolina answered, "We secede."

"In all history," said William Tecumseh Sherman to a southern friend in 1860, "no nation of mere agriculturists ever made successful war against a nation of mechanics.... You are bound to fail." Few in the South imagined failure in the spring of 1861. What did it matter that the North had more factories and more men? Confederate soldiers marching to their first battles would have told Sherman what they were telling each other: "One Southerner can lick ten Yankees!"

Their president, Jefferson Davis, knew that valor alone would not defeat the North. He commenced building a war economy from the ground up. When men ran short, the Confederacy conscripted them. States' rights would have to take a backseat if the South was to prevail.

### GETTYSBURG ADDRESS, 1860

We are now far into the fifth year, since a policy was initiated, with the avowed object, and confident promise, of putting an end to slavery agitation. Under the operation of that policy, that agitation has not only not ceased, but has constantly augmented. In my opinion, it will not cease, until a crisis shall have been reached, and passed. A house divided against itself cannot stand. I believe this government cannot endure permanently half slave and half free. I do not expect the Union to be dissolved—I do not expect the house to fall—but I do expect it will cease to be divided. It will become all one thing, or all the other.

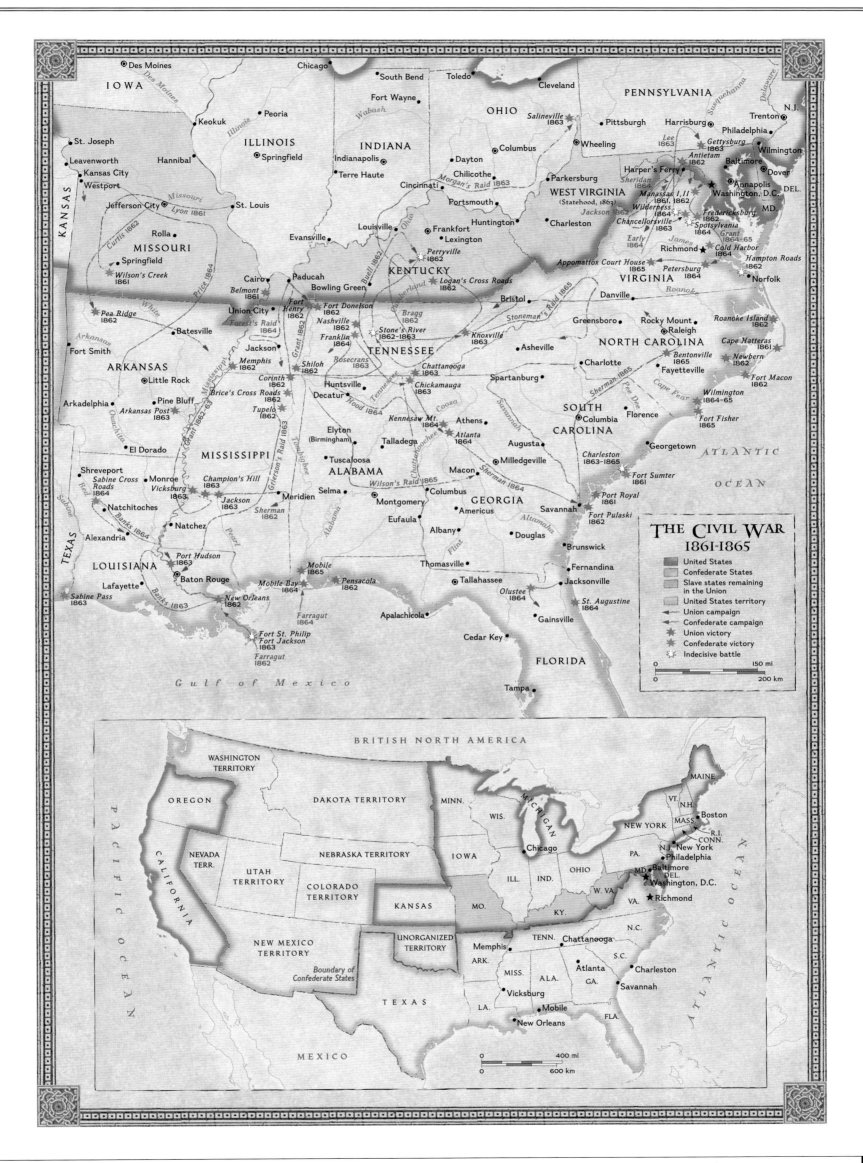

IOWA

Des Moines
Chicago
South Bend
Toledo
Cleveland
PENNSYLVANIA

Keokuk
Peoria
Fort Wayne
OHIO
Salineville 1863
Pittsburgh
Harrisburg
N.J.
Trenton

St. Joseph
ILLINOIS
INDIANA
Columbus
Wheeling
Lee 1863
Gettysburg 1863
Philadelphia

Leavenworth
Hannibal
Springfield
Indianapolis
Dayton
Parkersburg
Harper's Ferry
Antietam 1862
Wilmington
Baltimore
Dover

Kansas City
Terre Haute
Chilicothe
Sheridan 1864
Manassas I, II 1861, 1862
Washington, D.C.
Annapolis
DEL.

Westport
Cincinnati
WEST VIRGINIA (Statehood, 1863)
Wilderness 1864
MD.

Jefferson City
Lyon 1861
St. Louis
Portsmouth
Huntington
Charleston
Jackson 1862
Chancellorsville 1863
Fredericksburg 1862
Spotsylvania 1864

Louisville
Frankfort
Lexington
Early 1864
Grant 1864-65
Richmond
Cold Harbor 1864
Hampton Roads 1862

Rolla
Evansville
Appomattox Court House 1865
Petersburg 1864
Norfolk

MISSOURI
Springfield
Perryville 1862
KENTUCKY
VIRGINIA
Roanoke

Wilson's Creek 1861
Cairo
Paducah
Bowling Green
Logan's Cross Roads 1862
Bristol
Danville
Greensboro
Rocky Mount
Roanoke Island 1862

Belmont 1861
Fort Henry 1862
Fort Donelson 1862
Bragg 1862
Stoneman's Raid 1865
Raleigh
Cape Hatteras 1861

Pea Ridge 1862
Union City
Forest's Raid 1864
Nashville 1862
Stone's River 1862-1863
Knoxville 1863
NORTH CAROLINA
Bentonville 1865
Newbern 1862

Batesville
Franklin 1864
Rosecrans 1863
Chattanooga 1863
Asheville
Charlotte
Fayetteville
Fort Macon 1862

Fort Smith
Jackson
Memphis 1862
Shiloh 1862
Chickamauga 1863
Spartanburg
Wilmington 1864-65

ARKANSAS
Corinth 1862
Huntsville
SOUTH CAROLINA
Florence
Fort Fisher 1865

Little Rock
Brice's Cross Roads 1862
Decatur
Kennesaw Mt. 1864
Athens
Columbia

Arkadelphia
Pine Bluff
Tupelo 1862
Elyton (Birmingham)
Atlanta 1864
Augusta
Georgetown
ATLANTIC OCEAN

El Dorado
MISSISSIPPI
Talladega
Macon
Charleston 1863-1865
Fort Sumter 1861

Shreveport
Champion's Hill 1863
ALABAMA
Tuscaloosa
Milledgeville
Sherman 1864
Port Royal 1861

Sabine Cross Roads 1864
Monroe
Vicksburg 1863
Jackson 1863
Selma
Columbus
GEORGIA
Savannah
Fort Pulaski 1862

Natchitoches
Sherman 1862
Meridien
Montgomery
Americus
THE CIVIL WAR 1861-1865

Banks 1864
Natchez
Eufaula
Albany
Douglas
Brunswick

Alexandria
LOUISIANA
Port Hudson 1863
Thomasville
Fernandina

Lafayette
Baton Rouge
Mobile 1865
Pensacola 1862
Tallahassee
Jacksonville

Sabine Pass 1863
Banks 1863
Mobile Bay 1864
New Orleans 1862
Olustee 1864
St. Augustine 1864

Fort St. Philip Fort Jackson 1863
Apalachicola
Gainsville

Farragut 1864
Cedar Key

Gulf of Mexico
FLORIDA
Tampa

### THE CIVIL WAR 1861-1865

- United States
- Confederate States
- Slave states remaining in the Union
- United States territory
- Union campaign
- Confederate campaign
- Union victory
- Confederate victory
- Indecisive battle

0 | 150 mi
0 | 200 km

BRITISH NORTH AMERICA

WASHINGTON TERRITORY
MAINE

OREGON
DAKOTA TERRITORY
MINN.
VT. N.H.
Boston

NEVADA TERR.
WIS.
MICHIGAN
NEW YORK
MASS.
R.I. CONN.

UTAH TERRITORY
Nebraska Territory
IOWA
Chicago
N.J. New York

CALIFORNIA
COLORADO TERRITORY
ILL. IND.
OHIO
PA.
Philadelphia

KANSAS
MO.
W. VA.
MD. Baltimore
DEL.
Washington, D.C.

NEW MEXICO TERRITORY
UNORGANIZED TERRITORY
KY.
VA.
Richmond

Boundary of Confederate States
Memphis
TENN.
Chattanooga
N.C.

ARK.
MISS.
ALA.
Atlanta
GA.
S.C.
Charleston

TEXAS
LA.
Vicksburg
Mobile
FLA.
Savannah

New Orleans

MEXICO

0 | 400 mi
0 | 600 km

In the North, the question was, How to win the war?

Bring the North's resources to bear on the South, advised Lt. Gen. Winfield Scott. In 1860 the North had 110,000 manufacturing establishments; the South had 18,000. The North had 21,973 miles of railroad and 451 locomotives; the south had 9,283 miles serviced by just 19 locomotives. Scott advised: Blockade the South's ports; split it along the Mississippi. Blows to the Confederate States' commerce and communications would "bring them to terms with less bloodshed than any other plan."

The public scorned Scott's Anaconda Plan. It wanted battles won, fast. "Forward to Richmond!" it cried, and an ill-prepared Army of the Potomac marched to its first defeat at Bull Run.

The North fixed early on capturing the Confederate capital, Richmond. After Bull Run in 1861 the army returned in 1862 and was driven to retreat by Robert E. Lee's Army of Northern Virginia in the Seven Days' Battle. That autumn found the Army of the Potomac back across its namesake river.

Lee was not satisfied. His victories in Virginia had won little more than time. Defeating the Union Army on Union soil, however, might win the war. At least, some southern leaders hoped, it would bring European recognition of the Confederacy. His northward thrust into Maryland was stymied in the bloody Battle of Antietam.

Abraham Lincoln also had his eye on Europe. His preliminary Emancipation Proclamation, issued in September 1862, gave the rebelling states the choice of returning to the Union by January 1 or having their slaves declared free. Rejected by the South, Lincoln's terms had their intended effect. Opposed to slavery and dubious of Confederate success, France and Britain remained neutral.

The Army of the Potomac made Lincoln's proclamation ring hollow. It tried a third time for Richmond and again was pummeled by Lee; another attempt was turned back by nothing more than bad weather. A New Yorker mailed home discontent: "I am sick and tired of disaster and the fools that bring disaster on us."

In the West the Union was winning the war under a general who did not suffer fools

gladly, Ulysses S. Grant. Striking through Tennessee toward the Deep South, he handed the North its first strategic success in July 1863: control of the Mississippi.

That July also brought the Union good news from the East. Lee's invasion of Pennsylvania was stopped short at Gettysburg—and this time his army had been the one forced to limp back across the Potomac. Col. Josiah Gorgas, Confederate chief of Ordnance, had little doubt about what the stunning reverses portended for the rebellion: "The Confederacy totters to its destruction."

## Dueling Generals

Ulysses Simpson Grant, into whose initials admiring Northerners read the words "United States" and "unconditional surrender," arrived in Washington, D.C., in March 1864. The victor of Fort Donelson, Vicksburg, and Chattanooga had come east to assume command of all Union armies in the field

and to implement a strategy of total war against the South.

Grant would personally direct operations against Lee's army while Sherman's forces fought and burned their way through Georgia and the Carolinas. "We are not only fighting hostile armies, but a hostile people," wrote Sherman, "and must make old and young, rich and poor, feel the hard hand of war."

Audacious on the attack, superb in defense, Gen. Robert E. Lee had driven four Union generals from his native state—and from their commands—while leading the Army of Northern Virginia. His men held devout, soft-spoken Lee in awe, even in defeat. "We who live shall never see his like again," a soldier wrote.

If Lee embodied cavalier Virginia, his Union counterpart represented pragmatic Yankee stock. Ulysses S. Grant, wrote an officer, "wears an expression as if he had determined to drive his head through a brick wall...." Grant's strategy: "Find out where your enemy is, get at him as soon as you can and strike him as

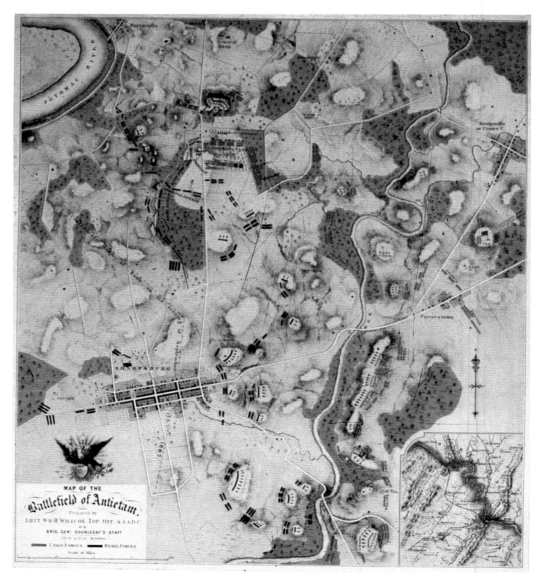

April 14, 1865—and another seed of vindictiveness was sown. President Andrew Johnson, a Tennessee Democrat who backed Lincoln's Reconstruction policy, could not win the support of Congress. The war had killed 623,000 men. Radical Republicans wanted to punish the South. "Dead men cannot raise themselves," raged Pennsylvania's Thaddeus Stevens. "Dead states cannot restore their existence 'as it was.'"

> ## INAUGURAL ADDRESS
> ## FEBRUARY 22, 1862
>
> It is with mingled feelings of humility and pride that I appear to take, in the presence of the people and before high Heaven, the oath prescribed as a qualification for the exalted station to which the unanimous voice of the people has called me.
>
> ...The first year in our history has been the most eventful in the annals of this continent. A new government has been established, and its machinery put in operation over an area exceeding seven hundred thousand square miles. The great principles upon which we have been willing to hazard everything that is dear to man have made conquests for us which could never have been achieved by the sword. Our Confederacy has grown from six to thirteen States...Our people have rallied with unexampled unanimity to the support of the great principles of constitutional government, with firm resolve to perpetuate by arms the right which they could not peacefully secure. A million of men, it is estimated, are now standing in hostile array, and waging war along a frontier of thousands of miles...although the contest is not ended, and the tide for the moment is against us, the final result in our favor is not doubtful...With humble gratitude and adoration, acknowledging the Providence which has so visibly protected the Confederacy during its brief but eventful career, to thee, O God, I trustingly commit myself, and prayerfully invoke thy blessing on my country and its cause.
>
> –Jefferson Davis

hard as you can, and keep moving on."

An enormous Yankee war engine—built by factories and fueled by deficit spending and the labor of immigrants and freed blacks—was arrayed against the South. Railroads shuttled goods and troops through strategic junctions such as Harpers Ferry, West Virginia.

Raised in an agrarian tradition, the Confederacy erected foundries, powder mills, and machine shops, primarily in the Deep South. Confederate armies ran short of butter before guns.

Grant drove hard into Virginia, giving furious battle to Lee in the Wilderness, at Spotsylvania Court House, Cold Harbor, and Petersburg. Lee's army was killing two for every man it lost—but was running out of men. Grant knew the numbers and sensed victory. "I purpose to fight it out on this line if it takes all summer," he wired Lincoln in mid-campaign.

Northern voters reacted to the mounting losses, too. Grant's "butcher bill," Democrats vowed, would be paid by Lincoln—with his presidency. Their nominee for the 1864 election was the dovish George McClellan, ex-commander of the Army of the Potomac. The South took heart. If Lincoln was ousted, all might yet be well. Confederate raids further sapped Union morale.

Total war claimed its first victim—Meridian, Mississippi—on February 14, 1864. Conquering General Sherman wrote, "Meridian, with its depots, store-houses, arsenals, hospitals, offices, hotels and cantonments no longer exists."

Then electrifying news fatal to McClellan's presidential hopes was telegraphed across the nation: Atlanta had fallen. All but unopposed, Sherman's legions seared a passage to the sea, reaching Savannah shortly before Christmas. "The simple fact that a man's home has been invaded," wrote Sherman, "makes a soldier in Lee's or Johnston's army very, very anxious to get home to look after his family and property." Thousands of Lee's men did just that, as news of Sherman's "hard war" filled desperate letters from home.

The Confederacy was finished, but the war raged on. New seeds of southern bitterness were sown with every farm razed by Sherman, seeds of northern vindictiveness with every boy killed at Petersburg. Reelected, Abraham Lincoln hoped to leave the war's grim harvest unreaped. "With malice toward none; with charity for all…," he urged in his Second Inaugural Address, "let us strive on to finish the work we are in; to bind up the nation's wounds…." His face was ravaged by worry. Advised in 1864 that a break from his duties might restore his health, Lincoln had responded, "I can not fly from my thoughts—my solicitude for this great country follows me wherever I go."

His dream of reuniting the country proved to be unfulfilled. John Wilkes Booth, self-described southern patriot, stilled the nation's most persuasive voice of union on

PAGE 86: *Regimental fife and drum corps.*
ABOVE: *Abraham Lincoln, here on the battle front, presided over a country divided.*
OPPOSITE: *Civil War battlefield Antietam, the bloodiest battle of the War.*

# EMANCIPATION PROCLAMATION

## Freedom for Slaves

"Thenceforward, and forever free." So proclaimed President Abraham Lincoln's Emancipation Proclamation on January 1, 1863. The proclamation referred only to slaves in the rebellious states over which Lincoln had no control, so the edict had little actual force. It did however, convert the struggle into a crusade against slavery, thus making European intervention impossible. It also allowed the Union to recruit black soldiers, nearly 180,000 of whom enlisted before the end of the war.

Shame had been the first weapon of antislavery agitators. Black leaders at an 1832 convention hoped to prick American consciences with the sight of "an *oppressed people,* deprived of the rights of citizenship, in the midst of an enlightened nation, devising plans and measures, for their personal and mental elevation, by *moral suasion* alone." Antislavery meetings, tracts, door-to-door calls, and mailing campaigns bombarded Americans with descriptions of life under slavery. The American Anti-Slavery Society alone distributed more than a million pieces of literature in 1835. In 1839 Theodore Dwight Weld, his wife, Angelina, and her sister Sarah Grimké published *American Slavery As It Is,* in which eyewitness accounts helped inflame antislavery sentiment. The book sold 100,000 copies its first year. Escaped slaves brought first-hand accounts to lectures. "I appear...this evening as a thief and a robber," Frederick Douglass told an 1842 audience. "I stole this head, these limbs, this body from my master, and ran off with them." The renowned antislavery orator and editor of the *North Star* demanded "emancipation for our enslaved brethren" and the vote for "nominally free" blacks.

Religion, notably Quakerism and evangelical Christianity, nourished abolitionism. Friend Elihu Embree of Tennessee had established the *Manumission Intelligencer* and the *Emancipator,* the first U.S. papers to deal exclusively with abolition, by 1820. Levi Coffin and Thomas Garrett, both Quakers, each sheltered more than a thousand fugitives.

Moral weapons, however, were blunted by economics and politics. Accounting for three-quarters of the U.S. export trade in 1850, cotton meant wealth—and slavery. The risk of provoking southern secession daunted many politicians. Black leaders despaired of attaining justice in the U.S.; some even

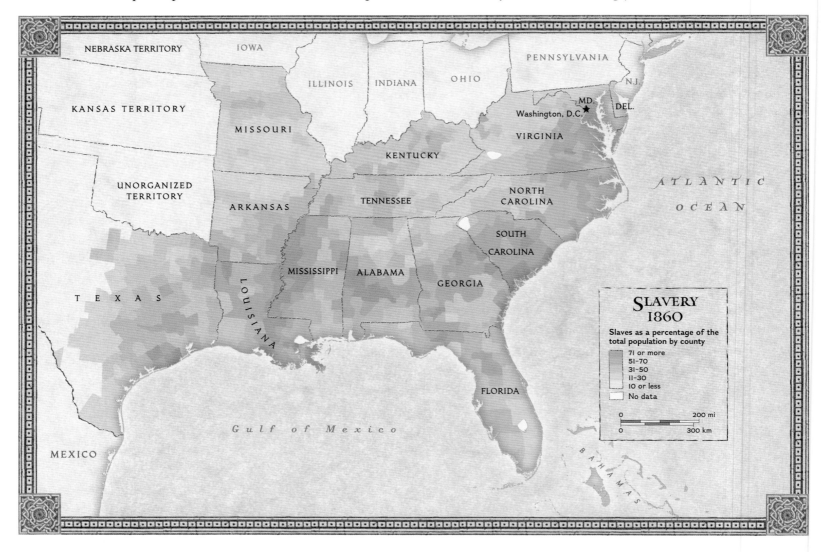

SLAVERY 1860

**Slaves as a percentage of the total population by county**
- 71 or more
- 51-70
- 31-50
- 11-30
- 10 or less
- No data

countenanced the once heretical idea of emigration to Africa. In the 1850s Martin Delany, an abolitionist editor, declared, "I must admit, that I have no hopes of this country—no confidence in the American people."

Abolitionists tried an old—and ultimately successful—strategy in 1848, after the war with Mexico. They fought to bar slavery from new territories. Through involvement in the Free Soil and, later, Republican Parties, combined with the inflammation of northern rage against slavery, abolitionists helped provoke the crisis they thought necessary to end slavery.

By 1860, jobs were drawing free blacks to mid-Atlantic cities and to Pennsylvania factories and mines. Ohio, with its strong antislavery sentiment and proximity to Canada, became a haven for runaways. Descendants of blacks freed after the Revolution farmed near Chesapeake Bay; in the 1790s ideals of universal liberty—and declining tobacco prices—had inspired many slaveholders to set their slaves free.

Those still in bondage sought freedom on foot. Harsh conditions, especially the forced separation of families, drove 40,000 slaves to flee the U.S. by 1860. As the abolition movement intensified in the 1830s, a thousand slaves escaped each year, although most were quickly captured. Northern cities held pockets of runaways, while southern swamps and hollows hid fugitive colonies.

Antislavery newspapers printed speeches, news from emigrants in Canada, and community notices. *Freedom's Journal,* published in the 1820s, was the first put out by blacks.

Speaking to an Ohio audience in 1851, Sojourner Truth said, "That man…says that women need to be helped into carriages, and lifted over ditches, and to have the best place everywhere. Nobody ever helps me into carriages, or over mud puddles, or gives me any best place, and ain't I a woman?…I have plowed, and planted, and gathered into barns, and no man could head me—and ain't I a woman? I could work as much and eat as much as a man (when I could get it), and bear the lash as well—and

I Sell the Shadow to Support the Substance.

SOJOURNER TRUTH.

ain't I a woman? I have borne thirteen children and seen them most all sold off into slavery, and when I cried out with a mother's grief, none but Jesus heard—and ain't I a woman?"

She was born sometime around 1797 in Ulster County, New York, and given the name Isabella Van Wagener. She answered what she felt to be a religious call to "travel up and down the land," so she took the name Sojourner Truth. She became a fervid abolitionist, a powerful preacher, and a strong proponent of the women's rights movement. She sang,

debated, and preached wherever she could, at churches, on street corners, at revival meetings.

She was one of the voices that propelled Abraham Lincoln, no abolitionist himself, to make his fateful decision. Full rights to citizenship would be granted in the 13th, 14th, and 15th Amendments.

---

ABOVE: *"I Sell the Shadow to Support the Substance,"* reads a carte-de-visite of Sojourner Truth. *The American evangelist and reformer sold the souvenir cards at lectures.*

# OIL and OILMEN

## Gushers and Texas Tea

The "black gold" that gushed from American soil powered personal fortunes as well as industry and transportation.

"Now they have come to harpoon Mother Earth," declared a reporter in western Pennsylvania in the 1860s, as whalers joined those flocking to cash in on newly accessible petroleum. They found far more than a replacement for their clean but expensive whale lamp oil. Kerosene distilled from the landlocked crude burned brightly and without the smoke and odor of lard or turpentine also being sold as illuminants. It soon took over the market—and refining plants—of the coal-oil industry, which had been crushing coal and distilling it into lamp oil.

The U.S. exported 32 million gallons of petroleum throughout the world in 1864. "It has crept round the globe in place of the moon—a light from the antipodes," a booster wrote the following year. "The Swiss cottager, smoking beside his petroleum lamp in the evening, rejoices in something better than a taper whereby to watch the faces of his wife and children. The German student studies better by it; or, gathered with his kind, drinks more madly, sings louder, under its radiant influence." Distilled crude also yielded naphtha, valuable as an anesthetic and solvent, a high-quality lubricant for machinery, and a wax for candles. By the late

1890s, 200 by-products accounted for half the oil industry's sales revenues.

Wood from plentiful forests fueled the nation's early development, from cooking to producing charcoal for iron foundries. Steam trains and river vessels demanded a less bulky fuel, and by 1885 coal had replaced wood as the main energy source. Concentrated in Pennsylvania, West Virginia, Kentucky, and Illinois, the fossil fuel was extracted and shipped to the burgeoning cities, often delivered to basements via coal chute. Still, it took at least two tons of coal to heat the average home during a Pennsylvania winter. Rising with wars and falling during the Depression, coal use gave way to natural gas and oil, the main fuels by 1950.

At Titusville, Pennsylvania, "Col." Edwin Drake's 1859 strike at 69.5 feet ushered in the modern oil industry. His well produced eight barrels a day, most of which became lamp oil.

The story goes that when businessmen sent John D. Rockefeller to Pennsylvania in 1860 to assess the infant oil industry, he found "chaos and disorder, waste and incompetence, competition at its worst." The dislike was mutual:

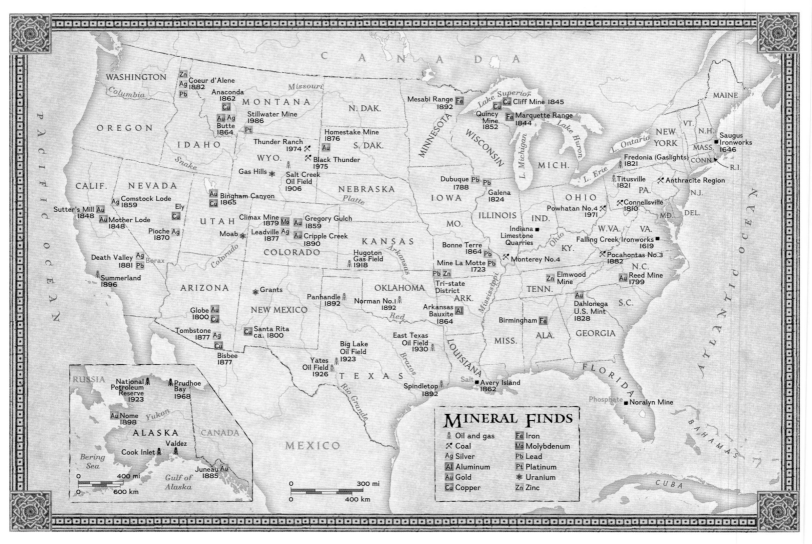

Boiler Avenue
April 23 1903
Edgerton

Roughnecks called the 21-year-old "that bloodless Baptist bookkeeper."

Rockefeller saw opportunity in refining oil into kerosene for the world's lamps, since whale oil was scarce and other illuminants burned poorly. He bought all but five of the competing refineries in Cleveland. To save money, he transported crude to refineries—and kerosene to freight yards—in his own barrels, on his own wagons. Railroads gave him kickbacks. Donkeys soon carried his kerosene in North Africa; elephants carted it in India.

By 1883 his Standard Oil Trust had captured more than 90 percent of the U.S. refineries and pipelines. When it seemed as if electricity would displace kerosene for lighting, along puffed and rattled a new contraption, the automobile. Rockefeller was still in the driver's seat.

Black Thunder, the most productive surface coal mine in the U.S., is just one of many in the Powder River basin, which stretches from Wyoming into Montana.

One of the most famous oil fields in the U.S. was Spindletop, discovered in southeastern Texas. In 1901 Capt. Anthony Lucas hit oil at 1,020 feet. The Spindletop gusher spewed thousands of barrels a day for nine days before it could be capped. By 1903 it was producing 20 percent of the U.S. total. More than 440 gushers came in there, making millionaires of some of the 50,000 fortune hunters who crammed into nearby Beaumont. Bank tellers shoveled silver dollars out to their flush customers. But life was risky in what some called Swindletop. Flash too big a roll and you'd end up a floater—in the river. Buyers subdivided their property for quick profits, until a lease was no bigger than a derrick floor. Boilers sat at the edges of the field, their steam lines running to the wells' rotary drilling engines. Racing under the "rule of capture"—get it before your neighbor does—the oilmen drained the field's gas pressure, and much of the available oil, by 1904.

Drilling into underlying salt domes brought a resurgence in the 1920s.

Chemists during the 1920s began experimenting with supplies of natural gas and liquid hydrocarbons recently available, producing new products for ravenous industrial and consumer markets. By the beginning of the 21st century, the U.S. was consuming 19.6 million barrels of oil per day, more than 25 percent of the world's total.

The U.S. produced enough oil to supply its own demand until 1970. The nation produces more than 10 percent of the world's oil, largely from both onshore and offshore fields along the Texas-Louisiana Gulf Coast, extending inland through west Texas, Oklahoma, and eastern Kansas, as well as in Alaska along the central North Slope.

ABOVE: *A forest of derricks sprouts at Spindletop in 1903, two years after the oil field was discovered in southeastern Texas. By then it was generating 20 percent of the petroleum produced in the U.S.*

# CAPTURING AMERICA *on* FILM

## *Daguerre, Brady, Curtis*

In the beginning there was the light, falling upon a continent's worth of blue mountains, red rocks, and big skies. Painters had been capturing the American landscape since the early days of colonization, but it awaited photographers to give Americans a true and detailed sense of their country.

Appropriately, the art of photography can be said to have been born in Paris, the City of Light. There the operator of a theater called the Diorama, Louis-Jacques-Mandé Daguerre, was experimenting with light. In 1825 he was showing paintings 71 by 45 feet long of various scenes. Subjects included episodes from Greek and Roman mythology and allegories and grand scenery. He lit the scenes imaginatively, creating the illusion that time was passing as the sun moved across the sky, or dark clouds could indicate changing weather, or even the images were themselves moved.

Like many painters of the time, he took advantage of the camera obscura—a darkened box with an opening and a lens through which light entered; there it formed an image on the box's opposite surface. The camera obscura helped painters get details right and make perspective convincing. But the image inside the box was fleeting; what was needed was a way to fix it there permanently.

The solution to the problem centered on finding a surface that was light sensitive; using a lens to form an image on it; then stopping the surface's further sensitivity so light wouldn't harm the image already created. Daguerre came up with iodine-treated, silver-plated, light-sensitive copper sheets. When put in a box and exposed to an image, the plate held the image. Warm mercury vapor made it magically appear and fixed it permanently on the plate. Daguerre named the resulting pictures for himself—Daguerreotypes.

A better inventor than businessman, Daguerre made little money from his new process. The materials were avail-

Bull Run nearby in the Virginia countryside, Brady journeyed out to see the fighting for himself. Confederates nearly captured him. An observer said that Brady showed "more pluck than many of the officers and soldiers who were in the fight." Seeing battle firsthand affected Brady deeply, and he determined to photographically record as much of the Civil War as he could. He sent Gardner and O'Sullivan and 20 more assistants into the field, each with a portable darkroom for processing the plates. Brady managed their efforts from his office in Washington.

By war's end Brady had some 10,000 plates of the soldiers and battlefields that he hoped the federal government would purchase as a permanent record of the War. But the government refused and Brady, broke, sold his New York City studio and declared himself bankrupt. In 1875 Congress finally acknowledged Brady's work and granted him $25,000, but by then he was depressed and still in debt. He became an alcoholic and died in the charity ward of Presbyterian Hospital in New York in January 1896.

An American photographer, Edward S. Curtis, who grew up among the Chipewa, Menomini, and Winnebago Indians of Minnesota would become the most successful and famous chronicler of the nation's diverse tribes. A boyhood interest in photography led to the purchase of a share of a Seattle photographic studio in 1891. An early sitter for a portrait was "Princess Angeline," one of Chief Seattle's daughters. In 1895 Curtis began a quest—to document all the major Native American tribes west of the Mississippi. Between 1896 and 1930 his cameras produced more than 40,000 negatives of Indians in 80 tribes.

Photography was employed by reformers as well. In 1890 Jacob Riis published *How the Other Half Lives,* a searing exposé of New York tenements that would spur the nation to outrage.

OPPOSITE: *The new art of photography brings Easterners sights from the West like Crazy Horse.* ABOVE: *Grand Review of the Union Army in Washington, D.C., in May 1865, by Matthew Brady.*

able to practically anyone, and copies of his instruction manual were soon available all over the world in various translations. Anyone who wanted to try to make a Daguerreotype was free to do so. And many in America rushed to do just that.

In the 20 years before the Civil War, photographic studios suddenly appeared everywhere, and Americans dressed themselves in their finery—cowboys with lassos and guns; soldiers in uniform; newlyweds posed stiffly in parlors—and received a small hard image as a remembrance. Often the pictures were encased in fine leather covers. Newspaper editors began relying on them for illustrations, as they copied engravings from them. They were popular but had some drawbacks. Each was an original with no negative from which copies could be made. They were heavy but still delicate and easily scratched. They were bright and shiny, so were difficult to look at in sunlight.

One of the American studios was the Daguerreotype Miniature Gallery in New York, opened in 1844 by Matthew Brady, who would become one of America's most famous and accomplished photographers. He soon had another studio in Washington,

D.C., where he concentrated on photographing famous Americans. Horace Greeley, Daniel Webster, John Calhoun, Thaddeus Stevens, Stephen Douglas, and many more sat for his portraits. He photographed Abraham Lincoln 35 times during the 1860 presidential campaign alone. When he won, Lincoln told friends, "Brady and the Cooper Union speech made me President."

When not yet 30, Brady's eyesight began to fail, and he started relying heavily on his chief assistants, Alexander Gardner and Timothy O'Sullivan. Gardner began utilizing a wet-plate system instead of the Daguerreotype. Both assistants would achieve wide renown as photographers during the Civil War and after.

War brought thousands of Union soldiers to Washington, D.C., and many of them journeyed to Brady's studio, proud in their new uniforms, to be photographed. Officers came too, and Burnside, Wallace, Sherman, Butler, Custer, Hooker, McClellan, and Farragut were some who had their likenesses reproduced in the Brady studio.

In July 1861, during the Battle of

# The
# RECONSTRUCTION

❧

## *Putting It All Back Together*

The collapse of the Confederacy brought suffering as well as freedom to the South's slaves. During the war, many had followed Union troops, camping in makeshift shacks, often sick and starving. Others looked for family members lost in the confusion of war. "I have a mother somewhere in the world," wrote the Reverend E. W. Johnson in an appeal for help to a newspaper. "I know not where. She used to belong to Philip Mathias in Elbert county, Georgia, and she left four of her children there about twenty-three years ago....Her name was Martha and I heard that she was carried off to Mississippi by speculators."

"We are scattered—stunned—the remnant of heart left alive within us, filled with brotherly hate. We sit and wait until the drunken tailor who rules…issues a

proclamation and defines our anomalous position," Mary Boykin Chesnut of South Carolina wrote of Lincoln's successor. Civil War was over, civil strife was not.

Yet Andrew Johnson was the white South's best ally. He led a minority coalition in an uncompromising platform: to seek a lenient peace that accorded dignity to the South. His opponents, Radical Republicans led by Thaddeus Stevens and Charles Sumner, did not trust white Southerners and northern Democrats to grant blacks equality. As proof they cited race riots in Memphis and New Orleans and newly enacted repressive "black codes."

In the battle of Reconstruction, Johnson drew first blood—his own—by departing from the prepared text of an 1866 speech long enough to call three Radical Republicans "traitors." Even the President's supporters were appalled by such abrasive behavior. A Republican Congress passed the Civil Rights Act and other laws over his veto. In 1868 the House impeached him; Johnson was spared removal by one vote in the Senate.

Ulysses S. Grant, winner of the war and the presidential election of 1868, had far less success in the campaigns of Reconstruction. His administration proved inept in dealing with economic turmoil and ineffective in coping with a united white front in the South.

After the war, three groups came to power in the South: One consisted of northerners who had moved South, some to help rebuild the region, some to make their own fortunes. Many carried suitcases made of carpet material—so were called "carpetbaggers." Also in power were southerners who had opposed secession—called "scalawags"—and newly enfranchised blacks. Most white Southerners opposed them all.

The South was not alone in struggling in the postwar era. In the North and Midwest, governments were unable to meet the needs of the emerging cities. Industrialization and a rapid influx of immigrants increased demands for municipal services. City bosses answered those needs with efficient political machines organized to trade patronage and favors for loyalty and votes. They corralled countless votes from the four million immi-

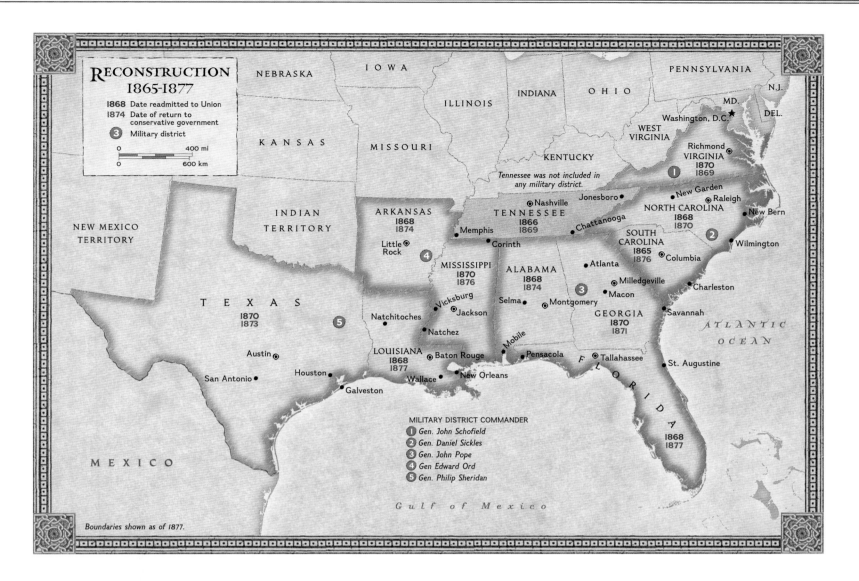

## RECONSTRUCTION 1865-1877

**1868** Date readmitted to Union
**1874** Date of return to conservative government
**③** Military district

0——————400 mi
0——————600 km

*Boundaries shown as of 1877.*

*Tennessee was not included in any military district.*

**MILITARY DISTRICT COMMANDER**
**①** Gen. John Schofield
**②** Gen. Daniel Sickles
**③** Gen. John Pope
**④** Gen Edward Ord
**⑤** Gen. Philip Sheridan

---

grants who landed in the 15 years after the Civil War. With the immigrants as their power base, most bosses operated as kingmakers without holding elected office. Among the noteworthy ones were Albert Ames in Minneapolis, Marcus Hanna in Cleveland, Martin Lomasney in Boston, George Cox in Cincinnati, and William Tweed in New York City. Anti-Tammany cartoons by Thomas Nast—what Boss Tweed called "them damn pictures"—helped turn public opinion against his machine in the 1871 election.

In the West deceit, theft, and neglect marked the government's policy toward the Indians. After the Civil War the Grant Administration began to drive them onto reservations. Put under the unyielding command of Gen. William Tecumseh Sherman, the Army destroyed the Indians' food supply, employing the same total-war tactics Sherman had used when he marched across the South in the Civil War.

The movement of Americans across the West was bad news for the plains bison. In 1871 a New York tannery developed a way to turn the soft hides into good leather, and soon hides brought $3.50 each in Dodge City, Kansas. By 1874 nearly all bison—some 1.5 million—had been slaughtered.

The 1876 presidential election was the final blow to Reconstruction. Republican Rutherford B. Hayes lost the popular vote to Samuel J. Tilden but won an electoral college victory by promising to remove troops from the South. Occupation of the South represented a compromise within the factious Republican Party. The intent was to coerce state governments into recognizing black political equality and accepting the 14th Amendment—the central requirement for readmission to the Union. The resistance of white southerners was strong. When the last federal troops left in 1877, with them went realistic hopes for black equality.

Standing between freed blacks and southern whites were agents of the Bureau of Refugees, Freedmen, and Abandoned Lands who worked to ease the transition from slavery to freedom.

Though it made gains in labor relations and education for blacks, the bureau was plagued by lack of staff and by insufficient funds, and in many states it was actively opposed by the Ku Klux Klan. Founded in early 1866 in Pulaski, Tennessee, by six former Confederate soldiers, the Klan killed black political leaders and burned Freedmen's Bureau schoolhouses. The bureau was dismantled by Congress in 1872, having fallen short of most of its major objectives.

As a policy of enforcing black rights in the South, Reconstruction was dead. The 13th, 14th, and 15th Amendments to the Constitution and the Civil Rights Acts of 1866 and 1875 were alive, but only on paper.

Tennessee was the first southern state to be readmitted to the Union in 1866. Arkansas, North Carolina, Alabama, Florida, Louisiana, and South Carolina rejoined in 1868. Last were Virginia, Mississippi, Texas, and Georgia in 1870.

---

OPPOSITE: *The Old South—and the New: In Georgia in the 1860s, Spanish moss dangles above two African American women, newly freed.*

# *The* RAILROADS

## *Webs of Transportation*

**B**altimore had problems. Its economic health was threatened by the Erie Canal and the busy wharves of Manhattan. Plans for other canals were afoot; one sought to connect the Potomac River to the Ohio. In 1826 Baltimore's merchants, bankers, and lawyers met to discuss a new technology that seemed to hold the answer to their city's uncertain prospects. Maps were consulted, computations rechecked, final agreement reached. The following year they incorporated their gamble as the Baltimore and Ohio Railroad Company.

Railroads had been developed in Europe. American engineers shook their heads, however, at trials of imported English locomotives: They could not pull heavy loads, and light-gauge tracks buckled under their weight. Underpowered and overweight locomotives might suffice in Britain, perhaps, which could afford to build expensive roadbeds for them. But American railroad companies had enormous distances to span and little money to do it with. But by the mid-1830s locomotives made by American master mechanics were at work on the B & O and scores of other railroads. Strong and lightweight, able to run on inexpensive track, they established the reputation of American locomotive engineering as the world's best.

By 1852 the B & O and three other northern railroads had reached beyond the Appalachians. There they found a disjointed system of midwestern railroads already in place and began buying as well as building. The B & O pioneered con-

nections to St. Louis and Cincinnati, the Pennsylvania Railroad to Dayton and Indianapolis. The city that proved to be the richest prize, Chicago, first was connected to the East in February 1852. Grange railroads fanned out from hub cities to bring crops to market. South of the Ohio, railroads made Richmond, Atlanta, Memphis, and Chattanooga entrepôts for tobacco and cotton—and objects of Union strategic attack during the Civil War.

In 1830 South Carolina pioneered steam passenger rail service in the U.S. and three years later completed a 135-mile railroad, then the world's longest. Connection with the Georgia Railroad transformed Terminus—renamed Atlanta in 1847—into the South's premier rail hub.

By 1860, 30,500 miles of railroad track had been laid—almost as much as the rest of the world combined. Two-thirds of it was in the North. While many railroads ran east and west, only three linked the North to the South in 1860. Eleven railroads met in Chicago, already the nation's rail hub. In 1862 Abraham Lincoln, anxious to cement California in the Union, signed into existence the Union Pacific Railroad and ordered it to link with the Central Pacific between Omaha and Sacramento.

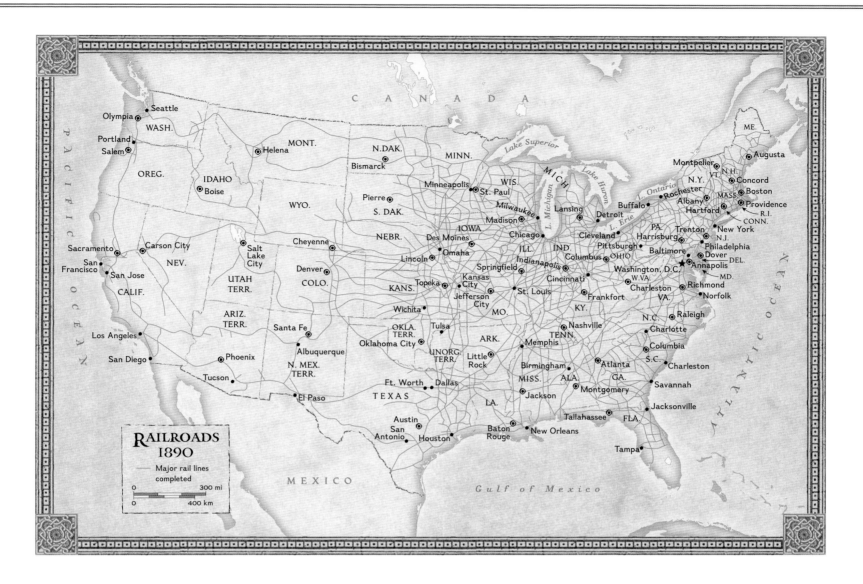

RAILROADS
1890

Major rail lines
completed

0           300 mi

0           400 km

The Union Pacific brought in more than 10,000 men. Most were Irish immigrants, some of them Civil War veterans. In California the Central Pacific recruited more than 10,000 Chinese immigrants to build its part of the line. Some had come to California because of the discovery of gold in 1848, but many had come to find jobs, planning to return home with the wages earned. Armed with picks, shovels, and sledgehammers, the railroad workers cleared and leveled land for the track.

On May 10, 1869, two locomotives stood nose to nose on tracks stretching to opposite horizons—"half a world behind each back," as a San Francisco editor put it. Bandmaster Capt. Charles Currier's description ended on a sober note: "Thus is the greatest undertaking of the 19th century accomplished. All honors to the resolute men who have 'put it through.'"

By 1883 four railroads crossed the West, making tracks for Dakota wheat fields, Rocky Mountain mining towns, California farmland, and Washington state timber; hauling out raw resources; and hauling in money, settlers, and goods.

"Rivers run only where nature pleases; railroads run wherever man pleases," noted a St. Louis newspaper in 1867. This was not news upstream in Illinois, where the Mississippi had been bridged a decade earlier at Rock Island, enabling trains to cross into Iowa.

St. Louis responded in 1874 with the engineering marvel of its day, the Eads Bridge, then the world's longest at 1,524 feet. Its top tier bore wagons and pedestrians; its bottom tier funneled the railroad traffic that allowed St. Louis to challenge even Chicago as a western gateway.

Railroading's golden age was under way. Pullman cars crossed the Great Plains, passengers leaning from windows to blaze away at herds of buffalo. Trains like the Empire State Express set standards of opulence and thrilled the public with full-throttle runs at record speeds.

Trains ran on time. Americans set their watches by them—first by choice, then by law. Railroad time became eastern, central, mountain, and Pacific time in 1883. Terminals like New York's Grand Central were monuments to efficiency. "Through this new gateway…," the New York Times

stated in 1913, "the entire population of the United States could pass in a single year without crowding and without confusion."

Efficiency and speed, however, were not exclusively railroad property—even if it seemed so through the turn of the century. In the 1920s railroads began losing passengers. A bus ticket cost less, and airplanes were faster. The automobile offered something more alluring than either: the open road.

By 1971 most intercity passenger trains were gone. The government consolidated the remaining major routes as Amtrak that year and modernized facilities and equipment. Profitable in heavily trafficked corridors, Amtrak still relies on subsidies.

OPPOSITE: A crew on the Northern Pacific Railroad takes a break somewhere in the American West. Crews could be diverse, with Irish, Chinese, and Mexicans working alongside one another. In carefully choreographed moves, they pounded ties and plates into position. Then 12 men hoisted heavy, 30-foot-long rails into place. Spike drivers hit each spike three times—there were ten spikes to a rail—and America crept westward.

# HOME
## *on the* RANGE

❧

## *American Ranchers*

Cattle crossed the Appalachians with settlers in the late 1700s. However, not until the introduction of high-milk-producing breeds such as Holsteins and Jerseys in the 1840s did dairy and beef producers begin to specialize. Before the Civil War three-quarters of the dairy industry was concentrated east of Ohio, and New York state alone contained one-third of the total. Chicago stockyards provisioned Union troops during the war. The Union Stockyards opened there in 1865, setting a pattern followed by large commercial meat-packers.

Cattle herding as a large-scale operation began early among British colonists on the Eastern Seaboard, particularly in South Carolina, and moved west over major migration routes. Anglo-style open-range techniques in the East, including branding and dog herding, blended with the Hispanic roping and riding styles of Louisiana and eastern Texas to produce a new ranching system that spread through the Great Plains.

During the 1870s and 1880s Texas cattlemen sent millions of head north on long drives to grasslands or railheads. By the end of the century fencing enclosed the ranges, and iron horses did the driving.

Cattleman Joseph G. McCoy began his 1874 account of the western cattle industry by assuring his readers that ranchers were divinely favored. "Sacred writ plainly tells us," he argued, "that Abel's offering being the product of his stock ranch was more acceptable to Deity than that of his agricultural brother."

As early as the 1840s those sons of Abel grazed hundreds of thousands of longhorns in Texas. At first the lanky cattle were valued only for hides, tallow, hooves, and horns. But after the Civil War eastern demand for meat made it profitable to drive herds north on such trails as the Chisholm to stops along the Kansas Pacific Railroad. From there they were transshipped to markets.

Every bit of a cowboy's equipment reflected active life under the open skies. His small, tough, sure-footed horse, a descendant of Spanish stock, could carry him 30 to 40 miles a day. His wide-brimmed hat protected him from the sun—and doubled as a pillow or water bucket. His red bandanna, worn as a mask, kept him from choking when riding dusty trails. Heavy leather chaps protected his legs in brushy country; gloves and cuffs helped prevent rope burn when working with his lasso. His vest provided handy pockets; the slicker, carried behind his saddle, kept him dry in

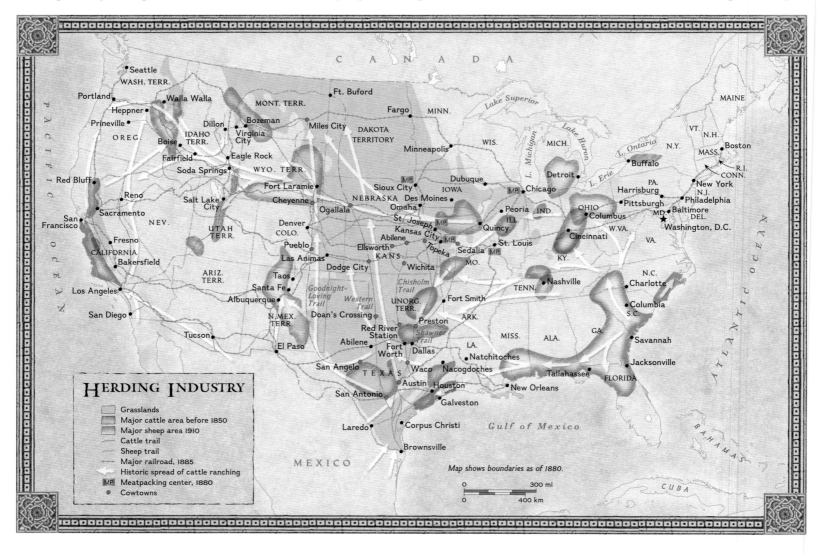

**HERDING INDUSTRY**

- Grasslands
- Major cattle area before 1850
- Major sheep area 1910
- Cattle trail
- Sheep trail
- Major railroad, 1885
- Historic spread of cattle ranching
- MP Meatpacking center, 1880
- Cowtowns

Map shows boundaries as of 1880.

0        300 mi
0        400 km

the rain—and was useful at night as a ground cloth. High-heeled boots held the stirrups. His six-shooter could be used to signal—or to blast rattlesnakes and rustlers.

Ranch hands rode the range for months at a time—from April "till the wagon made tracks through four-inch Christmas snow," according to one wife. At the end of the trail, cattle crowded the stockyards of East St. Louis, Omaha, Abilene, Kansas City, and Chicago. The yards flourished during the 20-year heyday of cattle driving, which began after the Civil War. A century later most big stockyards were gone, replaced by larger feedlots and scattered slaughterhouses.

The trail cowboy did not survive the century's last decade except in legend. Maybe in that bovine Valhalla he kept company with the apple-cheeked milkmaid, for dairying had become a market-driven industry even sooner. In 1850 more than 419 million pounds of butter and cheese were produced, and by 1860 rail lines in New England were speeding ice-cooled milk cans to cities and towns. By 1920 dairy operations had spread along an arc running from Vermont through New York and around the Great Lakes to Minnesota.

When Kit Carson drove 6,500 head from New Mexico Territory to California in 1853 the animals were sheep. In 1860, although most sheep were still in the East, flocks were growing in Texas, New Mexico, and California. By the 1880s sheepherders were moving their stocks into country along both flanks of the Rocky Mountains.

Between the 1860s and 1890s, as more ranchers, farmers, and sheepherders moved west, contests for rights to grazing lands from the Texas Panhandle to the Dakotas turned bitter. Cattlemen seized both public and Indian lands and wrote their own laws. Associations of stockmen briefly became unauthorized governments in the territories. Cattle companies strung barbed-wire fences around millions of acres of grazing land and shut out small farmers and ranchers from watercourses.

In 1883 a Galveston newspaper reported that 20 miles of barbed-wire fence on the property of the Hickey Pasture Company had been cut to bits, presumably by neighbors who refused to be denied a handy water supply. The first commercially successful barbed wire—there were eventually hundreds of types—was intro-

duced in 1874 by an Illinois farmer and inventor, Joseph F. Glidden. His most notable design, the Winner, had double-twist barbs on two strands of wire.

The fencing cost $100 to $200 a mile but paid for itself; ranchers needed fewer hands to care for cattle, and stock was kept from straying. As much as any six-shooter, barbed wire inflamed western conflicts. For more than a decade fence wars flared. "Range hogs" and cattle barons hired gunmen to protect their fences, while unlikely alliances of rangers, farmers, and cattle drivers armed with wire cutters fought for open access to the land well into the 1890s.

Farmers and ranchers were willing to buy unwatered land, then enclose it and drill wells as deep as 800 feet. Well water pumped by windmills into reservoirs allowed ranchers to safeguard against drought and to spread herds (which stuck close to water) over a much wider range.

ABOVE: *Farmers and ranchers clash on the Brighton Ranch in Custer County, Nebraska, around 1885, as masked gunmen cut the despised barbed wire that prevented the free ranging of their cattle.*

# FORGING *the* FUTURE

~

## *Steel and Steelmen*

It was a ridiculous idea—blowing air into molten iron to burn the carbon out and produce steel. Everyone knew that top-quality steel could only be made in small crucibles. Iron was the workhorse metal and always would be.

William Kelly thought otherwise. In the early 1850s he made soft and malleable steel without consuming the volumes of charcoal needed to puddle pig iron into workable wrought iron. Kelly made boiler plates for river steamboats,

steel, whose output was to be measured not in tons but in thousands of tons. The open-hearth furnace, developed in Europe and refined in the U.S. during the 1880s, boosted yearly output to millions of tons. It also removed phosphorus better than the Bessemer process, enabling greater use of the phosphorus-rich ore of the massive Great Lakes ranges and creating a stronger grade of steel. Located in northern Minnesota, Mesabi, which means "giant" in the language of the Ojibwa, is

THE VERDICT.

THE TRUST GIANTS' POINT OF VIEW.
"WHAT A FUNNY LITTLE GOVERNMENT!"

but he failed to patent his work until after an Englishman, Henry Bessemer, was granted British and U.S. patents for his own version, which brought him knighthood and enduring fame.

Alexander Holley ushered in modern American steelmaking in 1865, designing the nation's first viable Bessemer plant at Troy, New York. In 1890 the U.S. passed Great Britain as top steel producer.

Fiery 15-minute blasts of Bessemer converters signaled the end of iron's 3,000-year reign and the emergence of

the largest of the six Lake Superior iron ranges. Since 1892 it has yielded 3.5 billion tons of iron ore.

When anthracite coal began replacing charcoal as fuel in the 1830s, iron makers left rural iron plantations to locate furnaces near coal deposits. Cheaper transportation and demand for raw materials brought the mining of bituminous coal and led to larger, integrated manufacturing units.

The eventual result was an industrial complex of mines, ships, railroads, and steel plants. "Hell with the lid taken off,"

wrote a visitor to Pittsburgh in 1868. Commanding three rivers and surrounded by coal, Pittsburgh early on developed as the center of iron and steel manufacturing. By 1904, 34 separate iron-and-steel plants lined Pittsburgh's rivers. U.S. Steel owned two-thirds of the plants' capacity, wielding such power that it established a pricing system—Pittsburgh Plus—that dominated the entire industry until 1948.

Workers who lingered atop a blast furnace got drunk on carbon monoxide just before the vapors killed them. During the 12-hour turns at the open hearth, scrap metal might jam and 20-ton ladles spatter molten bullets. And yet, wrote a worker in 1919, "these ingots, when they come from the moulds virgin steel, are impres-

---

### ANDREW CARNEGIE

As a 13-year-old Scottish immigrant, Andrew Carnegie worked in a textile factory for $1.20 a week, but by 1901, when he sold his steel mill for $480 million, he was the wealthiest man in the world.

He founded the J. Edgar Thomson Steel Works near Pittsburgh, which eventually evolved into the Carnegie Steel Company. He built the first steel plants in the U.S. to use the new Bessemer system; detailed cost- and production-accounting procedures enabled the company to achieve great efficiencies. In the 1890s his mills introduced the basic open-hearth furnace into American steelmaking. By 1889 the Carnegie Steel Company dominated the American steel industry.

But Carnegie believed that a "man who dies rich dies disgraced," so after 1900 he devoted his life to giving away his fortune. All told, his trusts have given away some $350 million, both in Britain and the U.S. His money founded 281 public libraries, all over America, among other charities.

Living in what Mark Twain called the "Gilded Age," Carnegie received his share of criticism as a so-called robber baron. But, he argued, "it will be a great mistake...to shoot the millionaires, for they are the bees that make the most honey, and contribute most to the hive even after they have gorged themselves full...."

sive things—especially on the night turn. Then each stands up against the night air like a massive monument of hardened fire. Pass near them, and see what colossal radiators of heat they are. Trainloads of them pass daily out of the pit to the blooming-mill, to catch their first transformation." Their last transformation: into engines and rails, skyscrapers and bridges.

The industry grew in a helter-skelter fashion, and eventually some 800 plants fed America's appetite for steel. Andrew Carnegie's steel company was by far the largest but, at age 65, Carnegie wanted a new life of philanthropy and ease. The stage was set for the creation of the country's first billion-dollar corporation: U.S. Steel.

Famed banker J. P. Morgan brokered the deal, putting the finishing touches on it on the night of January 6, 1901, in his library at 219 Madison Avenue. Present were a representative of Carnegie; the controller of American Steel and Wire; and Morgan's partner, Robert Bacon. They consolidated those 800 steel plants into a company that would mine iron ore at one end and spew out all the finished steel the country could need at the other.

It remained to set a price for the Carnegie Steel Company and the smaller businesses. Morgan told Carnegie's rep, "If Andy wants to sell, I'll buy. Go and find his price." Approached after a round of golf, Carnegie jotted a figure on a piece of paper and sent it back to Morgan, who glanced at it and said, "I accept." It was a price of $480,000,000.

When Morgan and Carnegie met a year later on a steamship to Europe, Carnegie said: "I made one mistake, Pierpont. I should have asked you for $100 million more than I did." "Well," said Morgan, "you would have got it if you had."

The creation of U.S. Steel was the climax of the most massive and rapid burst of industrial concentration the world had ever seen. Between 1879 and 1897 there had been only 12 U.S. combinations with a total capitalization of $1 billion. A "combination" was the process whereby great interstate corporations, or "trusts," and later holding companies, were created and centrally administered by directors answerable only to the loose laws of a local entity, such as a small state. Their creation eventually led to the enforcement, by Theodore Roosevelt, the "trust buster," of the Sherman Anti-Trust Act of 1890.

Morgan's consolidation of U.S. Steel marked another new trend in American business: The robber barons were turning over their massive businesses to bankers and stock promoters. They, like Morgan, knew nothing of the individual industries they were controlling. They knew Business.

OPPOSITE: *With the White House in the palm of his hand, John D. Rockefeller controls both Washington and the oil market, according to an early cartoon. In the distance, government buildings appear as a part of his huge Standard Oil Company.*

ABOVE: *U.S. Steel used color coding in a 1903 map to distinguish its rail and steamship lines, iron ranges, coal and gas fields, smelters, and other properties.*

# ORGANIZING *the* WORKERS

❦

## *Labor and Unionization*

The 1876 Centennial Exposition in Philadelphia celebrated everything American—except her workers. Few visitors who marveled at the Corliss steam engine noticed its lone operator. But William Dean Howells did. He observed: "Now and then he lays down his [news]paper and clambers up one of the stairways…and touches some irritated spot on the giant's body with a drop of oil…." This was the new worker on display, manservant to a machine. The Exposition proclaimed the future, a vision that did not admit the army of carpenters, pickax men, and masons who had transformed 284 acres in less than two years.

Railroad workers were less easily forgotten. Stunned the following summer by a 10 percent pay cut, their third since a depression hit in 1873, workers on the Baltimore and Ohio line went on strike. Soon other lines struck, as did sympathetic factory workers and miners. Ordered to guard property, West Virginia militiamen refused to fire on the strikers and were replaced by federal troops. Rioting spread to Pittsburgh and Chicago. By the end of July rail yards across the country lay smoldering, and more than a hundred people lay dead.

The rail strike was broken, but the sympathy strikes signaled a growing cohesiveness among industrial workers. Work stoppages generally followed business cycles, increasing during periods of prosperity and diminishing when business activity declined and jobs disappeared. Samuel Gompers in 1881 began uniting craft unions and fighting for immediate economic goals. The AFL fought for bread-and-butter issues: shorter working hours, higher pay, and better working conditions. Gompers served as AFL president for almost 40 years, and his personal integrity played a large part in getting employers to sign contracts with federation unions. By 1900 his American Federation of Labor (AFL) spoke for most of the labor movement. Mass-production workers went largely unrepresented until John L. Lewis broke away in 1938 and organized entire industries under the Congress of Industrial Organizations (CIO). Yet the organization of labor had to fight business opposition every step of the way.

In 1868 pressure by the National Labor Union led to passage of a law establishing an eight-hour workday for "all laborers, workmen, and mechanics" employed in government work. Still, it took nearly a half century before the eight-hour workday became widely accepted by industry.

Labor unrest continued to be marked by violence. Some trade unions allied with anarchists, leading to the explosive Haymarket Square riot in Chicago on May 4, 1886. When police tried to disperse a mob of agitators, an anarchist threw a bomb that killed 8 policemen and wounded 67.

Unskilled workers remained unorganized and disregarded. Many were foreigners or women and children tending looms; most casual laborers of the big cities were foreigners. Horace Greeley in 1851 published data that showed that the minimum budget for a worker's family of five came to $10.37 a week. But only skilled workers received that much. Factory hands got $5 to $6, women $3 to $4.

By mid-century, festering slums, familiar in Europe but unknown in the U.S., grew up in U.S. cities. Each city had its own region; Five Points in New York was the prototype. In a study of Boston's Irish immigrants in mid-century, Oscar Hadlin describes the slum dwellings of the period.

"Built entirely beneath the street level, they enjoyed no light or air save that which dribbled in through the door leading down, by rickety steps, from the sidewalk above. Innocent of the most rudimentary plumbing, some normally held two or three feet of water, and all were subject to periodic floods and frequent inundations by the backwater of drains at high tide. Above all, there was little space. Some windowless vaults no more than eighteen feet square and five feet high held fourteen humans."

---

### The AMERICAN RED CROSS

"If Heaven ever sent out a holy angel, she must be one," wrote a surgeon of Clara Barton. She first gained fame for nursing the wounded on battlefields, then expanded to offer relief to the civilian victims of warfare.

Fittingly, she was a Christmas baby, born on Christmas Day in 1821 in Oxford, Massachusetts. By 15 she was a teacher. She first found a way to be of assistance during the Civil War, when she helped track and recover soldiers' lost baggage. After the first Battle of Bull Run she rounded up medicines and supplies for the wounded and even persuaded authorities to let her pass through the lines to search for missing soldiers, to pass out supplies, to succor the wounded. She had found her calling and carried on with relief work throughout the war.

She was vacationing in Europe when the Franco-German War broke out, and she again sprang into action organizing relief work for victims. In Europe she worked with the International Red Cross and, when she returned home, urged the U.S. to sign the Geneva Conventions. She founded the American Red Cross in 1881 and served as its president until 1904.

When soldiers in Cuba fighting the Spanish American war needed her, she was there, at age 77. But she turned cranky and suspicious as she aged, jealous of interference, authoritarian, and reluctant to cede any control. But her accomplishments survive, and she was often called the "angel of the battlefield." She died in Glen Echo, Maryland, on April 12, 1912.

Confronting giant corporations and trusts—in sugar, steel, tobacco, and oil—workers in the 1880s increased efforts to organize national unions. Employers fought these "muscle trusts" with injunctions, lockouts, blacklists, and armed guards. From 1865 to 1881 labor staged fewer than 500 strikes to press its demands. Between 1881 and 1894 there were 14,900 strikes, involving four million workers.

Rising affluence and legislation protecting the rights of workers gradually changed the battlefront from picket lines to bargaining tables. Fringe benefits such as medical care and tuition credits became part of complex agreements. By 1915, labor had united under the anthem: "It is we who plowed the prairies; built the cities where they trade; / Dug the mines and built the workshops; endless miles of railroad laid. / Now we stand, outcast and starving, 'mid the wonders we have made; / But the Union makes us strong. / Solidarity forever!... For the Union makes us strong."

Organizing minorities was more difficult. "So we must stand together to resist, for we will get what we can take— just that and no more," cap maker Rose Schneiderman exhorted her fellow garment workers in 1905. They were listening. The International Ladies' Garment Workers' Union would be founded in 1900; they had already won concessions by 1912. A three-month strike that began in 1909 gained a 52-hour workweek and wage increases. Women worked up to 14 hours a day in tenement lofts or in the city's thousands of "home factories." The middlemen often cut their meager wages for alleged garment imperfections or for rent on the sewing machines. As early as 1851 the shirt sewers' union, with no money for an advertisement, printed a broadside seeking public support for higher wages. Its workers, paid $2.50 a week, were "sewing at once with a double stitch, a shroud as well as a shirt." Shunned by some unions, women were actively recruited by others, including Terence Powderly's Knights of Labor, which had chartered 192 women's assemblies by 1886.

Black workers had far less success than did women in gaining acceptance into labor unions. Some unions had racial restrictions; others offered only segregated affiliation. Employers undermined organized labor in the early 1900s by recruiting southern blacks to come to northern cities as strikebreakers, a role some accepted because they were denied union membership. A. Philip Randolph gained new respect for blacks among unionists by organizing the Brotherhood of Sleeping Car Porters and winning national attention in 1928 with a threatened strike. Gradually responding to the CIO's aggressive recruiting, blacks began joining unions in substantial numbers in the 1930s. During World War II, Randolph and others created opportunities for blacks by calling for a massive march on Washington, D.C. The march was called off when President Franklin D. Roosevelt signed an executive order barring racial discrimination in defense industries.

---

ABOVE: *Signs of protest, in several languages, appear at the picket line of a garment workers' union strike in New York City around 1912. Shorter hours and higher pay were often the chief goals of early unions.*

# The LAWLESS LAND

## Gunfighters and Frontier Justice

"Three Men Hurled into Eternity in the Duration of a Moment," ran a headline of the *Tombstone Epitaph* one day in October 1881. There had been a deadly run-in in a vacant lot near the O.K. Corral when the town's Marshal, Virgil Earp, and his brothers Wyatt and Morgan shot it out with the Clanton and McLaury brothers, local cowboys. Doc Holliday, another famous name, fought alongside the Earps. The battle lasted only a minute or so but still shows up on movie and television screens and in books 125 years later. The combatants were typical of the shoot-outs that enlivened frontier towns of the Old West late in the 19th century: sheriff against outlaw, gambler against cowboy, city slicker against settler.

The West was a violent place then, with shoot-outs not uncommon. Sometimes it was hard to tell the good guy from the bad, as they often had more in common than not, men with high spirits and low morals. When they disagreed or had a score to settle, it was easy to reach for the six-shooter. Law and order lagged behind the westward advance of civilization, and the frontier was the home of itinerant cowboys, prospectors, railroad men, bad-tempered youths from the East, fugitives, and scam artists of every kind. They kept the undertakers busy.

The towns where they met and fought were dusty cattle, railroad, or mining towns, their wide unpaved streets lined with tents or flimsy wooden structures. The saloon might be nothing more than a tent, its bar a plank laid across two beer kegs. Tombstone, Arizona, was such a place, but wealth in the form of silver was pouring from mines in the surrounding hills. The town's population went from zero to 5,600 in just two years.

A young attorney found evidence that Tombstone was acquiring a touch of civilization. In a letter in 1880 he wrote that Tombstone had two dance halls, a dozen gambling places, and more than 20 saloons. "Still," he wrote, "there is hope, for I know of two Bibles in town."

Most fearsome of the western gunfighters were the men who rode in gangs—like the James brothers, Jesse and Frank. They were in it purely for the money and would swoop down on banks, trains, or stagecoaches to seize booty and rob passengers. They had learned about hit-and-run raids during their years in Confederate guerrilla bands during the Civil War, when they preyed upon Union troops along the Kansas–Missouri border. With peace, the James brothers organized fellow ex-guerrillas into a band that might number just three or four or as many as a dozen men. They planned their assaults carefully and struck swiftly, then vanished. The James gang flourished for 15 years, from 1866 to 1881, executing 26 raids in and around Missouri. They stole an estimated half a million dollars.

The Jameses' adventure ended in Northfield, Minnesota, when a bungled bank robbery in 1876 roused the citizens of the town; they fought back fiercely and in just 20 minutes or so virtually destroyed the gang, though Jesse and brother Frank escaped to the Dakota Territory.

Another gang leader, Henry Starr, who operated in Indian Territory, expressed the appeal of the gunfighter life. "Life in the open, the rides at night, the spice of danger, the mastery over men, the pride of being able to hold a mob at bay—it tingles in my veins. I love it. It is wild adventure."

Charged with keeping order in frontier towns were lawmen variously known as town marshal, county sheriff, state or territorial ranger, or federal marshal. Sheriff Bat Masterson called them "just plain ordinary men who could shoot straight and had the

For a while, justice in the courtrooms was as hit-or-miss as in the jails and on the streets. Many early judges lacked real learning in the law and were often tradesmen on the side. Without courthouses and courtrooms, they dispensed justice in stores or saloons. Informality reigned. In Dodge City, a judge opened a session by declaring: "Trot out the wicked and unfortunate, and let the cotillion commence."

An especially colorful figure of the Old West was Judge Phantly "Roy" Bean, who was born in Mason County, Kentucky, sometime around 1825. While still a teenager he and his brother hitched onto a wagon train to New Mexico, then spent several years wandering from town to town. Roy found himself in various troubles, some serious: He killed at least two men in duels. By 1882 he was west of the Pecos River running a bar, the Jersey Lilly, named for an actress he had fallen for. He had never received any real education but persuaded the Texas Rangers to let him set himself up as a Justice of the Peace. He began administering his form of eccentric justice with just one lawbook, *The Revised Statutes of Texas,* 1879. He dismissed the charges against an Irishman accused of murdering one of the Chinese railroad workers because, he said, after looking through his book of statutes, "Gentlemen, I find the law very explicit on murdering your fellow man, but there's nothing here about killing a chinaman. Case dismissed." On another occasion a corpse was found near the river and brought to Judge Bean's tavern. A pistol and $40 were in the dead man's pockets, so Bean fined him $40 for carrying a concealed weapon and used the money to pay the county for the man's funeral. His rulings, it was said, were "characterized by greed, prejudice, a little common sense and lots of colorful language." He could swear in both English and Spanish but forbade bad language in his courtroom. He died in 1903.

most utter courage and perfect nerve—and, for the most part, a keen sense of right and wrong." For the most part, perhaps, but some maintained second careers as practicing outlaws. The citizens of Laramie, Wyoming, hanged their head lawman when it was discovered that in his capacity as saloonkeeper he was drugging and robbing his patrons. Similarly, vigilantes hanged the sheriff of Ada County, Idaho, when he was found to be a horse thief.

In towns, the chief law officer was the marshal—in effect, the chief of police—who usually had a small force consisting of an assistant and a few policemen. He could also form posses or swear in deputies when needed.

There were also federal officers operating on a state- or district- or territory-wide basis.

Most were honest men and did make an impact on frontier justice, and many of the felons they arrested were professional criminals. In a typical month in Tombstone, Virgil Earp and his deputies made 48 arrests. Of these, 18 were drunk-and-disorderly charges, and 14 were for disturbing the peace. Only eight involved violence: four for assault, three for carrying concealed weapons, and one for resisting an officer.

ABOVE: *In Liberty, Missouri, frontier justice triumphs: On December 17, 1897, outlaw William Carr prepares to meet his maker.*

# NATIONAL PARKS

## Protecting Wild America

"In Europe people talk a great deal of the wilds of America," wrote Alexis de Tocqueville in 1832, "but the Americans themselves never think about them....Their eyes are fixed upon another sight: [their] own march across these wilds, draining swamps, turning the course of rivers, peopling solitudes, and subduing nature."

In the 19th century that began to change.

It started, it is generally conceded, with the artist George Catlin. On a trip to the Dakotas in 1832 he worried about the impact of America's westward expansion on Indian tribes, wildlife, and wilderness. They might be preserved, he thought, "by some great protecting policy of government...in a magnificent park...A nation's park, containing man and beast, in all the wild and freshness of their nature's beauty!"

His vision was partly realized in 1864 when Congress donated Yosemite Valley to California for preservation as a state park. The Park embraces a spectacular tract of mountain-and-valley scenery in the Sierra Nevadas, with waterfalls, meadows, and forests, including groves of giant sequoias. Writers, artists, and photographers spread the fame of the magnificent valley through the world, and a steady stream of visitors came on foot and horseback, and later by stage.

The move to preservation of the wild lands continued when Jim Bridger invited a credulous colleague to "come with me to the Yellowstone next summer, and I'll show you peetrified trees a-growing, with peetrified birds on 'em a-singing peetrified songs." Bridger also had serious tales for more serious ears, and he undertook three expeditions, in 1869, 1870, and 1871, to separate Yellowstone fact from fiction.

Even a mountain man's embellishments could scarcely top what they found: explosive geysers, mud volcanoes, scalding springs—one of the densest regions of thermal activity in the world. In 1872 Congress officially recognized the uniqueness of the area, passing "An Act to set apart a certain Tract of Land lying near the Headwaters of the Yellowstone River as a public Park." This Wyoming tract would be not only the nation's first national park but also the world's.

Fittingly, the first National Memorial honored Ulysses S. Grant, who had signed the act establishing the first National Park, Yellowstone, on March 1, 1872. After serving two terms as President, Grant settled

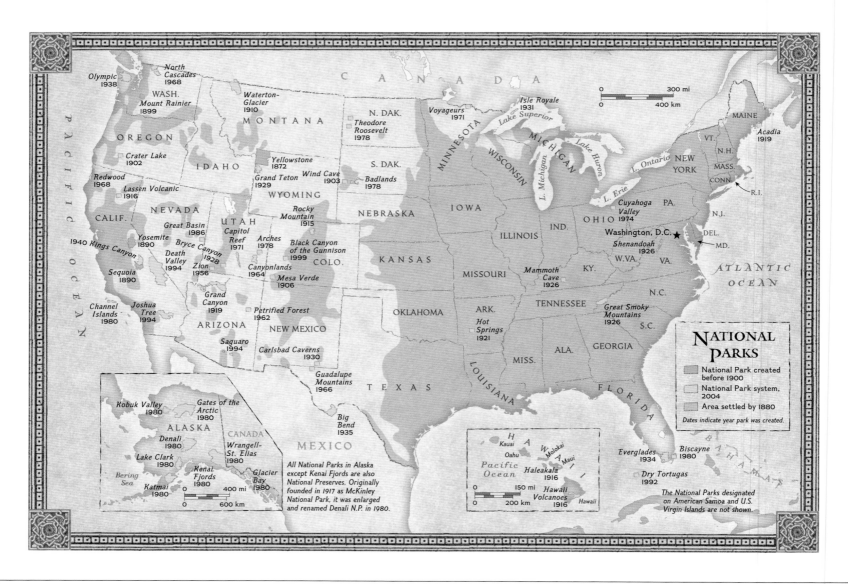

## JOHN MUIR

"Nature is a good mother," he wrote, "and sees well to the clothing of her many bairns—birds with imbricated feathers, beetles with shining jackets, and bears with shaggy furs. In the south, where the sun warms like a fire, they are allowed to go thinly clad; in the northland she takes care to clothe warmly."

He was born in Scotland but became one of America's most eloquent spokesmen for her wild treasures and lands. He emigrated from Scotland with his family to a farm near Portage, Wisconsin, in 1849, studied at the University of Wisconsin, and worked on mechanical inventions. But in 1867 an accident nearly cost him an eye, and he abandoned his career to thereafter devote himself to nature. He walked to the Gulf of Mexico and wrote a book about it: *A Thousand-Mile Walk to the Gulf.* In 1868 he went to Yosemite Valley in California and from there traveled into Nevada, Utah, Oregon, Washington, and Alaska, studying glaciers and forests

By 1876 he was urging the federal government to adopt a forest conservation policy, and, given impetus by two eloquent magazine articles in June and August 1897, he swung public and congressional opinion in favor of national forest reserves.

In 1908 the federal government established the Muir Woods National Monument in Marin County, California. Muir died in Los Angeles on Christmas Eve, 1914.

in New York City. There he died of throat cancer in 1885. Some 90,000 people donated more than $600,000 toward construction of a memorial, and in 1897 it was completed. Grant's Tomb, where both he and his wife, Julia Dent Grant, lie, was dedicated on April 27, 1897, and is still managed by the National Park Service.

The same year that Congress created the General Grant Memorial, it also established Sequoia National Park in California. But as there was not yet a National Park Service to administer parks, the Army was called in: Cavalry troops were given the job of protecting the big trees, and each year a company cantered out from San Francisco's Presidio to police the park.

After the establishment of Yellowstone National Park in 1872, conservation milestones began to occur regularly. That same year saw the first observance in Nebraska of "Tree-Planting Day" on April 10, which soon became Arbor Day. A year later Franklin B. Hough addressed the annual meeting of the American Association for the Advancement of Science and read his paper, "On the Duty of Governments in the Preservation of Forests." The first edition of *Forest and Stream* magazine appeared that same year. The joys of family camping were described in *Scribner's Monthly* in 1874 and 1875, and outdoor enthusiasts founded the Appalachian Mountain Club in Boston in 1876. New York in 1885 proclaimed that

the state's Adirondack Mountains "shall be kept forever as wild forest lands." In 1889 William Temple Hornaday published a report to the Secretary of the Smithsonian Institution called "The Extermination of the American Bison"; it chronicled the near extinction of the distinctive western beasts.

By 1916 there were 37 national parks and monuments, and responsibility for them was turned over to the Department of the Interior. President Woodrow Wilson signed the act creating the National Park Service on August 25. The Act called for those parks and others yet to be named to remain "unimpaired for the enjoyment of future generations."

Americans began to recognize the importance of the sites and artifacts of the country's Native Americans late in the 19th century; Arizona's Casa Grande Ruin was the first such site to be protected by Congress, in 1889.

President Theodore Roosevelt made the nation's forest reserves another point of national honor, tripling their size to 150 million acres. His goal was conservation of resources, not preservation of wilderness: "These reserves are, and should be, reserved for economic purposes." Leasing by the Forest Service, established in 1905, and the Bureau of Land Management, established in 1946, has been guided by the conservationist credo: multiple users for the land and sustainable yield of resources.

All national parks and national forests are carved from the Federal Domain, the lands left over after the rest of the continent had been disposed of. They comprise nearly a third of the nation: nearly 800 million acres, the majority west of the Mississippi River. A huge chunk was added with the purchase of Alaska from Russia in 1867.

By 2004 the National Park System had grown to 384 areas encompassing more than 83 million acres in 49 states.

ABOVE: *President Theodore Roosevelt and conservationist John Muir share the view at Glacier Point above Yosemite Valley, California, around the turn of the 20th century. Both fought to protect America's natural landscape and to preserve its wild lands.*

# The TELEGRAPH and TELEPHONE

⧫

## Lines of Communication

The first transatlantic calls were made by radio in 1927, and a cable was laid in 1956. In 1969 the first earth-to-moon call was placed, and by the 1970s calling the other side of the world via satellite had become routine.

The word "telegraph"—from the Greek *tele,* or distant, and *graphein,* or write—was apparently first used to describe an apparatus that looked like men waving their arms at one another, an 18th-century French optical semaphore invented by the Chappe brothers. Towers on the tops of hills were equipped with a pair of movable arms at the ends of a crossbeam—each with a shoulder and elbow. The arms could be maneuvered into several positions, and each position could be assigned a number or letter. Towers couldn't be more than about five miles apart and the cumbersome mechanical machinery was slow to operate, so only about three symbols could be sent per minute.

But the electric telegraph could not be developed before electricity was available. When Alessandro Volta of Italy invented the voltaic cell in 1800, it became possible to power electronic equipment more effectively, using low voltages and high currents.

Samuel F. B. Morse, a New York professor, took up the challenge of electric telegraphy in 1835. He contrived a system of dots and dashes that represented letters and numbers—and named it after himself, the Morse code—and in 1837 received a patent on an electromagnetic telegraph. The transmitter created dots and dashes by making and breaking contact between the battery and a wire to the receiver; the receiver imprinted them on a scroll of paper. Morse's partner Alfred Vail came up with the familiar make-and-break telegraph key and also refined the code by assigning the shortest sequences to the most frequently used letters. Their famous message—"What hath God Wrought!"—was transmitted on May 24, 1844, and inaugurated the age of the telegraph.

Newspapers quickly learned to use the new tool to transmit news from anywhere in the country, and in 1848 the Associated Press was formed to share telegraph expenses. By mid-century more than 50 telegraph companies were making the wires hum in the U.S. Several of them joined together in 1856 to form the Western Union Telegraph Company. Its first from coast-to-coast line was completed in 1861.

The invention of the telegraph not only killed off the Pony Express, it also showed that sounds could travel over wires. Alexander Graham Bell was listening.

Bell exhibited his telephone at the 1876 Centennial Exposition in Philadelphia. Though primitive, with an erratic transmission, it did well enough when Bell recited Hamlet's "To be or not to be" soliloquy into the instrument at one end of the hall with Dom Pedro II, Emperor of Brazil, listening at the other. The monarch exclaimed, "I hear, I hear."

Bell resigned from the telephone company in 1880 and used his profits to finance other inventions and his work with the deaf.

By 1887, a decade after the telephone was introduced to the world, a Manhattan

telephone pole might hold as many as 300 wires, each of which could carry only one call at a time. By then more than 180,000 subscribers were linked by at least as many miles of copper wire. Doctors, retailers, and other businessmen owned most of the phones, and monthly service cost more than half of the average worker's income.

Independent telephone companies, freed by the 1894 expiration of Bell's original patents, extended service to rural areas. By 1907 the greatest concentration of telephones per person was not in the East but in Iowa, Nebraska, Washington, and California. To gain residential customers, the telephone industry promoted practical uses such as ordering groceries and calling doctors. Only after World War I did the industry fully recognize the profit potential of encouraging people to do what they had always done: chat with family and friends.

In New York City outrage over the eyesore of overhead wires led to efforts as early as the 1880s to bury wires underground in insulated cables. In the 1980s the cables began giving way to bundles of optical fibers, threadlike strands of glass through which messages were sent by laser pulses. A single bundle could transmit 24,000 calls simultaneously.

One year after Alexander Graham Bell's first telephone call, in 1876, the Bell Telephone Company was established in Boston. More than 600 subscribers signed up despite early technical problems, including the need for "occasional repetition" to get a message through. Each private line was connected to only two or three other points—hardly a network. That design limitation, however, was soon remedied, and the first central exchange connected 21 subscribers of New Haven, Connecticut, in 1878.

Women operators held a monopoly until the 1960s. Young men worked the first switchboards in 1878, but the result was, as a visitor to the Buffalo exchange put it, "a perfect Bedlam." Men were known to swear at the poor equipment and novice subscribers.

For the user the telephone's greatest asset was its simplicity. It required no knowledge of codes, no dexterity, only speech. By 1881, 132,692 Bell telephones

were in service, and only nine cities with populations over 10,000 were without a telephone exchange. Rates were high—as much as $150 a year for business phones, $100 for residential. In 1919 a three-minute coast-to-coast call cost $16.50, more than $100 today. In 1987 the same call cost $1.14 due to improved technology, higher usage, and true competition after AT&T's breakup.

After 1890 AT&T's long-distance network grew steadily from its New England base, pushing west to Chicago by 1893. Expansion was boosted in 1900 with development of the loading coil, which reduced weakening of the long-distance signal. AT&T dominated toll lines, denying inde-

pendent firms access to them until 1913. Another technological milestone, electronic repeaters to amplify signals, made possible the first transcontinental line, opened between New York and San Francisco in 1915. By 1914 ten million telephones—70 percent of the world's total—were in the U.S.; by 1916 more than 70,000 communities were linked to the network.

OPPOSITE: *In 1892, Alexander Graham Bell makes the first telephone call from New York to Chicago.*
ABOVE: *Just a few years later wires needed for his apparatus crosshatch Lower Broadway. After 1900 underground routing buried most of them.*

# MANUFACTURING and MARKETING

❧

## Singer, McCormick, and Sears

In 1890 upstart Illinois passed venerable Massachusetts to take third place in gross value of manufactured goods and passed Ohio to become the leader in agricultural machinery. The industrial center of gravity was shifting westward.

The states north of the Mason-Dixon Line and the Ohio River and east of the Rockies produced about 85 percent of the industrial output. But southern industry was stirring, and new iron, cotton, and lumber mills were opening.

With panics in 1873 and 1893 bracketing a depression in 1883, the period was hardly tranquil. Even as rail routes expanded, allowing factories to disperse, corporate concentrations called trusts were being formed to control the economy and consolidate wealth. Meanwhile, nine-year-old children were commonly working 10 to 14 hours a day for two dollars a week.

The odd partnership of conservative lawyer Edward Clark and stage player, libertine, and machinist Isaac Singer led to the first U.S. company with large international sales to a huge base of individual consumers and clothing makers. Though Singer was an intuitive engineer and tinkerer, the partners' genius, especially Clark's, shone in sales and merchandising. Having negotiated a truce in the sewing machine patent wars of the mid-1850s, Clark brought the company's sales force under direct control; instituted the hire purchase system, an early version of installment buying; and established showrooms where women demonstrated the product.

By the late 1880s Singer had three sewing machine factories in the U.S. and others in Glasgow, Montreal, Hamburg, and Vienna. By 1914, 100,000 salespeople ranged the world, selling offspring of the first great American appliance.

This tribute, "The blacksmith is the universal mender and tinker: he must, through the cunning of his brain and the strength of his arm, be ready to shape anything and everything of iron," came from a Singer catalog of the late 1880s. Also, "The product of the Machine-Screw Department…would require the labor of several thousand skilled mechanics, were it not for the wonderfully ingenious machines constantly engaged [in making the screws]."

Such double vision, looking back to the skill of a single craftsman while pointing with pride to the newest quite literally labor-saving devices, reflected the state of American industry at the time. After 35 years of making sewing machines, Singer was finally making machines with truly interchangeable parts (while indulging in blacksmith nostalgia). Complete assembly-line mass production awaited the coming of Ford.

Management of Singer-size companies—and, most especially, of the rail-

roads—was like a business school whose lessons, curricula, and examinations changed daily. More changed than planning, fabrication, and scheduling techniques. A gigantic company could control every step of its manufacturing and marketing, starting from buying raw material in volume—the economies of scale. Yet that was but a corollary to a more important fact—the scale of the economy, an immense growth in the number of customers who had wages to spend.

The new tools that the farmer or the seamstress needed, or at least wanted, could not be supplied by the craftsman, the blacksmith, or the small-shop machin-

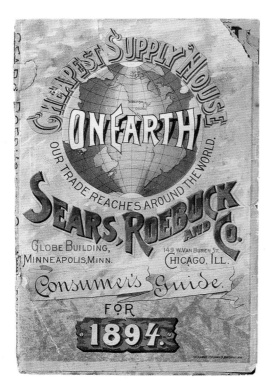

ist. Only the large manufacturer could make such tools and sell tens and hundreds of thousands at reasonable prices.

In 1850, in Illinois, there were 3.51 horses to every ox; in 1870 there were 43.19. Horses moved quickly enough to effectively pull new farm gear such as the McCormick reaper; oxen did not.

McCormick's reaper was not the first. Nor was it originally standardized—in the 1840s machines were built mainly by contractors. Yet the McCormick line, well advertised from the beginning, helped revolutionize both agriculture and industry. Even early machines could take the place of four men—the potential existed for three of them to leave the farm for work in factories.

Loyalty to the McCormick brand was built by company agents who stood by to repair machines at once during the critical time for harvest. In 1898, during the "harvester war," rival salesmen fought in an oversold market. McCormick merged with other competitors in 1902 to form International Harvester.

By 1900 Singer had 18 central offices supervising retail stores run by its employees, a more profitable system than paying commissions to agents.

The next step was to sell the world of customers not only tools but endless choices of finished goods. Enter the "Cheapest Supply House on Earth [and] The Most Progressive Concern of Its Kind in the World," Sears, Roebuck & Co. By 1897 customers could employ the services of "over 500 people devoted exclusively to out of town mail order trade" and order from its nearly 800-page catalog.

There, amid embroideries and millinery and bells "for farm, school house & elsewhere," were listed 22 baby carriages, 76 index entries under "Bicycle," and 110 men's pocket watches. Also offered were eight sewing machines (not from Singer) and one half-circle baler (not from McCormick). Competition, off brands, and price cutting had arrived with the claim that "by Reason of Our Enormous Output…we can secure the lowest possible prices. To this we add the smallest percentage of profit possible."

OPPOSITE: *Young women toil in a New York City hat factory around 1900.*
LEFT: *Their wares were marketed in the famous Sears Catalog, source of virtually everything a 19th-century family might need.*

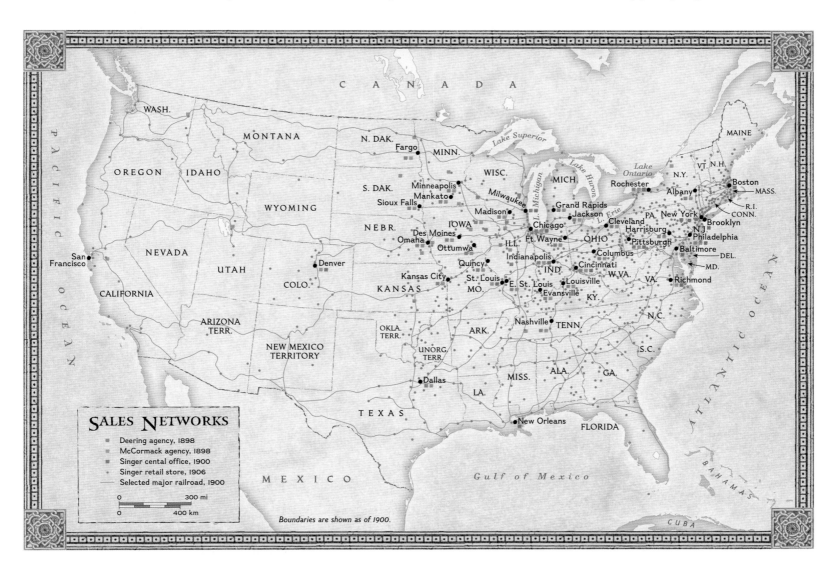

# PUTTING *the* RIVERS *to* WORK

❦

## *Hydroelectric Power*

"The dam did truly 'harness the mighty Colorado, as promised,'" said historian David McCullough. "The dam did truly make the desert bloom, and more. Orange groves would thrive, marquis lights would blaze, toasters turn on, and Hoover vacuum cleaners spring into action in far off Los Angeles, all because of the great Hoover Dam."

Hoover Dam had its first concrete poured on June 6, 1933, and the last on May 29, 1935. It contains 3.25 million cubic yards of concrete, enough to pave a standard highway, 16 feet wide, from San Francisco to New York City. Water rushing though its innards turns 17 main turbines that generate more than two million kilowatts of power. It generates more than four billion kilowatt-hours of power a year—enough to turn the lights on for 1.3 million people, mostly in Nevada, Arizona, and California.

Mankind began using the force of falling water to power machinery, such as mills, thousands of years ago. In the U.S. hydropower was in use as early as the 1700s for mills and pumps. Every brook and stream could be used to power the waterwheels that powered the grinding of grain or the sawing of logs. An enterprising entrepreneur could dig a channel called a mill race, to divert enough water to turn an overshot water wheel, the most common type in early America. The early textile mills of the Industrial Revolution all employed turbines driven by waterwheels.

At first dams were used simply to raise the level of a river or stream. Dams were used routinely when building canals to create long, navigable pools. With the growth of 19th-century cities, dams were employed to create reservoirs to supply clean drinking water for the cities' teeming hordes. These were connected by lengthy aqueducts, the oldest of which was the Old Croton Aqueduct, built in 1842 to supply burgeoning New York City. The first dam used to generate electricity was built in 1882 on the Fox River at Appleton, Wisconsin, and for 20 years provided the energy requirements of the community. Similarly, the dam at

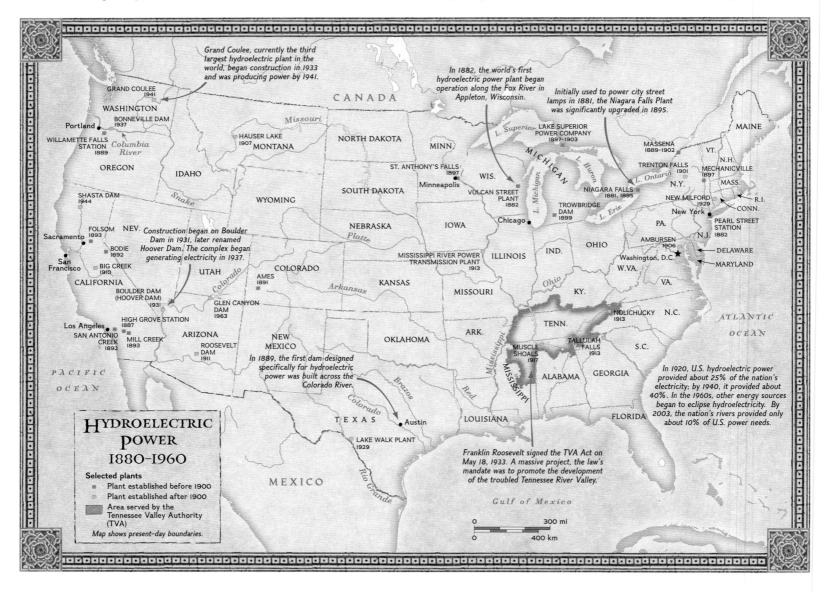

Grand Coulee, currently the third largest hydroelectric plant in the world, began construction in 1933 and was producing power by 1941.

In 1882, the world's first hydroelectric power plant began operation along the Fox River in Appleton, Wisconsin.

Initially used to power city street lamps in 1881, the Niagara Falls Plant was significantly upgraded in 1895.

Construction began on Boulder Dam in 1931, later renamed Hoover Dam. The complex began generating electricity in 1937.

In 1889, the first dam designed specifically for hydroelectric power was built across the Colorado River.

In 1920, U.S. hydroelectric power provided about 25% of the nation's electricity; by 1940, it provided about 40%. In the 1960s, other energy sources began to eclipse hydroelectricity. By 2003, the nation's rivers provided only about 10% of U.S. power needs.

Franklin Roosevelt signed the TVA Act on May 18, 1933. A massive project, the law's mandate was to promote the development of the troubled Tennessee River Valley.

### HYDROELECTRIC POWER 1880–1960

Selected plants
- ■ Plant established before 1900
- ■ Plant established after 1900
- ▨ Area served by the Tennessee Valley Authority (TVA)

*Map shows present-day boundaries.*

0   300 mi
0   400 km

Willamette Falls, Oregon, built in 1889, at first used a natural drop in water, but in 1894 a dam was added to provide more control and a steadier supply of water to the turbines.

Since then high-voltage lines have tied communities to power plants and to one another in a growing network known as interconnection. Because electricity cannot be stockpiled, interconnection gives regions the important ability to buy and sell power as local need fluctuates. That ability has, in turn, encouraged the development of larger, more efficient power plants to serve more consumers.

In the West, conditions were more favorable to the development of hydroelectric power. In the mountains, the rivers fall rapidly and the water, once it has turned the turbines, can be used for irrigation.

The Colorado River was first dammed for hydroelectric generation in 1893 near Austin, Texas, and provided nearly 15,000 horsepower of energy, a high figure for the time. But it was short-lived: In April 1900, heavy rainfall washed the dam and its turbines away. Near the turn of the century a hydroelectric dam was built at Massena, New York, that featured a powerhouse integral with the dam. Another, at Ogden, Utah, included some reinforced concrete in its construction and was also used for irrigation.

By the early 1900s America was getting more than 40 percent of its electricity from hydropower. That percentage has gradually declined with the development of other forms of generating electricity, and at the beginning of the 21st century just a tenth of the country's electricity was derived from dams and rivers.

Some early hydroelectric installations made use of natural differences in water level. A facility at Niagara Falls, New York, built in the 1890s to provide power for Buffalo, 26 miles away, is still producing power today. But there are few sites where such a natural fall of water can be used, and dams soon were built to provide a head of water. Three technologies—involving dam building, water turbines, and electric generators—came together at the close of the 19th century to produce reliable hydroelectric power.

The great floods and droughts of the 1930s led to the building of the huge multipurpose dams in the West: the Grand Coulee on the Columbia River, the Hoover Dam on the lower Colorado, the Central Valley Project in California. By producing cheap and plentiful power, these dams had a profound impact on the urban and industrial growth of the West.

Shortly after his 1933 inauguration Franklin D. Roosevelt signed the Tennessee Valley Authority Act. It created a federal corporation mandated to improve the Tennessee River's navigability and flood control, restore land in the valley, produce electric power, spur development, and operate the Muscle Shoals fertilizer factories.

In spite of objections from private companies, by 1939 TVA had built three dams and four more were underway. It employed some 13,000 people, and its agricultural programs reached more than 23,000 farmers. Wartime electricity needs spurred construction in the 1940s: Fontana Dam, 48 stories high, was completed in less than three years. TVA has grown into the largest power producer in the U.S. Its facilities include 11 fossil plants, 29 hydroelectric dams, three nuclear plants, a pumped-storage facility, and 17,000 miles of transmission lines. Through 158 locally owned distributors, TVA provides power to nearly 8.3 million residents in the Tennessee Valley.

Even though the terrain, watershed, and social conditions of the Tennessee Valley had certain parallels elsewhere, TVA legislation depended on the political momentum of Roosevelt's first hundred days in office. Never duplicated, TVA was an anomaly in government, born of a unique conjunction of geography and politics.

ABOVE: *Massive Hoover Dam—its concrete could form a monument a hundred feet square and two-and-a-half miles high—plugs a canyon of the Colorado River, creating Lake Mead behind it.*

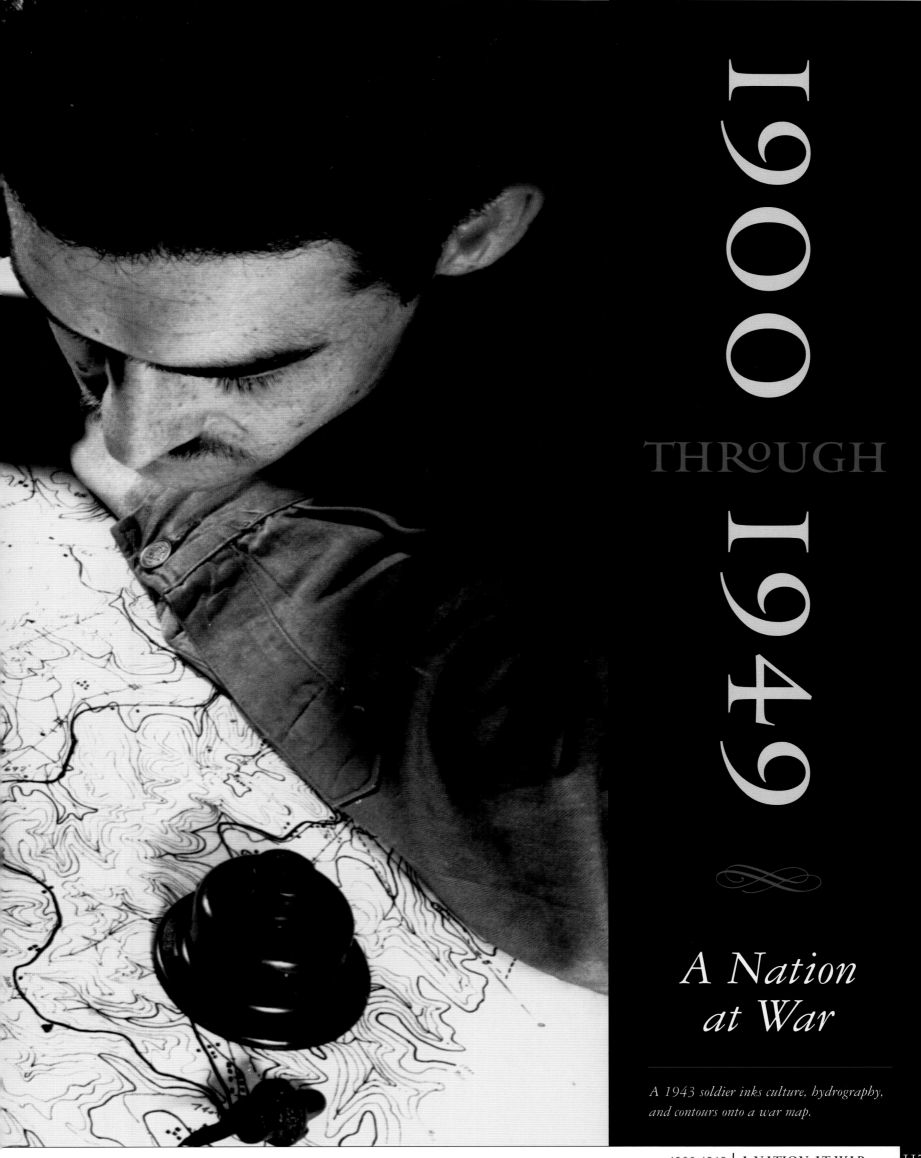

A 1943 soldier inks culture, hydrography,
and contours onto a war map.

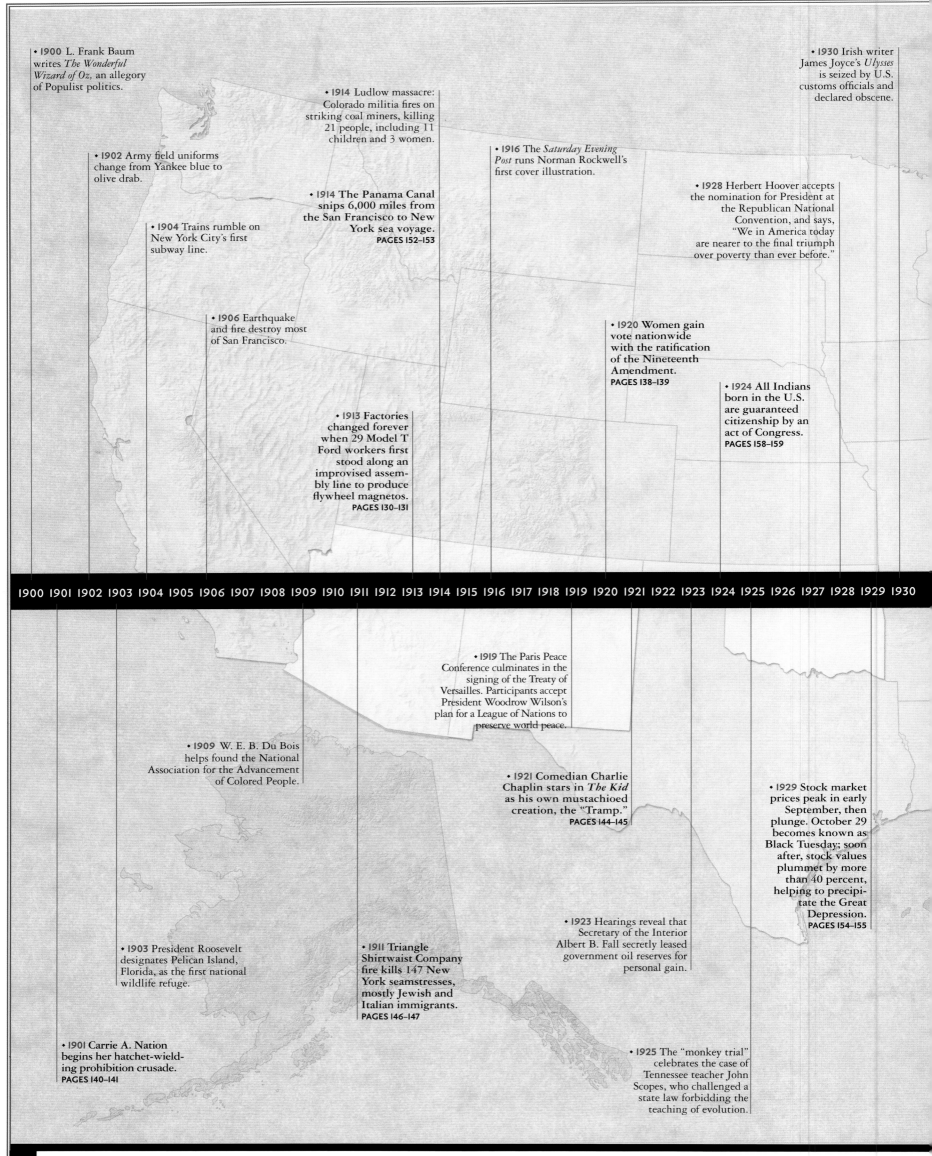

• 1900 L. Frank Baum writes *The Wonderful Wizard of Oz,* an allegory of Populist politics.

• 1914 Ludlow massacre: Colorado militia fires on striking coal miners, killing 21 people, including 11 children and 3 women.

• 1930 Irish writer James Joyce's *Ulysses* is seized by U.S. customs officials and declared obscene.

• 1902 Army field uniforms change from Yankee blue to olive drab.

• 1916 The *Saturday Evening Post* runs Norman Rockwell's first cover illustration.

• 1914 The Panama Canal snips 6,000 miles from the San Francisco to New York sea voyage.
**PAGES 152–153**

• 1928 Herbert Hoover accepts the nomination for President at the Republican National Convention, and says, "We in America today are nearer to the final triumph over poverty than ever before."

• 1904 Trains rumble on New York City's first subway line.

• 1906 Earthquake and fire destroy most of San Francisco.

• 1920 Women gain vote nationwide with the ratification of the Nineteenth Amendment.
**PAGES 138–139**

• 1924 All Indians born in the U.S. are guaranteed citizenship by an act of Congress.
**PAGES 158–159**

• 1913 Factories changed forever when 29 Model T Ford workers first stood along an improvised assembly line to produce flywheel magnetos.
**PAGES 130–131**

1900 1901 1902 1903 1904 1905 1906 1907 1908 1909 1910 1911 1912 1913 1914 1915 1916 1917 1918 1919 1920 1921 1922 1923 1924 1925 1926 1927 1928 1929 1930

• 1919 The Paris Peace Conference culminates in the signing of the Treaty of Versailles. Participants accept President Woodrow Wilson's plan for a League of Nations to preserve world peace.

• 1909 W. E. B. Du Bois helps found the National Association for the Advancement of Colored People.

• 1921 Comedian Charlie Chaplin stars in *The Kid* as his own mustachioed creation, the "Tramp."
**PAGES 144–145**

• 1929 Stock market prices peak in early September, then plunge. October 29 becomes known as Black Tuesday; soon after, stock values plummet by more than 40 percent, helping to precipitate the Great Depression.
**PAGES 154–155**

• 1903 President Roosevelt designates Pelican Island, Florida, as the first national wildlife refuge.

• 1911 Triangle Shirtwaist Company fire kills 147 New York seamstresses, mostly Jewish and Italian immigrants.
**PAGES 146–147**

• 1923 Hearings reveal that Secretary of the Interior Albert B. Fall secretly leased government oil reserves for personal gain.

• 1901 Carrie A. Nation begins her hatchet-wielding prohibition crusade.
**PAGES 140–141**

• 1925 The "monkey trial" celebrates the case of Tennessee teacher John Scopes, who challenged a state law forbidding the teaching of evolution.

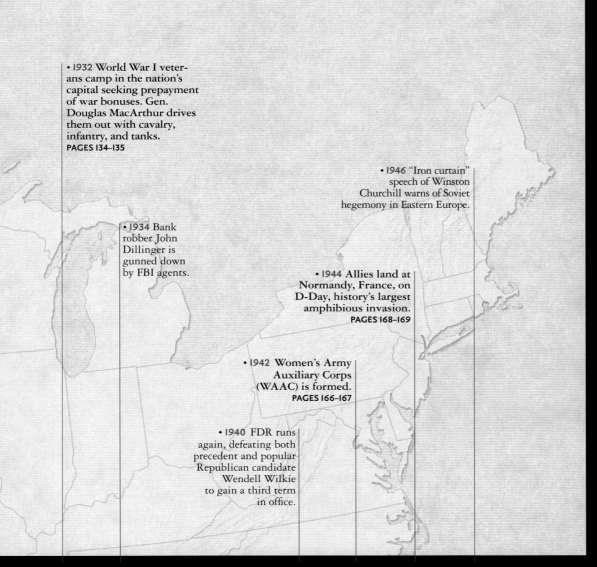

• 1932 World War I veterans camp in the nation's capital seeking prepayment of war bonuses. Gen. Douglas MacArthur drives them out with cavalry, infantry, and tanks.
**PAGES 134–135**

• 1946 "Iron curtain" speech of Winston Churchill warns of Soviet hegemony in Eastern Europe.

• 1934 Bank robber John Dillinger is gunned down by FBI agents.

• 1944 Allies land at Normandy, France, on D-Day, history's largest amphibious invasion.
**PAGES 168–169**

• 1942 Women's Army Auxiliary Corps (WAAC) is formed.
**PAGES 166–167**

• 1940 FDR runs again, defeating both precedent and popular Republican candidate Wendell Wilkie to gain a third term in office.

**1931 1932 1933 1934 1935 1936 1937 1938 1939 1940 1941 1942 1943 1944 1945 1946 1947 1948 1949**

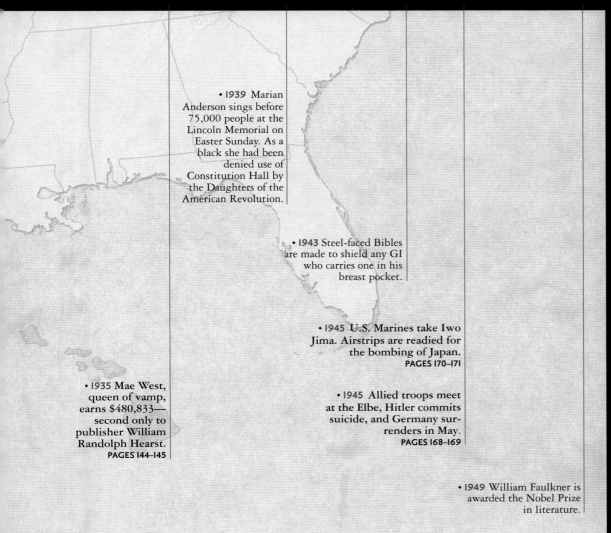

• 1939 Marian Anderson sings before 75,000 people at the Lincoln Memorial on Easter Sunday. As a black she had been denied use of Constitution Hall by the Daughters of the American Revolution.

• 1943 Steel-faced Bibles are made to shield any GI who carries one in his breast pocket.

• 1945 U.S. Marines take Iwo Jima. Airstrips are readied for the bombing of Japan.
**PAGES 170–171**

• 1935 Mae West, queen of vamp, earns $480,833— second only to publisher William Randolph Hearst.
**PAGES 144–145**

• 1945 Allied troops meet at the Elbe, Hitler commits suicide, and Germany surrenders in May.
**PAGES 168–169**

• 1949 William Faulkner is awarded the Nobel Prize in literature.

**M**ECHANIZED AMERICA thundered into the 20th century, inventing, building, and sometimes breaking down. "We guess a trestle will stand forever," a rail passenger told his aghast fellow traveler, Rudyard Kipling, before crossing a flimsy-looking bridge. "And sometimes we guess ourselves into the depot, and sometimes we guess ourselves into Hell."

Confidently bridging the oceans with its institutions, the U.S. guessed itself into possessions in the Caribbean and the Pacific. In 1916 President Woodrow Wilson looked across the Atlantic to a hell-in-progress, Europe's Great War. He hoped to keep the U.S. from it, saying, "God helping me, I will if it is possible."

"How Ya Gonna Keep 'Em Down on the Farm (After They've Seen Paree)?" Sophie Tucker sang in 1919 to doughboys returning from France. It wouldn't be easy.

By war's end, the U.S. was half rural, half urban, citifying fast, and a new world power to boot. Trains gave way to cars and planes and construction soared skyward as engineers built with new materials—and new visions. Women joined the men at the polls, then, flexing their muscles, deprived them of drink! At least for a while. Prohibition ended with a shrug. Immigrants poured through the Golden Door, and some Americans paused to give a helping hand to the exploited and the less fortunate. Labor unions fought for power. Radio gained listeners all over the world, and in the corner cinema, pictures talked!

The good times rolled. But it all came crashing down in the grim 1930s, and it would take another world war to put it back together again. An apocalyptic new force, created by splitting tiny atoms, illuminated mid-century; it would hover over Americans for their foreseeable future.

**1900–1949** *Saw the addition of three more states to the Union. Oklahoma in 1907 and New Mexico and Arizona in 1912.*

# The PIONEERS *of* AVIATION

## *Taking to the Skies*

"To fly, to fly—it was the oldest of dreams…," intoned historian David McCullough, host of a television show about the Wright Brothers. "And then one day it happened. Early in the new twentieth century at a remote spot on the outer coast of North Carolina, two young unknown Americans—brothers from Dayton, Ohio—succeeded as no human beings ever had. First one, then the other took off and landed in a flying machine—wings, propeller, gasoline engine, all of their own design. It was astounding, and though the world was slow to accept what they'd done as anything more than a stunt, the world was not to be the same again. If ever there was a turning point in history, it was this…."

The bachelor brothers lived at home with their preacher father in Dayton, where they ran a shop that built and repaired bicycles. They were unassuming midwestern young men, but, "while self-taught, were exceedingly serious aeronautical engineers—painstaking, resourceful, highly creative, truly brilliant and brave."

History gives them credit for accomplishing the world's first powered, sustained, and controlled airplane flight.

They went about it systematically in their workshop and on the beach at North Carolina, first experimenting with a series of gliders, then solving the problems of lift and control, and finally achieving powered, sustained flight. But others around the world were working on the same problems, and Orville and Wilbur devoted most of the rest of their lives to trying to make money from their invention and protecting their patents from others.

A combination of overwork and typhoid fever killed Wilbur. He died in bed on the morning of May 30, 1912. Orville outlived him by more than 30 years, dying of a heart attack on January 27, 1948.

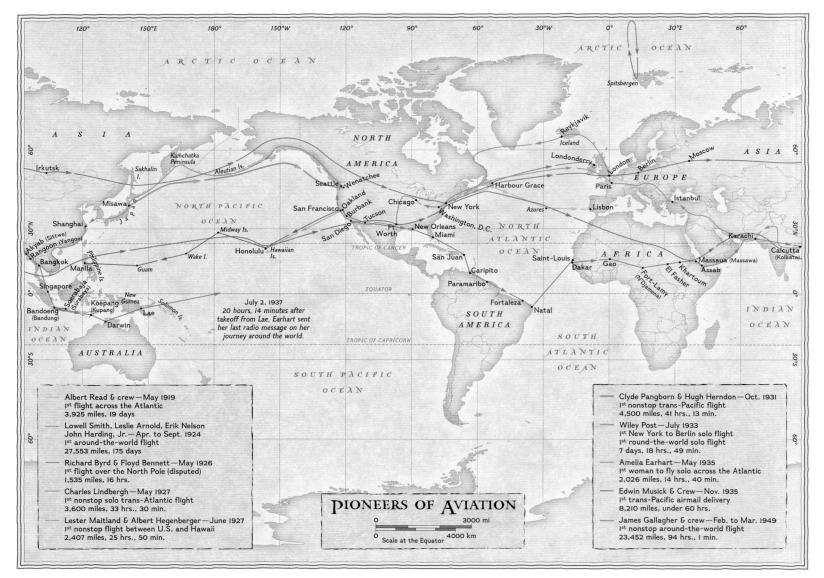

July 2, 1937
20 hours, 14 minutes after takeoff from Lae, Earhart sent her last radio message on her journey around the world.

Albert Read & crew—May 1919
1st flight across the Atlantic
3,925 miles, 19 days

Lowell Smith, Leslie Arnold, Erik Nelson John Harding, Jr.—Apr. to Sept. 1924
1st around-the-world flight
27,553 miles, 175 days

Richard Byrd & Floyd Bennett—May 1926
1st flight over the North Pole (disputed)
1,535 miles, 16 hrs.

Charles Lindbergh—May 1927
1st nonstop solo trans-Atlantic flight
3,600 miles, 33 hrs., 30 min.

Lester Maitland & Albert Hegenberger—June 1927
1st nonstop flight between U.S. and Hawaii
2,407 miles, 25 hrs., 50 min.

Clyde Pangborn & Hugh Herndon—Oct. 1931
1st nonstop trans-Pacific flight
4,500 miles, 41 hrs., 13 min.

Wiley Post—July 1933
1st New York to Berlin solo flight
1st round-the-world solo flight
7 days, 18 hrs., 49 min.

Amelia Earhart—May 1935
1st woman to fly solo across the Atlantic
2,026 miles, 14 hrs., 40 min.

Edwin Musick & Crew—Nov. 1935
1st trans-Pacific airmail delivery
8,210 miles, under 60 hrs.

James Gallagher & crew—Feb. to Mar. 1949
1st nonstop around-the-world flight
23,452 miles, 94 hrs., 1 min.

### PIONEERS OF AVIATION

0          3000 mi
0        4000 km
Scale at the Equator

A grandnephew, Wilkinson Wright, said, "They saw something they wanted to do, and they just did it. And if they didn't know the answer, they found other means to get the answer. The spirit of…not being afraid, of just going ahead and doing whatever had to be done is something that…I admire tremendously."

Charles A. Lindbergh made the first nonstop solo flight across the Atlantic Ocean, from New York to Paris, on May 20 and 21, 1927.

He was born in 1902 and grew up largely in Little Falls, Minnesota, and in Washington, D.C., where his father was a Minnesota congressman. He purchased a World War I Curtiss Jenny—his first plane—and in 1926 began flying the mail between St. Louis and Chicago. Several wealthy St. Louis businessmen put up the money that made it possible for him to compete for a prize that was being offered—$25,000 to the pilot who made the first successful nonstop flight between New York and Paris. In the simple, boxy monoplane *Spirit of St. Louis* he set off for Europe. En route, he wrote, "Now I've burned the last bridge behind me. All through the storm and darkest night, my instincts were anchored to the continent of North America, as though an invisible cord still tied me to its coasts. In an emergency—if the ice-filled clouds had merged, if oil pressure had begun to drop, if a cylinder had started missing—I should have turned back toward America and home. Now, my anchor is in Europe: on a continent I've never seen…. Now, I'll never think of turning back."

He made the flight in thirty-three and a half hours and immediately became a handsome and shy folk hero on both sides of the Atlantic. His daughter Reeve says, "People still tell me exactly where they were standing when they heard the news of his landing in Paris."

In May 1929 he married Anne Morrow, daughter of the U.S. ambassador to Mexico. In what was called the "crime of the century," their two-year-old son was kidnapped and murdered just a few years later. Speeches advocating American neutrality in World War II—

## ON LEARNING TO FLY AN AIRPLANE

Now, there are two ways of learning how to ride a fractious horse: one is to get on him and learn by actual practice how each motion and trick may be best met; the other is to sit on a fence and watch the beast a while, and then retire to the house and at leisure figure out the best way of overcoming his jumps and kicks. The latter system is the safest; but the former, on the whole, turns out the larger proportion of good riders. It is very much the same in learning to ride a flying machine; if you are looking for perfect safety, you will do well to sit on a fence and watch the birds; but if you really wish to learn, you must mount a machine and become acquainted with its tricks by actual trial.

—Wilbur Wright

ABOVE: *Wilbur Wright scurries to keep up with his airborne brother Orville, who is piloting the first sustained, controlled flight by a heavier-than-air craft. The two ushered in the Age of Flight near Kitty Hawk, North Carolina, on December 17, 1903.*

and one in which he blamed "the British, the Roosevelt Administration and the Jews" for unwisely advocating U.S. entry into the World War II—brought him considerable criticism, and he lived out his life in Hawaii, dying there in 1974. He had come to blame much of the degradation of the natural world and modern warfare on aviation technology and said, a few years before his death, "If I had to choose, I would rather have birds than airplanes."

Amelia Earhart was the first woman to fly alone over the Atlantic Ocean. She did it on May 20, 1932, almost exactly five years after the Lindbergh flight. Reaching Europe somewhat off course, she landed in an open field near Londonderry in northern Ireland. As she climbed from her plane, a man approached. "Where am I?" she asked him.

"In Gallegher's pasture. Have you come far?"

"From America," she said.

She made a series of flights across the United States and became involved in the movement that encouraged the development of commercial aviation. But she hungered for another adventure. "I have a feeling that there is just about one more good flight left in my system and I hope this trip is it. Anyway when I have finished this job, I mean to give up long-distance 'stunt' flying." But this stunt was a circumnavigation of the globe. She set out with navigator Fred Noonan on June 1, 1937, and set off around the world, from west to east. They got as far as Lae in New Guinea, but then the trail dims. The Coast Guard Cutter *Itasca* heard her final transmission: "KHAQQ calling *Itasca*. We must be on you but cannot see you…gas is running low…."

President Roosevelt authorized a search involving nine ships and 66 aircraft, but they never solved her disappearance.

## Taking to the Corridor Skyways

Early aircraft seemed to be magical toys, and until World War I they were mainly curiosities. After that conflict had proved their practicality, government officials, engineers, and entrepreneurs cooperated to exploit the speed of the airplane for civilian use.

The rapid development of air transport began in 1918, when the Post Office Department undertook regular airmail service. The first U.S. airmail flight took off in 1918. By 1927 mail was flown on 24 major routes. To beat the trains, mail planes had to fly at night and in all weather, which led to the development of instruments—such as accurate compasses, roll and pitch indicators, and precise altimeters—that made flights more reliable. Airmail service also accelerated the development of air routes, airports, and navigation systems.

In 1925 the post office contracted with fledgling private airlines to take over air-

mail service. By the nature of its subsidies it also encouraged the airlines to fly larger craft that could carry passengers. By the late 1920s transports were able to carry 12 passengers, and airlines were charting a nationwide network of routes. Flying speed and novelty appealed to business-people and the curious wealthy.

In these early days of commercial aviation, flying was an exotic and rare experience for most. Travelers dressed as for an evening out, and airlines vied to serve scrumptious on-board meals. Two airlines especially epitomized the glamour of long-distance flight. World War I pilot Juan Trippe founded Pan American World Airways—more familiarly PanAm—in 1927 and began carrying passengers from Key West to Havana. By 1930 PanAm's 12,000-mile route connected the U.S. with Cuba, Haiti, the Dominican Republic, Puerto Rico, Mexico, and several Central American countries. The famous *China Clipper* began transpacific flights from San Francisco to Manila in 1935, and in 1939

## BARNSTORMING

Theater companies who toured rural areas, often performing in barns for crowds of rustics, were called barnstormers. When pilots began entertaining crowds with their stunts, they took the same name.

The skilled maneuvers they performed had been learned in actual combat in the skies over Europe during World War I in dogfighting against the Germans. The Wright Brothers hired some flyers to show off the strength and safety of their planes, but their chief pilot in France, Eugène Lefebvre, was the first man ever to die while piloting an airplane. In fact, five of the original nine on the team of stunt pilots performing in Wright Flyers died in crashes.

Lincoln Beachey, barnstorming for the Glenn Curtiss exhibition team, earned fame by, among other famous stunts, flying over Niagara Falls, then under a nearby suspension bridge, finally diving into the gorge. He was the first stunt pilot to "loop the loop" as entertainment, though a Russian pilot, Petr Nesterov, had performed one during an actual dogfight in World War I. Young Winston Churchill looped the loop with Gustav Hamel, one of Britain's first stunt pilots.

After the war there were plenty of pilots and cheap planes but few jobs, so barnstorming offered an attractive alternative career. Barnstormers earned money by charging for short sightseeing tours or by charging admission to the rural fields where their planes took off and landed. Charles Lindbergh and Jimmy Doolittle were early barnstormers. Lindbergh even "walked the wing"—scrambled over the wings while holding on to struts and wires. Doolittle would become famous for another sort of daring: He led a bombing raid on Tokyo early in World War II.

PanAm inaugurated transatlantic service with the *Yankee Clipper,* flying between New York and Lisbon. By 1947 it was offering round-the-world service—New York to New York.

TWA—Trans World Airlines, which began flying on October 25, 1930—was lucky to be guided by Howard Hughes between 1939 and 1961. The eccentric but brilliant financier and aviation pioneer was principal stockholder in the 1950s when TWA flew throughout Europe, the Middle East, Africa, and Asia. In 1961 he lost control of the airline to Wall Street financial institutions.

After World War II, four-engine planes with pressurized cabins flew more people. The first tourist-class fares were sold in 1948, tapping a huge market, and by 1957 airliners carried more passengers per mile than did trains.

United Airlines hired the first flight attendants—called stewardesses then— in 1930. They enhanced the glamorous, elite image of flying. Dressed as the nurses they were, the women also were intended to reassure passengers about the safety of air travel—in an era when

flight in low-altitude airplanes was novel, noisy, and so bumpy that airsickness was common.

Sleek and rugged, the DC-3 was the most versatile and successful airplane in aviation history. Originally designed as a 14-berth "sleeper," it proved to be endlessly adaptable. It was a nonpareil airliner, a stalwart wartime transport, a Vietnam-era flying gun platform, a regular on overnight-delivery flights, and a drug smuggler's darling.

When new in 1936 it ruled commercial aviation. By 1938 it carried 95 percent of the nation's passenger traffic. The so-called Gooney Bird cruised at 180 miles an hour and carried twice as many passengers at far less the operating cost of its closest rival, the Boeing 247. Its 21-passenger capacity made it the first truly profitable airliner.

The Douglas Aircraft Company built 10,926 DC-3s and its military versions, the C-47 and C-53, before closing its assembly line in 1946. Foreign plants built several thousand more. In 1987 an estimated 1,500 of the workhorses were still in service.

Jetliners were introduced in 1958 and travel times, especially on coast-to-coast and overseas flights, fell sharply. Flight times from New York to Los Angeles shrank to six hours. Westward nonstops increased from nine daily in 1960 to 20 in 1987, while the total number of passengers was growing sixfold.

Flying had become indispensable to business, and millions vacationed by air. The jumbo jets of the 1970s, each hauling nearly 400 people, opened a new age of mass flying.

With the end of federal regulation in 1978 cozy arrangements that major carriers had enjoyed for 40 years evaporated. For the first time since the 1920s, major new airlines entered the market. Competition turned cutthroat, fares plummeted, ridership soared, and several famous lines either merged or crashed into bankruptcy.

ABOVE: *The* American Clipper, *here soaring over Manhattan, carried 44 passengers in the 1930s; it took the cushy plane nearly 17 hours to get from New York to San Francisco.*

OPPOSITE: *In 1933 Amelia Earhart was the first woman to fly solo across the Atlantic.*

# SOCIAL REFORM

❧

## *Reining in Capitalism*

Mary had a little lamb, And when she saw it sicken, She shipped it off to Packingtown, And now it's labeled chicken.

Terrifying fact underlay a jingle circulating after Upton Sinclair's fictional journey through the Chicago stockyards—*The Jungle*—was published in 1905. The book nauseated with revelations of rancid beef and tubercular pork destined for dinner tables. Humorist Finley Peter Dunne described Theodore Roosevelt, who denigrated sensational muckraking, as being "engaged in a hand-to-hand conflict with a potted ham" and hurling sausages from a White House window: "Since thin th' Prisidint, like th' rest iv us, has become a viggytaryan."

Largely because of the book, Congress passed the Pure Food and Drug Act and the Meat Inspection Act in 1906. The largest meat packers applauded the measures to restore public confidence—which drove many smaller competitors out of business.

A socialist, Sinclair had meant to provoke sympathy for the immigrants who toiled and died in slaughterhouses. Only eight of the book's 308 pages described the filth and confusion of the meat processing plant, where men toiled for 17 cents an hour and some-

times fell into the boiling vats and went out in Durham's Pure Leaf Lard. "I aimed at the public's heart," he wrote, "and by accident I hit it in the stomach."

Meatpacking was not the only industry to come under scrutiny. "Prosperity never before imagined, power never yet wielded by man, speed never reached by anything but a meteor, had made the world irritable, nervous, querulous, unreasonable and afraid." Henry Adams, descendant of two Presidents, vented the doubts of a nation. Industry had nurtured American trade and naval vigor but at great cost: cities darkened by poverty and political scandal as well as by smoke; colossal trusts that menaced cherished notions of fair play.

In 1911 there were more than 15,000 boys under the age of 16 working in Pennsylvania coal mines, picking slate out of coal from 7 a.m., to 5:30 p.m. At least two million children under the age of 15 were at work nationwide. Journalist Edwin Markham visited a cigarette factory: "One face followed me still, the gaunt face of a boy crouched like a cary-

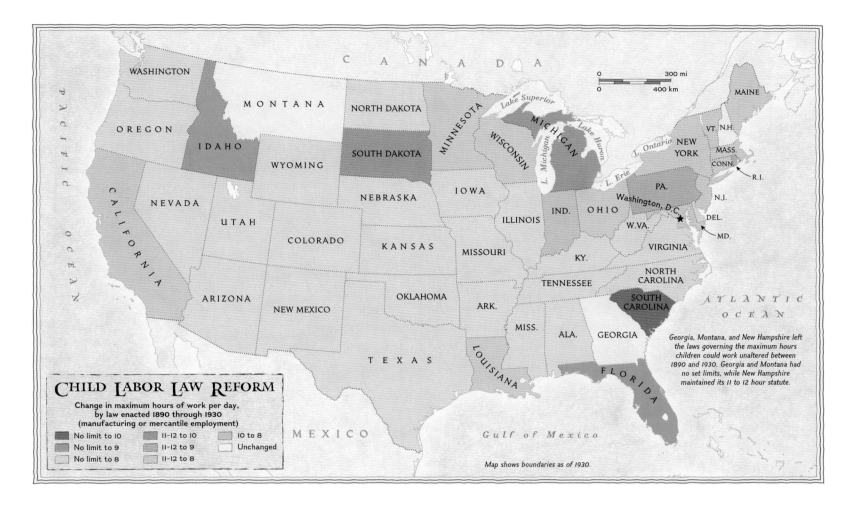

**CHILD LABOR LAW REFORM**

Change in maximum hours of work per day,
by law enacted 1890 through 1930
(manufacturing or mercantile employment)

- No limit to 10
- No limit to 9
- No limit to 8
- 11–12 to 10
- 11–12 to 9
- 11–12 to 8
- 10 to 8
- Unchanged

*Georgia, Montana, and New Hampshire left the laws governing the maximum hours children could work unaltered between 1890 and 1930. Georgia and Montana had no set limits, while New Hampshire maintained its 11 to 12 hour statute.*

Map shows boundaries as of 1930.

atid, pasting tiny labels on the margins of cigarette boxes. All day long he stuck little oblongs of paper marked with the runic words: 'Cork tips,' 'Cork tips,' 'Cork tips.' That was his message to the world. His pay was 25 cents a thousand and he sat there growing bent and haggard, and spending all his energies to promulgate to humanity this news about cork tips."

In 1916 Congress forbade employment of children under 14 in firms engaged in interstate commerce. This was ruled unconstitutional in 1918. Congress imposed an extra 10 percent tax on factories employing young children. This, too, was thrown out. It wasn't until the Fair Labor Standards Act of 1938 that the minimum age was set at 14 for employment outside of school hours in nonmanufacturing jobs; at 16 for employment during school hours in interstate commerce; and at 18 for occupations called hazardous by the secretary of labor.

So-called "sweatshops" often employed child labor. The term came from England, where as early as 1850 the word "sweater" described an employer or middleman who exacted monotonous work for very low wages. Sweatshops became widespread in the U.S. during the 1880s, when immigrants from eastern and southern Europe provided a large source of cheap labor. Sometimes they were in the home, where a family might contract to do piecework for pay and everyone pitched in. In addition to garments, they might be involved in shoe manufacture, soap making, cigar making, and the pasting together of artificial flowers. Sweatshops tended to be worse in large cities, where they could be hidden away in slum areas.

Muckrakers had found ample kindling. Lincoln Steffens exposed mismanagement and graft in *The Shame of the Cities;* Ida Tarbell attacked business "treated as warfare" in *The History of the Standard Oil Company.* Titles such as "Making Steel and Killing Men" told their own grim stories.

Journalists held no patent on righteous indignation. The reform spirit flourished across America. Women organized to gain the national vote, labor to demand better pay and work conditions, city dwellers to win better services—sidewalks, sewers, schools, parks, and transportation.

Calling themselves progressive, reformers clamored for change. In 1912, Democrat Woodrow Wilson declared "I am and have always been an insurgent" and called for reform. As President, Wilson made good on his promise, signing bills to refurbish the nation's banking system and to exempt labor unions from trust-busting laws.

---

### The JUNGLE

The line of the buildings stood clear-cut and black against the sky; here and there out of the mass rose the great chimneys, with the river of smoke streaming away to the end of the world. It was a study in colours now, this smoke; in the sunset light it was black and brown and grey and purple. All the sordid questions of the place were gone— in the twilight it was a vision of power. To the two who stood watching while the darkness swallowed it up, it seemed a dream of wonder, with its tale of human energy, of things being done, of employment for thousands upon thousands of men, of opportunity and freedom, of life and love and joy. When they came away, arm in arm, Jurgis was saying, "Tomorrow I shall go there and get a job!"

—Upton Sinclair

---

OPPOSITE: *Grimy boys, already gainfully employed while still in their adolescence, emerge from a coal mine somewhere in the eastern U.S. around 1910.*

# The AUTOMOBILE

## Hitting the Road

By 1895 Detroit was a growing industrial city, noted for steam and gas engines, stoves, and carriages. Entrepreneurs such as Ford, Durant, Leland, Olds, and the Dodge brothers quickly made it the auto capital of the country. In 1986 Michigan retained more auto-manufacturing facilities—114—than any other state and produced 30 percent of the cars made in the U.S. Ohio followed with 51 facilities; then Indiana, with 26.

Although initially rooted near basic suppliers and skilled labor, the industry soon decentralized. Parts and assembly

plants were located near regional and urban markets, saving transportation costs.

Henry Ford began this trend with a branch plant in Kansas City in 1912. By 1919 he had reached as far as Copenhagen, Denmark.

Motor vehicle assembly and parts plants nearly doubled in number between

1909 and 1927, when 1,373 were operating. After 1914 New York and Michigan lost plants to surrounding states. Competition, meanwhile, winnowed automobile firms, many of them former carriage or bicycle makers, from about 250 to 40.

By the 1920s Americans were growing tired of Henry Ford's black Model T, which had dominated the market since 1908. The electric starter, introduced in 1912, had encouraged women and older people to drive; the closed car and better roads had brought year-round driving. Motorists wanted more than basic transportation.

As head of General Motors, Alfred Sloan was ready to give it to them. GM was in business "to make money, not just to make motor cars," and Sloan organized its loosely knit units into a market-oriented team. He widened the product line, targeting models for sale to different classes of buyers, on the

company's installment plan if possible. In the 1920s GM developed its most important strategy, the annual model change. Sloan later said: "The 'laws' of the Paris dressmakers have come to be a factor in the automobile industry....The changes in the new model should be so novel and attractive as to create...dissatisfaction with past models." After World War I the so-called Big Three rose to dominate the automobile industry; in the U.S. Ford dominated with the Model T. In 1921, the depression shook the industry. GM was plunged into financial crisis, but Sloan,

---

### ROUTE 66

Designated officially in 1926, Route 66 ran diagonally across the West from Chicago to Los Angeles, linking hundreds of predominantly rural communities. John Steinbeck called it the "Mother Road" in *The Grapes of Wrath* and sent his Oakies hopefully along it. During the Great Depression thousands found work on it and it was reported "continuously paved" in 1938. Tourist courts, garages, and diners sprang up along its length; motels evolved from the earlier auto camps and tourist homes. It served its travelers well until the Interstate Highway System came along; the final section of the original was replaced by Interstate 40 at Williams, Arizona, in October 1984.

Among the postwar tourists who traveled Route 66 was Robert William Troup, Jr., of Harrisburg, Pennsylvania. Bobby was a former pianist with the Tommy Dorsey band and an ex-marine captain. In 1946, Bobby wrote a song about the highway:

*If you ever plan to motor west:*
*Travel my way, the highway that's the best.*
*Get your kicks on Route 66!*
*It winds from Chicago to L.A.,*
*More than 2,000 miles all the way,*
*Get your kicks on Route 66!*
*Now you go through St. Looey,*
*Joplin, Missouri!*
*And Oklahoma City looks mighty pretty.*
*You'll see Amarillo, Gallup, New Mexico,*
*Flagstaff...Barstow, San Bernardino.*
*Won't you get hip to this timely tip:*
*When you make that California trip,*
*Get your kicks on Route 66!*

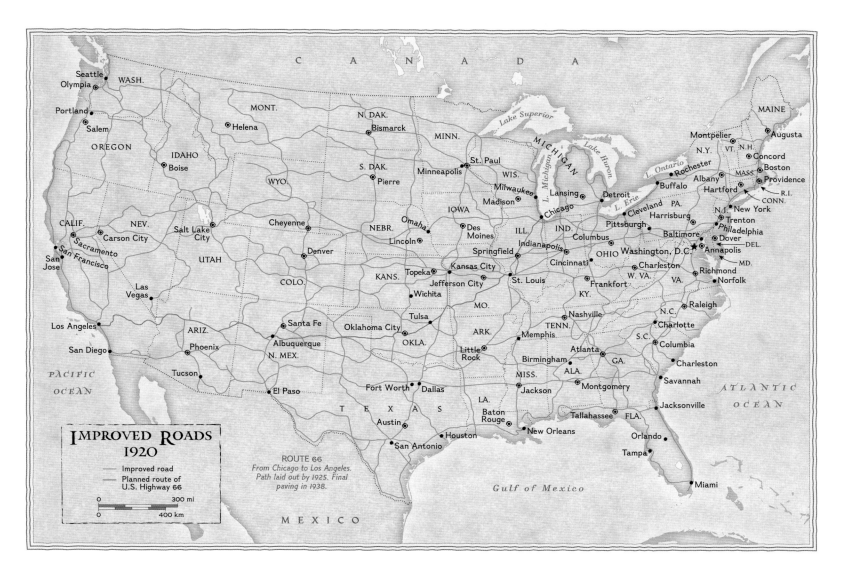

IMPROVED ROADS
1920

— Improved road
— Planned route of
U.S. Highway 66

ROUTE 66
*From Chicago to Los Angeles.
Path laid out by 1925. Final
paving in 1938.*

0        300 mi
0        400 km

who became president in 1923, introduced manufacturing innovations that made GM the unchallenged leader. Among other things, he gave the company a staff-and-line organization that featured autonomous manufacturing divisions. This facilitated the management of a large corporation and became the model of other companies.

The 1921 crash caught Henry Ford in the midst of constructing a large new plant and also in the process of buying out his stockholders. He weathered the storm, but many of his dealers, unable to sell cars and not permitted to return them, failed.

The third of the Big Three—Chrysler—was formed when the Maxwell Motor Company failed and Walter P. Chrysler was hired to reorganize it. It became the Chrysler Corporation in 1925 and grew enormously with the acquisition of the Dodge Brothers company in 1928. When Ford had to halt production for 18 months to switch from the Model T to the Model A, Chrysler broke into the low-priced market with the Plymouth.

By 1929 the Big Three were supplying three-fourths of the autos sold in the U.S. The five largest independents—Hudson, Nash, Packard, Studebaker, and Willys-Overland—produced most of the rest. But there were dozens of other manufacturers, most of whom were wiped out during the Great Depression of the 1930s. The depression also reduced the number of cars sold: Production declined from a peak of more than five million in 1929 to a low of just over a million in 1932. Production had still not reached the 1929 level when World War II broke out.

Eventually GM's vast, decentralized operation stretched from dozens of plants to thousands of retail dealers, producing a miraculous convergence. To assemble a 1961 Chevy in Baltimore on a Friday, chassis parts had to leave Detroit Monday afternoon. On Tuesday axles left Buffalo, and the engine left Flint. Wednesday, Cleveland sent the transmission. By Friday at 9 a.m., all were in Baltimore, with the right trim, color, and options.

Competition reduced automakers from 108 in 1920 to 12 in 1939; by 1963 only American Motors was independent of the Big Three. This "shared monopoly" grew into the nation's largest manufacturing enterprise, directly employing 2.3 million Americans by 1986. The late 1950s brought new competition: small, fuel-efficient European imports. Detroit was complacent, reflecting the arrogance that Chrysler's top executive, K. T. Keller, had expressed shortly after World War II. "Chrysler builds cars to sit in," he declared, "not to piss over." In 1980 Japan surpassed the U.S. as the world's leading auto producer. Chastened by market losses and plant closings, Detroit has faced increasing competition from other countries, yet autos remain America's "industry of industries."

OPPOSITE: *A 1905 pleasure drive turns anything but pleasurable as autos bog down in the rudimentary roads offered for the new sport of driving. Early roads were often either quagmires or dust clouds.*

## Building the Roads

The U.S. had more than three million miles of roads in 1920, but good ones were still exceptions. Only 35,000 miles of rural roads had been paved. Routes linking regions, such as the transcontinental Lincoln Highway, were privately funded. Road improvement and new construction averaged tens of thousands of miles each year.

By 1950, federal funds had built a basic network of 644,000 miles of highways. An additional 1.6 million miles of state and local roads had been surfaced with gravel or paved since 1920. Despite the progress, many new roads were outdated in design or overcrowded and unable to cope with the surge of growth that followed World War II.

When railroads took over most of the long-haul transport after 1850, America's roads fell by the wayside. Not until the automobile chugged into the foreground did demand for good roads become insatiable. It soon reshaped the land, the economy, and almost every aspect of life.

City streets were improving in 1900, but rural roads were mostly unimproved dirt tracks. The only maintenance many received was the halfhearted attention of farmers working off their road taxes. By 1904 only 144 miles of rural roads had any type of pavement. Primitive roads alternated between quagmires and choking dust, and some drivers in a 1904 New York to St. Louis tour abandoned Illinois roads for a better surface—freshly plowed fields. Service stations and road maps were as rare as pavement, so motorists had to be both mechanics and navigators. With each year, however, the number of cars shot upward, and road builders struggled to meet the demands of a sporting pastime become a national obsession.

As motor vehicles increased from 8,000 in 1900 to 9.2 million in 1920, drivers clamored for better roads. State and local governments improved thousands of miles annually and pressed for federal aid, which began in 1912 with a $500,000 appropriation. Most roads were merely graded and surfaced with gravel or clay and sand. The best were strips of concrete, brick, stone, or asphalt.

On came the flow of cars and trucks. Once dense cities sprawled as new suburbs and commerce geared to traffic lined the roads. By 1925 landscape and life-style were so transformed that an Indiana woman could say, "I'll go without food before I'll see us give up the car."

The first coherent system of federally funded roads was authorized in 1921; a grid of national highways was set in 1924; and uniform signs were adopted in 1925. High-speed divided highways with controlled access were adapted from European models. Bronx River Parkway in New York—the first scenic highway—opened in 1923. In 1940 the first 160 miles of the Pennsylvania Turnpike unfurled the concrete banner of the superhighway.

Returning triumphant from Europe after World War II, Gen. Dwight David Eisenhower remembered being impressed by the German Autobahn. "During World War II," he recalled, "I saw the superlative system of German national highways crossing that country and offering the possibility, often lacking in the United States, to drive with speed and safety at the same time." On June 29, 1956, Eisenhower, now president, signed the authorizing act for 41,000 miles of high-quality highways to tie the nation together. The mileage was later lengthened to 44,000 miles and intended to connect 90 percent of all cities of 50,000 people in all 50 states. Now virtually complete, the highways allow a motorist to drive from coast to coast without encountering a traffic light.

While some motorists complain that the interstates have contributed to the homogenization of the American landscape and steer clear of them, others find convenience and even beauty

in the graceful swoops and curves of the system.

In Phoenix, the interchange of I-10 and I-17 is called The Stack, completed in 1990. It consists of four levels, eight ramps, and 347 supporting piers, and is Arizona's first fully directional, multi-level, freeway-to-freeway interchange. *Arizona Highways* called The Stack "practical sculpture in concrete."

The I-35 parkway, delayed for more than 20 years by environmental and neighborhood groups, is now a part of the local and region transportation system in St. Paul, Minnesota, carrying 45,000 vehicles a day. The controversy of its beginnings resulted in a unique design: four lanes, no trucks weighing more than 9,000 pounds, a speed limit of 45 miles an hour, trees and shrubs in the median, and decorative fencing and lighting.

I-68 in Maryland, following the route

### RANSOM ELI OLDS

Olds was designer of the three-horse-power, curved dash Oldsmobile, the first American-made auto to be commercially successful; it was also the first to use a progressive assembly system, which was the beginning of modern mass-production methods.

Olds formed the Olds Motor Works in 1899 in Lansing, Michigan, and his first Oldsmobiles were marketed in 1901. Sales reached 5,000 in 1904, but that year, after an argument with his financial partner, Olds left the company. He formed the Reo Motor Car Company and built it into one of the industry's leaders, but after 1915 generally abandoned the auto business. He speculated in land in Florida and also marketed a lawn mower he had invented.

In April 2004, the last Oldsmobile rolled off the assembly line in Lansing, ending the line for the oldest automotive brand name in the U.S. It came off the assembly line at the Lansing Car Assembly plant, where the vehicles had been produced for nearly a century. Oldsmobiles had pioneered chrome-plated trim and gave Americans the Eighty Eight series, the front-wheel-drive Toronado, and the Cutlass.

Of the more than 35 million Oldsmobiles built, more than 14 million were built in Lansing.

of old U.S. 40, required a cut in Sideling Hill that removed 3.44 million cubic meters of shale, sandstone, and other rocks and created a gash that one magazine article called "an engineering marvel: a breathtakingly beautiful man-made rock wall, revealing in tilted, multi-colored layers of sedimentary rock 350 million years of geologic history." When I-68 opened in 1991, it included the Sideling Hill Exhibition and Tourist Information Center, which housed geological exhibits.

Because of concern about the endangered Florida panther, the construction of I-75 in Florida includes underpasses that allow the creatures and other wildlife to cross beneath the highway.

When construction began in the 1940s on the Henry G. Shirley Memorial Highway in Virginia, it was designed to accommodate traffic generated by the Pentagon, then also under construction. Now a part of the Interstate system as I-395, it is one of Washington, D.C.'s main traffic arteries and features the first exclusive bus lane built in the U.S.

Even Hawaii, isolated in the middle of the Pacific Ocean, has interstate highways: H-1, H-2, and H-3. The 24-kilometer H-3, the largest construction and public works project ever undertaken by the state, connects the Kaneohe Marine Corps Air Station to the Pearl Harbor defense bases, passing through the Koolau Mountains to do so.

ABOVE: *America's obsession with the auto produced even sheet music.*
OPPOSITE: *The New Jersey Turnpike, new in 1955, coiling upon itself.*

# HENRY FORD and C?

### Manufacturing for the Masses

Factories changed forever on April 1, 1913, when 29 Model T Ford workers first stood along an improvised assembly line to produce flywheel magnetos. Rather than assemble an entire magneto himself, each man now performed a single task and moved the unit to the next man. Assembly time immediately fell from 20 minutes per magneto to 13 minutes and, within a year, to 5 after engineers added a chain drive to the line and tinkered to find its optimum speed.

The experiment typified Henry Ford's relentless search to boost production of his "motor car for the great multitude." Back in 1909 Ford had decreed that he would build only the simple, sturdy Model T (though in several body styles). He spent freely to replace skilled labor with machinery and adapted techniques from other industries to achieve economies of scale. A key improvement came in 1910, when Ford fully deployed plant machinery by production sequence rather than by conventional grouping of similar machines.

"A slightly boyish figure with thin, long, sure hands incessantly moving," John Reed called Henry Ford, the son of an immigrant Irish farmer. He did not invent the automobile. Factories in France were producing autos five years before Ford made his first car. And other Americans were manufacturing automobiles at the same time. The year before Ford sold his first Model A, Ransom Eli Olds had made 2,500 "Merry Oldsmobiles."

Nor did he invent mass production, only perfected it. Cyrus McCormick had long been making his reapers by the mass production of standard parts, as had Isaac Singer with his sewing machines and Samuel Colt with his revolvers. But Ford's genius was to see that the automobile

could be more than a plaything of the rich; he was determined it could be made cheaply enough to sell to the masses.

A poll of college students named Ford the third-greatest figure of all time, trailing only Napoleon and Jesus. He flirted with the idea of a political career and even produced a ghost-written autobiography, *My Life and Work,* in 1922, which became an international best-seller. But he couldn't speak in public and a nascent paranoia was growing. The *Dearborn Independent,* avidly read by

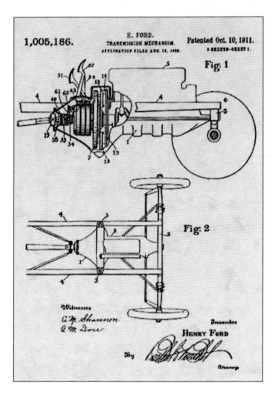

Adolf Hitler, preached his anti-Semitism. Henry Ford is the only American mentioned in *Mein Kampf.*

He liked to go "camping" with Harvey Firestone and Thomas Edison, others who had revolutionized American life. Firestone loved tours of flora and fauna, while Edison spent most of his time napping and reading. Ford liked to chop firewood and run foot races with the others.

With the success of the 1913 magneto

line, Ford engineers divided assembly into many steps. As the work came to each man, he did the same simple task over and over, "which the most stupid man can learn within two days," Ford wrote.

Engineers soon converted other operations to assembly lines. By April 1914 Ford was running three efficient lines for final assembly of the frame and power train. Production soared from 82,388 cars in 1912 to 230,788 in 1914, and the price of a typical car fell from $600 to $490.

The 60-acre Highland Park, Michigan, plant was designed by Albert Kahn for easy transit of raw materials and parts through a complex that employed 13,000 workers in 1914. Ford's array of 15,000 machines for metal forging, stamping, machining, painting, and baking produced

---

### The FORD THUNDERBIRD

One of the most beloved automobiles ever produced in the U.S. emerged a few years after the end of World War II and seemed to embody America's hunger for dazzle and elegance after the gray war years.

The Thunderbird—or T-Bird—first reached the market in September 1954. A two-seater, with a moderate engine and little trunk space, it was designed to compete with Chevrolet's Corvette. It was a huge success and people all over America stopped to stare—and yearn for one of their own. In subsequent models, Ford increased the trunk space by moving the spare tire to a hard case on the rear bumper and offering a larger engine as an option.

But the baby boom was producing larger families so Ford redesigned the T-Bird, making it a four-seater. In the 60s, with more and more government safety regulations in place, the convertible roof was abandoned and emissions standards dictated a smaller and less powerful engine. In the 1970s the T-Bird began looking very much like all other autos and lost much of its appeal. It was discontinued in the mid-1990s.

T-Bird fans, outraged, forced Ford to rethink their decision and in 1999 a completely redesigned T-Bird hit the market, looking much like the original Thunderbird of the 1950s.

parts—5,000 per car—so similar and reliable that few required hand finishing. Cars were simply started and driven off the line. The kind of interchangeability achieved in American plants was demonstrated dramatically in 1908 at the British Royal Automobile Club in London. Three Cadillacs were disassembled and the parts mixed together. Then 89 parts were removed at random and replaced from dealer's stock. The cars were then reassembled and driven 500 miles without trouble.

The Model T's springs, high undercarriage, and lightweight vanadium steel helped it survive the potholed roads of the time; its reliable 20-horsepower engine could be adapted to saw logs or grind corn. By 1914 nearly every other car in America was a Ford.

The moving assembly line revolutionized manufacturing, but workers hated it. After it was installed, they quit in waves. Turnover reached 380 percent late in 1913. Ford's response made him a folk hero. On January 12, 1914, he doubled the average pay of eligible employees to five dollars for an eight-hour shift—solving the turnover crisis at a stroke. "The chain system you have is a *slave driver*," one worker's wife wrote to Ford. "That five dollars a day is a blessing—a bigger one than you know but *oh* they earn it."

Not everyone agreed. The *Wall Street Journal* called the raise immoral, the application of "spiritual principles where they don't belong."

He utilized much immigrant labor and believed strongly in Americanizing them, even making English-language classes compulsory at his factories. "Our one great aim," he wrote, "is to impress these men that they are, or should be, Americans, and that former racial, national, and linguistic differences are to be forgotten."

The system of mass production and high wages enabled workers to become consumers themselves. What followed was an immense surge in productivity and workers with cash in their pockets as others quickly adopted Ford's methods.

Still, Ford bitterly resisted efforts of the unions to organize his workers.

By the end of the 1930s he was losing his magic touch. Prejudices filled his mind—hatred of Jews, Catholics, unions, even his son Edsel. His company trailed General Motors and Chrysler in production. His factories remained spotless and their safety record was superb. But wages had dropped. He turned over labor relations to Harry Bennett, a short, redheaded man that many considered a thug. Bennett's

"service department" hired spies to keep an eye on the workers, who developed what they called the "Ford whisper," a way of conversing with their heads down so they couldn't be reported by Bennett's spies.

Photographs taken of a fracas involving Walter Reuther, leader of the young United Automobile Workers union, exposed Bennett's tactics. In May 1937, Reuther went to Ford's River Rouge plant to hand out pamphlets; Bennett's men attacked him and his fellow unionists, punching and kicking, and hurling them down an overpass's steps.

Photographer James R. Kilpatrick of the *Detroit News* captured the episode. When Bennett's men demanded his film, he gave them film not yet exposed. The pictures were devastating to Ford's position. His son Edsel persuaded his father to allow the workers to vote. On May 21, 1941, nearly 70 percent of Ford workers voted to be represented by the UAW, and the rest chose a rival union.

---

ABOVE: *Innovations in mass production introduced by Henry Ford quickly spread throughout the industry, evidenced by these cars nearing completion at the Packard Motor Company.*
OPPOSITE: *Illustration of one of Ford's patents, this one for a transmission mechanism.*

# The
# REVOLUTION
# *in* MEXICO

## *Pancho Villa*

Crying *Tierra y Libertad*—Land and Liberty—Mexicans erupted in revolution in 1910. For the next ten years, bloody clashes between impassioned rebels and unscrupulous autocrats convulsed a nation in search of a new identity. It was the first massive social revolution of the twentieth century, and even as it fanned the flames of economic, cultural, and racial strife in a country exploited by oppressive officials and crippled by poverty, it offered hope to the long-suffering Mexicans. And it made rebel-outlaw Francisco "Pancho" Villa a legend in his time.

In American movies and newspapers of the time, Pancho Villa was portrayed as a Robin Hood, but with little justification. Mutual Films paid him $25,000 to allow its cameras at his battles. To help them, he promised to fight by daylight, and when the cameras weren't quite ready to attack the city of Ojinaga, he obligingly delayed the attack.

He was loved by his men for his bravery and his coarse humor. He abandoned the custom, then common in Mexico, of taking the women and children of the men along with the army, just one of his military innovations. He made swift forced marches with his cavalry, striking terror into opposing troops.

After Gen. Victoriano Huerta staged a bloody coup to seize control of Mexico in 1913, Mexican-American relations devolved into fiasco. Woodrow Wilson refused to recognize the "government of butchers" and helped engineer its downfall, leaving several factions contending for power. Civil war ensued. Out of this morass rode Francisco "Pancho" Villa and his troops.

Villa, the son of a field laborer, was orphaned at an early age. When one of the owners of an estate he worked on assaulted his sister, Villa killed the man and fled into the mountains, where he spent his adolescence as a fugitive. In 1909 he joined Francisco Madero's uprising against the dictator of Mexico, Porfirio Díaz. Mexico's peasants, fed up with the high cost of food and the continued mistreatment by rich landowners, turned to violence. Villa was voted a commander and led a force of 28 men.

In 1913, after a stint in the U.S., Villa returned to Mexico and formed a band of several thousand men which became known as the famous División del Norte—the Division of the North. Villa fought against the increasingly repressive and inefficient dictatorship of Huerta, winning several victories. In December 1913 he became governor of the state of Chihuahua.

President Wilson was a fan. In midsummer 1914, when Villa began a new round of civil war against his former revolutionary ally Venustiano Carranza, Wilson expected that Villa would win, so secretly encouraged him. He probably seemed an American sort of revolutionary to Wilson, on the side of the underdog peons but also respectful of the American property in the north. One reporter who rode with Villa said that he had "the eyes of a man who will some day go crazy." When he began losing

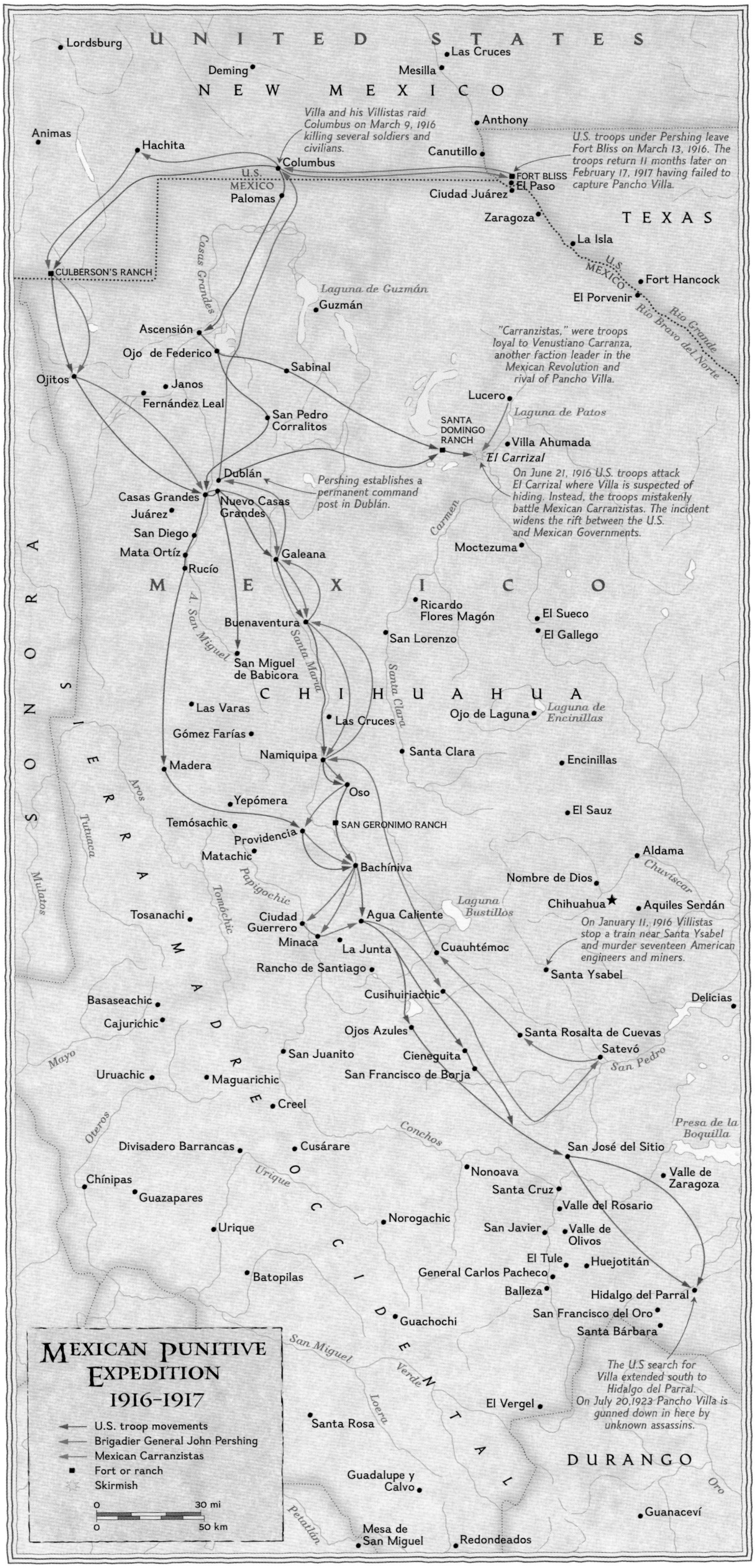
MEXICAN PUNITIVE EXPEDITION 1916–1917
U.S. troop movements
Brigadier General John Pershing
Mexican Carranzistas
Fort or ranch
Skirmish
0 30 mi
0 50 km
UNITED STATES
NEW MEXICO
TEXAS
MEXICO
CHIHUAHUA
SONORA
SIERRA MADRE OCCIDENTAL
DURANGO
Lordsburg
Las Cruces
Deming
Mesilla
Animas
Hachita
Anthony
Columbus
Canutillo
FORT BLISS
El Paso
Ciudad Juárez
U.S.
MEXICO
Palomas
Zaragoza
La Isla
Fort Hancock
El Porvenir
Rio Grande
Río Bravo del Norte
Villa and his Villistas raid Columbus on March 9, 1916 killing several soldiers and civilians.
U.S. troops under Pershing leave Fort Bliss on March 13, 1916. The troops return 11 months later on February 17, 1917 having failed to capture Pancho Villa.
CULBERSON'S RANCH
Casas Grandes
Laguna de Guzmán
Guzmán
Ascensión
Ojo de Federico
Sabinal
"Carranzistas," were troops loyal to Venustiano Carranza, another faction leader in the Mexican Revolution and rival of Pancho Villa.
Ojitos
Janos
Fernández Leal
San Pedro Corralitos
Lucero
Laguna de Patos
SANTA DOMINGO RANCH
Villa Ahumada
El Carrizal
Dublán
Pershing establishes a permanent command post in Dublán.
On June 21, 1916 U.S. troops attack El Carrizal where Villa is suspected of hiding. Instead, the troops mistakenly battle Mexican Carranzistas. The incident widens the rift between the U.S. and Mexican Governments.
Casas Grandes
Nuevo Casas Grandes
Juárez
San Diego
Mata Ortíz
Rucío
Carmen
Moctezuma
Galeana
Ricardo Flores Magón
El Sueco
El Gallego
A. San Miguel
Buenaventura
Santa María
San Lorenzo
San Miguel de Babicora
Santa Clara
Las Varas
Las Cruces
Ojo de Laguna
Laguna de Encinillas
Gómez Farías
Namiquipa
Santa Clara
Encinillas
Madera
Aros
Yepómera
Oso
El Sauz
Temósachic
SAN GERONIMO RANCH
Providencia
Matachic
Tutuaca
Bachíniva
Aldama
Nombre de Dios
Chuviscar
Mulatos
Papigochic
Tomóchic
Laguna Bustillos
Chihuahua
Aquiles Serdán
Tosanachi
Ciudad Guerrero
Minaca
Agua Caliente
La Junta
Cuauhtémoc
On January 11, 1916 Villistas stop a train near Santa Ysabel and murder seventeen American engineers and miners.
Santa Ysabel
Rancho de Santiago
Basaseachic
Cusihuiriachic
Delicias
Cajurichic
Ojos Azules
Santa Rosalía de Cuevas
Satevó
San Juanito
Cieneguita
San Pedro
Mayo
Uruachic
Maguarichic
San Francisco de Borja
Creel
Presa de la Boquilla
Oteros
Divisadero Barrancas
Cusárare
Conchos
San José del Sitio
Urique
Nonoava
Valle de Zaragoza
Chínipas
Santa Cruz
Guazapares
Valle del Rosario
Norogachic
Urique
San Javier
Valle de Olivos
El Tule
Huejotitán
Batopilas
General Carlos Pacheco
Balleza
Hidalgo del Parral
San Francisco del Oro
Guachochi
Santa Bárbara
San Miguel
Verde
The U.S search for Villa extended south to Hidalgo del Parral. On July 20,1923 Pancho Villa is gunned down in here by unknown assassins.
Loera
El Vergel
Santa Rosa
Guadalupe y Calvo
Oro
Guanaceví
Petatlán
Mesa de San Miguel
Redondeados

## BLACK JACK PERSHING

Even while hunting down Pancho Villa in Mexico, Brigadier-General Pershing railed against the "weak, chicken-hearted, white-livered lot" in Washington who were keeping America from joining in the European war against Germany. A year later, at the age of 56, he got his chance when he was appointed to head the American Expeditionary Force, even though he was junior to five other major-generals.

He had already fought against Apaches in Arizona, the Spanish in Cuba, and the Moros in the Philippines. While serving as a lieutenant instructor at West Point he earned the name "Nigger Jack" or "Black Jack" as a term of abuse, because he had led a black regiment in the war in Cuba. But the nickname came to represent his personal toughness. It was also while at West Point that he was treated to the "silence," a rare rebuke in which hundreds of cadets greet an unpopular officer entering the mess with absolute silence. When his wife and three daughters were killed in a fire, his personal toughness helped him survive. He told a friend, "About the only respite I have known is by keeping every minute occupied."

big battles Wilson switched his support to Carranza. The enraged Villa began raiding border towns and killing Americans. He stopped a train at Santa Ysabel in Mexico and murdered 17 American miners and engineers who were on board. Later he crossed the border to sack the town of Columbus, New Mexico. Nineteen Americans died before he was driven off.

His intention was to provoke America into war with Mexico so he could exploit the turmoil. He might have succeeded, but the President dispatched Gen. John J. Pershing on a "punitive expedition" in 1916, ostensibly in search of Villa. "Black Jack" Pershing and 12,000 men penetrated 400 miles into Mexico and remained ten months. Wilson's intervention in Mexico embittered relations for years.

OPPOSITE: *Mexican revolutionaries Pancho Villa, at left, and Emiliano Zapata share a cigarette break around 1911.*

# WORLD WAR ONE

## Into the Trenches

When the guns of August sounded in 1914, they heralded a war that would be called "great" until an even greater one came along.

World War I engulfed much of the world for four years and killed nearly 15 million people, either through direct fighting or through starvation and disease. Most of the casualties were in Europe, but European colonies around the world were also involved.

There had been a century of relative peace among the European nations, but that was ending as national rivalries created tensions. The action of one disturbed young man lit the fuse: On June 28, 1914, a Serbian nationalist assassinated Archduke Francis Ferdinand, the heir to Austria-Hungary's throne, in the city of Sarajevo. The great powers dithered and threatened, then tumbled almost inadvertently into war.

The Germans attacked across western Europe with more than a million men, fighting across Belgium to the Marne River, near Paris. There the French rallied with the help of the British and drove them back. The two armies dug in, facing each other in a double line of trenches 400 miles long. They devoted nearly four years to bloody attacks and counterattacks across no man's land, inflicting millions of casualties on each other. In the east, a huge Russian army moved against Germany but, after making a few gains against the smaller and better-led Germans, withdrew. Nonetheless, the fighting continued along an

ever shifting front from the Baltic Sea to the Black Sea.

In America, President Woodrow Wilson looked across the Atlantic to the hell-in-progress and hoped to keep the U.S. out of it, saying, "God helping me, I will if it is possible." He told the American people, "The United States must be neutral in fact as well as in name." But neutrality was difficult. The British set up a naval blockade to keep countries from trading with Germany; Germany responded with a new weapon, the submarine, and began sinking all enemy merchant ships found in the waters around Britain. When a German torpedo sank the British passenger ship *Lusitania* in May 1915, killing nearly 1,200 people, including 128 Americans, the country was enraged. Wilson warned Germany that if it sank any American ships, it would risk war with the U.S. Germany backed down.

In 1916, with the war in its third futile year, the people of Germany and Austria were on the verge of starvation,

cut off from supplies by British ships. The Germans resumed the submarine attacks, risking U.S. intervention. But they hoped to defeat Britain and France before the Americans had time to train an army and send it into battle.

On March 1, 1917, the British intercepted a telegram from Germany promising the Mexican government the return of Texas, New Mexico, and Arizona if Mexico would join the German side against the United States. American anger at Germany increased. Two weeks later the Russian people, wearied with hunger, ineffectual leadership, and unending bloodshed, rose up and swept away the ancient monarchy and Nicholas II, the tsar of Russia. It seemed likely that Russia's war effort would soon collapse.

Just three days after the tsar's fall, German submarines sank three American merchant ships. It was the last straw. In early April, at a special session of Congress, President Wilson asked for and got a declaration of war against the

Germans. The nation began mobilizing its resources, setting up camps all over the country to train soldiers, regulating private businesses—railroads, telephone companies, and factories—and dictating what people could buy, what they could eat, and how much fuel they could use.

Wilson had hoped he could build an army of volunteers in America, but three weeks after the declaration of war only 32,000 men had volunteered, not nearly enough. Conscription, common in all the major European countries except Britain, was hated by many. To Democratic Speaker Champ Clark there was little difference between a conscript and a convict. One senator predicted that the streets would run with blood if the government began drafting America's young men. But Wilson and his secretary of war

ABOVE: *An American gun crew inches forward during the Meuse-Argonne offensive in France in the autumn of 1918. Nearly 120,000 Americans fell in this costly battle.*

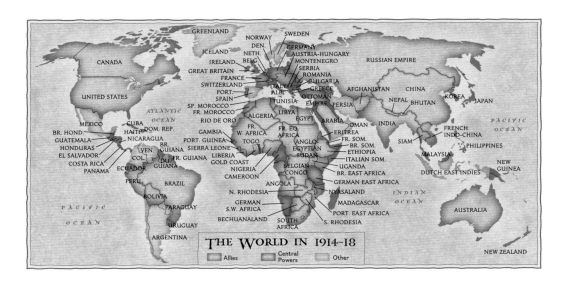

**THE WORLD IN 1914–18**
Allies — Central Powers — Other

Newton Baker got the Selective Service Act through Congress. They then built a movement of the public mood in their favor; draftees were made into heroes by parades and patriotic festivals, while dissenters were labeled "slackers." Every male between the ages of 21 and 30 was required to register on June 5, 1917, and nearly 10 million did. On July 20 Secretary Baker drew black capsule "258," the number assigned to a different draftee in each precinct, from a goldfish bowl. By mid-December 516,000 draftees had been sent to camp, and Sergeant Irving Berlin had even written a song for them: "Oh, How I Hate to Get Up in the Morning."

Brigadier-General Black Jack Pershing, who impressed superiors with his incisive mind and strength of character, was appointed to head the American Expeditionary Force. He had learned his fighting skills against the Apaches in Arizona, the Spanish in Cuba, and the Moros in the Philippines. He was a strict disciplinarian: He once kept troops waiting in the rain for hours, then complained that their boots were muddy. He was frustrated by the slow buildup of men and arms. Eleven months after America's entry into the war he could barely field one division for combat.

## Total War

Despite fears that African Americans would resist the draft, 400,000 served among the 3.7 million American troops in France. They had served well in the Spanish-American War but in this latest conflict were mostly used for menial work as longshoremen, supply troops, orderlies, and musicians, and none was allowed to rise above the rank of captain. Still, New York's 396th Infantry, the "Harlem Hellfighters," won more than 150 Croix de Guerre decorations and paraded proudly home through the streets of Harlem.

The buildup accelerated throughout 1918, with more than a million Americans engaged in combat by the end of the year. But America had no Air Force squadrons in 1917 and only eight in May 1918, all equipped with French airplanes. The government made the mistake of trying to design new planes and guns instead of adapting British and French weapons already being manufactured by American factories. Artillery, planes, and machine guns all had to be bought or borrowed from the French. Pershing's army received American guns just in time to fire a salute of celebration at the armistice.

After the war, a British historian, Captain Liddell Hart, wrote of the achievement of Pershing and his men: "It is sufficient to say there was perhaps no other man who would or could have built the structure of the American Army on the scale he planned. And without that army the war could hardly have been saved and could not have been won."

Meanwhile, amid growing unrest in Russia, a group of Bolshevik, or Communist, revolutionaries led by V. I. Lenin took control of the government. The new government, eager for peace, quickly acquiesced to harsh German demands and withdrew from the war.

This allowed Germany to move thousands of troops from the eastern front to the west to wage all-out war against the French and British.

But by the spring of 1918 troopships were delivering nearly 100,000 American soldiers a month across the Atlantic to help the Allies. They reached the battlefields of France in time to help block the last great German offensive in early June 1918. Germany's government collapsed, and Kaiser Wilhelm, the German ruler, went into exile. The German leaders who replaced the Kaiser accepted a peace offer from the Allies, and all fighting ended at 11 a.m. on November 11, 1918.

"This war is an End, and, also, a Beginning. Never again will darker people of the world occupy just the place they have before." So black scholar W. E. B. Du Bois characterized the effects of World War I. But African American veterans

## The FOURTEEN POINTS

1. Open covenants of peace openly arrived at
2. Freedom of the seas in peace and war
3. Removal of trade barriers
4. Disarmament
5. Impartial adjustment of all colonial claims, based on the principle that the interests of the population have equal weight with those of the power
6. Evacuation of Russia by the Germans and self-determination for the Russian people
7. Evacuation and restoration of Belgium
8. Restoration of France, with restitution of Alsace-Lorraine, taken in 1871
9. Readjustment of Italian frontiers along recognizable lines of nationality
10. Establishment of autonomy for the subject nationalities of Austria-Hungary
11. Evacuation and restoration of Romania, Serbia, and Montenegro
12. Emancipation of Turkey's subject peoples
13. Establishment of an independent Poland with access to the sea
14. Formation of a general association (league) of nations to be formed under specific covenants for the purpose of affording mutual guarantees of political independence and territorial integrity to great and small states alike

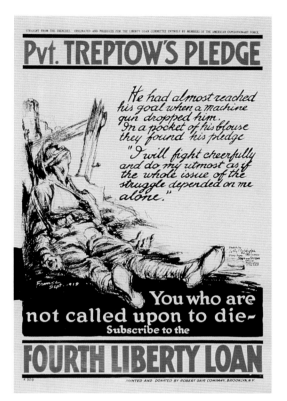

**Pvt. TREPTOW'S PLEDGE**

*He had almost reached his goal when a machine gun dropped him. In a pocket of his blouse they found his pledge "I will fight cheerfully and do my utmost as if the whole issue of the struggle depended on me alone."*

**You who are not called upon to die—**
Subscribe to the

**FOURTH LIBERTY LOAN**

returned from the war to find a rejuvenated Ku Klux Klan and segregation spreading northward with the movement of blacks into industrial cities. The Great War fed the Great Migration, an exodus of 400,000 southern blacks to cities of the North and West between 1916 and 1919.

In December 1918 President Wilson journeyed to Paris to help the Allies prepare a peace treaty that he hoped would lead to limits on arms, fairer colonial policies, and a "League of Nations"—an assembly where all member countries could meet regularly to discuss how to settle quarrels without going to war. His "Fourteen Points" speech on January 8, 1918, was received as a deliverance by millions of civilians and soldiers sick of war on both sides of the trenches. It was reprinted in 60 million pamphlets distributed all over the world.

Wilson was in good spirits on the way to Europe. On the ship, he watched Charlie Chaplin in *A Dog's Life* and joined the sailors in mess for a singalong. He shook hands with some 800 sailors. But, he brooded, "People will endure their tyrants for years, but they tear their deliverers to pieces if a millennium is not created immediately. Yet these ancient wrongs, these present unhappinesses, are not to be remedied in a day or with a wave of the hand. What I seem to see—I hope I am wrong—is a tragedy of disappointment."

When he arrived in Paris with his wife Edith he was greeted as a hero: "Paris," Mrs. Wilson wrote, "was wild with celebration. Every inch was covered with cheering, shouting humanity.... Flowers rained upon us until we were nearly buried."

Despite Wilson's promise of a just peace that would leave no hard feelings, the treaty signed at the Versailles Palace on June 28 forced Germany to give back a large territory it had taken from France 48 years earlier, as well as lands to the east. It was forced to disband most of its armed forces, admit that Germany alone was to blame for starting the war, and pay billions of dollars in reparations.

The harsh terms embittered the defeated Germans even more and planted the seeds of another and even bloodier conflict to come.

---

BELOW: *Red Cross workers, fleeing a German bombardment, scramble to get orphans into a sandbagged bunker in Belgium.*
ABOVE: *A poster hopes to raise money for the war effort from noncombatants at home.*

# WOMEN GO *to the* POLLS

## Suffragette Movement

"Taxation without representation is tyranny," declared some proponents of votes for women. "Give women suffrage," claimed others, "and all wars will cease." Local campaigns supplemented pickets at the White House, hunger strikes, even imprisonment.

By 1910 females composed more than one-fifth of the nation's work force. Women increasingly demanded political liberation to match their newfound financial independence. They shared the vote with men in 11 states by 1914—Wyoming was the first state to grant the vote, in 1869—but nationwide suffrage seemed a distant goal. Advocates wanted a constitutional amendment; male lawmakers sidestepped the issue in Congress, claiming the states should decide.

Women suffragists met formidable opposition from their own sex and from a liquor industry that feared enfranchisement would lead to prohibition.

In the first decade of the 20th century, a solidarity movement began among American women. They began calling themselves feminists around 1912, but some, including, surprisingly, Eleanor Roosevelt, initially opposed female suffrage, arguing that women could do more good working in the social organizations they formed.

Jane Addams (1860-1935) worked from her base in her community house in the slums of Chicago, striving to reform factory hours, sanitation, and health care. At the 1912 convention of the Progressive party, the only major party to support women's suffrage, she seconded the nomination of Teddy Roosevelt.

Alice Paul learned militant tactics in the votes-for-women campaign in London and brought them back to America. By age 23 she had been in prison three times. She and her group picketed the White House, drawing attention to the hypocrisy of President Wilson, who fought for worldwide democracy but would not extend it to American women.

Jeannette Rankin was elected to Congress in 1916, a Republican from Montana. There, a few years later, she got the House to pass the 19th Amendment for female suffrage—by one vote.

Florence Kelley, daughter of a Pennsylvania congressman and close friend of Susan B. Anthony, combined

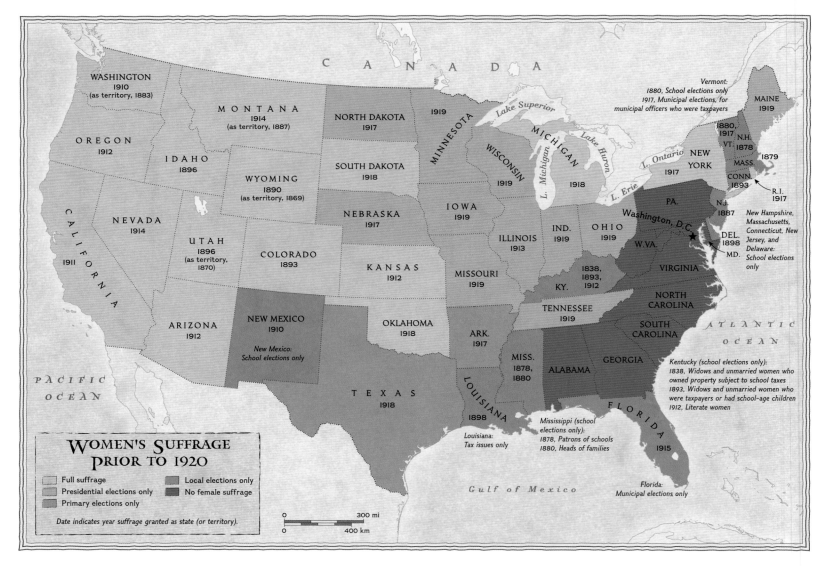

### WOMEN'S SUFFRAGE PRIOR TO 1920

- Full suffrage
- Presidential elections only
- Primary elections only
- Local elections only
- No female suffrage

*Date indicates year suffrage granted as state (or territory).*

WASHINGTON 1910 (as territory, 1883)
OREGON 1912
MONTANA 1914 (as territory, 1887)
IDAHO 1896
NORTH DAKOTA 1917
SOUTH DAKOTA 1918
WYOMING 1890 (as territory, 1869)
NEVADA 1914
UTAH 1896 (as territory, 1870)
CALIFORNIA 1911
NEBRASKA 1917
COLORADO 1893
KANSAS 1912
IOWA 1919
MINNESOTA 1919
WISCONSIN 1919
MICHIGAN 1918
ILLINOIS 1913
INDIANA 1919
OHIO 1919
ARIZONA 1912
NEW MEXICO 1910
OKLAHOMA 1918
MISSOURI 1919
KENTUCKY 1838, 1893, 1912
W.VA.
PA.
VIRGINIA
NEW YORK 1917
NEW JERSEY 1887
DEL. 1898
MD.
Washington, D.C.
ARK. 1917
TENNESSEE 1919
NORTH CAROLINA
SOUTH CAROLINA
TEXAS 1918
LOUISIANA 1898
MISS. 1878, 1880
ALABAMA
GEORGIA
FLORIDA 1915
MAINE 1919
VT: 1880, 1917
N.H. 1878
MASS. 1879
CONN. 1893
R.I. 1917

*New Mexico: School elections only*

*Vermont: 1880, School elections only 1917, Municipal elections, for municipal officers who were taxpayers*

*New Hampshire, Massachusetts, Connecticut, New Jersey, and Delaware: School elections only*

*Kentucky (school elections only): 1838, Widows and unmarried women who owned property subject to school taxes 1893, Widows and unmarried women who were taxpayers or had school-age children 1912, Literate women*

*Mississippi (school elections only): 1878, Patrons of schools 1880, Heads of families*

*Louisiana: Tax issues only*

*Florida: Municipal elections only*

CANADA
Lake Superior
Lake Michigan
Lake Huron
L. Ontario
L. Erie
ATLANTIC OCEAN
PACIFIC OCEAN
Gulf of Mexico

0 — 300 mi
0 — 400 km

passion for social justice with a firm belief in the power of facts. Like a whirlwind,

## SUSAN B. ANTHONY

Susan Anthony, severe in her gold spectacles, black dress and tight austere bob of hair, is the stereotype of the "old maid" reformer of the Gilded Age. She was, in fact, tough, canny, funny in private, difficult to shock and pungent in her rhetoric: "Women," she said, "we might as well be great Newfoundland dogs baying to the moon as to be petitioning for the passage of bills without the power to vote." And again, "For a woman to marry a man for support is a demoralizing condition. And for a man to marry a woman merely because she has a beautiful figure is a degradation." Nor have all the issues she and nineteenth- and early-twentieth-century feminists fought gone away in a hundred years. Argument has hardly ceased over a woman's right to control her reproduction, equality in the workplace, political and legal status or the right, even, to dress as she likes.

–Harold Evans, 1998

she stormed into the sweatshops and tenements of Chicago to learn for herself how women and children were being exploited. *Hull-House Maps and Papers* of 1895 documented what she found. In New York in 1899 she became general secretary of the new National Consumers' League and organized boycotts of products from rogue employers. She helped develop a model statute of minimum wage laws, which were enacted in 13 states and the District of Columbia.

Women were second-class citizens in other respects as well. They could not divorce drunken or abusive husbands. They could not go to college. They could not exert property rights without their husbands' support. American law still followed an interpretation of jurist Blackstone's dictum that "the husband and wife are one, and that one is the husband." Between 1893 and 1908, according to scholar Nell Irvin Painter, suffragists waged 480 separate campaigns just to get the issue of suffrage on state ballots and succeeded only 17 times. Of these only three passed—Colorado (1893) and Idaho and Utah (1896).

The major roles played by women during the fighting in World War I did much to break down the final resistance to women's suffrage. Amendments to the Constitution giving women the vote had been introduced into Congress in 1878 and 1914, but both were soundly defeated. By 1918, just after the war, both major political parties were committed to women's suffrage, and the amendment was carried by the necessary two-thirds majorities in both the House and the Senate in January 1918 and June 1919, respectively

On August 26, 1920, women gained the right to vote with ratification of the 19th Amendment to the Constitution. "The right of citizens of the United States to vote shall not be denied or abridged by the United States or by any State on account of sex."

ABOVE: *A patriotically festooned auto carries a group of young girls to a suffrage meeting around 1920. Looking ahead to a time when they would be eligible to vote, two carry a placard reading "Votes for Us When We Are Women."*

# GOING DRY

## Prohibition and Repeal

**B**essie Laythe Scovell, president, addressed the annual convention of the WCTU, the Woman's Christian Temperance Union, in Mankato, Minnesota, at the end of the 19th century.

"Beloved Comrades: We are met in our twenty-fourth annual convention in the historic city of Mankato, where nearly four decades ago, thirty-nine of the five hundred Indian prisoners, captured by Col. Sibley, were executed. This act ended the Sioux War, which had been the terror to the inhabitants of three states. More than seven hundred white people had been massacred and many thousands driven from their homes. Today we are met to execute plans (not Indians) to carry on our peaceful war for 'God and Home and Native Land.' There is an enemy in the land more stealthy than the Indian, more deadly in its work—the alcoholic liquor traffic. It is killing thousands annually and destroying hundreds of homes. We toil and sacrifice today to hasten the tomorrow when this enemy will be executed upon the gibbet of public opinion, and the liquor traffic be as dead as the Indians buried in yonder mound."

In the U.S. an alcoholic beverage was defined as any drink with more than 0.5 percent alcohol. Beer had 3 to 8 percent, wine 10 to 20. The move to ban its manufacture and sale arose during a period of strong religious revivalism in the 1820s and 1830s when idealists were hopeful of eliminating the flaws from human beings. Drunks were considered highly flawed.

The places where they drank—dark, rough, all-male saloons and bars—were thought to be destructive of family life and factory discipline. Prostitutes hung out in them, wages were gambled away, and ward

---

### F. SCOTT FITZGERALD

"**T**hey were careless people, Tom and Daisy—they smashed up things and creatures and then retreated back into their money or their vast carelessness, or whatever it was that kept them together, and let other people clean up the mess they had made." In *The Great Gatsby* Fitzgerald wrote of the love and death of a wealthy bootlegger, as told by a curious young cousin who was a spectator.

Young, handsome, and socially privileged, Fitzgerald acted out the legend of "the sad young men" who made up Gertrude Stein's "lost generation." Disillusioned youths who flouted traditions and taboos cherished by their parents, they and their girls were the flappers of the Jazz Age. "The very rich are different from you and me," he wrote. "They possess and enjoy early and it does something to them, makes them soft where we are hard, and cynical where we are trustful in a way that, unless you were born rich, it is very difficult to understand. They think, deep in their hearts, that they are better than we are...." Fitzgerald and his troubled wife Zelda threw themselves into having fun—"I had everything I wanted and knew I would never be so happy again."

But beneath the fun-filled surface a poignancy emerged. Fitzgerald ended *Gatsby* "So we beat on, boats against the current, borne back ceaselessly into the past."

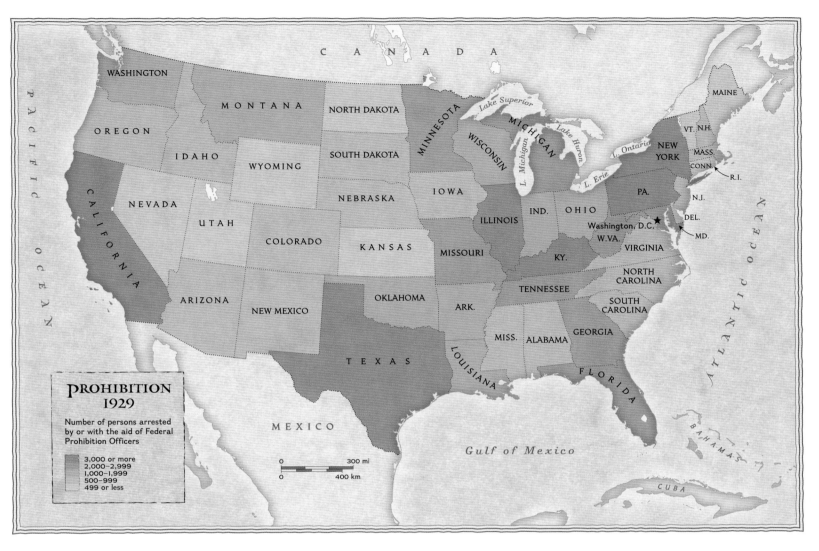

PROHIBITION
1929

Number of persons arrested
by or with the aid of Federal
Prohibition Officers

3,000 or more
2,000–2,999
1,000–1,999
500–999
499 or less

bosses visited to buy votes on election day.

The first prohibition law was passed in Maine in 1846, and a number of state legislatures followed suit before the Civil War. By January 1920 prohibition was already in effect in 33 states. The 18th Amendment to the Constitution went into effect on January 29, 1920—and the country went into shock.

Prohibition was not popular and, as a result, not very firmly enforced. Police were easily bribed to overlook the beer that was still being brewed, and one federal agent, Izzy Einstein, reported that in most American cities it took just half an hour to find alcohol. In Chicago, he said, it took 21 minutes, Atlanta 17, Pittsburgh 11—and in New Orleans the search occupied just 35 seconds! (His taxi driver provided it.) Bootleggers imported much of their illegal bounty from Canada and shipped in the rest. Ships carrying liquor anchored just outside New York's jurisdiction, and bootleggers used their ingenuity to get it ashore. Some liquor, according to historian Harold Evans, "came in as fruit, some was flown in and dropped in lakes, some was fired ashore in torpedoes."

Illicit bars called speakeasies screened their clientele at the door and hid their liquor from the occasional raid by police. New York's "21" on 52nd Street still displayed, in 1996, a cellar stacked with bottles hidden behind a brick wall that slid aside at the touch of a secret button.

On December 5, 1933, Utah provided the two-thirds majority needed when it voted for the 21st Amendment to the Constitution—which repealed the 18th, Prohibition. It was the first, and so far the only, time a constitutional amendment has been repealed.

Prohibition was not a complete failure. Public drunkenness virtually disappeared, and while some people died or went blind from bad moonshine, diseases and deaths from alcohol declined. The head of the Hudson Guild in New York said, "A great number of men who always stopped in at the saloon on the way home and almost emptied their pay packets now bring their wages home. They and their families are living more peaceably than they did before."

But Prohibition spawned the organized crime families that still exist. Chicagoan John Torrio, the father of mod-ern American gangsterism, made bootlegging a multimillion-dollar business by doing deals with the big brewers, bribing the police and politicians, and getting the Chicago gangs to agree to divide up the bootlegging turf. In 1923 a Democrat, Judge William E. Dever, was elected mayor and set out to enforce Prohibition. His crusade set off a storm of gangland killings as bootleggers, suffering shrinking profits, cut into one another's territories. A rival shot Torrio, who survived and fled home to Italy but not before handing over to Al Capone his breweries, speakeasies, and brothels worth tens of millions of dollars.

Even women, who had been among the most vociferous "drys," organized for the repeal on the grounds of individual freedom. After the repeal of Prohibition, several states continued independently to ban liquor, but by 1966 all had bowed to the inevitable.

OPPOSITE: *Chief result of Prohibition: the proliferation of illegal saloons, or speakeasies. A sign on the pavement shows the way to one, around 1925.*

# LIFE in MENLO PARK

### The Genius of Thomas Edison

There is no substitution for hard work," said Thomas Edison. And also, "Genius is one percent inspiration and ninety-nine percent perspiration." Having graduated from what was then known as the "school of hard knocks," he knew what he was talking about. And his hard work paid off. By the time of his death he had 1,093 patents to his name, the most productive inventor in the history of the human race.

He was born in 1847, youngest of seven children, and had a harsh childhood, frequently beaten by his father. He may sometimes have deserved disciplining: At six he set a fire in the barn "just to see what it would do." At 12, with just three months of schooling behind him, he dropped out and began working on a train, selling newspapers and other items on the run between Port Huron, Michigan, where he lived, and Detroit. Then he found the Detroit Free Library and spent hours there, devouring everything that came his way.

Progressive deafness—evidently caused by a bout of scarlet fever and untreated ear infections—began to plague him early on but did not interfere with his first real job—as a telegrapher. He spent several years knocking around the country, working at outposts of Western Union. His work as a telegrapher led to his first successful invention, a recording stock ticker, useful to investors and speculators. He manufactured the tickers himself, and made enough money to hire his first assistant, John Ott, who would be with him through all the great discoveries.

By the spring of 1876, prosperous and pushing 30, he bought land in Menlo Park, a New Jersey hamlet 25 miles southwest of New York City. Along with fame and money had come lawsuits, and to give himself a quiet place to concentrate and work, he built what his biographer Matthew Josephson called "the first industrial research laboratory in America, or in the world, and in itself one of the most remarkable of Edison's many inventions."

His staff was expected to work nearly round the clock, as did their boss. He had mastered the art of the catnap and could doze off for a few minutes virtually anywhere and anytime. "My children grew up without knowing their father," said John Ott. "When I did get home at night, which was seldom, they were in bed."

His most original invention came out of experiments with an embossing recorder for telegraphy, in 1877, when he happened onto the principles of the phonograph. Simply put, he found that if he took a vibrating diaphragm from an experimental telephone, attached a

blunt pinpoint to it, ran a piece of waxed paper under it, and shouted into the transmitter, the pinpoint would leave indentations in the wax. It would follow, he surmised, that if he ran the paper through another machine with a similar stylus and diaphragm, he would get the sound back.

On July 18, 1877, the primitive phonograph worked. Edison yelled "Halloo!" into the device and heard a recognizable human response. Four months later an improved machine, made of brass and iron with a revolving cylinder turned by a hand crank, worked even better. Edison's high-pitched voice could be clearly heard reciting one full stanza of "Mary Had a Little Lamb." He hauled the machine to Washington, where he demonstrated it to the representatives and senators and even to President Rutherford B. Hayes.

In the summer of 1878 Edison took his first vacation, traveling to Wyoming to observe a total eclipse of the sun. An idle conversation with a traveling companion led him to begin considering the idea of a workable electric light. Sir Humphry Davy had demonstrated an arc light in London 70 years earlier, and since then many people had recognized the potential of electricity for illumination.

He worked himself and his men up to 20 hours a day for weeks on end and, in the end, made an incandescent lamp that glowed red and burned for 40 hours. It would have burned longer, but Edison deliberately increased the voltage to see how much it would support and, like all lightbulbs, it burned out. More inventions were needed to generate electric power and somehow deliver it to the consumer, a high priority to Edison, always the practical inventor. Devices for sealing the bulbs, screw-in sockets, light switches, safety devices, meters, and a host of other contrivances had to be developed.

But in just three years the basic work was done. He bought some rundown real estate in lower Manhattan and built his first power station. It opened on September 4, 1882, with one dynamo servicing 85 subscribers. The Electric Age was upon us.

He grew imperious and crusty with age and, in the 1920s, tried to develop a domestic source of rubber. He settled on goldenrod, and hybridized a plant that grew 14 feet tall. This engrossed him in his final years. He and his wife were close friends of the Henry Fords, vacationing together for 25 years. They enjoyed "camping," along with Harvey Firestone. Naturalist John Burroughs originally guided them as, they said, they escaped "fictitious civilization." When they grew

too old for camping, the Edisons and Fords vacationed together to Florida. In 1931, as Edison lay dying, Ford asked one of the inventor's sons to capture his father's last breath in a vial, which Ford kept at his estate for many years.

It may have taken uremia, Bright's disease, diabetes, and a gastric ulcer to finish him; he died on October 18, 1931, only 40 hours before the 52nd birthday of the electric light.

## MENLO PARK

A tower built to commemorate the anniversary of the development of the incandescent light was built at Menlo Park in 1929. It was said to resemble a giant beanpole with an enormous light bulb on top of it. An eternal light—electric, not a flame—burned at its base. The tower stood in the middle of the field where the Edison laboratory had once stood. A more permanent and attractive tower was under construction in 1936 when a severe storm swept through the region, knocking down not only the original tower but the newer one under construction. The eternal light remained alight, powered by batteries. The new tower was finally completed in 1938 and dedicated on what would have been Thomas Edison's 91st birthday.

At a dedication of a plaque at the sight in 1925, Mina Edison, the inventor's second wife, spoke: "I, who have had the privilege of living with a great mind, a remarkable personality, a true husband and a devoted lover for nearly forty years, wish, in paying my tribute, to congratulate 'the old pioneers' upon having had the opportunity of working...with one of the greatest workers of all time....him whom we all hold so dear."

The laboratory buildings where Edison did his work at Menlo Park are no longer there, having been removed in 1929 by Henry Ford to his Greenfield Village Museum in Dearborn, Michigan.

ABOVE: *A picture of brooding genius, Thomas Edison glares at one of his inventions, probably an early phonograph. He received more than a thousand patents for his inventions, which included the lightbulb.*
OPPOSITE: *The bulb's ubiquity can be seen from space in a nighttime portrait of the U.S.*

# PICTURES *That* TALK

## *Movies in America*

**G**o hire some girls, any girls, so long as they're pretty, especially around the knees." Thus did filmmaker Mack Sennett explain how he found bathing beauties to appear in his films. Sitting in the dark, watching flickering images on the screen before them, Americans learned who they were and what it meant to be an American. During an average week in 1938, when the country was still struggling to shake loose from the Great Depression, America's population of 130 million people bought 80 million movie tickets. Life on the silver screen was richer, fuller, more exciting, and filled with girls with pretty knees.

From fumbling beginnings around the turn of the 20th century, movies evolved from "peep shows" to complex, full-length spectacles shown in luxurious movie palaces that seated thousands. By early in the 1920s movies had become America's fifth most lucrative industry.

With film that required a lot of light for exposure, the fledgling industry resettled from New York to an obscure section of Los Angeles called Hollywood, where the sun was more reliable and the temperatures conducive to working outside, all year round. Ironically, Hollywood—which came to be known for its sinful stars—was laid out by a developer who hoped the subdivision would reflect his sober religious principles. Horace Wilcox was a prohibitionist real estate developer from Kansas who laid out Hollywood in 1887 and named it for the home of a Chicago friend. In 1910, worried by its scant water supply, the residents voted to become a part of Los Angeles.

There the first moguls—mostly ambitious, hard-charging Jewish immigrants or sons of immigrants who had begun in the business running nickelodeons—invented the modern studio system. They saw the new medium's potential—a rich but inexpensive source of entertainment for working-class Americans—and moved away from the cheap and slightly disreputable one-reelers that New York filmmakers had been turning out. They founded studios that controlled stables of producers, directors, writers, and stars. Films got longer and better.

*The Count of Monte Cristo* of 1908 was one of the first narrative movies; it had a plot. Filming on it was begun in Chicago and completed in Hollywood. Hollywood's first studio was built on a lot on Sunset Boulevard a few years later, and soon some 20 companies were filming in the area. Cecil B. DeMille, Jesse Lasky, and Samuel Goldwyn made *The Squaw Man* in 1914 in a barn just a block from today's Hollywood and Vine. By 1916 the center of America's film industry had moved from New York to Hollywood. Well-known authors—F. Scott Fitzgerald, Aldous Huxley, Evelyn Waugh, William Faulkner—all took jobs in Hollywood, writing screenplays for what they considered unseemly sums of money. But "Hollywood money isn't money," said writer Dorothy Parker. "It's congealed snow, melts in your hand, and there you are."

Early comedies, like those of Mack Sennett, who improvised hundreds of one- and two-reel films, often working on several simultaneously, tickled America's funny bone. Inept policemen who careened around corners clinging to their jalopies, riots of pie throwing, sight gags that were ingenious and sometimes dangerous, the high and mighty slipping on banana peels and falling face-first into mud puddles—all kept moviegoers rolling in the aisles. Charlie Chaplin rejected slapstick in favor of subtle characterizations and a wistful sadness.

Producers at first tried to keep actors anonymous, fearing that if they got to be famous they would ask for more money. And did they ever! Cute Mary Pickford, who could convincingly play a 10-year-old when she was in her late 20s, was a shrewd and iron-willed negotiator, and by 1915 she had negotiated her pay to

### CLARA BOW

**C**lara Bow's beauty made her a silent-era star, but her voice killed her career. She was born poor in Brooklyn in 1905. In high school she won a beauty contest and set out for Hollywood. A small part in *Beyond the Rainbow* in 1922 brought her to the attention of producers, and she was soon featured in silent films like *Mantrap* and *Dancing Mothers*. She became the country's "It Girl" in 1927 when she starred in the film of Elinor Glyn's novel *It*. With bobbed hair and big eyes, she came to personify the public's idea of the sexy, free-living flapper of the 1920s.

She was living a wild life to match her image, and when scandals broke, her career suffered. And when "talkies" came along and fans heard her thick Brooklyn accent, it ended. She moved to a cattle ranch in Nevada with her husband, former Western star Rex Bell, and lived there peacefully until her death in 1965.

$10,000 a week. Chaplin and Douglas Fairbanks were soon at the same level, and in 1919, to head off a salary squeeze by the studios, the three banded together with director D. W. Griffith to form their own company, United Artists. Said one executive: "The lunatics have taken charge of the asylum."

Stars powered the system. Britain's Lord Louis Mountbattan said of Mary Pickford and Douglas Fairbanks: They were "treated like royalty, and in fact they behaved in the same sort of dignified way that royalty did." When the first great "Latin lover," Rudolph Valentino, died in 1926 of peritonitis, 30,000 fans swarmed his funeral. There were reports that at least a dozen overwrought fans committed suicide.

When the movies learned to talk, much changed. Stars with thick European accents disappeared and trained Broadway actors took over. Directors emerged as the new stars, with men like Alfred Hitchcock, Cecil B. DeMille, and Otto Preminger choosing the cast for their films, hiring technicians, coaching the actors, making deci-

sions about lighting and camera angles and the final editing. Movie magazines fed fans' desire to know everything about their favorite stars, and the studio publicity machines cranked out features that made their stars seem like ordinary people, on the one hand, and exotic creatures of wealth and luxury on the other. Spectacular features from directors like Victor Flemming and David Lean crowded the screen with "casts of thousands." A new generation of comics like the Marx Brothers inspired mayhem on the screen, and the "screwball" comedies—described by a term from baseball, a pitch that darts up and dips down in unexpected ways—included Frank Capra's *It Happened One Night,* and, in 1938, Howard Hawks's *Bringing Up Baby* with Cary Grant and Katharine Hepburn. Jack Lemmon and Tony Curtis starred with Marilyn Monroe in Billy Wilder's rollicking *Some Like It Hot,* playing nearly the entire film in drag as female musicians.

Musicals, war movies, gangland pictures, mysteries, and horror films all attracted moviegoers to the box office. But perhaps nowhere did the movies so

eloquently speak to Americans and their past as in the Westerns. The genre chronicled the progression of the pioneers across the continent—and incidentally the destruction of the native population, who served merely as convenient villains until well into the 20th century. Iconic figures such as Alan Ladd in *Shane* or Gary Cooper in *High Noon* or John Wayne in *Stagecoach* represented Americans as they thought they might have been. Only later did the movies begin to reflect upon the effects of Manifest Destiny on the national character and the violence born there that still plagues America.

After World War II, more and more filming was done on locations around the world, emptying Hollywood studios and sound stages. They became the production sites of many television shows. By 1960 Hollywood had become the source of much of American network television.

---

ABOVE: *Moviegoers flock to see* City Lights, *the latest Charlie Chaplin film around 1931.*
OPPOSITE: *Studios soon learned what fans wanted, issuing autographed studio portraits of early stars such as Clara Bow.*

# WAVES *of* NEW AMERICANS

## *Immigration to the States*

Immigration patterns have strongly reflected changes in U.S. policy. Record keeping began in 1820, when ships' masters were required to report arriving alien passengers. The designation "immigrant" was first made in 1868. Only "paupers, vagabonds and possible convicts" were excluded until the immigration ban on Chinese in 1882. Minimum health qualifications were set in the 1890s.

With the end of the Napoleonic Wars in 1815, German farmers and Irish peasants fled hunger caused by overpopulation and by blight on a native New World crop—the potato. The more fortunate, such as English craftsmen, came for better opportunities in America.

The principal immigration reception center in the U.S. was a small island off the southwestern tip of Manhattan named for merchant Samuel Ellis, who owned it in the 1770s. Between 1892 and 1954, 17 million immigrants entered the U.S. through its portals. First was a 15-year-old Irish girl named Annie Moore, who was at the head of the line when the facility opened on January 1, 1892. Her two brothers were right behind her.

Tragically, just five years after opening, a fire on Ellis Island burned the immigration station completely, killing no one but destroying many years of federal and state immigration records dating back to 1855. In December 1900, a new facility opened—built of fireproof brick and stone.

Of the 17 million immigrants who were processed at Ellis Island, five million were first- and second-class passengers. They were not required to undergo the inspection process on Ellis Island but were given a cursory inspection aboard ship, then passed through. The government theorized that these wealthier pas-

## MRS. O'LEARY'S COW

"Late one night, when we were all in bed, Mrs. O'Leary lit a lantern in the shed. Her cow kicked it over, Then winked her eye and said, 'There'll be a hot time in the old town tonight!'"

Maybe she did and maybe she didn't. Kate O'Leary supposedly told several people the morning after the blaze that she was in the barn when one of her cows kicked over a lantern. In fact the 1871 fire did almost surely begin in the vicinity of a crowded family barn owned by the O'Leary family at 137 DeKoven Street, where a horse, a calf, and five cows were kept, one of them named Daisy. Or Madeline, or Gwendolyn, in other tellings. And curiosity seekers claimed to find broken pieces of such a lantern in the ashes behind her cottage.

But there is testimony that Kate was in bed early that evening, and the official inquiry by the city found no proof of her guilt. And the broken lamp disappeared, "borrowed" by an Irish servant who never returned it. Additionally, when the 40th anniversary of the fire rolled around a police reporter named Michael Ahern claimed, in the *Chicago Tribune,* that he and two friends had concocted the whole story. The two friends, now dead, couldn't comment.

Over the years, other theories emerged: Some boys were having a smoke. A meteor fell to Earth, breaking into fragments as it fell and igniting blazes not only in Chicago but also in Wisconsin and Michigan the same night. Or maybe it was spontaneous combustion. Or maybe Daisy really did it all by herself.

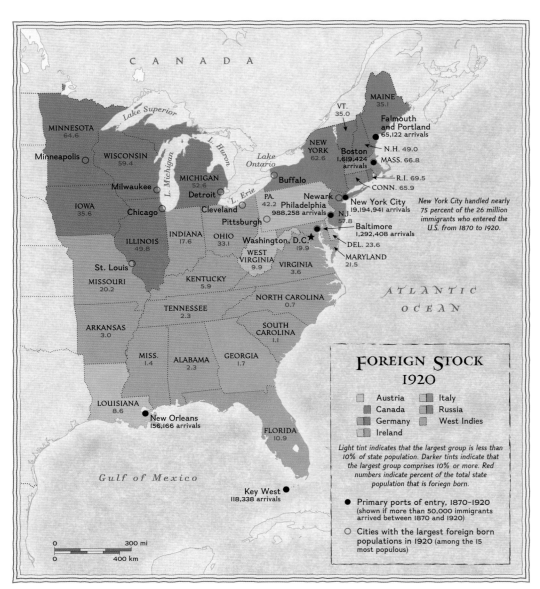

FOREIGN STOCK 1920

- Austria
- Canada
- Germany
- Ireland
- Italy
- Russia
- West Indies

*Light tint indicates that the largest group is less than 10% of state population. Darker tints indicate that the largest group comprises 10% or more. Red numbers indicate percent of the total state population that is foreign born.*

● Primary ports of entry, 1870-1920 *(shown if more than 50,000 immigrants arrived between 1870 and 1920)*

○ Cities with the largest foreign born populations in 1920 *(among the 15 most populous)*

*New York City handled nearly 75 percent of the 26 million immigrants who entered the U.S. from 1870 to 1920.*

sengers were less likely than their poorer brethren to become public charges due to illnesses or legal problems. Only steerage and third-class passengers were sent through Ellis Island, where they underwent a medical and legal inspection.

Doctors would scan every immigrant that came off the ship for obvious physical ailments and by 1916 had become adept at conducting "six second physicals." In those few seconds, they boasted they could spot various medical conditions—anemia, tuberculosis, varicose veins, rickets, "feeble-mindedness"—that would bar an immigrant from entry. Only about two percent were excluded, most because the inspector decided on his own that the immigrant was likely to end up on American welfare rolls, or because of a contagious disease. Still, it was heartbreaking for the immigrant to have come so far only to be turned away at the last minute.

The flood of immigrants into the country reached a peak, and Quota Laws were passed in 1921 and the National Origins Act in 1929. These attempted both to slow immigration and to control its character: Quotas of immigrants allowed in were based on a percentage of the number of an ethnic group already here. The ethnic flavor of the "old immigrants" was protected.

The Irish, having left a homeland one observer called "a complete pauper warren," crowded into northeastern cities. Jobs paying as little as $1.50 a week were welcome. Despite low pay, each year they sent millions of dollars home to buy passages for relatives. By 1845 the potato blight in Ireland had become the potato famine. In six years a million people died of disease and starvation, many of them buried in mass graves. Nearly a million more came to the U.S., making up 45 percent of all immigrants in the 1840s. The number of Irish immigrants peaked in 1851, when 221,253 of the unfortunates arrived.

The Germans—skilled craftsmen, shopkeepers, and farmers—followed the frontier to cheap land. After the failed 1848 revolution, political refugee "forty-eighters" joined the influx, which soon surpassed even that of the Irish. Few, except those lured by Texas land offers, settled in the South, where labor was slave and land was scarce. Although clustering in the Midwest, German settlements sprang up wherever opportunity occurred. In the peak year 1882 America welcomed more than 250,000 Germans.

Welcome for immigrants was tempered by the expectation that they would, as John Quincy Adams put it, "cast off their European skin" and assimilate. The Irish, however, had to contend with a sometimes violent anti-Catholicism that gave rise to the nativist Know-Nothings. Partly in defense, partly by preference, the Irish began to consolidate political power in northern cities. Even there they often faced prejudice—signs read "No Irish need apply"—and many turned to city politics. Others had careers in labor unions or the church. By

ABOVE: *Immigrant families huddle on the deck of the S. S. Pennland in 1893, en route to a new life in America. Between 1890 and 1914, nearly 16 million European immigrants arrived in America.*

living in tiny dark rooms lacking windows or any means of sanitation. Men worked long hours in factories with dangerous work conditions. Seamstresses worked in sweatshops that became notorious on March 25, 1911, when a fire broke out at the Triangle Waist Company, killing 146 laborers.

## Becoming a Citizen

"Wide open and unguarded stand our gates, / And through them presses a wild motley throng." Things were already changing in 1892 when Thomas Bailey Aldrich's poem, "The Unguarded Gates," appeared in the *Atlantic Monthly*. The newly opened facilities at Ellis Island in New York Harbor were scrutinizing arrivals as never before. There 16 million immigrants in all were not so much welcomed to the country as asked to prove their worthiness to enter. Still, in the 21st century, such free and welcoming portals seem unimaginable.

New York City handled the lion's share —75 percent—of the 26 million immigrants who entered from 1870 to 1920. In the busiest decade, 1900 to 1909, nine million people arrived. Numbers from northern Europe were at an apogee, from southern and eastern Europe still rising. The facilities that greeted immigrants ranged from federal efficiency at Ellis Island to laxness at New Orleans. Ports competed for the transoceanic traffic—and made sure that not too many immigrants lingered; railroads ran right onto wharves. The first American soil an immigrant set foot on might be in St. Louis.

Chain migration—the tendency to follow in the footsteps of friends and relatives—gave ports different ethnic character. The Irish preferred Boston; Germans, Baltimore; Italians, New York and Philadelphia. Gulf of Mexico ports drew on Cuba and the Caribbean rim. The West Coast extended an ambivalent welcome across the Pacific. Chinese laborers surged into San Francisco until their exclusion in 1882. From 1900 to 1909, 139,712 Japanese came to the U.S., half

1870 the Irish had become the largest foreign-born group in California.

There was money in immigrants, and promoters of states, railroads, and steamship lines fanned the flames of "America fever." A Minnesota pamphlet cajoled, "Exchange the tyrannies and thankless toil of the old world for the freedom and independence of the new." Scandinavians came. Even though their new life might be hard, they sent prepaid tickets home. Norwegians, Swedes, and Danes (in that order by total immigrants) arrived in great numbers after the Civil War, forced out of the homelands by exploding populations and a shortage of good farmland. Norway was second to Ireland in the loss of its 19th-century population to the U.S. Scandinavians, many of them farmers, lumbermen, and miners, settled mainly in the upper Midwest. Later many went to the Pacific Coast in search of land and jobs. "This is just like Norway!"

wrote one Norwegian describing Washington State's Puget Sound area.

The English blended in easily. At first many aimed to become independent farmers; some started utopian communities in the Midwest. Yet their greatest impact was new skills and technology brought to mines and factories. Drawn to Mormonism, so many settled in Utah that by 1890 one out of seven residents of Salt Lake City was English. Migration peaked in the 1880s with a wave of young industrial workers.

As industry grew, more laborers came alone. British workers sought higher pay in the U.S. factories, while Canadians fled economic depression. Nineteen million people immigrated in the 19th century, enabling the U.S. to populate the West and become the world's industrial leader.

Such massive waves of new immigrants, most of them farmers, led to exploitation. In cities, hundreds of poor families were crammed in tenements, of them to Honolulu. In 1920, 43 percent of Hawaii's population was Japanese.

The great wave of immigrants that peaked as the century turned consisted of those "pulled" and those "pushed." The pulled followed economic incentives and often came alone, later returning home or using their savings to bring home to them, family member by family member. Italians poured in, four million by 1920. Most were males, intending to return to Italy, and almost half did. Greeks, Romanians, and Serbs returned in even greater percentages.

Among those "pushed" were three million Jews driven from Russia by edict and pogrom. Nearly one-third of Eastern Europe's Jews had arrived by 1924. Their ghettos became springboards into industry and the professions, just as the Old Country neighborhoods of Poles and Czechs, Latvians and Turks, provided berths before those groups edged into the cultural mainstream.

Beyond the "arched gateway" of New York's harbor lay work in the industrial boomtowns extending west to the Mississippi River. By 1920 the northern states east of the river, taken together with the West Coast, held 91 percent of the foreign-born population. Immigrants held majorities in many major cities, though they were being gained on by

---

## The NEW COLOSSUS

On a Plaque at the Statue of Liberty:
*Not like the brazen giant of Greek fame,*
*With conquering limbs astride from land to land;*
*Here at our sea-washed, sunset gates shall stand*
*A mighty woman with a torch, whose flame*
*Is the imprisoned lightning, and her name*
*Mother of Exiles. From her beacon-hand*
*Glows world-wide welcome; her mild*
     *eyes command*
*the air-bridged harbor that twin cities frame.*
*"Keep ancient lands, your storied pomp!"*
     *cries she*
*With silent lips. "Give me your tired, your poor,*
*Your huddled masses yearning to breathe free,*
*The wretched refuse of your teeming shore.*
*Send these, the homeless, tempest-tost to me,*
*I lift my lamp beside the golden door!"*

–Emma Lazarus

---

native-born Americans—and by their own children—everywhere but in the southern New England states.

Seventy-five percent of immigrants settled in the cities of a nation that was 50 percent rural. Though no group formed a majority in any major city, Jews and Italians had a plurality in New York and Philadelphia, Polish in Chicago and Cleveland, Germans in Pittsburgh and Milwaukee, Irish in Boston and San Francisco. Factory owners found cheap, tractable labor among the recent arrivals, replacing Germans and Irish with Eastern Europeans. One Pittsburgh mill owner advertised, "Syrians, Poles, and Romanians preferred."

Following the huge influx of immigrants from southern and eastern Europe in the first decade of the 20th century, the Immigration Act of 1924 was passed. Besides adopting a system of quotas based on national origin and excluding many Asians, the act set an annual ceiling on immigration.

In 1924 ethnic quotas all but closed the gates on eastern and southern Europe. Only after World War II would the Mother of Exiles again find a place in her heart for refugees, welcoming them by the hundreds of thousands from war-torn Europe, from behind the Iron Curtain, from Cuba, and, after 1975, from Southeast Asia.

A 1965 law kept a ceiling but scrapped preferences and exclusions, favoring only relatives of those admitted and persons with certain skills. Since 1965 most immigrants have come from Asia, Latin America, and the West Indies.

The gates that opened wide for refugees closed to a crack on those fleeing simple poverty. They came anyway: at least 300,000 illegal entrants a year in the 1970s and 1980s, most slipping across the Mexican border, an often hazardous tactic that demonstrates the desperation of many new arrivals. Today's gatekeeper might be named Fiorelli or Kukowski, today's entrant Salgado or Liu, but otherwise that most American of dramas, the immigrant saga, plays on with the same plot and provokes the same passions as in 1892.

---

OPPOSITE: *Squalid tenements welcomed many immigrants to America, including this New York family of 1888.*

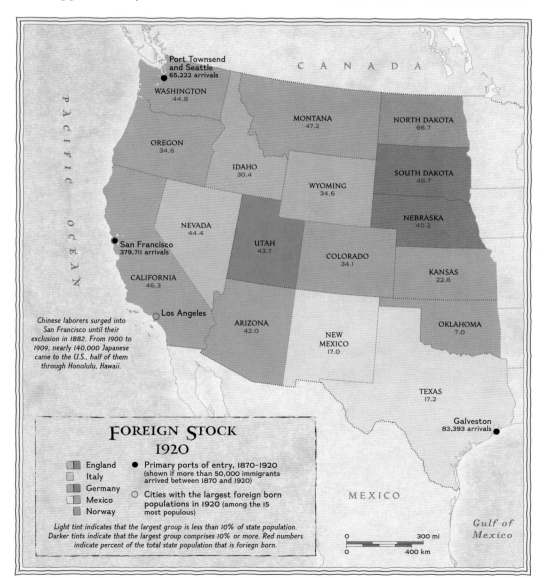

Port Townsend and Seattle
65,222 arrivals

CANADA

WASHINGTON
44.8

MONTANA
47.2

NORTH DAKOTA
66.7

OREGON
34.6

IDAHO
30.4

SOUTH DAKOTA
48.7

WYOMING
34.6

NEBRASKA
40.2

NEVADA
44.4

UTAH
43.7

COLORADO
34.1

KANSAS
22.6

San Francisco
379,711 arrivals

CALIFORNIA
46.3

Los Angeles

ARIZONA
42.0

NEW MEXICO
17.0

OKLAHOMA
7.0

*Chinese laborers surged into San Francisco until their exclusion in 1882. From 1900 to 1909, nearly 140,000 Japanese came to the U.S., half of them through Honolulu, Hawaii.*

PACIFIC OCEAN

TEXAS
17.2

Galveston
83,393 arrivals

MEXICO

Gulf of Mexico

**FOREIGN STOCK 1920**

- England
- Italy
- Germany
- Mexico
- Norway

● Primary ports of entry, 1870-1920
(shown if more than 50,000 immigrants arrived between 1870 and 1920)

○ Cities with the largest foreign born populations in 1920 (among the 15 most populous)

*Light tint indicates that the largest group is less than 10% of state population. Darker tints indicate that the largest group comprises 10% or more. Red numbers indicate percent of the total state population that is foreign born.*

0       300 mi
0    400 km

# RIDING *the* AIRWAVES

⤬

## *Radio Reaches America*

U.S. Patents 841,387 and 879,532 went to Lee de Forest. In 1907 his Audion vacuum tube used electric power to amplify electromagnetic waves, an important step in transmitting the human voice. De Forest installed the first radiophones on U.S. Navy vessels. Radios used vacuum tubes, which could be replaced separately, until smaller, cheaper, and more durable transistors took over in the 1960s.

Riding airwaves, we mock mountains, scorn rivers, shove plains aside. Radio

though a good set soon cost almost $100, by 1924 Americans had bought 2.5 million. Radio commercials began in August 1922; ten minutes on WEAF (later WNBC) cost $100. Sponsors underwrote many popular programs. The first regular licensed broadcasting began on August 20 of that year.

Radio brought rural families closer to news and weather reports in the 1920s and 1930s. Radio networks used program circuits, AT&T lines akin to telephone wires. Only 583 stations—all AM—were oper-

The first U.S. President to recognize the enormous power that radio gave him—to enter America's living rooms and address the people directly—was FDR. He gave scores of "fireside chats" during his years in office, the first on Sunday night, March 12, 1933, the day before the country's reorganized banks, which had been closed a few days before for a four-day "bank holiday," were to reopen. An estimated 60 million hung on his every word as he explained the banking system in warm and friendly tones and with candor and thoroughness. The next day confidence was restored when the banks reopened.

He used fireside chats effectively to belittle critics, explain complex issues, and rally the American people to policies. On one occasion he said, "Here is one third of a nation ill-nourished, ill-clad, ill-housed—now!

defies geographic barriers that once slowed news, isolated communities, and daunted all but the hardiest travelers.

Citizens band radio *(comin' atcha, good buddy; ten-four!)* proved a useful tool for private communication, as had marine VHF and amateur short-wave radio.

Originally made as hobby items, radios started appearing in stores in 1920. Even

ating in 1934. To cut down on interference, regulations reduced the number of stations broadcasting at night by half.

On December 6, 1923, President Calvin Coolidge addressed Congress and for the first time a presidential address was broadcast; Orson Welles's radio dramatization of *War of the Worlds* caused a nationwide panic on October 30, 1938.

## EDWARD R. MURROW

"This...is London," intoned Murrow nightly, from his posting in Europe. Millions imitated his preamble, allowing a second of hesitation between the first word and the second. He grew up in the Northwest and studied drama at Washington state. He came to New York to work for CBS in 1935 and two years later was posted to Europe, just in time for World War II. His first broadcast was from Vienna in 1938, where he reported the Anschluss, Austria's capitulation to Germany. Everyone recognized his voice. He was the first journalist to employ radio to its fullest and most dramatic extent. During the war he broadcast regularly from Europe, keeping Americans up-to-date on the progress of the war and on the battering the city of London was taking during the Blitz in 1940. Listeners could even hear the sounds of sirens, anti-aircraft fire, and real bombs falling. By 1943 his was the principal voice describing the war to millions of Americans in their living rooms across the country. He saw himself not just as a broadcaster but also as an educator, telling people what they needed to know and providing information they could not acquire on their own.

A constant chainsmoker, his ever-present cigarettes finally killed him in 1965.

"Here are thousands upon thousands of farmers wondering whether next year's prices will meet their mortgage interest—now!

"Here are thousands of men and women working for long hours in factories for inadequate pay—now!

"Here are thousands upon thousands of children who should be in school, working in mines and mills—now!...

"If we would keep faith with those who had faith in us, if we would make democracy succeed, I say we must act—now!"

But mostly radio meant entertainment. Music of all sorts came across the airwaves. Big bands broadcast from dance halls in every corner of the country. Guy Lombardo and his Royal Canadians became a New Year's Eve fixture. On Christmas Day, 1931, the Metropolitan Opera began its long run of Saturday afternoon broadcasts. In 1937 NBC brought another cultural icon to the air when it put together a symphony orchestra designed especially for Maestro Arturo

Toscanini and hired him to conduct it in their studios. For 18 years he and his orchestra performed the classic symphonic and operatic repertoires on the air. Recordings of broadcasts are still available.

In 1941 Martin Block became the first disc jockey, on "The Make Believe Ballroom." He played recordings while describing a hall with bands and singers.

Radio dramas captured large audiences. Soap operas like "Just Plain Bill" and "Romance of Helen Trent" began broadcasting in 1932 and 1933. Mystery dramas came along, too: "The Shadow" in 1930, "Inner Sanctum" in 1941, and "The Whistler" in 1942.

In 1939 broadcasters were devoting just 7 percent of air time to news, but that increased to 20 percent by 1944. Still, music had by far the dominant programming. Twenty million American homes owned a radio in 1934, 30 million in 1942, and in 1950 some 40 million.

When the Federal Communications

Commission approved stereo broadcasting early in the 1960s, FM, with better sound quality, gained fans among music lovers. The AM spectrum was full in most major markets by 1962, and new stations, especially in suburban areas, turned to FM.

After two decades of rapid growth, FM in 1977 was the medium of broadcast on 2,873 commercial and 870 nonprofit stations, up from 960 and 194 in 1962. By the end of the 1970s, FM reached a larger audience than AM, which nevertheless led in stations and profitability. Most stations were devoted to country music in 2003—slightly more than 2,000—than any other format; news/talk was second with about 1,800.

ABOVE: *Radio listeners could hear American jazz musician Louis Armstrong and his band, the Hot Five.*

OPPOSITE: *The public got news from journalist Elmer Davis broadcasting from Washington, D.C., during World War II.*

# BIGGER, TALLER, LONGER

❦

## *Great Engineering Feats*

From mud huts and simple logs laid across a stream, the art and architecture of constructing buildings and bridges has advanced with mankind. Though the centuries, materials became more durable as structures achieved greater and greater height and span. Interiors of houses became more and more livable. Machinery replaced muscle power in the construction business.

David Macaulay wrote that bridges "are in a sense three-dimensional diagrams of the work they do" and that the thing most bridges have in common "is that they were…built to span water—a challenge that seems to have an enduring appeal to those of us with neither wings nor gills."

In 1869, President Ulysses S. Grant signed a bill approving the plans to build a bridge from Manhattan to Brooklyn,

and work began on January 2, 1870. It was the first bridge to use steel for cable wire. Chief engineer and designer John Roebling died from an accident shortly after work began, and his son, Washington Roebling, took up the task of building the bridge. He too was nearly killed by an attack of the bends brought on by his working in the highly pressurized caissons. But he carried on, supervising construction from his apartment in Brooklyn, watching the workmen with binoculars, and dispatching instructions and messages to the site via his wife, Emily.

The bridge opened in 1883, thirteen years after construction began. Between 20 and 30 workmen died during construction. The twin towers rose 276.5 feet above the water, just a few feet shy of

the then tallest building in New York, the spire of Trinity Church at 281 feet. Toll for the bridge was one cent on opening day and three cents thereafter. Some 150,000 people crossed on opening day.

A host of awe-inspiring bridges would follow in its wake. The Golden Gate Bridge, arguably the most beautiful in the world, was built across San Francisco Bay's Golden Gate in 1937. The site presented daunting difficulties for builders: Tides raced through the narrow mouth of the bay, fogs and storms swept in from the Pacific Ocean, and foundations had to be strong enough to withstand the region's frequent earthquakes. The U.S. Navy demanded that the height of the bridge at its center be 220 feet to ensure clearance for its fleet. Despite the many difficulties—both engineering and human—the bridge was completed in less than five years. Strauss commemorated its opening with a poem: *At last the mighty task is done; / Resplendent in the western sun,…* that included a slap at his many critics. *Launched 'midst a thousand hopes and fears, / Damned by a thousand hostile sneers, / Yet ne'er its course was stayed….*

Macaulay attributes the growth of skyscrapers partly to a sense of competition among their builders—who can build the tallest? The impulse began in

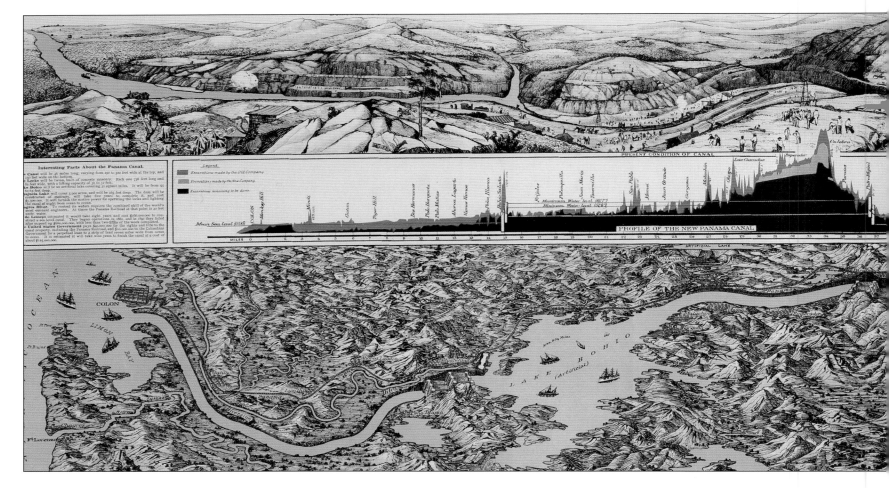

## FRANK LLOYD WRIGHT

"The physician can bury his mistakes, but the architect can only advise his client to plant vines," wrote Frank Lloyd Wright, prickly genius of American architecture. Wright was born in Wisconsin and left high school before completing his senior year. But he attended the University of Wisconsin as a Special Student in civil engineering. In 1887 he moved to Chicago and worked at architectural detailing. His Midwestern roots emerged as he and other like-minded architects founded the "Prairie School" of architecture. It replaced the boxlike structures of most of the houses of the era with low buildings, flat roofs, and bands of windows that turned corners. Inside, the main rooms often merged into one large, continuous space.

Wright designed about 800 buildings. Of the 400 actually built, 280 are still standing. The most famous perhaps is "Fallingwater" in Pennsylvania. It protrudes magically over a small waterfall, and it brought Wright fame and commissions from all over the world.

Wright believed that buildings should be in harmony. "No house should ever be on any hill or on anything. It should be of the hill, belonging to it, so hill and house could live together each the happier for the other."

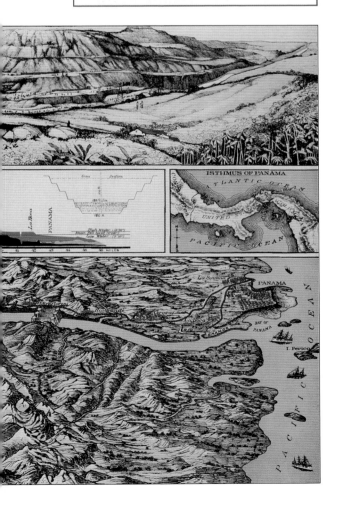

Chicago, after the great fire of 1871 destroyed much of the city. With downtown space running short, developers began building upward. In 1893, when several buildings exceeded two hundred feet in height, officials, fearing the tall boxes would turn the sunny streets into dark canyons, imposed a ten-story limit on all new construction. So the skyscraper moved east. Within 25 years the tallest buildings in the world rose above Manhattan's grid. Sixty years would pass before Chicago could once again lay claim to the country's tallest building.

Within the tight confines of the island of Manhattan, the skyscraper flourished. Landmark buildings such as the triangular Flatiron Building (1903) and 793-foot Woolworth Building (1913) led to the construction of the handsome Chrysler Building (1930). It was the tallest building in the world for only two years, succeeded by the Empire State Building. Its distinctive shape stemmed in part from city zoning regulations and site limitations. One required tall buildings to be stepped back at certain predetermined heights, based on the width of the adjacent streets, to assure a minimum amount of light and air at street level. Another stated that the portion of a building above its 30th floor could be any height as long as the square footage of any individual floor did not exceed 25 percent of the area of the site. Its chief designer, William Lamb, had notions of his own: One, that no worker be more than 25 feet from a window. An ideal was to provide as much floor space as possible,

but each increase in floor space required more elevators; and the more elevators Lamb provided the more floor space they consumed. The more floor space they consumed, the more floors he had to add. By the time everyone was satisfied, the building rose to 86 stories.

Yet the engineering marvel of the half-century was the Panama Canal, slashed through swamps and mountains across the narrow Isthmus of Panama. The French had tried and given up. President Theodore Roosevelt was the force that finally got the canal built. Six thousand men worked on it for seven years, many dying of malaria. The first ship passed through on January 7, 1914. From Atlantic to Pacific, the length of the canal is about 45 miles—it's another few miles to deep water on both ends—and it saves ships from having to round Cape Horn at the bottom of South America, shortening their voyages by 8,000 nautical miles.

In 1974 the title of world's tallest building returned once more to Chicago. Built for the Sears, Roebuck Company the Sears Tower reaches 110 floors and a height of 1,450 feet, excluding broadcast antennas and their supports at the very top. Vertical tubes of welded steel frames provide the rigidity needed to limit the sway from Chicago's legendary winds.

LEFT: *Map of the Panama Canal—"topographic, diagrammatic, and illustrative"—was drawn in 1903. Its bottom panel showed how the completed canal would look.*
ABOVE: *A bolter finishes part of the Empire State Building's 57,000-ton steel frame.*

# The STOCK MARKET CRASH

## A Roaring Silence

The Gin and Jazz Age, the Dollar Decade, the Roaring Twenties—the era was all of those. Hemlines came up, inhibitions went down. Flappers with bobbed hair danced the night away. A hot sound called jazz caught on. Bands led by the elegant Duke Ellington, Fletcher Henderson, and others played at exotic nightclubs. In New York City's Harlem, the Cotton Club was tops.

After a post-World War I recession, big business started booming in 1922. Steel and automobile manufacturing grew through the decade, but small businesses—more vulnerable to economic swings than large companies—failed by the tens of thousands.

As their wages declined, coal miners, textile workers, and farmers could ill afford new products. But if cash was not available for luxuries, credit was—for radios and vacuum cleaners as well as cars.

Speculation in stocks inflated the value of businesses, and the bubble of false prosperity burst in the crash of 1929. Throughout the late 20s, the stock market had been climbing, fueled by exuberant speculation. After reaching a high in August 1929, share prices began to fall during September and early October, but investors continued to buy. Then on October 18 the market began a dramatic plunge.

The next day, Black Thursday, six leading Wall Street bankers met at the House of Morgan to work out a way to save the bull market. But by 11:00 a.m. the market had lost $9 billion in value. A reporter described the traders on the floor of the Stock Exchange: "Some stood with feet apart and shoulders hunched forward as though to brace themselves against the gusts of selling orders which drove them about the floor like autumn leaves in a gale."

The Big Six bankers had pooled assets to save the market, and after their meeting Richard Whitney, vice president of the Exchange, bought 10,000 shares of U.S. Steel. Then, still trying to prop up the market, he walked the floor, purchasing 200,000 shares of several stocks for $20 million. Late in the day the market rallied somewhat, and at close was down just $3 billion.

But after a calm weekend, Black Monday loomed. By now the market was so overvalued that no one group of bankers could control it or stop it from falling. And, at the opening bell, fall it did. General Electric dropped 48 points; Eastman Kodak 42; U.S. Steel 18. When the president of National City Bank, Charles Mitchell, was seen to be smiling as he emerged from Morgan's Bank in the afternoon, it was taken to be a hopeful sign; but he had been there to arrange a loan to cover his own losses. The Big Six were quietly selling.

Black Tuesday, October 29, was, according to economist John Kenneth Galbraith, "the most devastating day in the history of the New York stock market and it may have been the most devastating day in the history of markets." By the closing bell, $32 billion had been lost as investors dumped more than 16.4 million shares.

Over the years, the legend grew that many Wall Street brokers had committed suicide by jumping from their office windows during the Crash, but apparently only one person did, a 51-year-old woman named Hulda Browaski. She was chief clerk of the bond department of a brokerage house, but she was not an investor. Her savings were safe in government bonds. She was simply depressed by working long days and nights processing the trading orders that overwhelmed every brokerage.

The Great Depression descended upon the United States. A Kansas City insurance salesman named John Schwitzgebel, sitting in his club, dropped the financial page he had been reading and shouted: "Tell the boys I can't pay them what I owe them" and shot himself twice in the chest. Hardest hit were investors who had played the market by putting down 10 percent in cash and borrowing the rest—buying "on margin."

Some famous people were hit hard by the crash. The Rockefeller family lost four-fifths of its fortune. Groucho Marx lost $240,000 and Winston Churchill $500,000. The Vanderbilt family lost $40 million in railroads alone.

Overnight the American dream became a nightmare. Investors lost as much money on October 29 as the U.S. had spent fighting World War I. By 1932 nearly a third of all American workers were unemployed and national output was cut in half. By 1933 a fourth of all the nation's farmers had lost their land.

"Dear Mr. President: I'm a boy of 12 years.... My father he staying home. All the time he's crying because he can't find work.... I don't know why they don't help us Please answer right away because we need it. will starve." Stricken Americans wrote daily to the White House asking for work. The poor grew poorer, while once prosperous families fell victim to bank failures. It seemed that the national anthem had become "Brother, Can You Spare a Dime?" Men

and women alike grew tired, shabby, and discouraged in their often fruitless search for work. Shantytowns made of cardboard and corrugated metal popped up on urban fringes. They were nicknamed Hoovervilles, for the President who believed Americans should be able to provide for themselves.

Those ragged suburbs could take only so many. More than a million other souls— 200,000 of them children—drifted along, large numbers riding the rails.

But as bread lines grew, so did movie lines. The talking pictures were still new, and families flocked to see the heroes and villains of screen adventures. Some 110 million tickets were sold weekly in 1930, and in spite of the depression, Hollywood produced 500 movies a year. A 1933 cartoon, *Three Little Pigs,* had the nation singing "Who's Afraid of the Big Bad Wolf?" when wolves were at many doors.

Americans turned, too, to such fads as miniature golf, backgammon, and pin-

ball. Bingo halls were packed and the Irish Sweepstakes made front-page news.

Even nature seemed to conspire against the American dream. In good years when it rained in the Oklahoma-Texas Panhandle country farmers plowed the grasslands under. The bad years came in the 1930s, and the winds tore at land left exposed by dying crops. The loose soil blew into big "black blizzards" or "rollers."

The Dust Bowl's soil was swept airborne—some of it settling on ships 300 miles out in the Atlantic Ocean. Soil in the Southeast was heading for the ocean too. It was washed out by rains running across abused farmland. The soil came off in sheets, especially on hillsides of naked, plowed ground. Hard rains cut a nick in the soil, then a notch, then a slash, then a gully. Gullies linked with gullies, and miniature Grand Canyons webbed nightmarish landscapes across the South.

Erosion resulted from too little water in some parts of the country, too much

in others. What happened was no mystery. By 1935 Congress had passed the Soil Conservation Act. In 1939 Hugh Hammond Bennett wrote in *Soil Conservation:* "National habits of waste in this country have nowhere been exhibited more flagrantly than in the use of agricultural land."

A large influx of farmers were forced off their farms and into the Pacific region. Demand for lumber, the most popular wood produce from the nation's forests, plunged when the Depression halted housing construction. Immigration from abroad declined dramatically as Europeans thought twice about hitching their wagons to the American star.

ABOVE: *Black Tuesday, October 29, 1929: Workers flood the streets of New York following Wall Street's crash. It helped cause the Great Depression, when millions went hungry.*
OPPOSITE: *Unemployed men receive soup and a slice of bread in Los Angeles in 1930.*

# The
# NEW DEAL

## Picking up the Pieces

Americans used to making their own way were hard hit by the world-wide economic depression. Rightly or wrongly, they largely blamed their president, Herbert Hoover, voted him out of office, and replaced him with Franklin Roosevelt, who ran on the promise that if he were elected, the federal government would step in to end the Depression. "I pledge myself," he said, "to a new deal for the American people." He declared in his inaugural address on March 4, 1933: "The only thing we have to fear is fear itself."

His frenetic first hundred days took peo-

getting started. He sent $500 million to the states for direct relief, saved a fifth of all home owners from foreclosure, and refinanced farm mortgages. Perhaps the most far-reaching programs of the New Deal were the Social Security measures of 1935 and 1939, which provided old-age and widows' benefits, unemployment compensation, and disability insurance. Additionally, the government was put in the business of generating electric power by the establishment in 1933 of the Tennessee Valley Authority (TVA), which would tap the rivers of a seven-state area and supply cheap electricity, prevent floods, improve navigation, and pro-

approval was a blue eagle, a stylized depiction of a Navajo thunderbird clutching a cog wheel in one talon and six lightning bolts in the other; its slogan: "We do our part."

FDR's New Deal included an alphabet soup of employment programs designed to put Americans back to work.

The Public Works Administration, or PWA, set up under the National Industrial Recovery Act, hired workers to build projects ranging from New York's Lincoln Tunnel to the University of New Mexico's library. New courthouses, schools, and hospitals sprang up everywhere.

Not everyone felt that such reform projects were the answer. Critics complained that the federal government had too much control over business and spent too much money.

Nevertheless the PWA and other programs continued to generate millions of jobs. In 1935 the Works Progress Administration (WPA), under energetic Harry Hopkins, aimed to employ many in building golf courses, playgrounds, parks, and airports for communities across the country. Congress appropriated a healthy $4,880,000,000 to provide work for the country's vast army of unemployed men. The money had a "pump-priming" effect on the economy and the private sector during the Depression, though the whole endeavor was naturally troubled by disorder, waste, and the inevitable dishonesty and cronyism of politicians. Hopkins also developed programs for authors, artists, and musicians. Writers hired by the Federal Writers' Project (FWP) researched and wrote guidebooks to the states and regions. They also were put to work indexing newspapers, researching sociological and historical questions, and organizing historical archives. Participants appreciated the work; a young writer named John Steinbeck reported taking a dog census on California's Monterey Peninsula.

Unemployed artists went to work for the Federal Arts Project (FAP) in hundreds of public buildings, including schools and post offices, painting murals and canvases and sculpting statues and friezes. Musicians launched community symphony orchestras and singing groups.

The Civilian Conservation Corps (CCC) put to work 2.5 million unem-

ple's breath away with revolutionary initiatives. He completed the rescue of the banking system with deposit insurance, regulated the stock exchanges, coordinated the faltering rail system, and went off the gold standard to raise prices. And he was just

duce nitrates. The last great act of the hundred days was the National Industrial Recovery Act (NIRA), which fostered partnership between business and the state; it established the National Recovery Administration (NRA) whose seal of

ployed youths by the end of the decade; they built roads and bridges in national parks, planted trees, and constructed dams. One historian noted that "the CCC left its monuments in the preservation and purification of the land, the water, the forests, and the young men of America."

The typical CCC enrollee was between 18 and 19 years old, had completed eight years of schooling, and had been without a job for seven months. Raymond Burr, the actor who would later win fame as Perry Mason on television, was an enrollee at Camp Whitmore in California. "We Can Take It" was the unofficial motto of the young men of the CCC. The program was disbanded on June 30, 1942, seven months after the U.S. entry into World War II.

Workers with a craft, such as carpentry or plumbing, could join unions, which would help improve their wages, but unskilled laborers had no one to represent them. Forced to accept low wages for long hours, they were helped in 1935 when Congress passed one of the New Deal's most important laws, the National Labor Relations Act. It guaranteed the right of workers to organize and to bargain as a group with their bosses.

By June 1943, when it was officially terminated, the WPA had spent $11 billion on nearly 1.5 million projects, giving work to more than 8,500,000 unemployed Americans. In eight years those Americans had built, repaired, or improved 853 airports, 8,192 parks, 125,110 public buildings; they had also laid out 651,087 miles of highways, roads, and streets.

Intellectuals questioned whether capitalism could be, or should be, saved. As the American dream turned into an economic nightmare, leftist thinkers were drawn to communist ideals of community and cooperation. Many were later repulsed by the reality of purges and sham trials in Joseph Stalin's Soviet Union. But the Red Scare was loose again. In 1938 the House Committee on Un-American Activities (formed to monitor Nazi and Fascist agents) under Congressman Martin Dies of Texas focused on "Reds," among them writers, artists, New Deal liberals, and labor leaders.

---

### MAIN STREET

Mrs. Dawson opened the meeting by sighing, "I'm sure I'm glad to see you all here today, and I understand that the ladies have prepared a number of very interesting papers, this is such an interesting subject, the poets, they have been an inspiration for higher thought, in fact wasn't it Reverend Benlick who said that some of the poets have been as much an inspiration as a good many of the ministers, and so we shall be glad to hear—"

The poor lady smiled neuralgically, panted with fright, scrabbled about the small oak table to find her eye-glasses, and continued, "We will first have the pleasure of hearing Mrs. Jenson on the subject 'Shakespeare and Milton.'"

—Sinclair Lewis

---

ABOVE: *To get people back to work, the PWA, or Public Works Administration, hired workers on every sort of project, all around the country.*
OPPOSITE: *Around 1935, in one project, workers in an unknown city widen a street by removing curb stones.*

# On the
# RESERVATION

❧

## The Bureau of Indian Affairs

With guns and horses, aggressive tribes of Native Americans ruled the untamed West, menacing white interlopers and less warlike natives. "Something must be done to keep those Indians quiet," exclaimed one government agent.

Gold mines, oil fields, and an abundance of rich farmland drew settlers onto earth formerly allotted to Indians by treaties. Railroads spanned the prairies; from train windows, travelers shot the buffalo upon which Plains people relied,

leaving the carcasses to rot. Armies corralled tribes onto reservations.

By the Civil War's end in 1865, nearly 20,000 soldiers manning western forts stood ready to hush the natives. As the Army struggled to contain Apache and Navajo in New Mexico, determined Sioux under Red Cloud closed the Bozeman Trail, dictating peace terms to U.S. troops at Fort Laramie in 1868.

Mere paper would not avert a nation's will. Soon armed columns began carving inroads into Indian refuges. Each

side tasted calamity: Lt. Col. George Custer's "last stand" in 1876, the doomed 1,700-mile flight of Chief Joseph and the Nez Perce in 1877, the slaughter of women and children at Wounded Knee in 1890. When the dust settled and the bodies were removed, U.S. dominion sprawled unchallenged across the breadth of North America.

Reformers and missionaries sought to wean Indians from tribal customs and to assimilate them into mainstream society. Under the Dawes Act of 1887, termed the Indian Magna Carta by humanitarians, reservations were parceled out to individuals, and the "sur-

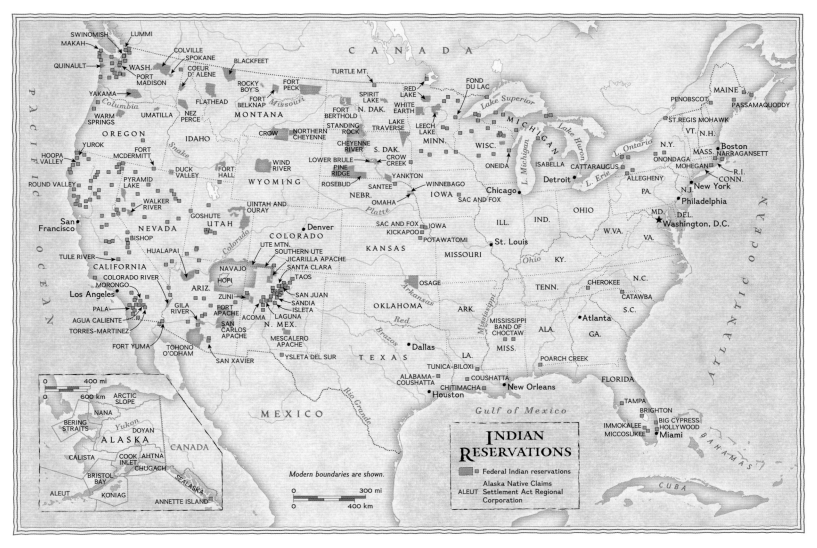

Modern boundaries are shown.

## Indian Reservations

■ Federal Indian reservations
Alaska Native Claims
ALEUT Settlement Act Regional Corporation

plus" lands were sold off. The Indian Reorganization Act reversed Dawes in 1934 and signaled the kindling of a new desire—to preserve America's native culture. But by then two-thirds of America's remaining Indian property had passed into white hands.

Since its creation in 1824, the Bureau of Indian Affairs—once an instrument of federal policies to subjugate and assimilate the tribes and their people—has tried to manage America's Native Americans amid shifting philosophiess. Conferral of citizenship on Indians after World War I improved access to legal redress, but the unique status of tribes cast questions of title in a jurisprudential twilight zone.

In the thirties, FDR's "Indian New Deal" under BIA head John Collier introduced congressional measures to protect reservations and to forestall the erosion of aboriginal customs. The Indian Reorganization Act halted allotment of tribal lands to individuals and encouraged native religious practices, including the controversial consumption of peyote in the Southwest.

Increased public interest sparked a renaissance in such neglected arts as weaving, pottery, sculpture, and crafting jewelry and masks.

Yet his policies of assimilating Indians into American culture, though devised with the best of intentions, infuriated most Indians, and the policy of assimilation became to them synonymous with the death of their culture. "How can we plan our future when the Indian Bureau threatens to wipe us out as a race?" asked a tribal chairman.

During the 1950s Collier's successors tried to reverse his programs, urging an end to reservations, to federal acknowledgment of tribes, and to special treatment of Native Americans. Federal relocation brought thousands of Native Americans into the cities, where it was thought enhanced job prospects would improve their welfare. These policies, it was thought, would "free" Indians by speeding their absorption into mainstream society. In practice it helped free land for exploitation.

Policy changed again in the 1960s. Some ignored tribes were officially rec-

ognized, and many land claims were settled. Yet by popular standards—wealth, education, longevity—descendants of the earliest Americans still lagged behind all other major ethnic groups, falling well below national averages. Alcoholism and unemployment plagued many on and off the reservations. Discouraged and militant Indians staged demonstrations and armed takeovers to focus attention on their people's unrest. In 1969 members of Indians of All Tribes seized Alcatraz Island, a former penitentiary in San Francisco Bay, for 19 months. They declared the site "more than suitable for an Indian Reservation.... It would be fitting and symbolic that ships from all over the world, entering the Golden Gate, would first see Indian land, and thus be reminded of the true history of this nation."

OPPOSITE, BELOW: *Heavy losers in the American dream, Native Americans stood little chance against the white onslaught. This delegation of Mandan and Arikara Indians journeyed to Washington in 1874.*
OPPOSITE, ABOVE: *Treaties signed there did little to protect them from land grabs.*

# The SUPERHEROES

*Comic Books Take Flight*

An innovation that marked the beginning of the modern comic book appeared more than a hundred years ago in an illustrated book called *The Yellow Kid:* the characters had a new element, a balloon, a space where the author wrote what the characters said, and even thought, and that pointed to their mouths with a kind of tail.

With that, comics assumed their modern form, and they developed into a genre of original drawings and stories. Their golden age was from the middle 1930s to the late 1940s. They became famous for their covers, which equaled circus posters in their flamboyance, energy, and lettering.

Most of the first comics were compilations of newspaper funnies. One of the earliest and most successful was Foxy Grandpa, whose adventures appeared in more than two dozen books between 1901 and 1916. It featured a clever old duffer who continually outfoxed his two prankish nephews.

A Manhattan firm, Cupples & Leon, was the largest and most successful publisher of comic books during the first 30 years of the century. Between 1906 and 1934, they issued more than a hundred different series of comics, all reprinted from newspapers, with no original material. Such books survive today in reprints of popular newspapers strips either in paperback or hardcover. Issues of *Dilbert,*

*Garfield,* and *Calvin and Hobbes* are published regularly.

Major Malcom Wheeler-Nicholson, a dapper former U.S. Cavalry officer with spats and a cane, first conceived a line of comic books featuring nothing but original material. The company he founded would become DC Comics, a leader in the field. His first magazine was called *New Fun* and differed from what had been tried before by including action, intrigue, and mystery stories such as were becoming popular in newspaper strips in the mid-1930s. The first issue's cover was in color, but the interior 32 pages were black and white. The adventures, which were all "to-be-continued," included *Sandra of the Secret Service, Jack Andrews, All-American Boy,* and *Cap'n Erik.* But Major Nicholson's magazine didn't sell very well. The comic book boom had not really begun yet, and distributors were reluctant to handle comic books, and newsstands even more reluctant to give them rack space.

His *Detective Comics* got off to a modest start early in 1937. The first issue featured a bright crimson cover from which a sinister Oriental glowered at the

reader. Its subscription ad promised, "Here is a magazine crammed full of color, action, plot and punch. You'll see why crime does not pay, why the police always put the finger on the criminal."

*Star Ranger* was chock full of nothing but cowboys, both serious and whimsical, and was one of the two original comic books devoted entirely to the West.

With adventure and Westerns, comic books began growing up. Flash Gordon, Dick Tracy, and Tarzan all made their appearance. The first superhero was born when Superman appeared in 1938. Superman forever changed the look and content of four-color magazine. He was introduced in *Action Comics* in a 13-page story that listed his birthplace only as "a distant planet" and made no mention of his adoptive parents. It also introduced mild-mannered Clark Kent and his fetching co-worker, Lois Lane, who was already giving him the cold shoulder. By 1941 Action Comics was selling 900,000 copies a month. A separate *Superman* comic, begun in 1939, soon reached a circulation of 1,250,000 a month.

In 1939 Batman made his first appearance in *Detective Comics #27*. In a short six-page story, the new hero's pointy ears looked a little lopsided on his cowl and his batwing cape doesn't appear to fit quite right. The next year he acquired his youthful sidekick, Robin the Boy Wonder.

The best-selling superhero of the 1940s turned out to be another character with a dual identity: Captain Marvel was the World's Mightiest Mortal, but he was really a teenager named Billy Batson who needed the magic word "Shazam" to turn into a superman. He returned to his own identity when the trouble had passed. He was drawn to look like actor Fred MacMurray, a Hollywood leading man of the 1930s and early 1940s.

During the 1940s publishers sought to expand their audience in both directions—with true crime and sexy women for older readers, and more wholesome fare, especially humorous, for the children. Humor ranged from clever satires through slapstick to whimsy. Many featured animals.

Disney was king. Comic books featuring his animated cartoon characters

had been appearing since the mid-1930s. Walt Disney's *Comics & Stories* appeared in the autumn of 1940, with Donald Duck the star. He appeared, often with his trio of nephews, on all but two of the first hundred covers.

*Looney Tunes* and *Merry Melodies* featured stars of the Warner Brothers animated cartoons. Stories were devoted to Porky Pig, Elmer Fudd, and Bugs Bunny. In *Coo Coo Comics* readers found the world's only Supermouse, whose "great powers, you know, stem from his SUPERCHEESE." Superkatt starred in *Giggle,* wearing a hero costume consisting of a baby bonnet,

a bow tie, and a diaper; he had a mutt dog for a sidekick.

By 1944, the comic book industry was thriving. *DC Comics* was publishing 19 different titles and selling more than 8,500,000 copies a month. And the superheroes had gone to war. Nazis and squinty-eyed Japanese regularly met their doom at the hands of comic-book heroes. On the cover of *Action #17* Superman is lifting a tank on a battlefield, and on *#21* he's attacking a U-boat. *Heroic Comics* deemphasized superheroes and devoted its covers and most of its stories to real war heroes.

In the 1950s a backlash developed against comic books, which some considered to be bad for American's youth. Frederic Wertham's *The Seduction of the Innocent* accused comic books of causing youthful corruption, violence, and juve-

nile delinquency. The industry developed a "comics code" to rule on what could or could not appear in the pages of comics. It ended virtually all the horror titles.

The 50s also saw the birth of *Classic Comics,* illustrated versions of the classics of literature. Many who grew up in the 1950s recall first making the acquaintance of the Count of Monte Cristo and the Hunchback of Notre Dame in the pages of *Classic Comics.*

## "GOOD GIRL" ACT

The term refers not to comics about good girls, but rather to comics that featured good drawings of pretty girls—most often scantily or provocatively clad.

In the late 1930s some publishers came to realize that a large portion of their audience was made up of adolescent boys. They responded in two ways: the more sedate added adolescent boy characters, hence Robin the Boy Wonder. Others, such as Fiction House, featured sparsely clad young women on their covers. From August 1940 onward, Sheena the Queen of the Jungle, in her familiar leopard-skin costume, appeared on every cover of Jumbo Comics. Inside, she battled rampaging savages, evil slave traders, and greedy ivory hunters.

An imitation Tarzan named Kaanga, another Fiction House hero, had a dark-haired young woman named Ann as his mate. She wore a two-piece leopard-skin costume. Sometimes she served as rescue victim for Kaanga, but other times she took part in his battles and skirmishes.

Mysta of the Moon, Futura, Tiger Girl, Firehair—the "Flame Girl of the Wild West"—appeared in the 1940s. Firehair had been raised by Indians after the death of her parents and adopted by a Dakota tribe.

Wonder Woman appeared on the cover of the first edition of Sensation Comics in January 1942, and every subsequent cover until 1951. Her only serious rival was Mary Marvel, Captain Marvel's teenage sister.

OPPOSITE: *Comic books provided generations of American youth with adventure and amusement.* ABOVE: *Their heroes even made the transition to the movies. Here Superman faces off against Atom Man.*

# FEEDING
# *the* NATION

## *Farms and Farmers*

In 1850 there was one farm for every 16 people in the United States—in 1984 only one for every 100. As farm size began to grow in the 1930s, when agriculture became capital intensive, the number of farms began to decline. Increased mechanization reduced the need for human labor, causing farm employment to plummet. In 2002 there were just 2,158,000 farms, averaging 436 acres each, in the U.S.

Advances in the first half of the 20th century made American farmers more efficient and more productive. The arrival on the scene of the lumbering tractor late in the 19th century was one. At first tractors were simple four-stroke gasoline engines sitting stationary; then wheels were added to make them portable. Their number increased from 600 in use in 1907 to almost 3,400,000 by 1950. A major innovation was the power takeoff, introduced in 1918, which allowed power from the tractor's engine to be transmitted directly to another implement through a shaft.

The corn picker, which came into use in the U.S. corn belt following World War I, increased the yields of corn, the most important single crop in the U.S. But new crops were being developed, too. The soybean was critical. It had been grown in the U.S. since 1804 but only as a garden plant. It wasn't until the early 1930s, when an oil processing method eliminated a disagreeable odor from the processed bean, that it began to find use in shortening, margarine, mayonnaise, salad oil, and other foods.

Even the farm animals were altered. American hogs of the late 19th century were heavy animals that, when rendered,

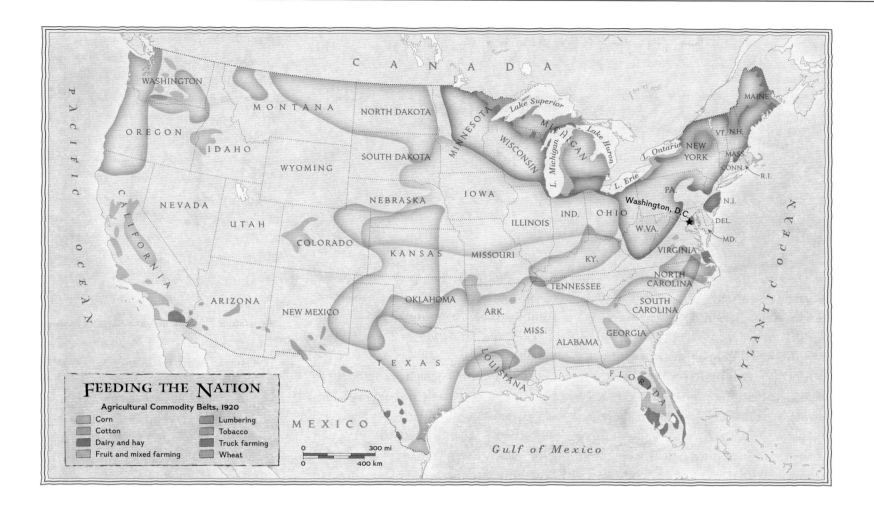

**FEEDING THE NATION**
Agricultural Commodity Belts, 1920
- Corn
- Cotton
- Dairy and hay
- Fruit and mixed farming
- Lumbering
- Tobacco
- Truck farming
- Wheat

300 mi

400 km

yielded a lot of lard. But in the 1920s cheaper vegetable oils began to supplant lard as a source of fat in American diets. Hogs that produced leaner, less fatty meat became more popular, and farmers and meat packers encouraged their development.

The Great Depression hit farmers hard, as even the weather conspired to produce years of drought in the Great Plains and West. By 1940, some 3.5 million farmers had abandoned their homes and hit the road, headed mostly for California. They were called "Okies," because many came from Oklahoma, or "exodusters." If they reached the Golden State, many became migrant workers, picking and boxing fruit or baling cotton. They were generally paid about $350 to $400 a year, about half of what California judged was a subsistence income.

After the Great Depression, farmers could afford improved equipment, pesticides, commercial fertilizers, and stronger plant varieties to increase yields. Expensive chemicals and machinery made large-scale farming more profitable, forcing farmers to "get big or get out." Exceptions have been a growing number of small farms that cater to specialty markets.

Modern applications of science to farming caused U.S. production to soar after World War II, resulting in the most significant changes in agriculture since colonial times—an American green revolution. Farmers doubled and tripled their yields by using hybrid drought- and disease-resistant seed and applying liquid nitrogen and other commercial fertilizers. Between 1945 and 1970 the production of beef rose by 110 percent and soybeans by 480 percent. Crop dusting became so widespread that Flying Farmer clubs were formed. By 1986 farmers spent ten billion dollars a year on agrichemicals.

By the 1980s farmers were facing increased competition from low-cost Third World producers and reduced demand on world markets. Economic pressures were forcing midsize farms to evolve into large family corporations of "briefcase farmers" or small farms largely supported by off-farm income. In the process thousands of family farms went under as they failed to adapt to a complex system dependent not on hard work but on the bottom line.

California epitomizes the success of the American farmer—though it was not always so. "No one will ever be able to make a living here from the land," a visi-

tor to the state is said to have remarked in the early 19th century. The fertile San Joaquin Valley, today the state's most productive region, was then considered a desert. For years after the gold rush Californians grappled with an arid land where eastern farming techniques simply did not work. They developed new irrigation practices and experimented with exotic crops, but most grazed cattle until European demand fueled a wheat boom in the 1870s.

The emphasis had shifted to fruits, nuts, and vegetables by the turn of the century. The new transcontinental railroad system, the refrigerated railcar, and the development of the canning industry had expanded the markets for California produce all the way to the East Coast.

California became the country's top producer in 1947, and 40 years later it supplied half the nation's fruits, nuts, and vegetables and led in the production of 56 crops ranging from olives to avocados.

OPPOSITE: *Bountiful cornucopia crowds a display table near Marinette, Wisconsin, in 1895. The image appeared in* Northern Wisconsin, A Hand-Book for the Homeseeker, *which demonstrated "agricultural and horticultural possibilities" in the state.*

# SPENDING *the* RESOURCES

## *Whose Water Is It?*

Land is plentiful for the City of Angels—hence its spread across nearly 500 square miles—but water is not. To secure a supply, the city bought—secretly—property along California's Owens River and built an aqueduct that runs more than 200 miles, having successfully survived sabotage by bitter Owens Valley residents. Most of them farmed and ranched, and they were anticipating economic good times once the Reclamation Service completed its Owens Valley irrigation project. But

William Mulholland and his partner Fred Eaton—through a combination of normal land purchases and near bribery, determination, and deceit—managed to capture enough land and water rights to block the Owens Valley project. Instead of onto farmers' fields, the water went to Los Angeles.

The East is wet and the West is dry, and they meet at the 100th meridian. While the East withdraws nine times

more water for industry than the West, the West withdraws nine times more for irrigation.

Until the 1860s what is now called the Great Plains was better known as the Great American Desert. It was thought to be a natural boundary "up to which population and agriculture may advance, and no further." Much wishful thinking and little evidence were knitted after the Civil War into curious theories about human modification of rainfall and climate on the Great Plains. A speculator in town property and dabbler in science, Nebraskan Charles Dana Wilber put it most succinctly: "Rain follows the plow."

During the 1880s the regional population of Kansas, Nebraska, and the Dakotas nearly doubled. Then came the droughts of the 1890s. According to hydrographer Frederick H. Newell in 1896, those "unfortunate settlers" who kept farming with humid-region techniques "if not driven from the country,

alternate between short periods of prosperity and long intervals of depression."

One answer was irrigation: in the Great Basin from surface water; in the Far West by impounding snowmelt and mountain rain and sending them along by way of aqueduct, canal, and ditch; and later, in the Plains from underground sources.

By 1890 farmers had irrigated some 3.7 million acres of western lands by simple diversion of watercourses. In the Midwest much of Indiana, Ohio, and Illinois was still in marshland, but large-scale drainage was under way. By 1900

## WILLIAM MULHOLLAND

From humble beginnings, William Mulholland rose to become one of the wealthiest—and most reviled—characters in California history. The route from his birthplace in Belfast, Ireland, in 1855, to Los Angeles was complex . He arrived in New York in the early 1870s as a sailor, and made his way to Michigan where he worked in lumber camps; then a dry goods business in Pittsburgh; then Arizona, where he was a miner. In Arizona he even served a stint as a paid fighter of the Apaches.

He found a job as a ditch cleaner for a private Los Angeles water company, learned the ins and outs of the water business, and somehow ascended to head the city's Department of Water and Power. From there, he and his cronies orchestrated the theft of the waters of the Owens River Valley for the City of Angels.

It took a massive construction project. Thousands of workers spread out across two hundred miles of California terrain, running power lines, laying tracks, building roads, and digging sluiceways. In eight years, by 1913, they had completed the Los Angeles Aqueduct.

Mulholland's scheme centered on producing more water than the city actually needed, so he was able to pipe the excess to the arid San Fernando Valley. There more cronies and partners had been buying up land, waiting for the increase in value once there was water for it.

But the St. Francis Dam collapsed in 1928, killing nearly 500 and covering much of Ventura County in muck. Water 75 feet high and two miles wide rushed to the sea. Mulholland had supervised the construction of the dam, and he was forced to resign in disgrace. He died in 1935.

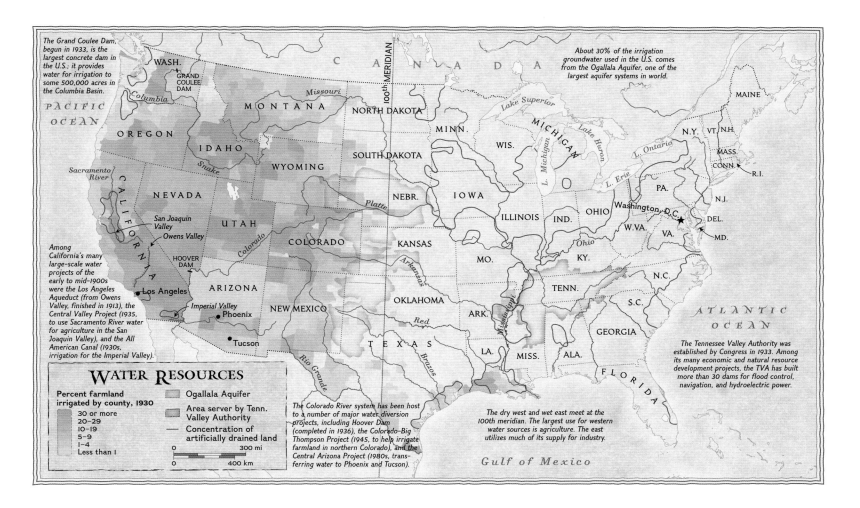

The Grand Coulee Dam, begun in 1933, is the largest concrete dam in the U.S.; it provides water for irrigation to some 500,000 acres in the Columbia Basin.

About 30% of the irrigation groundwater used in the U.S. comes from the Ogallala Aquifer, one of the largest aquifer systems in world.

Among California's many large-scale water projects of the early to mid-1900s were the Los Angeles Aqueduct (from Owens Valley, finished in 1913), the Central Valley Project (1935, to use Sacramento River water for agriculture in the San Joaquin Valley), and the All American Canal (1930s, irrigation for the Imperial Valley).

The Colorado River system has been host to a number of major water diversion projects, including Hoover Dam (completed in 1936), the Colorado-Big Thompson Project (1945, to help irrigate farmland in northern Colorado), and the Central Arizona Project (1980s, transferring water to Phoenix and Tucson).

The dry west and wet east meet at the 100th meridian. The largest use for western water sources is agriculture. The east utilizes much of its supply for industry.

The Tennessee Valley Authority was established by Congress in 1933. Among its many economic and natural resource development projects, the TVA has built more than 30 dams for flood control, navigation, and hydroelectric power.

### WATER RESOURCES

Percent farmland irrigated by county, 1930
- 30 or more
- 20–29
- 10–19
- 5–9
- 1–4
- Less than 1

- Ogallala Aquifer
- Area server by Tenn. Valley Authority
- Concentration of artificially drained land

0   300 mi
0   400 km

---

some six million acres across the nation had been drained—about 80 percent as many as those irrigated.

After the Reclamation Act of 1902, federal policy was directed at providing water for agriculture in dry western lands. Costs per reclaimed acre rose as much as ten times original estimates by 1920.

The Colorado River has had its waters fought over, debated about, and siphoned off practically since settlement began. Historian Marc Reisner says, "…it is the most legislated, most debated, and most litigated river in the entire world. It also has more people, more industry, and a more significant economy dependent on it than any comparable river in the world.…The river system provides over half the water of greater Los Angeles, San Diego, and Phoenix; it grows much of America's domestic production of fresh winter vegetables; it illuminates the neon city of Las Vegas,…"

In 1922, Arizona, Nevada, California, Wyoming, Utah, Colorado, and New Mexico, the seven states that make up the Colorado River drainage, signed the Colorado River Compact. It divided among the states 15 million of the estimated 17 million acre-feet of water that

flowed past Lees Ferry in Colorado. In 1944, Mexico was assigned 1.5 million acre-feet of what was left. But little makes it to Mexico. Reisner points out that the Colorado is so depleted that only a "burbling trickle" reaches the Gulf of California, "and then only in wet years."

By the 1940s California agriculture had been largely remade. By the 1970s great circles of center-pivot irrigation, one of man's most visible marks on the planet, were spread upon the plains like checkers.

Percolating through sand and gravel or held by porous rock, often in large formations called aquifers, groundwater must be pumped like oil. From Texas through Nebraska the Ogallala aquifer underlies the High Plains and provides 25 percent of the nation's irrigation water. With as much water as Lake Huron, the formation, full of fossil water collected over thousands of years, is being drained much faster than it is being replenished—a consequence of farming in dry lands.

The first half century was also the great age of dam building. Massive projects were built across the country, particularly in the West. The Hoover Dam, built in 1935, was among the first, taming the

Colorado River. Of the numerous dams on the Columbia River in the Northwest, the Grand Coulee (1941) is the largest in the United States.

Less showy than dam building, drainage of farmland by 1930 had affected nearly 50 million acres—two and a half times as many as the 19.5 million acres under irrigation. About 20 percent of all U.S. cropland was drained by the 1980s.

Damming, digging, dredging, and other kinds of management have long been agenda items in debates on water use. The central question has been: Has it all amounted to rain barrel or pork barrel? One historical answer: Funding follows the plow.

Water management has made supplies more reliable, but the chancy nature of agriculture in dry regions remains: Less rainfall and high evaporation leave dry ground vulnerable to erosion, a potential for disaster.

OPPOSITE: *Partners in speculation—from left, J. B. Lippincott of the U.S. Reclamation Service, Los Angeles Mayor Fred Eaton, and William Mulholland—got rich by manipulating supplies of Los Angeles water, a commodity as precious as gold in the arid West.*

# WORLD WAR TWO

## The Greatest Conflict

With rationing, with restrictions on railway travel *(is this trip necessary?)*, and despite shortages of cars and toys and nylons and bacon *(meatless Tuesdays)* and tires and alarm clocks *(don't you know there's a war on?)*, the U.S. in World War II managed to turn out guns and churn out butter. When the prewar "arsenal of democracy" became the arsenal for survival, results were stupendous. By 1942 U.S. industrial output equaled the combined production of the Axis powers. By 1944 it doubled it.

When war came, patriotism meant going to work as much as going to battle. More than eight million more civilians were employed in 1944 than in 1939, and 11 million others were in uniform. The ranks of the unemployed—9.5 million had been out of work in 1939—were absorbed.

The workweek increased from 38 to 45 hours, and industrial output grew—by 132 percent. New plants, new production techniques, and information pooling increased efficiency, and productivity grew—by 11 percent. What energized the long, hard hours was that most powerful motivator, the incentive to win the war *(praise the Lord and pass the ammunition)*. Duty required putting the government in debt (through war bonds) to keep the economy armed, fueled, and running. The government made more personal income subject to taxation and introduced a withholding tax. Although the tax base was broader than ever, taxes paid less than half the cost of the war.

Whereas Germany had elaborate plans to conscript women for war work, it did not succeed. The U.S. had no conscription but recruited with propaganda that played on widespread don't-let-our-troops-down sentiment that was also a recurrent theme in popular magazine fiction.

More than three million American women worked in war production, and by 1945 some 258,000 served in the armed forces. The culture of the postwar era expected that real-life Rosie the Riveters would leave the factories now that the fighting was over. For many women the independence, the pay, the respect were not soon forgotten.

American children helped the war effort, too. They grew vegetables for the family in "victory gardens." They collected scrap paper, tin cans, foil from chewing-gum wrappers, and other materials to be used in making planes, tanks, and weapons. They loaned part of their allowance to the government to help pay for the war. Each week millions of schoolchildren bought a 25-cent stamp to paste in a special book. When the book was filled, it would be traded for a $25 Defense Savings Bond.

On the home front, Americans, who had been going without since the 1929 stock market crash had triggered the Great Depression, rolled up their sleeves, tightened their belts a notch more. It was a time, remembered one journalist, when "you just felt that the stranger sitting next to you in a restaurant…felt the same way you did about the basic issues."

Old tires, doormats, and raincoats went to the war effort when President Franklin D. Roosevelt asked the nation to contribute rubber, critically short after Japanese conquests in the Far East. The response totaled 450,000 tons. Gas rationing followed, its intent less to save gas than to reduce tire wear. Growing domestic production of synthetic rubber ended the crisis.

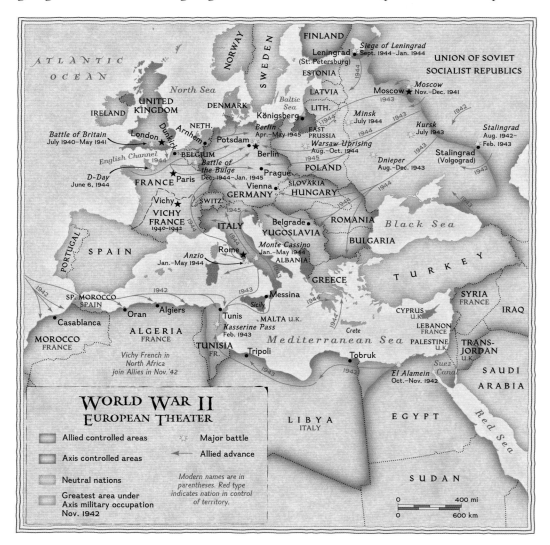

### WORLD WAR II
### EUROPEAN THEATER

- Allied controlled areas
- Axis controlled areas
- Neutral nations
- Greatest area under Axis military occupation Nov. 1942
- Major battle
- → Allied advance

*Modern names are in parentheses. Red type indicates nation in control of territory.*

Nearly 120,000 Japanese Americans spent much of the war in internment camps. Radio brought home front and war front closer together. Hollywood exported cheery slices of Americana and fabricated slices of foreign conflict: *Casablanca, Thirty Seconds over Tokyo, Winged Victory.* Newsreels sought to explain the geopolitics of a war that girdled the globe.

With Liberty ships, mass production of freighters to supply troops across four oceans became a reality. Construction time was eventually cut to 111 hours. More than 2,700 Liberty ships were built at about 1.6 million dollars each; 195 were lost at sea.

As for bombers, load-carrying capacity required ever larger sizes, stronger airframes, and more powerful engines. Bomber development pointed the way toward civilian airliners. The first American-designed bomber, the Martin MB-1, served from 1918 to 1923. The B-17 Flying Fortress, first all-metal, four-engine U.S. bomber, was later derived from an airliner design; 12,000 of the craft flew in World War II.

Mobilization was not without its confusions, dislocations, profiteering, and plain miscalculations. Early in the war, the rush to mobilize was so overpowering that too much in the way of scarce materials was being used to build factories; not enough was being reserved to build munitions.

U.S. industrialists understood the geopolitics. Their factories were keeping Allied armies supplied in western Europe, in the Soviet Union, and in China—as well as fully provisioning a U.S. military force of more than 16 million. It was a performance to make even Soviet leader Joseph Stalin raise a glass to toast American production, without which the Allies "never could have won the war."

Toward the war's end, another concern arose: Would victory lead to depression? Between May and August 1945, jobs in the aircraft, ammunition, and shipbuilding industries dropped by nearly 50 percent, or 1.2 million people. Two and a half million more war workers were laid off in September 1945. A million and a half military personnel were demobilized by the year's end.

Yet the economy did not collapse. Swift reconversion to peacetime industry only began to meet a huge backlog of demand. Postwar production instead turned out cars, appliances, houses, and babies.

## Armies on the Move

"We are alive, rudely awakened," wrote a young newspaper editor, Jonathan Daniels. Pearl Harbor acted on the Depression-ridden nation "like a reverse earthquake," wrote *Time* magazine, "that in one terrible jerk shook everything disjointed, distorted, askew back into place."

ABOVE: *In the mud of Europe, American troops man antitank artillery in 1944. By war's end, Generals Patton, Bradley, and Eisenhower had distinguished themselves as leaders of brave fighting men.*

the rebellion-torn China in 1931, some leaders spoke out, but none chose to act. While Hitler armed his new Germany, the allies who had beaten the old Germany watched, nervous but disunited. Many wanted to appease the aggressors, allowing them a few conquests in hopes they would not seek more.

But they did. Japan sought to rule "Greater East Asia." Italy claimed Ethiopia in 1935 and Albania in 1939. Germany and Italy, linked to form the Axis powers, grew bolder. Germany seized Austria, Czechoslovakia, Poland, Denmark, Norway, the Netherlands, Belgium—and, in 1940, France. The Nazis ruled half of France; their French collaborators at Vichy, the other half.

As Europe exploded into war, Japan joined the Axis alliance and seized more European-held lands in Asia and the Pacific Ocean. The world took sides. From Denmark's 15,000 troops to America's 12 million, the Allies mustered a mighty force to face the Axis nations in fighting that spanned the globe.

American troops had to bide their time before joining the fighting in Europe. Months of preparation were needed before they could invade Hitler's stronghold. Finally, on June 6, 1944, U.S. and British troops crossed the English Channel and struggled ashore on Normandy's beaches. They came in nearly 5,000 ships and landing craft; 11,000 planes provided cover overhead; troop strength numbered some 176,000. Their invasion covered nearly 60 miles of coastline and met fierce resistance from embattled Germans. After a few days of fighting, the Allies had secured a foothold, and within seven weeks more than a million men had landed. Throughout the rest of 1944 the Americans advanced, liberating Paris and then sweeping the Germans out of France.

By September Belgium and Luxembourg had been liberated. In mid-December a strong German counterattack—the Battle of the Bulge—pushed the Americans back briefly, but in the spring of 1945 the offensive went forward again. On April 25, American soldiers advancing to the east and Russian soldiers fighting their way west met near the German town of Torgau. Five days later, with Russians fighting

A world again at war left few nations neutral in 1941 when Japan attacked Pearl Harbor and drew the U.S. into the conflict.

The alliances that bound the warring nations had been taking shape for decades. When Japan seized Manchuria from

**World War II
Pacific Theater**

Allied controlled areas
Axis controlled areas
Land conquered by Japan, 1931–42
Neutral nations

——— Limit of Japanese expansion in the Pacific, Aug. 1942
✳ Major battle
←—— Allied advance

*Modern names are in parentheses. Red type indicates nation in control of territory.*

0        1500 mi
0        2000 km

Germans in the streets of Berlin, Hitler committed suicide in his bunker. A week later the war in Europe was over.

Following the shock of the attack on Pearl Harbor, the Americans found their Pacific forces crippled, with many sailors and marines killed and many ships sunk or disabled. Japan, on the other hand, held much of the Pacific Ocean. Its rule reached some 4,500 miles from its mainland in Asia to the Solomon and Gilbert Islands. The American Navy scored an early victory at the Battle of Midway in 1942 as carrier-based planes defeated a Japanese fleet sent to seize the island as a base, effectively halting the Japanese Pacific offensive and serving as a turning point in the War. The Japanese lost four of five heavy carriers in the battle. During a six-month stretch of 1942–43, the Guadalcanal campaign built on the advantage created by Midway; the campaign forced the Japanese to begin a retreat from which they never recovered. Losses were heavy on both sides, but the U.S. was able to replace ships and airplanes; the Japanese were not. Before long, Americans were fighting from island to island, or "leapfrogging"—one

thrust headed toward the Philippines, another through the central Pacific to bring troops and bombers within range of Tokyo.

Islands like Iwo Jima and Okinawa saw bloody battles as the Allies drove by land, sea, and air toward Japan. On February 19, 1945, after 72 days of continuous, if somewhat ineffectual, air strikes, 60,000 U.S. Marines went ashore on Iwo Jima. The operation used in total 800 warships, and sent 110,000 men ashore, supported by another 220,000 men on the water. The island's capture was to have taken 14 days. In the end, it took 36 days, and made casualties of a third of the Marine force: 5,931 dead, 17,372 wounded. Fleet commander Adm. Chester W. Nimitz's words are inscribed on the monument to the battle outside Washington, D.C.: "Uncommon Valor was a Common Virtue."

By 1945 the U.S. Marine forces in the Pacific had perfected the art of amphibious warfare. Specially trained troops landed on beaches throughout the Pacific. Tanks, artillery, and men stormed ashore in waves from landing craft, covered by supporting fire from the air and sea. The beachhead would first be secured

by American troops and machinery, then troops would advance inland.

Early amphibious efforts in another arena, the North African campaigns of November 1942, were not so skillful. Overburdened men drowned, and the transfer of armor and artillery from large ships to small landing crafts was ineffectual and cumbersome. Ninety-four percent of the first wave of landing craft was lost at Algiers; 35 percent was lost at Casablanca. Due to the element of surprise, however, the landings of the campaign were successful.

By the summer of 1944 the Americans had advanced close enough to reach Japan by air, and Japanese cities began to feel the fury of American bombs. Over the following months, Japan's situation became hopeless, but the country's military leaders wanted to fight to the end to resist an invasion of their homeland.

On August 6, 1945, an American bomber, the *Enola Gay,* dropped an atomic bomb on the city of Hiroshima. It blotted out the city in a blinding flash. Three days later another bomb was dropped on Nagasaki. Five days later Japan surrendered, and World War II was over.

Tomorrow couldn't come soon enough for the Americans returning home to claim their Miracle Houses in the suburbs. Others remained overseas, while the wartime alliance with the Soviet Union unraveled over Soviet expansion in eastern Europe. The cocksure grin of the GI was fast becoming a fixture overseas; his cigarettes, soft drinks, and chewing gum were giving the world a taste for things American. A peace made prosperous by the U.S. economy—and kept by U.S. monopoly of the atom bomb—seemed assured.

OPPOSITE, ABOVE: *On the other side of the world, war raged against Japan. Pilots aboard the Japanese carrier* Kaga *study a last-minute sketch of attack routes chalked on the deck, preparing to attack American forces at Pearl Harbor in Hawaii.*

OPPOSITE, BELOW: *At Pearl Harbor, small two-man Japanese midget submarines infiltrated the harbor. One carried this chart showing harbor depths and a proposed route around Ford Island.*

# The MANHATTAN PROJECT

❧

## *Igniting the Air*

"We knew the world would not be the same. A few people laughed, a few people cried. Most people were silent. I remembered the line from the Hindu scripture, the *Bhagavad gita*....'I am become Death, the destroyer of worlds.' I suppose we all thought that, one way or another."

Robert Oppenheimer was reflecting on the vision he saw as he looked upon the havoc he helped to release at a desolate spot in the New Mexico desert in July 1945.

The Manhattan Project, which created atomic weapons, presents a dual paradox: With it the United States unlocked the mysteries of the atom, but it also introduced to the world the most destructive form of warfare known to man. It has been controversial for more than half a century.

It was born in the midst of World War II in an atmosphere of hurried alarm: There was evidence that Hitler's Nazi scientists were attempting to harness the atom for their own nefarious reasons. Much of the early research for the project was done in New York City by the Manhattan Engineer District of the U.S. Army Corps of Engineers—so it took the name the Manhattan Project. It would take four

years of work, from 1942 to 1945, and $1.8 billion 1940s dollars to design and build three atomic bombs. "Gadget," the first, was exploded as a test; "Little Boy," the second, destroyed much of Hiroshima, Japan; and "Fat Man" did much the same to Nagasaki. The Project was unusual in that it involved cooperation among scientists, military officers, and civilians. Conducted in great secrecy, it efficiently produced the desired result. Ironically, many of the scientists who worked on it had fled the persecution of Hitler's Germany.

The essential fissionable component of an atom bomb is Uranium 235, which cannot be separated from its natural companion, the much more plentiful uranium 238, by chemical means; the atoms must be separated by physical means. One method, the electromagnetic process, was developed at the University of California at Berkeley under Ernest Orlando Lawrence; the diffusion process was developed under Enrico Fermi at Columbia University. Both required large, complex facilities and enormous amounts

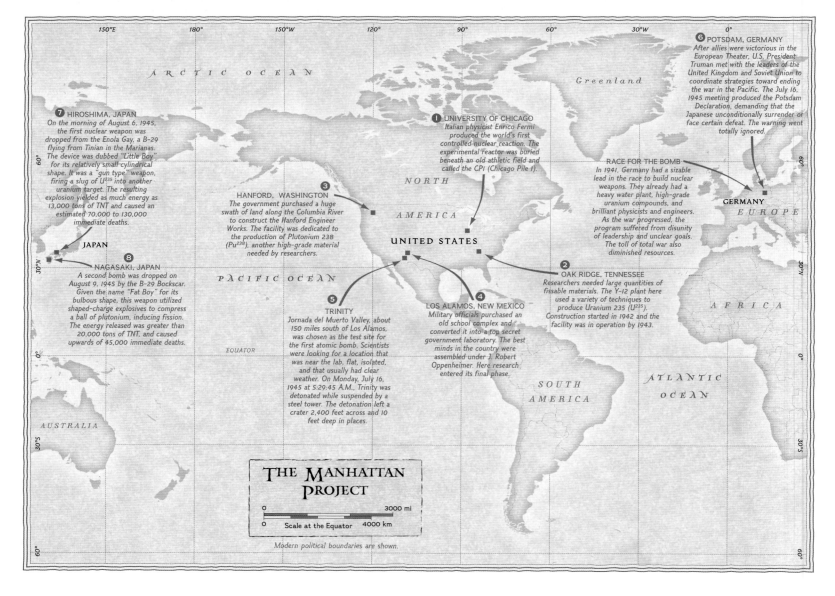

**THE MANHATTAN PROJECT**

0 — 3000 mi
0 — Scale at the Equator — 4000 km

*Modern political boundaries are shown.*

**❼ HIROSHIMA, JAPAN**
On the morning of August 6, 1945, the first nuclear weapon was dropped from the Enola Gay, a B-29 flying from Tinian in the Marianas. The device was dubbed "Little Boy" for its relatively small cylindrical shape. It was a "gun type" weapon, firing a slug of U²³⁵ into another uranium target. The resulting explosion yielded as much energy as 13,000 tons of TNT and caused an estimated 70,000 to 130,000 immediate deaths.

**❽ NAGASAKI, JAPAN**
A second bomb was dropped on August 9, 1945 by the B-29 Bockscar. Given the name "Fat Boy" for its bulbous shape, this weapon utilized shaped-charge explosives to compress a ball of plutonium, inducing fission. The energy released was greater than 20,000 tons of TNT, and caused upwards of 45,000 immediate deaths.

**❶ UNIVERSITY OF CHICAGO**
Italian physicist Enrico Fermi produced the world's first controlled nuclear reaction. The experimental reactor was buried beneath an old athletic field and called the CP1 (Chicago Pile 1).

**❸ HANFORD, WASHINGTON**
The government purchased a huge swath of land along the Columbia River to construct the Hanford Engineer Works. The facility was dedicated to the production of Plutonium 238 (Pu²³⁸), another high-grade material needed by researchers.

**❺ TRINITY**
Jornada del Muerto Valley, about 150 miles south of Los Alamos, was chosen as the test site for the first atomic bomb. Scientists were looking for a location that was near the lab, flat, isolated, and that usually had clear weather. On Monday, July 16, 1945 at 5:29:45 A.M., Trinity was detonated while suspended by a steel tower. The detonation left a crater 2,400 feet across and 10 feet deep in places.

**❹ LOS ALAMOS, NEW MEXICO**
Military officials purchased an old school complex and converted it into a top secret government laboratory. The best minds in the country were assembled under J. Robert Oppenheimer. Here research entered its final phase.

**❷ OAK RIDGE, TENNESSEE**
Researchers needed large quantities of fissable materials. The Y-12 plant here used a variety of techniques to produce Uranium 235 (U²³⁵). Construction started in 1942 and the facility was in operation by 1943.

**❻ POTSDAM, GERMANY**
After allies were victorious in the European Theater, U.S. President Truman met with the leaders of the United Kingdom and Soviet Union to coordinate strategies toward ending the war in the Pacific. The July 16, 1945 meeting produced the Potsdam Declaration, demanding that the Japanese unconditionally surrender or face certain defeat. The warning went totally ignored.

**RACE FOR THE BOMB**
In 1941, Germany had a sizable lead in the race to build nuclear weapons. They already had a heavy water plant, high-grade uranium compounds, and brilliant physicists and engineers. As the war progressed, the program suffered from disunity of leadership and unclear goals. The toll of total war also diminished resources.

of electricity to produce even small amounts of separated uranium 235; their production began on a 70-acre tract near Knoxville, Tennessee—Oak Ridge.

An atomic bomb is powerful and destructive because of fission, the chain reaction that occurs when exploded. Fission occurs when the central part of an atom, the nucleus, breaks into two equal fragments. The fragments release other neutrons that break up more atoms, and a chain reaction takes place—in millionths of a second.

Test director Kenneth T. Bainbridge settled on an isolated site near Alamogordo, New Mexico, a valley called the Jornada del Muerto, to build the bomb. Oppenheimer selected the name by which the site would be known: Trinity.

While work went on at Alamogordo, the rest of the world was oblivious to developments there. President Roosevelt, whose health had been deteriorating for some time, suddenly died and his successor, President Harry Truman, who had never heard of the bomb, had to be

brought into the undertaking and fully briefed. Then the Germans surrendered in Europe, ending the war there and concentrating the world's attention on the Pacific front. There were unanswered questions about the practicality of an atomic bomb: Fermi seriously wondered if the explosion might escape from its handlers and ignite the atmosphere.

On July 16, 1945, the first test was conducted. Observers about 10,000 yards from the blast site, wearing welders' glasses and suntan lotion, watched the equivalent of 20,000 tons of TNT explode. At ground zero the temperature rose to between 3000° and 4000° C. Everyone pronounced the test a success.

But now disagreements arose about whether the bomb was truly necessary to end the war. And if it was, should it be used on only military targets—or on a Japanese city? Some argued that the Japanese should be shown a demonstration of the bomb's power; perhaps they would be cowed into surrender. Others

insisted that only the destruction of the Japanese homeland would provide the shock that would lead to their surrender.

In the end, the proponents of the bomb won out: Its use, they pointed out, would save thousands of Allied lives by removing the necessity of invading of the Japanese islands. President Truman ordered their use. On August 6, 1945, a B-29 Flying Fortress named the *Enola Gay*—for the pilot's mother—dropped Little Boy on the city of Hiroshima. It missed its primary target by several hundred feet but still destroyed much of the city and killed 70,000 people; many thousands more would later die from radiation poisoning.

After Fat Man was dropped on Nagasaki, Japan surrendered. A new age had begun.

ABOVE: *Nearly wiped from the face of the Earth, the Japanese city of Hiroshima bears grim witness to the power of the atomic bomb. This photograph was taken the day of the blast, August 6, 1945.*

# INTEGRATING SPORTS

*Playing the Game*

Baseball player Satchel Paige offered advice on how to stay young. "Avoid fried meats which angry up the blood. If your stomach disputes you, lie down and pacify it with cool thoughts. Keep the juices flowing by jangling around gently as you move. Go very light on the vices, such as carrying on in society. The social ramble ain't restful. Avoid running at all times. Don't look back. Something might be gaining on you."

Satchel Paige was a tremendous baseball player, but he and his fellow African American players truly were in a league of their own. After the Civil War, when baseball began growing in popularity across the country, the players were strictly segregated—whites on white teams, blacks on black.

In the late 1880s black teams were organized into the League of Colored Baseball Clubs. Teams included the Boston Resolutes and the Lord Baltimores. One team, the Cuban Giants, were not from Cuba at all but called themselves that to avoid the racism directed at black teams.

It took a far-sighted owner, Branch Rickey of the Brooklyn Dodgers, to break the color barrier. He hired a 28-year-old infielder named Jackie Robinson and on a cold, rainy afternoon in April 1947 sent him to bat—the first black player in Major League baseball. With calm dignity he faced taunts, indignities, bean balls, and even death threats from many fans. His first year he batted .297, scored 125 runs, and lead the team in stolen bases with 29.

The traditionally all-white sport of golf long limited African Americans to roles as caddies and country club staff, but notable exceptions broke from the ranks. George Grant invented the golf tee in 1899. Rhonda Fowler, a pioneering black woman golfer, was Women's Eastern Champion in 1935, and in 1948 three black men—Theodore Rhodes, Bill Spiller, and Madison Gunther—filed a lawsuit against the PGA for civil rights violations. The PGA changed to a "by-invitation-only" format to avoid having to admit blacks, but the lawsuit was an early salvo in the civil rights movement.

In the 19th century, many African American men were successful jockeys. Willie Simms is the only one to have won all of the Triple Crown classics. He and Isaac Burns Murphy were elected to the National Museum of Racing Hall of Fame in Saratoga Springs, New York, the only two blacks so honored. In 1892 Alonzo "Lonnie" Clayton, then 15, riding a horse named Azra, became the youngest jockey ever to win the Kentucky Derby.

Another trailblazer was Jesse Owens. He not only rose from a poor background to become a world-famous athlete, but he also made ridiculous the racial theories of the world's most brutal dictator.

He was born in Alabama in 1913 and grew up in Cleveland, Ohio. His name was James Cleveland, and his friends and family called him J. C. until an early teacher, on his first day of class, thought she heard him say Jesse instead of J. C.—so Jesse he forever remained. He discovered a love and talent for running early on, set state and national records in high school and world records in college at Ohio State. Like other black athletes there he was not allowed to live on the campus, and when the team traveled he and his black teammates could not eat with the whites; they either ordered carryout or found black restaurants. Also, most white hotels would not accept them as guests, and those that did required them to enter from the alley and stay out of the elevators. Up the stairs they climbed. Despite all this, Jesse set three world records and tied a fourth at a Big Ten meet in Ann Arbor, Michigan, on May 25, 1935.

In 1936 he journeyed to Berlin for the Olympic Games. Hitler hosted the games, expecting to show the world the superiority

of his so-called Aryan German athletes. "I wanted no part of politics," said Jesse. "I'd learned long ago…the only victory that counts is the one over yourself." While Hitler fumed in the stands, Jesse won the 100-meter dash, the 200-meter dash, and the broad jump. Of his final jump, he said, "I decided I wasn't going to come down. I was going to fly. I was going to stay up in the air forever." In track and field competitions, he was the first American to win four gold medals in a single Olympics.

By the time of their deaths—Jackie died in 1972, Jesse in 1980—blacks were commonplace in all professional sports.

In baseball, Willie Mays, Reggie Jackson, and Henry Aaron excelled. Aaron retired with a record 755 career home runs, as well as career marks for most games, at bats, total bases, and RBIs—and managed a .305 average for his 23 seasons. Jackson—the Yankees' "Mr. October"—hit three homers in one Series game. Mays, with 660 home runs, followed only Babe Ruth and Aaron on the all-time list—until Mark McGwire hit 70 homers in 1998. African American Barry Bonds topped even that in 2001, hitting 73 home runs for the season.

In professional football, one of the earliest black superstars was fullback Jim Brown of the Cleveland Browns. His size, speed, elusiveness, and power seemingly allowed him to run around or through anyone. His 1957-65 career rushing record of 12,312 yards endured into the 1980s.

For the title of "the Greatest," two black athletes might argue. "I am the greatest," Cassius Marcellus Clay, Jr., of Louisville, Kentucky, proclaimed, from the beginning of his boxing career. "Float like a butterfly, sting like a bee," became his mantra. As a brash 18-year-old, he won a gold metal in the Olympics in 1960, then became a flamboyant world champion. He found a new religion with the Black Muslims and a new name, Muhammad Ali. He successfully defended his title nine time, but was stripped of the championship and sentenced to five years in prison in 1967 for refusing to submit to the draft. Ill with Parkinson's disease, he retired in 1981 but returned to carry the torch at the Atlanta Olympics in 1996.

Michael Jordan is widely considered the finest basketball player the game has ever seen—black or white. In 1998 Frank Deford wrote in *Sports Illustrated,* "If there is a heaven on earth, it certainly includes a vision of Jordan at the height of his powers." He led the U.S. to Olympic gold medals in 1984 and 1992. He twice led the once hapless Chicago Bulls to three consecutive championships. Even one of his rivals, Boston Celtics great Larry Bird, called him "God disguised as Michael Jordan." He benefited from something earlier blacks would have only wondered at: endorsements. When Nike introduced Air Jordan shoes in 1984, his first pro season, it hoped to sell $3 million worth in three years. But thanks to His Airness they sold more than $130 million in that year alone. His fame made him the highest paid athlete ever.

Sportswriters named Native American Jim Thorpe the greatest male athlete of the first half of the 20th century. He earned gold in the 1912 Olympics for the decathlon and pentathlon, then excelled in professional football and baseball. As an Indian he endured many of the same slights and inequities as blacks.

ABOVE: *Jackie Robinson, far right, the man who broke the color barrier in major league baseball in 1947, poses with fellow Brooklyn Dodgers in 1950.*

OPPOSITE: *Jesse Owens dazzled crowds at the 1936 Berlin Olympics, winning four gold medals and infuriating Hitler, who boasted of the racial superiority of his so-called Aryan people.*

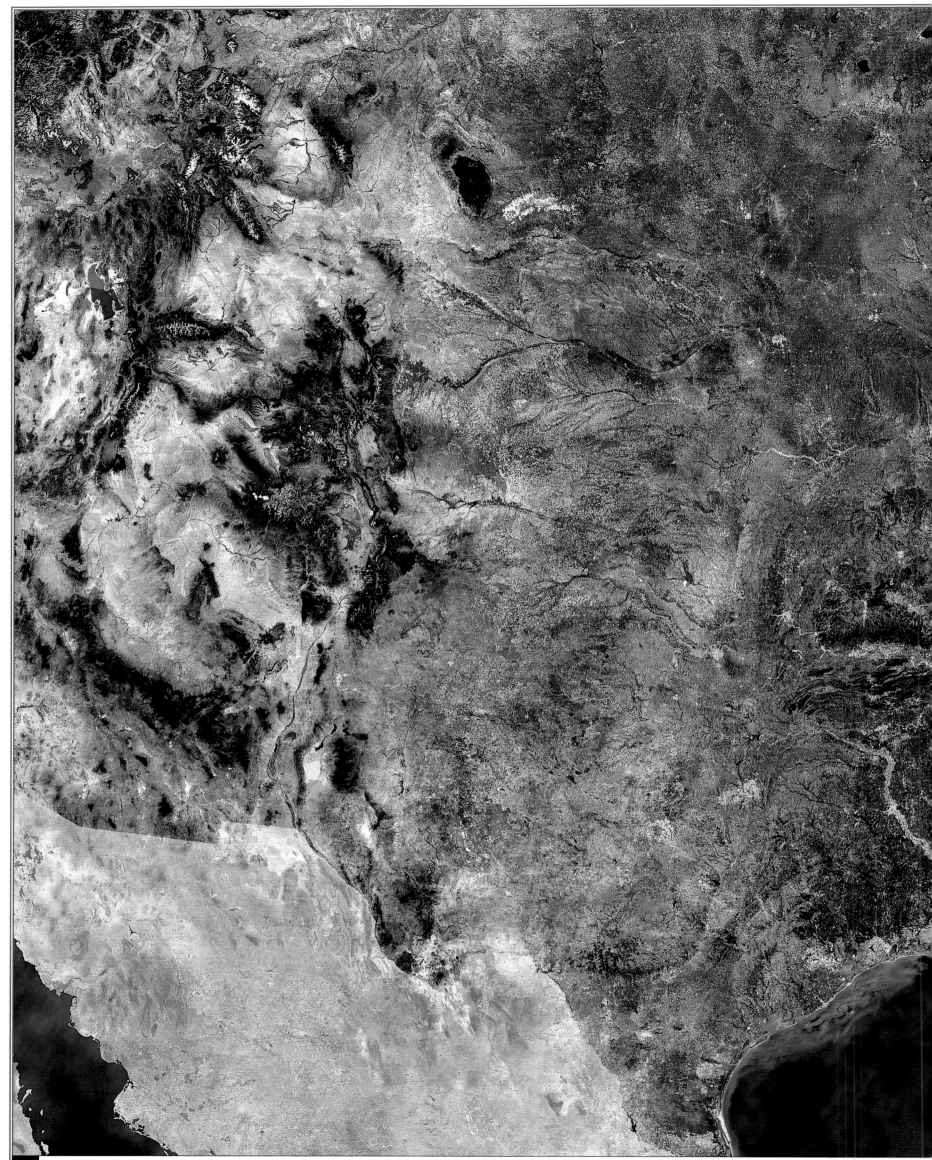

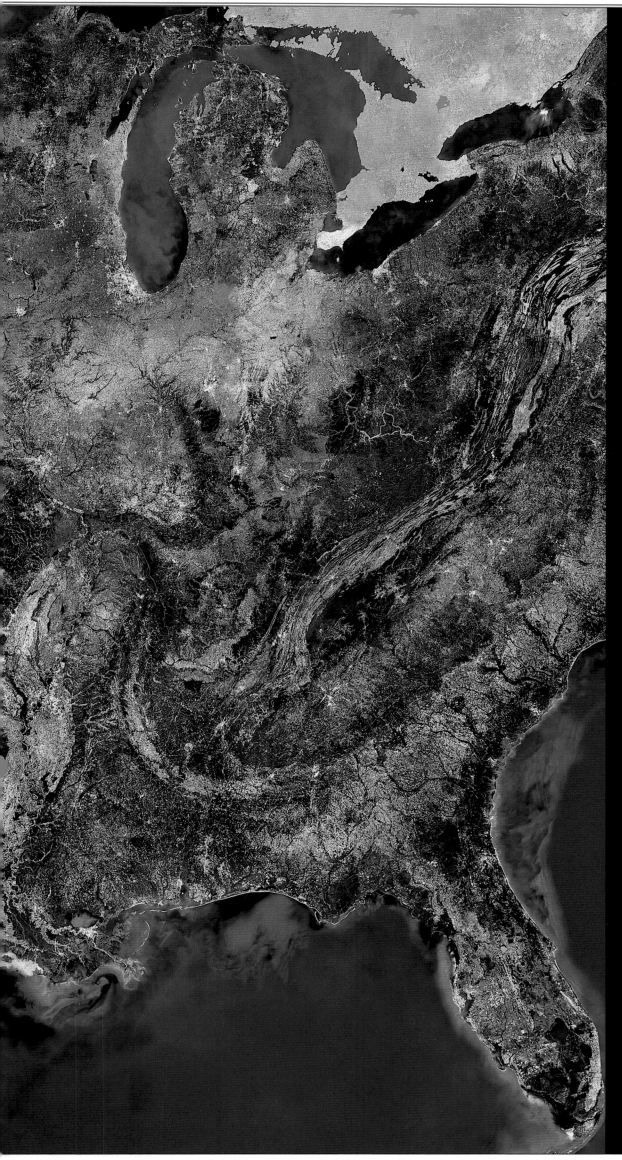
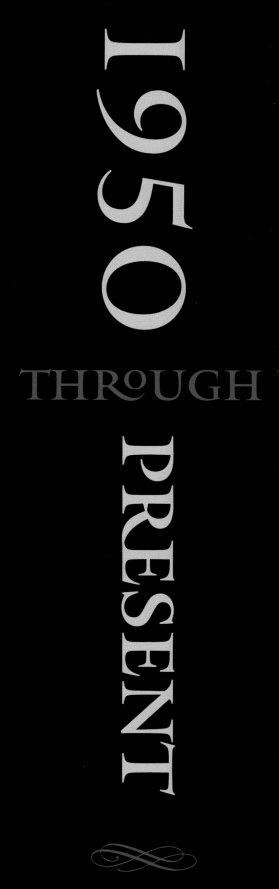

# 1950

## THROUGH

## PRESENT

*Decades of Change*

America enters the digital age; a mosaic of
432 images combine for a cloud-free portrait.

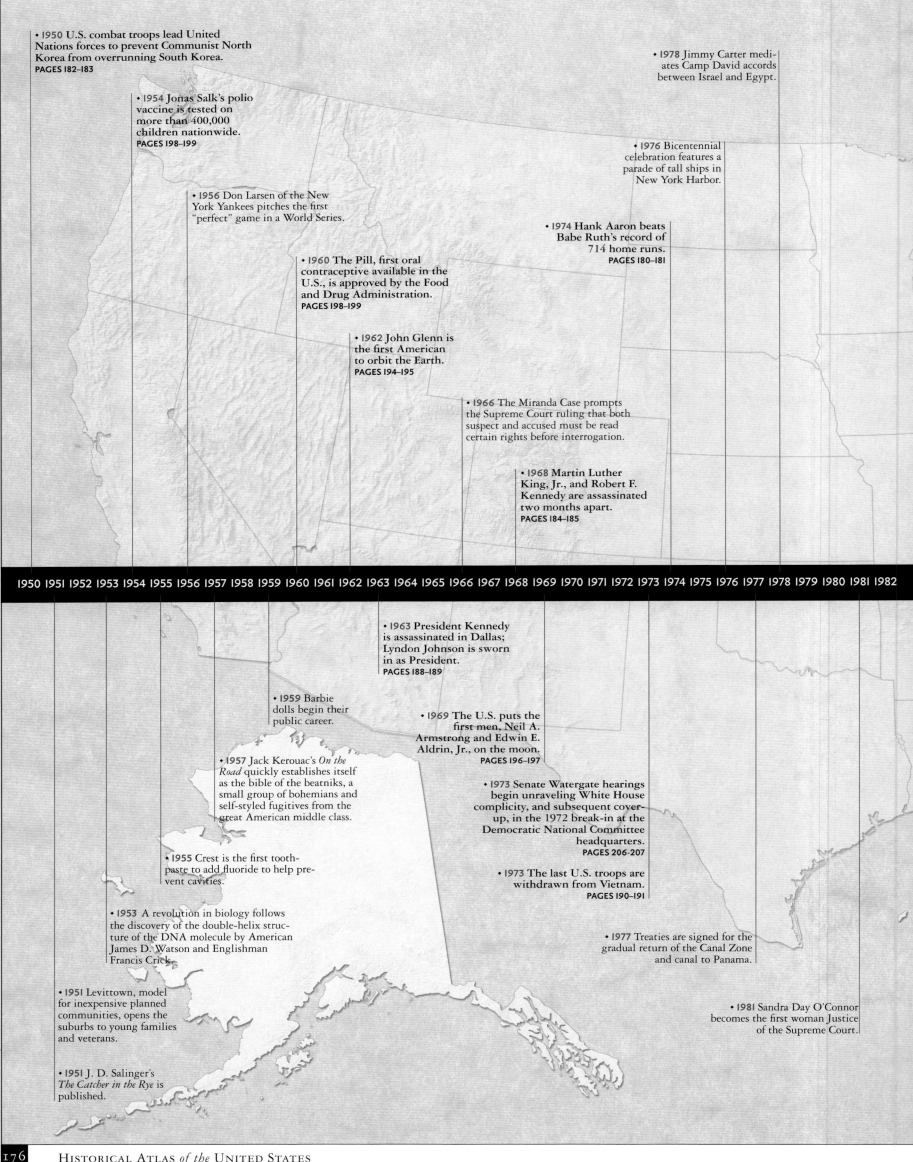

• 1950 U.S. combat troops lead United Nations forces to prevent Communist North Korea from overrunning South Korea. **PAGES 182–183**

• 1978 Jimmy Carter mediates Camp David accords between Israel and Egypt.

• 1954 Jonas Salk's polio vaccine is tested on more than 400,000 children nationwide. **PAGES 198–199**

• 1976 Bicentennial celebration features a parade of tall ships in New York Harbor.

• 1956 Don Larsen of the New York Yankees pitches the first "perfect" game in a World Series.

• 1974 Hank Aaron beats Babe Ruth's record of 714 home runs. **PAGES 180–181**

• 1960 The Pill, first oral contraceptive available in the U.S., is approved by the Food and Drug Administration. **PAGES 198–199**

• 1962 John Glenn is the first American to orbit the Earth. **PAGES 194–195**

• 1966 The Miranda Case prompts the Supreme Court ruling that both suspect and accused must be read certain rights before interrogation.

• 1968 Martin Luther King, Jr., and Robert F. Kennedy are assassinated two months apart. **PAGES 184–185**

1950 1951 1952 1953 1954 1955 1956 1957 1958 1959 1960 1961 1962 1963 1964 1965 1966 1967 1968 1969 1970 1971 1972 1973 1974 1975 1976 1977 1978 1979 1980 1981 1982

• 1963 President Kennedy is assassinated in Dallas; Lyndon Johnson is sworn in as President. **PAGES 188–189**

• 1959 Barbie dolls begin their public career.

• 1969 The U.S. puts the first men, Neil A. Armstrong and Edwin E. Aldrin, Jr., on the moon. **PAGES 196–197**

• 1957 Jack Kerouac's *On the Road* quickly establishes itself as the bible of the beatniks, a small group of bohemians and self-styled fugitives from the great American middle class.

• 1973 Senate Watergate hearings begin unraveling White House complicity, and subsequent cover-up, in the 1972 break-in at the Democratic National Committee headquarters. **PAGES 206-207**

• 1955 Crest is the first toothpaste to add fluoride to help prevent cavities.

• 1973 The last U.S. troops are withdrawn from Vietnam. **PAGES 190–191**

• 1953 A revolution in biology follows the discovery of the double-helix structure of the DNA molecule by American James D. Watson and Englishman Francis Crick.

• 1977 Treaties are signed for the gradual return of the Canal Zone and canal to Panama.

• 1951 Levittown, model for inexpensive planned communities, opens the suburbs to young families and veterans.

• 1981 Sandra Day O'Connor becomes the first woman Justice of the Supreme Court.

• 1951 J. D. Salinger's *The Catcher in the Rye* is published.

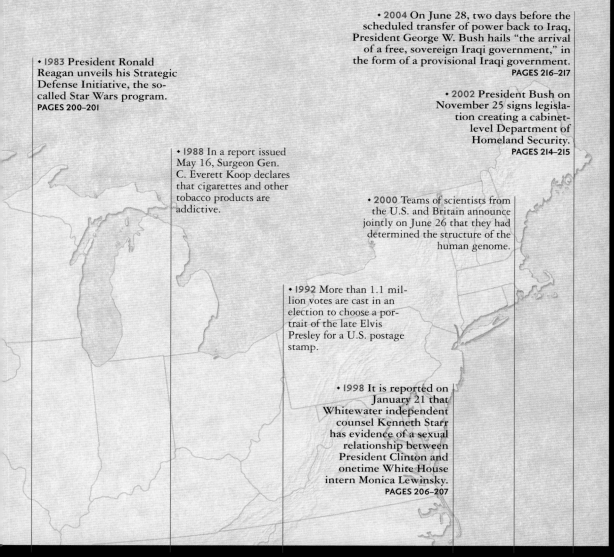

• 1983 President Ronald Reagan unveils his Strategic Defense Initiative, the so-called Star Wars program.
**PAGES 200–201**

• 2004 On June 28, two days before the scheduled transfer of power back to Iraq, President George W. Bush hails "the arrival of a free, sovereign Iraqi government," in the form of a provisional Iraqi government.
**PAGES 216–217**

• 2002 President Bush on November 25 signs legislation creating a cabinet-level Department of Homeland Security.
**PAGES 214–215**

• 1988 In a report issued May 16, Surgeon Gen. C. Everett Koop declares that cigarettes and other tobacco products are addictive.

• 2000 Teams of scientists from the U.S. and Britain announce jointly on June 26 that they had determined the structure of the human genome.

• 1992 More than 1.1 million votes are cast in an election to choose a portrait of the late Elvis Presley for a U.S. postage stamp.

• 1998 It is reported on January 21 that Whitewater independent counsel Kenneth Starr has evidence of a sexual relationship between President Clinton and onetime White House intern Monica Lewinsky.
**PAGES 206–207**

1983 1984 1985 1986 1987 1988 1989 1990 1991 1992 1993 1994 1995 1996 1997 1998 1999 2000 AND BEYOND

• 1993 A great summer flood inundates eight million acres in nine Midwestern states leaving 50 dead.
**PAGES 204–205**

• 1997 Timothy McVeigh is convicted of conspiracy and murder, June 2, for the 1995 Oklahoma City bombing.
**PAGES 214–215**

• 1999 Dr. Jack Kevorkian, who claimed he had helped 130 people kill themselves, is convicted of 2nd-degree murder on March 26; on April 13 he is sentenced to 10 to 25 years in prison.

• 1989 Just before a World Series game, October 17, an earthquake strikes the San Francisco Bay area, causing 62 deaths.
**PAGES 204–205**

• 1987 More than 200,000 gays, lesbians, and sympathizers march on Washington, D.C., to demand civil rights and stronger action against AIDS, an affliction first reported in the U.S. in 1981.

• 1983 U.S. servicemen are attacked in the Marine barracks in Beirut, Lebanon, by an Arab-driven truck bomb; 241 die.

"A MERICA IS A LARGE FRIEND-ly dog in a small room," Arnold Toynbee wrote, in 1954. "Every time it wags its tail it knocks over a chair."

Throughout the second half of the 20th century America seemed to be constantly knocking over chairs. Wealthier and more powerful than ever, America couldn't decide whether to be the world's policeman or its banker. It seemed to some that the harder America tried, the more enemies she made. "It bewilders Americans to be hated," wrote Lance Morrow in 1980.

American armies went to Korea and Vietnam and Iraq. The Peace Corps went everywhere. American streets became riot zones, as Americans protested wars and inequalities. Assassins' bullets felled revered leaders. At the same time, steps were taken into space, the final frontier. New technologies led to medical breakthroughs and, on the Internet, revolutions in the dissemination of knowledge.

When 1976 rolled around it was time to observe the Bicentennial of the most venerable of democratic nations that had been born in revolution. The president of France came to help celebrate what Lafayette had helped start. Valéry Giscard d'Estaing said: "It is not for us to predict what role you will actually play in the future. That…remains to be heard. I assure you of this: We are all listening."

Americans huddled nervously around their radios and TVs when the new millennium arrived, fearing the worst and hoping, as always, for the best. The new century brought some of both.

Back in 1900 Scottish critic William Archer had written, "The United States is a self-conscious, clearly defined, and heroically vindicated idea, in whose further vindication the whole world is concerned…. The United States of America, let us say, is a rehearsal for the United States of Europe, nay, of the world."

**1950–Present** *Saw the addition of the final two states to date to the Union, Alaska in January and Hawaii in August 1959.*

# The SMALL SCREEN

### The Birth of Television

Watching the first *See It Now* episode on November 18, 1951, viewers saw Edward R. Murrow pointing to two television monitors, one showing the Atlantic Ocean, the other the Pacific. Each coast could see the other—the North American continent shrunk to fit a small screen.

TV's largest early studio was opened in 1946 by DuMont, which linked New York and Washington, D.C., in the first commercial network. DuMont soon lost out to NBC, CBS, and ABC.

Transcontinental TV broadcasting began in 1951. AT&T's new coast-to-coast TV link (shared by the networks) transmitted President Harry Truman's address to the San Francisco peace conference that officially ended the war with Japan.

Television changed American society in many ways. In 1954 frozen TV dinners hit the market, and families found themselves perched in the flickering darkness, eating and watching TV at the same time.

In 1954, Wisconsin Senator Joseph McCarthy was feverishly pursuing his publicity-drenched hunt for Communists in government. During the televised hearings he charged U.S. Army Joseph Welch's law firm with employing a Communist. Welch responded, "I think I never really gauged your cruelty or your recklessness" and refuted the charge. McCarthy's power began to crumble, and he was condemned by his Senate colleagues.

Many consider the 1950s the Golden Age of American television. Vaudeville, in essence, made the leap from the stage to the small screen as variety shows featured comic skits, acrobats, and singing and dancing.

Milton Berle—Uncle Miltie—first came on the air in June 1948, and reigned supreme throughout the fifties, often in drag. *Your Show of Shows* with Sid Caesar debuted in February 1950 and ran until June 1954. Ninety minutes long, it featured Imogene Coca, Carl Reiner, and Howard Morris. Writers for the show

included such young talents as Woody Allen, Mel Brooks, Neil Simon, and Larry Gelbart. The smooth and relaxed Perry Como hosted an hour-long show between 1955 and 1963. "Dream Along With Me," he would sing at the beginning of each show. The Peter Gennaro dancers and the Ray Charles singers were regulars. *The Colgate Comedy Hour* was first to be telecast in color, on November 22, 1953. It featured rotating hosts such as Martin and Lewis and Abbott and Costello. *Your Hit Parade,* from 1950 until 1959, presented the seven most popular songs of the week.

But there were more than variety shows. *Today* premiered on January 14, 1952, and *Tonight,* with Steve Allen, in 1954. Several studios presented 90-minute original dramas each week. Paddy Chayefsky's *Marty* was broadcast in May, 1953, with Rod Steiger as the lonely Bronx butcher.

Later in the fifties westerns became popular. *Gunsmoke,* the first adult western, ran from 1955 to 1975 on CBS. *Bonanza* had Sunday nights on NBC, in color on the Ponderosa, from 1959 until 1973.

Politicians quickly learned the benefits of appearing on television, though some learned more slowly than others. In September 1960 candidates Richard Nixon and John Kennedy held the first presidential debate on TV, an occasion considered disastrous for the unphotogenic Nixon, whose five o'clock shadow famously cost him votes.

On September 9, 1956, pop singer and early American idol Elvis Presley appeared on the Ed Sullivan variety show, which showed the famous hip-swiveler only from the waist up.

In an emerging quiz show scandal, Columbia University Professor Charles Van Doren admitted to a U.S. House Subcommittee that he had been coached before appearances on NBC's *21* in 1956 in which he had won $129,000. His name became synonymous with "cheater," and the networks scrambled to clean up all their quiz shows.

Another generation watched the Vietnam "living-room war" in all its nightly news horror. And on July 20, 1969, the world

watched man's first steps on the moon—a giant leap for television and its audience.

TVs became focal points during crises. In 1963 President Kennedy's assassin was also assassinated—on live TV. Four days of nonstop coverage that started with three shots in Dallas became for many, including writer Marya Mannes, "total involvement....I stayed before the set, knowing—as millions knew—that I must give myself over entirely to an appalling tragedy, and that to evade it was a treason of the spirit."

Ownership of television sets had become widespread by the early 1960s. Most local stations depended on affiliation with one of the three major networks. The medium's novelty was color, and in December 1966 consumers for the first time bought more color than black-and-white sets.

Of the 106.7 million homes (98 percent of U.S. households) that owned at least one TV set in 2003, 100 percent had color; 34 percent had two sets; 41 percent had three or more sets; 91 percent had a VCR; 70 percent received basic cable, 48 percent received premium cable.

The average American in 2002 watched 30 to 35 hours of TV per week.

The top-rated show in 1950-51 was *Texaco/Star Theatre,* watched by 10,320,000 households. The top-rated show of all time was the final episode of *M\*A\*S\*H,* broadcast on February 28, 1983, when 50,150,000 households tuned in. Just 41,470,000 watched to see who shot J. R. on *Dallas* on November 11, 1980.

Cable television, which was begun in the 1950s so remote communities could share a large antenna, was boosted in the 1970s by satellites relaying TV signals. In 1981 a quarter of American households received cable TV; in 1987 half did. That rocketing trajectory and the rise, though much slower, of independent stations eroded the old-line networks' hegemony.

OPPOSITE: *Desi Arnaz gives his real-life wife, Lucille Ball, a peck on the cheek on the set of their television show,* I Love Lucy.

ABOVE: *Quiz shows had great popularity. A guest and his expert confer inside an isolation booth during a session of* The $64,000 Question, *around 1957. The quiz-show genre disappeared for a number of years when some shows were found to be rigged.*

# The MAJOR LEAGUES

*~*

## Play Ball!

"Whoever wants to know the heart and soul of America had better learn baseball," wrote Jaques Barzun. For more than 150 years Americans have peered into the game of baseball and seen themselves and their country reflected. A democratic game, it balances between individual accomplishments and team efforts—*e pluribus unum,* out of many, one. It is a national pastime that is for many a passion. Jane Forbes Clark, Chairman of the National Baseball Hall of Fame and Museum, wrote, "Reaching across generations and bridging different heritages, baseball embodies fair play, ingenuity, and teamwork—core attributes of the American character."

The myth that baseball was invented by Abner Doubleday during the Civil War has been pretty well put to rest. In fact, baseball was popular by 1855 and spread across the country during the war. The first baseball book designed for fans, *Beadle's Dime Base-Ball Player,* appeared in 1860. In 1868, an estimated 200,000 people attended baseball games.

The National League emerged in 1876, and by then many of the rituals of the game were in place. Newspapers carried intricate box scores that concisely summarized the previous day's play. Complex statistics, like batting averages and RBIs, allowed fans to measure players against one another. Fans with scorecards could keep a meticulous record of each play during a game. An early Edison electric lightbulb was displayed at a night game in Massachusetts in 1880. President Chester A. Arthur welcomed a group of athletes to the White House at the start of the 1883 season, declaring, "Good ballplayers make good citizens." And beginning in 1894, the Compton Electrical System took play-by-play results from a telegraph and relayed them to 10-by-10-foot displays depicting a baseball diamond. Fans could stand and watch a game progress. One of Edison's first movies, *The Ball Game,* appeared in 1898.

Pittsburgh radio station KDKA went on the air in November 1920 and in

its first summer carried a Pirates game live from Forbes Field. In 1922 Westinghouse touted its radios as a way for customers to hear Grantland Rice broadcast games from the Polo Grounds in New York. By the late 1920s five Chicago stations were carrying the Cubs home games. Some baseball executives feared that broadcasting the games would lessen the crowds at the ball parks, but the opposite happened: The more the fans heard of the games, the more they wanted to see them. When television came along it used the same tactics to sell sets: By 1947, 3,000 New York City bars had installed television, which carried the games.

The World Series—a ritual that is strictly American—was born in 1903, with the first meeting of the National and American Leagues. Pittsburgh in the National and Boston in the American played a best-of-nine competition for what they called the world's championship. Boston won in eight games, more than 100,000 fans attended, and the owners gave the players a share of the gate.

For the first decades of the century, the baseball was heavier, giving rise to the term Deadball Era. A young pitcher turned slugger, Babe Ruth, changed the face of the game with a then-record 29 home runs in 1919. He would go on to lead the New York Yankees, considered the greatest team of all time, to multiple World Series. The game became known for its great sluggers, including Lou Gehrig, Jimmy Foxx, and Rogers Hornsby.

During the days of World War I "The Star Spangled Banner" became a pregame fixture. Now some people say the last two words of the anthem are "Play ball!" During World War II some of the game's biggest stars were in uniform. Joe DiMaggio, Ted Williams, Hank Greenberg, and Bob Feller all did their part. Williams gave up four and a half seasons in the prime of his career to serve during both World War II and the Korean War.

After the war more people attended, and baseball saw several innovations, including racial integration of the game in 1947 and the rise of the minor leagues. The nation's interest became riveted on the inner-city rivalry between the Yankees and once lowly Brooklyn Dodgers. In a dramatic series of years in the 1950s, Brooklyn cried, "Wait till next year!" until finally they beat the Damn Yankees in the 1955 World Series.

The postwar boom didn't last long, however. Americans had other things to do—in their new suburbs with their new wealth. Additionally, there were no major league clubs west of St. Louis or south of Washington, D.C., so much of the population couldn't attend a game if they wanted to. And many ballparks were in city centers and not convenient for suburbanites. Attendance began to drop.

The first franchise changes since 1903 occurred in the 1950s. In 1953 the Braves, always in the shadow of the Red Sox, moved from Boston to Milwaukee, and the following year the St. Louis Browns moved to Baltimore. But the thunderbolt came in 1958, when the Dodgers and the Giants moved from New York City to California—the Dodgers to Los Angeles and the Giants to San Francisco. The decade of franchise movement was followed by several rounds of expansion that lasted into the 1990s, and the 154-game season was expanded to 162 in 1961 in the American League and 1962 in the National.

Players from many nations and ethnic backgrounds play alongside one another. There are Caucasians and Hispanics, men from the Dominican Republic, Puerto Rico, Cuba, Mexico, Venezuela, Nicaragua, and other Caribbean nations, as well as Japan, on the field. In the Dominican Republic baseball was a national sport and a national passion shortly after it was introduced there in the 1880s. Boys begin playing young, and they live in a tropical climate that allows for year-round play. Today, approximately 10 percent of all players in the major leagues are from the Dominican Republic.

---

ABOVE: *Yankee Clipper Joe DiMaggio shows his form after signing a $100,000 contract in 1950; the deal made DiMaggio the highest paid player in baseball.*

OPPOSITE: *Another star, Los Angeles Dodgers lefty Sandy Koufax, makes a pitch against the Minnesota Twins. His three-hit shutout gave the Dodgers the deciding game of the 1965 World Series.*

# STEMMING *the* COMMUNIST TIDE

## *The Korean Conflict*

After World War II, the U.S. and the Soviet Union agreed to joint occupation of Korea. Two young American colonels—one of them Dean Rusk—had half an hour to find a place to cut Korea in half. They chose the 38th Parallel, which put Korea's capital Seoul and 21 million people in the South and 9 million people and most of its industry in the North.

Edgy about communism, the Americans chose 70-year-old Syngman Rhee, who had been living in the U.S. since 1904 to govern the South; a Moscow-trained communist, 33-year-old Kim Il Sung, was put in place in the North. Both Rhee and Sung were in place by 1948, when the U.S. and the Soviet Union withdrew from Korea. It was a situation bound to fail. When Stalin gave Kim Il Sung permission to "liberate" the South, North Korean troops poured across the 38th Parallel.

"By God," said President Truman, on June 24, 1950, "I'm going to let them have

it." On June 27 the United Nations Security Council voted 7 to 1 to join the war on South Korea's side. It was the first time the UN had attempted to uphold international law by force of arms. The U.S. would contribute the bulk of the forces, followed by South Korea, Britain, Canada, Turkey, and Australia. American troops departed for the Korean Peninsula.

The fighting lasted from June 25, 1950, to July 27, 1953. At first the North Korean troops nearly swept the defending armies of South Koreans and American soldiers off the peninsula, capturing the capital of Seoul on June 27. To lead American troops, Truman sent 70-year-old Gen. Douglas MacArthur, who mobilized American ground forces from Japan. But they were underequipped, both militarily and emotionally, for the fight. Demoralized units repeatedly threw down their weapons and ran. They finally dug in, with their backs to the sea, at the southeastern port of Pusan. The tide was turned by a masterstroke by MacArthur, who made an amphibious landing at Seoul's seaport of Inchon, 200 miles behind the backs of the North Koreans. The 1st Marine Division retook Seoul.

The next phase of fighting took MacArthur and his men across the 38th Parallel into North Korea. But when they approached North Korea's border with China, thousands of Chinese troops, who had been waiting in North Korea's canyons and desolate valleys, attacked on all sides, often at night, in waves of bugle- and whistle-blowing masses. Even with their dead piled three deep they kept coming. They destroyed South Korean regiments and forced the Americans to retreat south across the Chongchon River. Farther east, another American force was beaten back in the longest retreat in American history, some 120 miles. Unflappable General Oliver Smith, asked about the retreat, said, "Gentlemen, we're not retreating. We are just advancing in a different direction."

American counterattacks pushed the Chinese back above the 38th Parallel and there a long, futile war of attrition began.

Peace talks began on July 10, 1951, but fighting continued for two more years. America lost 54,246 troops, the Chinese perhaps a million, South Korea 47,000. At

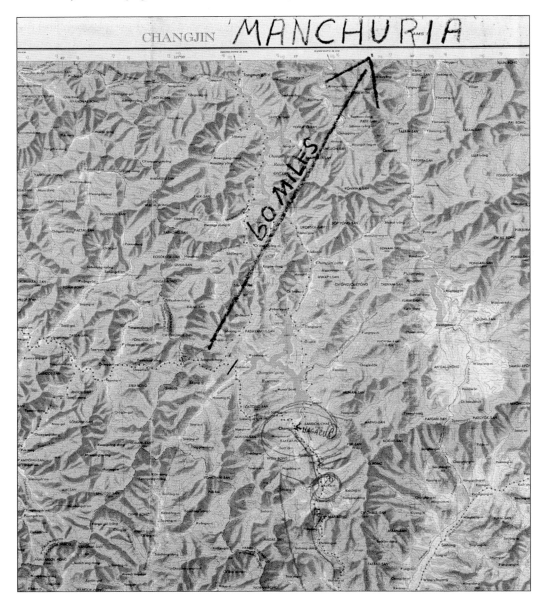

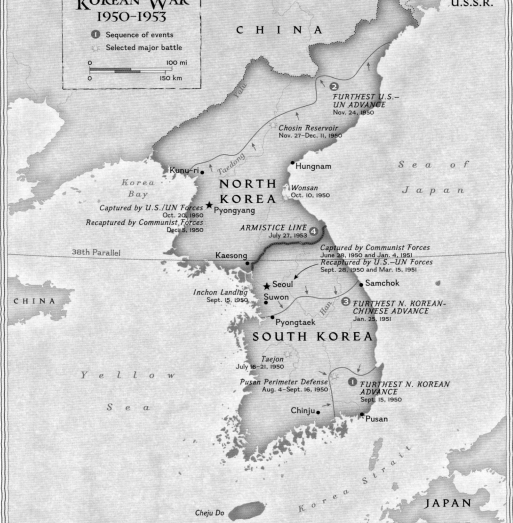

**KOREAN WAR**
**1950–1953**

- Sequence of events
- Selected major battle

0 — 100 mi
0 — 150 km

**CHINA**

**U.S.S.R.**

② FURTHEST U.S.–
UN ADVANCE
Nov. 24, 1950

Chosin Reservoir
Nov. 27–Dec. 11, 1950

Kunu-ri

Hungnam

*Sea of*

*Japan*

*Korea*
*Bay*

**NORTH**
**KOREA**

Wonsan
Oct. 10, 1950

Captured by U.S./UN Forces
Oct. 20, 1950
Pyongyang
Recaptured by Communist Forces
Dec. 5, 1950

ARMISTICE LINE
July 27, 1953 ④

Captured by Communist Forces
June 28, 1950 and Jan. 4, 1951
Recaptured by U.S.–UN Forces
Sept. 28, 1950 and Mar. 15, 1951

**38th Parallel**

Kaesong

**CHINA**

Inchon Landing
Sept. 15, 1950
Seoul
Suwon

Samchok

③ FURTHEST N. KOREAN–
CHINESE ADVANCE
Jan. 25, 1951

Pyongtaek

**SOUTH KOREA**

Taejon
July 16–21, 1950

*Yellow*

Pusan Perimeter Defense
Aug. 4–Sept. 16, 1950
① FURTHEST N. KOREAN
ADVANCE
Sept. 15, 1950

*Sea*

Chinju

Pusan

Cheju Do

*Korea Strait*

**JAPAN**

the end there were still two Koreas, separated by the 38th Parallel; communism ruled the North and capitalism the South.

A sidebar to the Korean drama played out between President Truman and his commander, Douglas MacArthur. MacArthur, cranky as he approached the end of a half-century career, chafed under civilian control. He argued vociferously for total war on Communist China. He requested 26 atomic bombs to be dropped on North Korea and China. He committed numerous acts of insubordination, disobeying orders that only Korean troops approach the Chinese border; bombing bridges over the Yalu River when directed to not bomb within five miles of the border; giving press interviews that undermined administration policy; publicly disagreeing with UN policies regarding reunification of the Koreas. He was frighteningly ready to risk global nuclear war.

Finally he read a message from Truman: "I deeply regret that it becomes my duty as Commander-in-Chief of the United States military forces to replace you as Supreme Commander, Allied Powers...." General Eisenhower, who had long known and disliked MacArthur, said, "I am going to maintain silence in every language known to man." MacArthur disliked Eisenhower equally. He described him as the apotheosis of mediocrity and the best clerk he ever had.

When MacArthur arrived back in San Francisco, half a million people lined the streets to cheer him, and in New York seven million attended a ticker tape parade. He gave an emotional 34-minute address to Congress. Truman described it as "nothing but a bunch of damn bullshit." At the end, MacArthur said: "I still remember the refrain of one of the most popular barrack ballads of that day, which proclaimed, most proudly, that 'Old soldiers never die. They just fade away.' And like the soldier of the ballad, I now close my military career and just fade away—an old soldier who tried to do his duty as God gave him the light to see that duty....Goodbye."

ABOVE: *Broadcast journalist Edward R. Murrow interviews a U.S. Marine on the Korean front. The conflict took forces perilously near Communist China.*

OPPOSITE: *A topographical map bears a Marine officer's marking showing the proximity of his position at Chosin Reservoir to Manchuria.*

# The FIGHT for CIVIL RIGHTS

## The Early Stirrings

Following the Civil War, the first years of freedom brought little economic change to landless freedmen trapped in the sharecropping system, though new political power gave hope to many. The 14th and 15th Amendments guaranteed equal citizenship and gave black men the right to vote. With the help of northern carpetbaggers and southern scalawags, blacks organized to win elective office. By the late 1870s, however, with the "redemption" of the South by traditional Democrats and the abandonment of Reconstruction by northern Republicans, hopes for true equality were crushed.

By 1908 all southern states had effectively barred blacks from the polls by such devices as literacy tests, property qualifications, and poll taxes. As political rights vanished, black leaders like Booker T. Washington stressed self-help and solidarity. Black-owned businesses—including banks, real estate firms, and insurance companies—catered to black communities, often with the support of black churches.

The Ku Klux Klan, founded in 1866 by former Confederate officers, underwent a resurgence as a nativist political force and spread its influence throughout the country in the 1920s. Catholics and Jews as well as blacks were among its targets. The Klan's political clout helped elect sympathetic governors in 11 states—seven of them in the Midwest and West.

Grotesque caricatures of black people were well entrenched as ordinary forms of white humor before the Civil War. Both white and black minstrels painted with blackface and half-moon smiles performed skits, songs, and jokes that portrayed blacks as mincing, frolicking fools. By the 1870s advertisements and

### JIM CROW

Shabby stereotypes of blacks were born early. One came from a popular ditty: "Wheel about, turn about, / Do jis so, / An' ebery time I wheel about / I jump Jim Crow." Clad in tatters and painted in blackface, Thomas D. Rice, a white man, sang and danced in the 1830s to that tune, breathing a kind of life into his hapless black character—to the great amusement of white northern audiences. Rice's character earned such fame that it later gave name to the growing body of segregation laws.

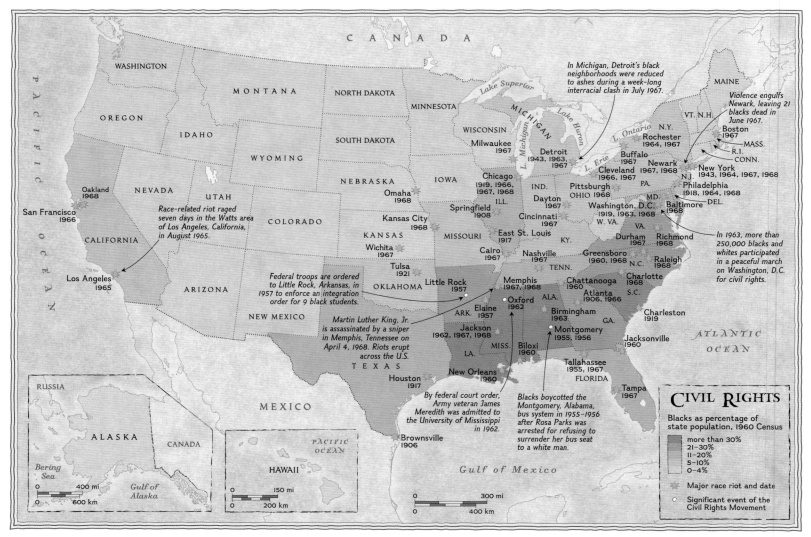

In Michigan, Detroit's black neighborhoods were reduced to ashes during a week-long interracial clash in July 1967.

Violence engulfs Newark, leaving 21 blacks dead in June 1967.

In 1963, more than 250,000 blacks and whites participated in a peaceful march on Washington, D.C. for civil rights.

Race-related riot raged seven days in the Watts area of Los Angeles, California, in August 1965.

Federal troops are ordered to Little Rock, Arkansas, in 1957 to enforce an integration order for 9 black students.

Martin Luther King, Jr. is assassinated by a sniper in Memphis, Tennessee on April 4, 1968. Riots erupt across the U.S.

By federal court order, Army veteran James Meredith was admitted to the University of Mississippi in 1962.

Blacks boycotted the Montgomery, Alabama, bus system in 1955-1956 after Rosa Parks was arrested for refusing to surrender her bus seat to a white man.

**CIVIL RIGHTS**

Blacks as percentage of state population, 1960 Census

- more than 30%
- 21–30%
- 11–20%
- 5–10%
- 0–4%

✳ Major race riot and date

● Significant event of the Civil Rights Movement

packaging often showed blacks with saucer lips and bulging eyes.

Black fictional characters such as Sambo, Uncle Remus, Aunt Jemima, Amos 'n' Andy, and the roles of film actor Lincoln Perry Monroe, who took the name "Stepin Fetchit," entered popular culture through various media. Those "humorous" depictions and other representations of blacks as servants or cooks or mammies perpetuated the idea that blacks were suited only for menial jobs. Intended or not, such portrayals reinforced notions of white racial superiority.

Unlike other minorities such as the Irish, who rose from the butts to the tellers of jokes, blacks had no recourse against public comedy aimed their way. Black comedy with sharp edges stayed underground or in small clubs before times began to change in the 1950s, and original voices such as Dick Gregory's were heard.

In *Uncle Tom's Cabin,* the character of Uncle Tom was a figure of kindness and dignity—a good stereotype. To militant blacks in the 1960s, however, calling some- one "Uncle Tom" was an insult, meaning

an obsequious black toady to whites. Stereotypes had come full circle.

In the early 20th century groups like the National Association for the Ad- vancement of Colored People (NAACP) pursued civil rights, defending victims of race riots and protesting discrimination against black soldiers during World War I. Black veterans returned from the war to find a rejuvenated Ku Klux Klan and segregation spreading northward with the movement of blacks into indus- trial cities. Freedom's business was still unfinished.

Separation of the races by law was still the rule in 1950. In many states blacks remained cut off from whites in virtually every phase of existence. The Supreme Court's "separate but equal" doctrine, aris- ing from the 1896 *Plessy* v. *Ferguson* case, applied to public transportation and accommodations, yet it was used as a rationale to establish segregation much more broadly. Local ordinances, usually even more restrictive than state laws, sanc- tioned what had already been the practice.

Newspaper reports of alleged black crimes contributed to vigilantism. Charges

involving rape or murder by black men were frequently sensationalized. Lurid accounts of such attacks were used to jus- tify lynchings, especially in the South. Of the 4,743 lynchings reported between 1882 and 1958, nearly 75 percent of the victims were black.

From its founding in 1909, the NAACP carried a large burden in the struggle for black equality. Using nonvi- olent political and legal actions, the NAACP prompted many important civil rights acts and Supreme Court decisions. For example, in 1944, it was declared that primary elections could not be closed to blacks, ruled in *Smith* v. *Allwright*. In 1948 restrictive covenants requiring homeowners to sell only to whites could not be enforced in the courts, decided in *Shelley* v. *Kraemer*. In 1954 public school segregation, curtailed by earlier cases that had required specific schools to take black

---

ABOVE: *Eerily matter-of-fact, a crowd gathers on a hot August evening in Marion, Indiana, in 1930 to gawk at a lynching. Between 1889 and 1918, some 2,500 blacks were lynched in the U.S., 50 of them women.*

students, was ruled unconstitutional in *Brown* v. *Board of Education, Topeka, Kansas.*

In 1957 the Civil Rights Commission, a bipartisan advisory committee, was created by Congress. The Civil Rights Act of 1957 was the first civil rights legislation of the 20th century. The act pledged that voting rights would be enforced by federal officials if courts found a "pattern or practice" of disfranchising blacks in a state or locality. In 1964 it pressed further, prohibiting discrimination in jobs and public places and empowering the attorney general to sue the offender.

And other legislation would continue to be passed. In 1962, discrimination in housing projects funded by the federal government was banned by a presidential executive order. A few years later, 1968's Federal Fair Housing Law prohibited racial discrimination in the sale and rental of most housing. Poll taxes were outlawed by the 24th Amendment, passed in 1964. A year later the Voting Rights Act eliminated literacy tests, provided for federal registrars to enroll blacks unlawfully deprived of the right to vote, and specifically outlawed intimidation of blacks trying to register or vote. Extension of the Voting Rights Act for five more years was signed by President Richard M. Nixon in 1970.

## Into Public Office

"Anyone looking for the civil rights movement only in the streets is mistaken. Politics is the civil rights movement of the 1970s. It is the first hurrah of the economically and politically oppressed." So in 1974 Atlanta's first black mayor, Maynard Jackson, described the changing tactics of the movement to secure full civil rights for Americans of African descent.

Legal demolition of the "separate but equal" doctrine of segregation came in 1954. Legal demolition of voting barriers came with the Civil Rights Act of 1964 and the Voting Rights Act of 1965. With the effective right to vote came the opportunity to win public office. It was taken by a new generation of black politicians, many of whom had apprenticed in

the civil rights movement. Their first hurrah was to run in—and often win—elections at the local, state, and federal levels. Among their number was the Rev. Jesse Jackson, who competed on equal terms with other candidates in his 1988 campaign for the Presidency.

In 1964 elected officials numbered just over a hundred; in 1987 almost 7,000 held public office. Black legislators helped enact policies to improve education, employment, and entrepreneurial and housing opportunities—civil rights issues had become bread-and-butter issues. Most visible politically were black mayors in major cities, who faced problems that had multiplied during decades of urban neglect.

Many blacks benefited from economic gains growing out of political gains. An expanding middle class was better educated, better paid, and better housed than ever before. Equal opportunity and affir-

mative action had opened many doors. Many rose to high positions in the armed forces, where a disproportionate number died while serving in Vietnam. The military services became the most thoroughly integrated of all the federal institutions.

Despite progress, an underclass was left behind in the inner cities—people isolated from examples of stability and hope: family, church, and community organizations. Since the 1950s drugs and violence have blighted lives already afflicted by unemployment and decaying housing.

Despite advances in the law, many blacks were frustrated by slow progress in reality. From the 1940s through the early 1970s, blacks first used civil disobedience to assert their rights, then increasingly vented their rage in riots.

Peacably enough, in 1955 and 1956, blacks boycotted the Montgomery,

Alabama, bus system after Rosa Parks was arrested for refusing to surrender her seat to a white man. In 1961 the Congress of Racial Equality (CORE) dispatched freedom riders throughout the South to test whether transportation facilities there were in fact desegregated. And in 1963 more than 250,000 blacks and whites participated in a peaceful march on Washington, D.C., for civil rights.

And even as education desegration made political gains such as the 1962 federal court order that Air Force veteran James Meredith be admitted to the University of Mississippi, other attempts needed armed support: In 1957, President Dwight D. Eisenhower ordered federal troops to Little Rock, Arkansas, to enforce an integration order for nine black students in Central High School.

By the mid-1960s there were often outbreaks of violence by those frustrated by the delay in being granted full civil rights. A race-related riot raged for six days in the Watts area of Los Angeles in June 1965. Two years later reports of police brutality in Newark, N.J., sparked riots that claimed the lives of 21 blacks and marked the beginning of the "long hot summer," and, in Michigan, Detroit's black neighborhoods were reduced to ashes during a week-long interracial clash in July.

"Put on your marching shoes. Walk with me into a new dignity," Martin Luther King, Jr., had challenged his followers. He had grown up in Atlanta, a bold and persistent child. His dreams emerged as he matured. He dreamed of help for the poor—on dirt farms in the South, in ghettos in the North. He dreamed of peace. After the bus protest in Montgomery, which he helped organize, he became the transcendent figure in the civil rights movement. He preached nonviolence and conciliation. During the 1963 March on Washington, he held a huge audience spellbound as he described his vision of America. In 1964 he won the Nobel Peace Prize.

In 1968 Martin Luther King, Jr., president of the Southern Christian Leadership Conference, civil rights leader, and Nobel Peace Prize laureate, was assassinated by a sniper in Memphis, Tennessee, on April 4. His death sparked riots in several cities.

## BROWN *v.* BOARD *of* EDUCATION

In approaching this problem, we cannot turn the clock back to 1868 when the [Fourteenth] Amendment was adopted. We must consider public education in the light of its full development and its present place in American life throughout the Nation. Only in this way can it be determined if segregation in public schools deprives these plaintiffs of the equal protection of the laws....

Whatever may have been the extent of psychological knowledge at the time of *Plessy* v. *Ferguson*, this finding [that segregation has a tendency to retard the educational and mental development of black children] is amply supported by modern authority. Any language in *Plessy* v. *Ferguson* contrary to this finding is rejected.

We conclude that in the field of public education the doctrine of "separate but equal" has no place. Separate educational facilities are inherently unequal.

ABOVE: *Federalized Arkansas National Guardsmen provide cover as five African-American girls enter Central High in Little Rock. The desegregation, ordered by the U.S. Supreme Court, took place on October 2, 1957.*
OPPOSITE: *Dr. Martin Luther King, Jr., greets participants in the March on Washington, August 28, 1963.*

# TRAGEDY *and* LOSS

## *Assassination Plagues the Nation*

On April 3, 1968, Dr. Martin Luther King, Jr., gave a speech. "Like anybody, I would like to live a long life. Longevity has its place. But I'm not concerned about that now. I just want to do God's will. And He's allowed me to go up to the mountain and I've looked over, and I've seen the promised land. I may not get there with you. But I want you to know that we, as a people, will get to the promised land. And so I'm happy tonight. I'm not worried about anything. I'm not fearing any man. Mine eyes have seen the glory of the coming of the Lord."

The next morning, Dr. King stepped out onto a balcony of the Lorraine Motel in Memphis, Tennessee, and was shot by a 39-year-old career criminal named James Earl Ray. The Rev. Ralph Aber-nathy, a friend and colleague, was at King's side in a moment, cradling his head and patting his cheek, murmuring, "This is Ralph, this is Ralph, Martin, don't be afraid." But the wound was fatal.

Dr. King's assassination was one of a number of such killings—including those of John F. and Robert Kennedy—in the 1960s that shook Americans to their souls. Many wondered if the streak of violence that had haunted the country's history—from slavery and the elimination of whole tribes of Indians to the hair-triggered gun-slingers of the old West—was still haunting the country. Was the American dream unraveling?

Tragedy would again visit the Kennedy family two months after the assassination of Dr. King. Robert F. Kennedy, younger brother of JFK, had declared himself a candidate for president. He had been addressing a predominantly black rally in Indianapolis when he heard of King's death; he announced it to the crowd and appealed to them to uphold Dr. King's legacy of nonviolence. He quoted a fragment from Aeschylus that had comforted him after his brother's murder: "In our sleep, pain which cannot forget falls drop by drop upon the heart until, in our own despair, against our will, comes wisdom through the awful grace of God."

Coming late to the presidential race, he campaigned hard, and by June 4, the time of the California primary, he was nearly exhausted. But on the day of the primary, buoyed by optimism as the evening wore on and the vote turned his way, he left his suite in the Ambassador Hotel to deliver a rousing speech to some 1,800 supporters in the hotel's ballroom. He exited through the hotel's pantry, where, just after midnight, a slim Palestinian named Sirhan Sirhan fired eight shots from a .22-cal. revolver, and, before horrified onlookers, Kennedy sprawled in a growing pool of blood.

Labels on the image:
TEXAS BOOK DEPOSITORY
CAMERAMAN NIX
TREE SHADED KNOLL
POINT OF IMPACT FATAL BULLET
ACTUAL POSITION OF VEHICLE
200 FT.
100 FT.

## MALCOLM X

He spent his first few years on the mean streets of Lansing, Michigan, as Malcolm Little, son of a murdered father and an institutionalized mother. In and out of trouble and detention homes, he moved to Boston to live with a sister in his early teens.

While in prison for burglary, he converted to the black Muslim faith and, released from prison, journeyed to Chicago to meet the sect's leader, Elijah Muhammad. He became Malcolm X—the X representing his long-lost African name.

He embraced the asceticism of Islam and began touring and speaking on race and religion. With bitter eloquence he railed against the white exploitation of blacks. He was contemptuous of the civil-rights movement and rejected both integration and racial equality. In mesmerizing speeches, he called for black separatism, black pride, and black self-dependence. He never encouraged any specific violent act, but he ridiculed Martin Luther King's nonviolence as suicidal.

He broke with Elijah in 1963 and returned from Mecca convinced that Islam embraced all colors and that the Black Muslims were wrong. "He was trapped somewhere between his utopian black nationalism with its ties to Mother Africa, and the competing chimera of Martin Luther King's completely integrated, beloved community, and the conflict would tear him apart before it made him a saint," wrote one historian.

He was assassinated by rivals on February 21, 1965, as he was preparing to speak in New York.

The death of JFK stunned Americans and left them, half a century later, still remembering exactly where they were and what they were doing on November 22, 1963, when they heard the awful news from Dallas. *Time* magazine correspondent Hugh Sidey had been traveling with the President in a press bus when he heard three sharp, strange sounds "from an ugly building 50 yards in front of us. CBS correspondent Robert Pierpoint, who had covered the Korean War, leaped to his feet and said, 'Those sounded like gunshots'." The news was confirmed later at Parkland Hospital when a priest blurted out, "He's dead, all right." Official word came a few minutes later and millions of Americans watched on television as a clearly distraught Walter Cronkite fumblingly read the statement.

For four days, Americans huddled around their television sets and watched as the unbelievable drama played out: The President's wife, Jackie, in blood-stained suit; his son John John saluting his father's casket; the assassin himself assassinated; the gathering of world leaders marching in the streets of Washington at the slain President's funeral.

The assassin was a former marine named Lee Harvey Oswald. The mystery of why he would kill such a vibrant president deepened two days later when he himself was shot by Jack Ruby, a Dallas businessman.

For decades following the killing, conspiracy theories abounded as Americans grappled with the truth: that a single disturbed young man could so profoundly alter history.

Violence would continue to plague American politics. On September 5, 1975, Lynette Fromme was arrested after a botched assassination attempt on President Gerald Ford. A further attempt was made on Ronald Reagan on March 31, 1981. John Hinckley's bullet instead paralyzed the President's press secretary, James Brady. This tragic moment would lead to the passage of the Brady Act, a law limiting the sale of firearms.

OPPOSITE: *With only moments to live, President John F. Kennedy waves from the rear of his limousine during a motorcade through the streets of Dallas, Texas. His shooting, on November 22, 1963, set off waves of conspiracy theories.*

ABOVE: *An aerial view of the site of John F. Kennedy's shooting was used in an attempt to disprove the "second gunman" theory of the assassination.*

# The WAR in SOUTHEAST ASIA

## Vietnam Conflict

I t was the longest war in America's history," Harold Evans has written, "in the end the most unpopular war, and the first modern war America lost. Vietnam was a watershed. It ended the liberal consensus that America had a duty to fight everywhere abroad for freedom. It destroyed the illusion of American omnipotence. It demoralized the armed forces. It polarized the country as nothing had since the Civil War…And it shattered everyone's faith in the honesty and credibility of government, since every administration involved systematically deceived the people."

The four presidents most deeply involved with Vietnam—Eisenhower, Kennedy, Johnson, and Nixon—were haunted by a domino theory born in World War II. As Poland, France, Belgium, Holland, Norway, and Denmark had fallen to Hitler's Nazis after he was allowed to take Czechoslovakia, then surely Thailand, Burma, Malaysia, Indonesia, and perhaps even India might go communist if they were allowed to take Vietnam. From there, communism's spread would be unstoppable. Lyndon Johnson said that if America lost Vietnam it would find itself defending the beaches of Waikiki. So American troops would go to war in far-off Southeast Asia.

It began with economic and military aid provided by the U.S. to the South Vietnamese. Secretary of State John Foster Dulles had assured the government that Americans need not die in far-off Asia—victory could be had merely by assisting the South Vietnamese. But the North Vietnamese troops—the Viet Cong—continued to infiltrate the South. President Kennedy authorized additional noncombatant military personnel, called advisers, and by the end of 1962 there were 11,000 in South Vietnam. If attacked, they were authorized to defend themselves with force.

Early in August 1964, in the Gulf of Tonkin, a U.S. destroyer reported being fired upon by North Vietnamese patrol boats. It was the second time such an attack had occurred there, President Johnson reported—erroneously. He persuaded Congress to endorse the Gulf of Tonkin Resolution, authorizing the President to take "all necessary measures to repel attacks." On his orders, U.S. planes began bombing North Vietnam.

After 1965 there was no more pretense that the U.S. was merely providing support; American troops poured into the country and fighting escalated. Military leaders maintained that the war could be won with a little more materiel and a few more troops. It was assumed that failure by the U.S. would lessen American credibility throughout the world. By June 1965, 50,000 American troops were fighting with the South Vietnamese, expanding to 180,000 by year's end.

But they were having little success: As is often the case, U.S. military leaders were refighting the last war—when massed armies met on clear-cut battlefields. The Viet Cong used different tactics: surprise attacks, ambushes, stealth,

communist forces, North Vietnam, South Vietnam, and the U.S. was reached. Signed on January 27, 1973, it put in place a cease-fire. It called upon an international force to keep peace; North Vietnamese troops could remain in the South but could not be reinforced, and the South would have the right to determine its own future. All prisoners of war would be released. U.S. troops would withdraw and their bases torn down.

In August 1973 the U.S. Congress voted against any further U.S. military activity in Indochina, and by year's end few U.S. military personnel remained there.

On July 2, 1976, the two Vietnams were finally united as the Socialist Republic of Vietnam. Its capital is Hanoi. Saigon was renamed Ho Chi Minh City.

and concealment. The U.S. sought to win with superior firepower and helicopters.

Still the number of U.S. troops climbed, to 389,000 in 1967.

Then came a major surprise. At the time of the lunar new year—Tet—in 1968, the North Vietnamese and Viet Cong launched coordinated attacks throughout the South, hitting 36 major cities and towns. Even in Saigon the fighting was fierce. The casualties the North suffered were enormous but so was their victory: a growing conviction in America that the war was foolish and could not be won. Protests against it grew in volume and number. Many Americans even wondered if the U.S. was morally justified in interfering in a conflict that looked very much like a Vietnamese civil war. But on it dragged.

President Richard Nixon in 1969 put in place a new policy called "Vietnamization." It sounded much like the policy that had launched the war: The U.S. would provide arms, equipment, air support, and economic aid, and the South Vietnamese would fight. American field commanders were ordered to keep casualties to "an absolute minimum," and they decreased considerably. In the meantime the peace talks underway between Hanoi and the U.S. in Paris made little progress.

In the spring of 1970, U.S. and South Vietnamese troops crossed the border into Cambodia to destroy Viet Cong bases there. U.S. planes appeared in the skies over northern Laos and bombed and napalmed North

Vietnamese troops battling American-supported Vientiane government troops.

By the end of 1971, U.S. withdrawal was proceeding quickly, and soon only 160,000 American troops were left.

In Paris, after years of negotiations, an agreement between the South Vietnamese

OPPOSITE: *A U.S. medical helicopter emerges from a pink cloud, smoke used to mark a drop zone, to evacuate wounded of the 173rd Airborne Regiment, ambushed in Vietnam in 1965.*
ABOVE: *Years later, in 2000, veterans marked this map with points showing where they had been based.*

VIETNAM WAR
1946-1975

Selected major battle

0    200 mi
0    300 km

Modern names are in parentheses.

## Protesters Take to the Streets

A parallel war to the one in the jungles of Southeast Asia was fought on the streets and campuses of the U.S. As the war in Vietnam grew, so did doubts about it at home. Into the mid-1960s, most Americans supported the involvement in Vietnam. But as the fighting dragged on, public opinion became bitterly divided. Why, many people asked, were Americans spilling blood in a war in far-off Asia? Students took to the streets and taunted President Johnson with the chant, "Hey! Hey! LBJ! How many kids did you kill today?"

The U.S. had been gradually drawn into a war for reasons that were not entirely clear. Growing numbers of young people began to burn draft cards. They organized antiwar marches, wore peace symbols, waved the North Vietnamese flag. Other Americans watched the protests with shock and anger. Bitter arguments took place among family members. Not since the Civil War had Americans been so divided.

On April 30, 1970, President Nixon announced that a massive American-South Vietnamese offensive into Cambodia was in progress. "We take these actions," he said, "not for the purpose of expanding the war into Cambodia, but for the purpose of ending the war in Vietnam, and winning the just peace we all desire."

The next day, students across the country rallied to protest what they saw as an escalation of the war. At Kent State, some 500 students gathered. Later that night a spontaneous rally began on the Strip, an area of downtown Kent with a number of bars. Passing police cruisers were hit with beer bottles; some windows were broken, primarily of "political targets": banks, loan companies, and utility companies.

On May 2, the mayor ordered a dusk-to-dawn curfew and alerted the Ohio National Guard of possible unrest. That night, 2,000 marchers swarmed across the Commons and surrounded the ROTC building. Twice the students set the building afire and twice firemen, hampered by rock throwing and hose slashing, brought it under control. Police surrounded the building and dispersed the students with tear gas. Arrival of

National Guard units inflamed them once again, and this time they succeeded in burning the ROTC building to the ground. (In the first two weeks of May, 30 ROTC buildings were burned nationwide.) Using tear gas and drawn bayonets, the Guard dispersed the students.

Ohio National Guard troops and armored personnel carriers were stationed throughout the campus. A feeling of uneasy, mutual hostility existed between the soldiers and students. Ohio Governor James Rhodes arrived in Kent and held a news conference, claiming that the demonstrators were the handiwork of a highly organized band of revolutionaries who were out to "destroy higher education in Ohio." They were "the worst type of people we harbor in America, worse

than the brown shirts and the communist element…. We will use whatever force necessary to drive them out of Kent." A National Guard commander told his troops that Ohio law gave them the right to shoot if necessary. That night, a crowd gathered and the Guard announced a new curfew and began to disperse the students. Tear gas was fired from helicopters hovering overhead. The crowd headed toward town and staged a spontaneous sit-in at an intersection. They demanded that the mayor and the Kent State president speak with them about the Guard's presence on campus. Again, helicopters and tear gas were used, and some of the

students were injured by being bayoneted and clubbed by the Guardsmen. Helicopters with searchlights hovered overhead all night.

On Monday, May 4, a crowd of 1,500 had gathered by noon. Ohio's Assistant Adjutant General Robert Canterbury ordered the Guardsmen to disperse them. Over 100 men, armed with loaded M-1 rifles and tear gas, formed a skirmish line and forced them into a wider area on a practice field. For some time, Guardsmen would advance and students retreat, then students advance and Guardsmen retreat. As many students assumed the confrontation was over, a dozen members of Troop G simultaneously turned, aimed, and fired into the crowd in the parking lot. Four students were killed and nine wounded.

Campuses all over the country exploded in rage. More than 400 shut down as two million students went on strike.

In 1977, Kent State proceeded with the construction of a gymnasium annex over a large part of the site of the May 4 confrontation. One hundred and ninety-two protesters were removed and arrested.

The first antiwar protests had been tentative affairs that didn't get much attention. One in Boston in 1965, for instance, drew only a hundred people. But as the nation endured the greatest turmoil since the Civil War, protesters soon made Washington, D.C., the fulcrum for antiwar forces. Every year from 1967 until 1973 a major march occurred in the District, including four of the largest antiwar demonstrations in American history.

"It was a time in which there was a very great deal of turbulence on the one hand," said Marcus Raskin, a public policy professor and former protester, "but also a period in which citizenship took on the form of real action." The first major antiwar rally in the District was staged by students on April 17, 1965, just a month after the U.S. had sent its first Marines to Vietnam. About 16,000 people picketed the White House and marched on the Capitol. Only four arrests were made.

Two years later, on October 21, 1967, the March on the Pentagon became a defining moment of American history. Norman Mailer won a Pulitzer Prize for chronicling it in *Armies of the Night*. By the time of the

march, 13,000 Americans had died in Vietnam, and the draft had become a serious bone of contention. The Youth International Party—the Yippies, led by Abbie Hoffman and Jerry Rubin—announced that they planned to "exorcise" the Pentagon. About 100,000 protesters rallied at the Lincoln Memorial, then marched across the Potomac to the Pentagon, where more than 2,500 Army troops stood. Marchers pressed forward to place flowers in the barrels of their M-14 rifles. Tear gas was unleashed and the crowd began running. "The Pentagon's steps were spattered with blood," wrote the *Washington Post.*

The Moratorium rally on November 15, 1969, was the biggest antiwar demonstration in American history with more than 250,000 protesters—some estimates as high as 500,000—pouring down Pennsylvania Avenue and spilling onto the Mall between the Capitol and the Washington Monument. Lyndon Johnson, whom war protesters hated, was gone and President Nixon was trying to "Vietnamize" the war, so some of the energy of earlier protests was lacking. Too, the gov-

ernment had developed plans for handling huge crowds: 3,000 police officers, 9,000 Army troops, 200 lawyers, and 75 clergymen were on hand to keep the peace.

Kent State re-ignited the fury, and demonstrators vowed to shut down the federal government on May Day, 1971, by blocking the flow of traffic into the District and preventing civil servants from getting to their jobs. But President Nixon had vowed to keep the city running.

Two weeks before May Day events began peacefully with more than 200,000 people attending rallies. The Vietnam Veterans Against the War camped on the Mall; many threw their combat medals and ribbons at the Capitol building to demonstrate their fervor. "The aim of Mayday actions is to raise the social cost of the war to a level unacceptable to America's rulers," a protesters' tactical manual said. But the police were ready.

They created fill-in-the-blank field-arrest forms to replace lengthier forms; they had Polaroid cameras in the police vans so an officer could be matched with

the people he arrested; new "lexi-cuff" handcuffs, prenumbered with badge numbers of the arresting officers, were available to the officers.

The police launched a preemptive strike. By 8:00 a.m., they had arrested 2,000; lacking jail space they held them on a Washington Redskins practice field. By day's end they had arrested a record 7,000.

Protest leader Rennie Davis, struggling to articulate what had happened, said the day's events were "almost the most major nonviolent demonstration" in the nation's history.

Clearly the Vietnam War protests had some influence in bringing an earlier end to the war, but the extent of that influence is still in dispute.

OPPOSITE: *Demonstrators rally in Washington, D.C., in 1967.*
ABOVE: *Protest turns bloody: Kent State University student Mary Ann Vecchio kneels over the fallen body of Jeffrey Miller, killed when Ohio National Guard troops fired at antiwar demonstrators.*

# The FIRST SMALL STEPS

*Space Exploration*

When the day came for U.S. Air Force test pilot Chuck Yeager to attempt to break the sound barrier, he didn't tell his superiors that a few days earlier he had broken something else—some ribs, in a fall from a horse. On October 14, 1947, he strapped himself into a Bell X-1 rocket—a craft shaped like a .50-caliber bullet—and dropped from beneath the belly of a specially modified B-29 bomber over California's Mojave Desert. When the engine ignited, the craft leaped forward and soon hit a speed of more than 600 miles an hour, the first time man had flown faster than the speed of sound. "It was as smooth as a baby's bottom," Yeager said. "Grandma could be up there sipping lemonade." His aplomb showed he had "the right stuff," in writer Tom Wolfe's memorable phrase—a characteristic that would survive in future astronauts as the U.S. began its first tentative steps into outer space.

Just 43 years after Robert Goddard successfully flew the first liquid-fueled rocket, Americans would be walking on the moon, an effort launched eight years before, when President Kennedy had committed the U.S. to landing a man on the moon "before the end of the decade."

The space age began with a tiny aluminum capsule called Sputnik 1. It began orbiting the Earth and beeping its taunt back to American scientists in October 1957. It was a Soviet satellite, not American. The United States' number one rival had taken the first step toward exploring outer space. The following month the Soviets took an even larger step, testing the effects of space travel on a dog, Laika, who was sent into orbit.

High schools across the nation scrambled to redo science curricula in the face of this perceived humiliation. After several explosive failures, in January 1958 the U.S. sent its own satellite into orbit, and in July created an agency to oversee the exploration of space—NASA, the National Aeronautics and Space Administration. Still, the U.S. in the early years of exploration remained a few steps behind.

In April 1961 the Soviets scored another triumph by being first to launch a man, Yuri Gagarin, into space. The personable young cosmonaut said, "To be the first to enter the cosmos, to engage, single-handed, in an unprecedented duel with nature—could one dream of anything more?" He was the first human to experience weightlessness in outer space, when his notebooks and pens floated loose in the Vostok capsule.

The next month Alan Shepard became the first American in space, with a 15-minute suborbital flight in a capsule named *Freedom* 7. He was a crack test pilot and engineer, and had been chosen for the first Mercury flight by vote of his fellow astronauts and NASA officials. Inside his nine-and-a-half-foot-tall capsule, he quickly rocketed to a speed of 5,180 mph and rose to 116.5 miles above the Earth's surface; there the engines cut off and the astronaut and his capsule hurtled through space and dropped down into the Atlantic Ocean a mere 40 miles from their target.

Within a year John Glenn circled the Earth tucked inside a Project Mercury cap-

Astronaut Gus Grissom was well liked and hard working but cursed with bad luck. Born in Indiana in 1926, he flew 100 missions for the Air Force during the Korean War. After the war he worked as a test pilot before being chosen as one of the original seven Mercury astronauts. He was the second American to fly in space. Even his Mercury mission had problems. At splashdown, the capsule's hatch blew prematurely, letting ocean water pour in. Grissom, perhaps panicking, abandoned ship and the capsule sank to the bottom of the Pacific. The inquiry exonerated him but cast a shadow upon his career. He later wrote, "I felt reasonably certain that I wouldn't have a second space flight."

Selected as a crew member for the first Apollo mission, Grissom was practicing for the flight with fellow crewmen Ed White and Roger Chaffee in 1966 when disaster struck. Sealed into their capsule, they spent a long day rehearsing. Then a seemingly casual report came from Chaffee. "Fire, I smell fire." Then more urgent calls came. By the time staff removed the capsule door, all three astronauts were dead.

sule named *Friendship 7*. Americans stayed riveted to their television sets as a serious glitch developed during Glenn's mission. An alarm indicated that the crucial heat shield was loose and liable to come off during the fiery re-entry. Glenn was advised to keep the retro-rockets in place instead of jettisoning them to help keep the heat shield in place. As he plummeted toward Earth at 15,000 mph at the end of his short mission, flaming pieces of the retropack flew past his window. But he splashed down safely nearly five hours after liftoff.

The six Mercury astronauts flew on their backs, wedged into the wide end of their bell-shaped craft. Since the quarters were cramped, all the original astronauts were less than 5 feet 11 inches tall. The next generation of American spacecraft—Gemini— were designed to carry two crewmen.

The Gemini program taught NASA skills it needed before it could land astronauts on the moon: more about maneuvering a spacecraft in orbit, rendezvousing with another spacecraft, and working in space outside the vehicle. Though the capsule was larger, each astronaut had less space—from 55 to 40 cubic feet—than in Mercury. Gemini accomplished a number of "firsts": the first space walk by Ed White, the first

rendezvous of spacecraft, and the first manned docking with a target vehicle. During its ten missions, Gemini showed that people could live in space as long as two weeks—more than time enough to get to the Moon and back—and could accomplish tasks during space walks. For the first time, astronauts were true pilots, using onboard computers and rockets to maneuver in space.

## To the Moon

Though a Soviet spacecraft was the first to land intact on the moon, an American craft carried the first astronauts there. On July 20, 1969—just before the end of the decade, as President Kennedy had decreed—Neil Armstrong planted the first human footprint on the moon. "That's one small step for a man," he said, "one giant leap for mankind."

OPPOSITE: *Looking truly alien in their spacesuits, the original seven astronauts of the Mercury Program greet the public in 1959.* ABOVE: *An aeronautical forebear, Chuck Yeager, broke the world's speed record in a* Tell X-1A *aircraft in 1953. He had been first to break the sound barrier in 1947.*

The Apollo program built upon the success—and failures—of previous programs. The giant Saturn V rocket that would boost astronauts toward the moon evolved from rockets developed by the German rocket pioneer Wernher von Braun, who came to the U.S. after World War II. It was ready to go by 1967. Its ability to lift payload was about 100 times greater than that of the rocket that had lifted Alan Shepard aboard Mercury in 1961.

The Apollo program included many unmanned test missions and 12 missions with astronauts aboard: three Earth orbiting missions (Apollo 7, 9, and Apollo-Soyuz), two lunar orbiting missions (Apollo 8 and 10), a lunar flyby (Apollo 13), and six moon landing missions (Apollo 11, 12, 14, 15, 16, and 17). Two astronauts from each of the final six missions walked on the moon, the only humans yet to have set foot on another body in the solar system.

The Apollo 8 mission, the first manned flight using a Saturn launch vehicle, was launched early December 21, 1968. The three astronauts on board—Frank Borman, James Lovell, and William Anders—journeyed 200,000 miles to orbit the moon, the first humans ever to travel there. They entered moon orbit on December 21 and broadcast stunning pictures back to Earth. Their orbit would take them to the far side of the moon, out of radio communication with Earth, and the world held its breath for half an hour of silence. Finally came Lovell's voice: "Go ahead, Houston, Apollo."

Because it was Christmas Eve, the astronauts made a radio broadcast back to Earth. Anders read, "In the beginning God created the heaven and the earth," and the crew took turns reading more verses from Genesis. Borman ended, "…and God saw that it was good. And from the crew of Apollo 8, we close with good night, good luck, a Merry Christmas, and God bless all of you—all of you on the good Earth."

Apollo 8's mission lasted 7 days and included 10 orbits around the moon.

Apollo 9 spent 10 days in Earth orbit, testing equipment and procedures. Apollo 10, launched on May 18, 1969, was a 10-day dress rehearsal for the actual first landing. It entered orbit around the moon, and its lunar module Snoopy descended to within nine miles of the lunar surface with two astronauts on board. They tested the lunar module's radar and ascent engine and surveyed the landing site for Apollo 11.

Apollo 11, launched on July 16, 1969, made its historic landing. A camera in the lunar module watched and conveyed a fuzzy image back to Earth as Neil Armstrong climbed down the ladder to the surface. The spacecraft was in two stages, one for descent, the other for ascent. The descent stage provided the engine used to land and had four legs, a storage area for scientific experimental equipment, and the ladder for the crew to climb down to the moon's surface. It also served as the launch platform for the ascent.

The astronauts found they had little difficulty walking on the moon's surface, though they bounced comically in the reduced gravity. Their back-mounted, portable life-support systems controlled the oxygen, temperature, and pressure inside their suits. They spent a total of two and a half hours on the surface of the moon, collecting soil and rock samples to return to Earth.

They left an American flag, of rigid construction to simulate waving, on the surface when they departed for home. They splashed down in the Pacific Ocean on July 24, 1969, 15 miles from their recovery ship, U.S.S. *Hornet*.

Novelist Vladimir Nabokov wrote, in the *New York Times,* "Treading the soil of the moon, palpitating its pebbles, tasting the panic and splendour of the event, feeling in the pit of one's stomach the separation from terra—these form the most romantic sensations an explorer has ever known."

But an actor in the London production of *Hair* ad-libbed, "I loved the moon—until they trod on it."

The final U.S. mission to the moon was Apollo 17, which entered lunar orbit on December 10, 1972. The astronauts commemorated the culmination of the moon program by unveiling a plaque. Beneath drawings of Earth's two hemispheres and

## RIDE, *Sally* RIDE

"Our future lies with today's kids and tomorrow's space exploration," said Dr. Sally Ride, first American woman in space. At Stanford she accumulated a stack of degrees—including a Ph.D. in physics. She saw an ad in a newspaper calling for astronaut volunteers. More than 8,000 men and women applied, and Sally was among the 35 individuals who were accepted; six were women. During the second and third flights of the space shuttle *Columbia* in 1981 and 1982 she served on the ground as a communications officer, but when *Challenger* lifted off for an six-day mission in 1983 she was aboard. All told, she logged more than 343 hours in space. At touchdown she said, "I'm sure that's the most fun I'll ever have in my life."

a central moon map, the text read, "Here man completed his first explorations of the Moon December 1972 AD. May the spirit of peace in which we came be reflected in the lives of all mankind."

For years, various robotic satellites had been launched into space, complex tools to plumb the mysteries of our nearest cosmic neighbors. The dream of a permanent home in space took a leap with Skylab program, designed to give workers an orbiting scientific laboratory. Skylab 4 clocked 84 days in space during which its crew circled the planet 1,260 times and covered 34.5 million miles, the equivalent of a flight to Mars. But Skylab 4 is most famous for rattling the citizens of Australia when, in July 1979, its mission ended, it broke up over the continent, scattering debris across the Outback.

The International Space Station was first proposed in 1869, when an American novelist wrote of a "brick moon" that orbited the Earth and helped ships navigate at sea. In 1923 Romanian Hermann Oberth was the first to use the term "space station" to describe a wheel-shaped facility that would serve as a jumping-off place for a human journey to the moon and Mars. In 1952 Dr. Wernher von Braun published his concept of a space station that would have a diameter of 250 feet, orbit more than 1,000 miles above the Earth, and spin to provide artificial gravity. In 1998 the first two modules of the International Space Station were launched and joined together

in orbit. Other modules soon followed and the first crew arrived in 2000.

America's exploration of space took a dramatic turn early in 2004, when President Bush proposed a goal of sending astronauts back to the moon as a first step toward manned missions to Mars. Various unmanned probes have been sailing off into the distances of space for years. Drawing their energy from solar panels and their instructions via radio from home, they send back data and photographs that let us peek into the mysteries of deep space.

During its two-year mission, the Mariner 10 spacecraft transmitted more than 12,000 images of Mercury and Venus. It's still orbiting the sun more than 25 years after launch. Voyager 1 and 2 were sent to explore the giant outer planets. Both craft visited Jupiter and Saturn, and Voyager 2 continued on to Uranus and Neptune. In the spring of 1990, Voyager 2 transmitted images looking back across the span of the entire solar system. Magellan, launched in 1989 from the space shuttle, measured the surface height of features on Venus. Gallileo, also launched from the shuttle, made a six-year journey to Jupiter.

A future mission called Dawn will rendezvous and orbit the asteroids 4 Vesta and 1 Ceres, observing the asteroids' internal structure, density, shape, size, composition, and mass; it will also return data on surface morphology, cratering, and magnetism. Dawn will be launched from Florida on May 27, 2006, and spend four years traveling to reach Vesta on July 30, 2010, which it will orbit for 11 months. On July 3, 2011, it will sail away from Vesta and reach Ceres on August 20, 2014, where it will again orbit for 11 months. From the data, scientists hope to be able to determine which meteorites found on Earth came from asteroids.

The project, sure to take decades and many billions of dollars, faced an uncertain future as Americans tried to sort out their priorities in the reach toward space.

---

BELOW: *A 1959 Soviet Union photograph, from their moon-circling Lunik Three satellite, revealed lunar features never before seen.*
OPPOSITE: *Astronaut Edwin Aldrin makes tracks on the lunar surface during the Apollo 11 mission on July 20, 1969.*

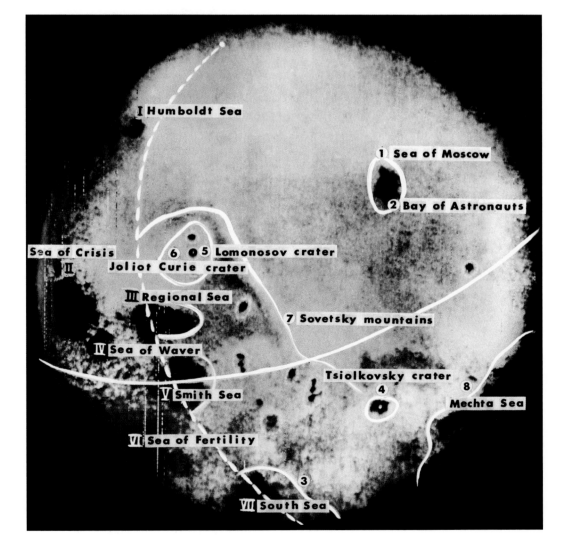

# COMMONPLACE MIRACLES

## Modern Medicine

Celsus wrote an account of the origin of rational medicine: "Some of the sick on account of their eagerness took food on the first day, some on account of loathing abstained; and the disease in those who refrained was more relieved. Some ate during a fever, some a little before it, others after it had subsided, and those who had waited to the end did best…. Occurring daily, such things impressed careful men, who noted what had best helped the sick, then began to prescribe them. In this way medicine had its rise from the experience of the recovery of some, of the death of others, distinguishing the hurtful from the salutary things." Experience was the first teacher of medicine.

In the 1950s death was defined as a cessation of the heartbeat, yet for surgeons to operate successfully on the heart it had to be deliberately stopped. Doctors had to "kill" their patients before they could save them. The solution came through the invention of the heart-lung machine, or pump, which kept the blood circulating through the lungs, where it picked up oxygen, and then throughout the body. The idea of the pump was first conceived by John Gibbon in 1931, but a quarter of a century passed before he had developed his machine to the point where he could perform his first operation in 1955. A surgeon wrote, "Gibbon's idea and its elaboration take their place among the boldest and most successful feats of man's mind—the invention of the phonetic alphabet, the telephone or a Mozart symphony." The next logical step was the first heart transplant, by Christiaan Barnard, in 1967. This looked for a while like a dead end, for the following year a hundred transplants were performed across the

globe and not a single patient survived. But years of advances in techniques, drugs, and equipment have made the operations routine, and now thousands of successful transplants are performed each year. The first successful kidney transplant had occurred a few years earlier. The transplant itself was fairly simple, involving lit-

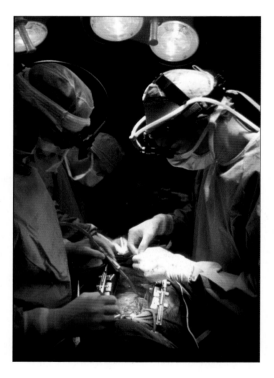

tle more than connecting the blood supply of the donated kidney to the recipient's. But the body's ability to distinguish between the "self" and the "non-self" meant the body's immune system attacked the invader. Once drugs were found to temporarily suppress the immune system, kidney transplants became routine.

A desire to help infertile couples bear children led to the first "test-tube baby," Louise Joy Brown, born in 1978. Again, the difficulties did not seem great. The eggs of a woman with blocked fallopian tubes cannot pass from the ovary down into the uterus to be fertilized by the husband's sperm. The solution: obtain an egg

from the ovary, add the sperm, then place the fertilized conceptus back into the uterus. But Bob Edward of Cambridge University and his collaborator Patrick Steptoe at Oldham General Hospital worked for seven heartbreaking years before succeeding with little Louise. In the following two decades, 40,000 pregnancies resulted from their work.

Some advances in medicine raise moral and ethical issues that will take years to sort

---

### TOMORROW'S DISEASES in HIDING

Regardless of the medical miracles that we tend to take for granted, nature sometimes seems intent on catching mankind by surprise.

Epidemics—which kill far more people than war does—don't emerge in the cities, where they are most lethal, but often in what the *New York Times* calls "biological caldrons in some of the world's most obscure places"—the partially logged jungles of Africa, the mud flats of Bangladesh, the steamy restaurants of southern China.

AIDS and Ebola come from apes, SARS from the palm civet. Cholera pandemics historically have begun on the banks of the Ganges. Creutzfeldt-Jakob comes from eating mad cows, who got mad cow disease from eating sheep infected with scrapie; all are caused by misfolded proteins called prions. We don't know where scrapie comes from.

It takes time for researchers to put the clues together. Two years passed before doctors noticed that the "gay cancer" affecting men in California had the same symptoms as "slim disease" in central Africa. The bloodiest hemorrhagic fevers like Ebola are difficult to study because they thrive in countries that are often dangerous and lack safe and adequate laboratories. Other epidemics attract little attention. The red rash of Lyme disease was noted by dermatologists in the 1800s but dismissed as "unexplained."

Dr. Howard Markel, a medical historian, points out that for centuries pandemics traveled simultaneously with word of them: Travelers carrying the news often carried the microbes. Now, as SARS showed, illnesses race abroad by jet, arriving in people who clear customs before they even feel feverish.

out. Cloning—producing an individual from a single cell of its parent, and which is genetically identical to it—is within the realm of possibility, but makes many people uneasy. Human beings could, in effect, begin to manage their own evolution.

Most Americans—76 percent—oppose attempting to clone humans, but nearly a quarter believe it has already been done. Two-thirds approve of using reproductive genetic testing to help parents have a baby free of a genetic disease. Men are twice as likely as women to be supportive of reproductive genetic technologies. The biggest fear is that cloning is "playing God."

Similar uneasiness confronts stem cell research. Stem cells—found in human embryos, placentas, and umbilical cords—can be induced to grow into an array of different types of body tissues and could one day be useful in treating a variety of ailments. New treatments might be devised for heart disease, Alzheimer's disease, diabetes, cancer, and spinal cord injuries. But because harvesting the cells often involves destroying a human embryo, many conservatives and anti-abortion Americans say it is unethical.

The introduction of powerful new drugs has kept pace with accomplishments in the surgery. A doctor setting up a practice in the 1930s had about a dozen proven remedies for treating the diseases he encountered. By the 1960s those dozen remedies had increased to more than 2,000, and today there are many thousand more. Many were discovered by accident. Drugs used to treat one condition were found to relieve another, or found to have side effects that could be turned to therapeutic advantage. One medical historian wrote, "The origins of virtually every class of drug discovered between the 1930s and the 1980s can be traced to some fortuitous, serendipitous or accidental observation." The explosion of medical technology that accompanied the development of new drugs happened for the opposite reasons. Whereas most drugs were discovered by accident, technological solutions were highly intentional, specific answers to well-defined problems. For sustaining life, dialysis, pacemakers, ventilators, and intensive care have been developed; for diagnosing illnesses various scanners, including CT,

MRI, and PET have joined ultrasound, angiography, and cardiac catheterization; and in the surgery, we've seen joint replacement, introcular lens implants, cochlear implants, and endoscopy.

The future promises even more dazzling innovations, as computers and robots take over in the operating room; as scientists further unlock the secrets of genetics and experiment with stem cells—at the same time they grapple with new ethical considerations. But their aspirations are noble. As one medical historian said, "The basis of medicine is sympathy and the desire to help others, and whatever is done with this end must be called medicine."

BELOW: *Patient William Schroeder takes his first tentative steps following the implantation of an artificial heart into his chest. The 1985 operation took more than six hours and replaced Schroeder's failed heart with a Jarvik-7 synthetic organ. Schroeder lived 20 months before dying of a stroke.*
OPPOSITE: *More recently, doctors at the UCLA Medical Center perform a heart transplant in 1996.*

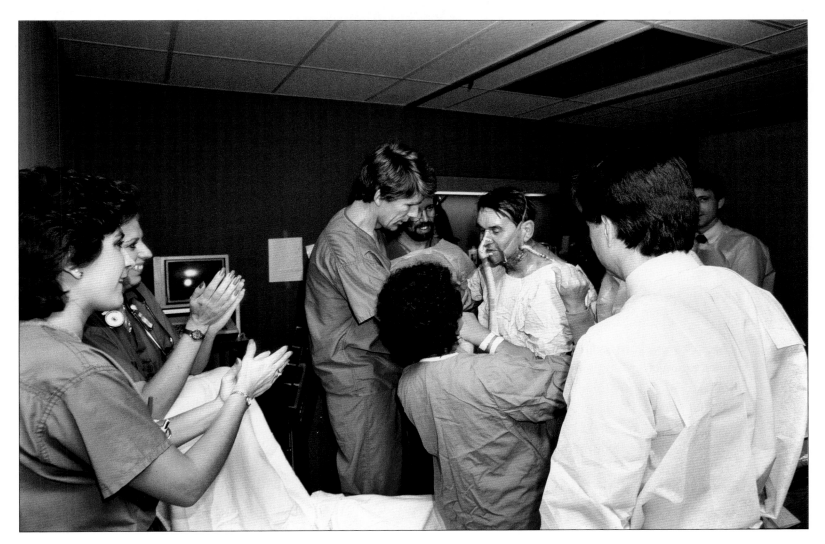

# The NEW GLOBAL TENSIONS

## Cold War and Iron Curtain

At the end of World War II, an exhausted planet heaved a sigh of relief and hoped that peace would reign. But almost immediately the peace turned uneasy. The United States and the Soviet Union and their respective allies squared off in open yet restricted rivalry.

Within a few years of war's end, the Soviet Union was deeply involved in those

Secretary of State George C. Marshall, lent billions of dollars to countries of Western Europe, solidifying allegiance to the U.S. In June 1948 the Soviet Union cut off all land traffic into the zones of Berlin occupied by the Western allies. The allies responded with an airlift, delivering food and supplies to stranded Berliners. After 11 months the Soviet Union ended its blockade. In

Korean War brought the two superpowers into direct conflict. In 1961 the Soviets built a wall across Berlin to protect East Berliners from the West and stop the steady flow of German refugees fleeing westward.

In 1952 and 1953 both powers successfully tested a hydrogen bomb, a vastly more powerful nuclear weapon. They also began developing ballistic missiles that could deliver the weapons across continents and oceans. In 1962 the Soviets began secretly installing the missiles in Cuba, just 90 miles from American shores, resulting in the Cuban Missile Crisis. President Kennedy ordered a naval blockade, threatening to stop and board any Soviet ship trying to bring

MISSILE EQUIPMENT
MARIEL PORT FACILITY
4 NOVEMBER 1962

4 MISSILE TRANSPORTERS

OXIDIZER TRAILERS

OXIDIZER TRAILERS

FUEL TRAILERS

countries of eastern Europe that its army had liberated: Communist governments were put in place. By 1950 Poland, Czechoslovakia, Bulgaria, Romania, and Hungary had communist governments taking orders from Moscow. Occupied Germany became split between East and West, communist and democratic. The U.S. under Truman fought back with money and aid: The Marshall Plan, named for

1949 the U.S. and 11 other countries formed the North Atlantic Treaty Organization (NATO) to protect one another from communist aggression. The Soviet Union formed its allies into the Warsaw Pact.

In 1949, the Soviets exploded their first atomic warhead, ending the U.S. monopoly on the weapon, and the Chinese communists came to power in mainland China. The balance of power seemed more precarious. The

## NIXON in CHINA

One of Richard Nixon's first acts as president was to dictate into a small recorder, on February 1, 1969, a memo to his National Security Adviser, Henry Kissinger, urging him to explore the possibility of opening a diplomatic door to Communist China. Nearly two years later, while visiting Pakistan, Kissinger faked a stomachache and accepted an invitation from the country's president, Yahya Khan, to spend a few days at a rest house in the hill station of Nathiagali. On July 9, 1971, Kissinger's motorcade drove off. Disguised, Kissinger flew to China for a secret meeting with Chinese Prime Minister Zhou Enlai. On July 11 he reappeared in Islamabad and cabled Nixon one word: "Eureka!" A few days later Nixon announced Kissinger's trip and his acceptance of an invitation to visit Beijing.

Nixon expected to widen the growing breach between China and the Soviet Union. Nixon was taking a great risk. At home he might alienate the Republican right wing and especially friends of Taiwan in Congress. He flew to China without an appointment with Chairman Mao Zedong, who was bedridden, and he might have been publicly rebuffed. But Mao dragged himself from bed and met with Nixon. The meeting tipped the balance of power toward the West nor did it lose Taiwan; Nixon was correct that China would not risk the new American friendship to attack the island.

The trip has been called Nixon's finest hour.

nist North Vietnam from overrunning South.

In the 1960s and 1970s, the world became more subtly complicated. A split occurred between the Soviet Union and China, shattering the unity of the communist bloc. Western Europe and Japan emerged as economic forces. With the Stategic Arms Limitation Treaties (SALT), the two superpowers set limits on missile systems, though they continued massive arms buildups. With the arrival of Soviet Leader Mikhail S. Gorbachev and his reforms in the late 1980s, the Soviet Union's days were numbered. In late 1991 it collapsed altogether, and the Cold War ended.

OPPOSITE: *Photographic evidence of missiles in Cuba—missile transports, oxidizer trailers, and fuel trailers—took the Soviet Union and the United States to the brink of nuclear war in 1962. The Soviets backed down and removed the missiles, but tensions between the two superpowers remained high.*

ABOVE: *Soviet Secretary General Mikhail Gorbachev and President Ronald Reagan meet for the first time in Geneva in 1985; they "abandoned four decades of confrontation" and began a surprising and welcome cooperation.*

weapons. With Russian freighters nearing the blockade line, Premier Nikita Khrushchev backed down and ordered the missiles removed. Neither superpower was ready to use nuclear weapons for fear of retaliation.

Throughout the Cold War, both went to pains to avoid military confrontation, choosing to resort to combat operations only to stop allies from defecting or to overthrow them

after they had done so. Soviets troops preserved communist rule in East Germany in 1953, Hungary in 1956, Czechoslovakia in 1968, and Afghanistan in 1979. The U.S. helped overthrow a government in Guatemala in 1954, staged an unsuccessful invasion of Cuba in 1961, invaded the Dominican Republic in 1965 and Grenada in 1983, and undertook to prevent commu-

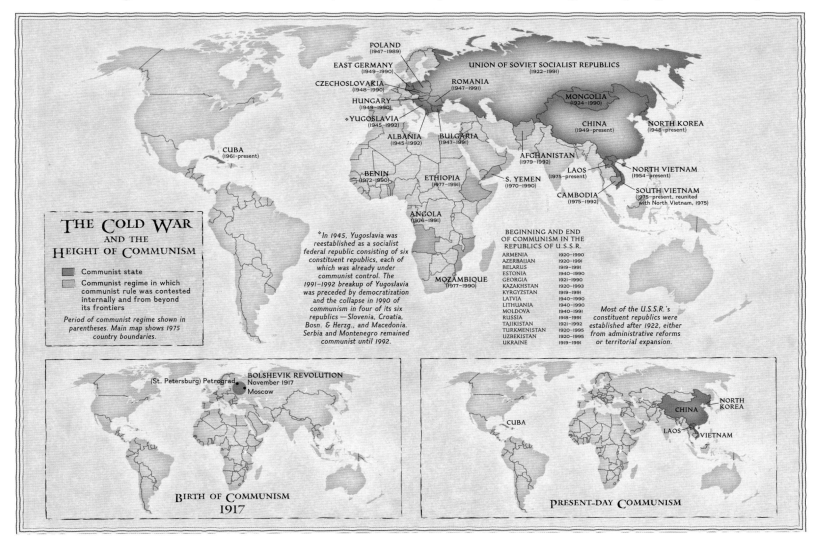

THE COLD WAR
AND THE
HEIGHT OF COMMUNISM

■ Communist state
□ Communist regime in which communist rule was contested internally and from beyond its frontiers

*Period of communist regime shown in parentheses. Main map shows 1975 country boundaries.*

*+In 1945, Yugoslavia was reestablished as a socialist federal republic consisting of six constituent republics, each of which was already under communist control. The 1991–1992 breakup of Yugoslavia was preceded by democratization and the collapse in 1990 of communism in four of its six republics — Slovenia, Croatia, Bosn. & Herzg., and Macedonia. Serbia and Montenegro remained communist until 1992.*

BEGINNING AND END
OF COMMUNISM IN THE
REPUBLICS OF U.S.S.R.

| | |
|---|---|
| ARMENIA | 1920–1990 |
| AZERBAIJAN | 1920–1991 |
| BELARUS | 1919–1991 |
| ESTONIA | 1940–1990 |
| GEORGIA | 1921–1990 |
| KAZAKHSTAN | 1920–1993 |
| KYRGYZSTAN | 1919–1991 |
| LATVIA | 1940–1990 |
| LITHUANIA | 1940–1990 |
| MOLDOVA | 1940–1991 |
| RUSSIA | 1918–1991 |
| TAJIKISTAN | 1921–1992 |
| TURKMENISTAN | 1920–1995 |
| UZBEKISTAN | 1920–1995 |
| UKRAINE | 1919–1991 |

*Most of the U.S.S.R.'s constituent republics were established after 1922, either from administrative reforms or territorial expansion.*

BIRTH OF COMMUNISM
1917

BOLSHEVIK REVOLUTION
November 1917

PRESENT-DAY COMMUNISM

# The AMERICAN HOSTAGES

※

## 444 Days in Iran

One of the most frustrating foreign-affairs dramas of the 20th century played out as one U.S. administration ended and another began.

It began far away in Iran early in 1979, when conditions there were deteriorating as various factions fought to oust the Shah of Iran from power. He had begun his reign in 1941, succeeding his father. In a 1953 power struggle with his prime minister, he gained American support to prevent nationalization of Iran's oil industry. In return for assuring the U.S. a steady supply of oil, the Shah received economic and military aid from eight American presidents.

Early in the 1960s, the Shah announced social and economic reforms but refused to grant broad political freedom. Iranian nationalists accused him of "westernizing" Iran. In 1963, the Shah suppressed riots and arrested many of his opponents. Among them was a popular religious nationalist and bitter foe of the U.S., the Ayatollah Ruhollah Khomeini.

The Shah formed a new government to replace the military administration then in power, but the main opposition force, headed by Khomeini, refused to either join or cooperate with it. The Shah spent billions of oil dollars on military weapons, but at the cost of popular support. His regime collapsed in revolution. The Shah fled into exile and, denied entry into the U.S., settled in Egypt.

In February 1979, the exiled Khomeini returned to Tehran and whipped discontent into furious anti-Americanism. American leaders little understood how deep was Iranian resentment of generations of exploitation by one foreign power or another, and how much the Shiite Muslim clergy detested the growing influence of Western culture—everything from the status of women to rock 'n' roll—on their country. Roused by the Ayatollah's ranting about "foreign devils," waves of militants daily beat against the iron gates of the embassy, chanting for the death of President Jimmy Carter and the Shah.

November 4, 1979: It was raining moderately at the time.... After arriving at the residence I had my hands tied behind my back so tightly with nylon cord that circulation was cut off. I was taken upstairs and put alone in a rear bedroom and after a short time was blindfolded....they tried to feed me some dates and I refused to eat anything I couldn't see. I strongly protested the violation of my diplomatic immunity.... I was taken to the Embassy living room on the ground floor where a number of other hostages were gathered. Some students attempted to talk with us, stating how they didn't hate Americans—only our U.S. Government, President Carter, etc. We were given sandwiches and that night I slept on the living room floor. We were not permitted to talk to our fellow hostages and from then on our hands were tied day and night and only removed while we were eating or had to go to the bathroom.

November 5, 1979: I was taken into the Embassy dining room and forced to sit on a dining room chair around the table with about twelve or so other hostages. Our hands were tied to each side of the chair. We could only rest by leaning on the dining table and resting out head on a small cushion. The drapes were drawn.... Our captors always conversed in stage whispers.... I slept that night on the floor under the dining table with a piece of drapery for a cover.

September 26, 1980 (328th Day!) This morning had another fight to get breakfast and to make the terrorists understand what we wanted, yet breakfasts are always the same—bread, butter, jam, tea and orange juice!... Jerry and I were taken outdoors for an hour of sunshine in the vegetable garden enclosure. It was really delightful, as the sun at this time of the year is mellow and warm, without being hot, and we did get our full hour!

January 21, 1981: The voice came over the Algerian plane's speaker: "You are now leaving Iranian air space!" What a cheer went up....

—Robert C. Ode
Retired Foreign Service Officer,
on temporary duty in Tehran

The U.S. State Department evacuated families of embassy personnel, and urged other Americans to leave Iran. On October 22, 1979, the Shah was allowed to enter the U.S. for gall bladder surgery, and this further infuriated his opponents in Iran. On November 4, thousands of students, demanding the return of the Shah to face their justice, overran the U.S. embassy in Tehran and took 90 people captive. Later, they freed some of them, including women, non-Americans, and African Americans.

In order to apply pressure on the Iranians, President Carter halted oil imports from Iran and froze Iranian assets in the U.S. When neither had much effect, he severed diplomatic relations with Iran and imposed a complete economic embargo on the country in April 1980.

Every day Americans watched impotently as television images showed mobs of Iranians, burning the Stars and Stripes, shouting abuse, intensifying fears for the lives of the hostages.

Operation Eagle Claw was planned to free them. To practice the mission, a model of the Teheran embassy was built at Fort Bragg, North Carolina; then officers figured out how to infiltrate 118 Delta force commandos at night. In the desert of Arizona, the men practiced scaling walls, blowing doors, scanning darkened rooms with infrared glasses. They memorized 53 faces of the hostages, making allowance for the growth of beards, afraid they might accidentally shoot an American sitting next to a guard. Six Hercules C-130s would fly them from Egypt to Desert One, an uninhabited spot about 250 miles southeast of Teheran. There they would rendezvous with eight large RH-53D Sea Stallion helicopters from the carrier *Nimitz* in the Gulf of Oman. They would refuel, then fly the commandos to Desert Two 50 miles southeast of Teheran. From there the commandos would travel by trucks, in the night, to the embassy.

Secretary of State Cyrus Vance called it "a damn complex operation," and opposed it. The mission almost immediately began to fall apart. One helicopter cracked a rotor blade and was abandoned. A sandstorm blew up.

Another chopper's gyroscope failed. The remaining choppers flew to Desert One, the last one landing almost three hours later. A pilot now reported failed hydraulics, reducing the number of choppers to five. Back in the White House, Carter deliberated and prayed, then approved the withdrawal of Eagle Claw.

In the black of night, one of the Sea Stallion pilots nudged his craft into the air to go around a C-130. Blinded by the whipped-up dust, he let his rotor blade slash into a C-130; the two craft exploded and burned. Eight men died. They and the helicopters were abandoned in the desert as survivors rushed to get out before daybreak. Secretary Vance resigned.

The debacle rattled America and contributed to the defeat of Carter, running for a second term. The Shah's death in July and the invasion of Iran by Iraq in September further complicated the situation. Fearful of the incoming administration, Iran began new negotiations to free the hostages, asking for $24 billion in return for the captives. On Inauguration Day, January 20, 1981, Carter stayed in the White House, trying to complete financial arrangements for a release. International calls flew between Algiers, Teheran, and London. In Teheran, the hostages were moved nearer the airport, and buses stood ready to take them to the planes. At 10:45 a.m. Carter's wife Rosalynn forced him into his rented morning clothes and they departed for the Inauguration ceremony.

Before it was over, Iran had settled for $8 billion, a promise by the U.S. to lift trade sanctions, and an agreement giving Iran immunity from lawsuits arising from the incident. The hostages had been held captive 444 days.

On January 21, the day after Ronald Reagan's Inauguration, former President Jimmy Carter flew to West Germany as the new President's emissary to personally greet the now homeward-bound former U.S. hostages.

OPPOSITE: *Americans held hostage, blindfolded employees of the U.S. embassy in Iran are led from the building on the first day of captivity, November 4, 1979.*

# NATURAL DISASTERS

*Devastation of the Nation*

The first volcanic event in the contiguous 48 states in 63 years was a beauty. At 8:32 a.m. on Sunday, May 18, 1980, in Washington, a magnitude 5.1 earthquake triggered a blast that blew away the top 1,300 feet of Mount St. Helens crest. The massive eruption took dozens of lives, imperiled thousands of others, and devastated 200 square miles, triggering floods and mudflows and sending ash clouds rolling across the Northwest. Its force equaled that of 500 Hiroshima atomic bombs.

For many weeks the mountain had teased scientists as it seethed and trembled and produced minor eruptions. They placed instruments on and around the mountain: seismometers to record quakes, gravity meters to gauge vertical swellings, tiltmeters and laser targets to detect outward bulging. Everyone wanted them to predict what the mountain was going to do, but Mount St. Helens, a composite of alternating layers of ash and lava, resisted.

By May 10, the pulse of the mountain was quickening—some small quakes approached 3.0 on the Richter scale, and infrared aerial photos showed several hot spots in the crater and on the flanks. Most alarmingly, the mountain's north slope began to bulge ominously.

Then, in just a few seconds on the 18th, the bulge blew itself outward. Like a nozzle, the new crater funneled much of the initial blast northwest and northeast, its hurricane wave of scalding gases and hot debris traveling 200 miles an hour. Douglas firs 150 feet tall were uprooted or snapped like toothpicks as far as 17 miles from the mountain. It amounted to a clear-cut of 200 square miles.

The disintegrating north wall and cascades of rock, riding on a cushion of hot gases, tobogganed down over the North Fork of the Toutle River, burying it to an average depth of 150 feet beneath new fill. The debris flowed downstream in a 15-mile-long river of muck and mud. Dozens of houses were inundated or swept away, Weyerhaeuser rail lines were wiped out and railcars swept away. Weyerhaeuser estimated that it lost 36,500 acres of commercially harvestable timber, plus 26,000 acres of young trees.

Soon the nozzle on the side of the mountain turned upward, and a roiling pillar of ash thrust 12 miles into the sky, its interior lit by spooky flashes of orange lightning. It climbed quickly to 50,000 feet, then 60,000, its top flattening out like an anvil. The dark cloud spread eastward, casting Yakima, 85 miles away, into midnight darkness at 9:30 a.m. Over the next month, workers would remove an estimated 600,000 tons of ash from downtown Yakima. Motorists across central and eastern Washington could not get home that day, immobilized by the heavy ash fall that their headlights could not penetrate. Police and emergency vehicles helped herd them off the hazardous highways into makeshift refugee centers.

The roar of the eruption was heard 200 miles away. Some electric grids failed as ash caused transformers to arc and short out. The explosive scythe killed an estimated 5,000 black-tailed deer, 1,500 elk, 200 black bears, and 15 mountain goats, plus unknown numbers of smaller mammals, birds, and fish.

In the early 1990s other natural disasters rattled the nerves of Americans. The most destructive hurricane on record in the U.S. began quietly as a small tropical wave off the west coast of Africa on August 14, 1992. Two days later it spawned a tropical depression that became tropical storm Andrew. On August 20 vertical wind shear nearly killed it, but it held together and by the next day was halfway between Bermuda and Puerto Rico and turning westward. It became a category 4 hurricane on August 23rd and roared across southern Florida on the 24th. It continued westward across Florida into the Gulf of Mexico, then turned northward, reaching the central Louisiana coast on August 26 as a category 3 hurricane. It continued to the northeast, gradually losing strength.

Andrew was the third most powerful hurricane to hit the U.S. since records have been kept. Its central barometric pressure at landfall in Homestead, Florida, was 27.23 inches. Its peak winds in southern Florida couldn't be directly

## HARRY TRUMAN

Profane and crusty, 84-year-old Harry Truman refused to leave the area where he had lived for 50 years, despite warnings from scientists. He and his wife Edna had built a lodge and cabins on the shores of Spirit Lake, a popular destination for two generations of vacationers. When Edna died some years earlier, Harry closed the lodge but rented a few cabins and boats each summer. Urged to leave when the volcano began acting up, Harry said, "I'm going to stay right here because, I'll tell you why, my home and my ——— life's here. My wife and I, we both vowed years and years ago that we'd never leave Spirit Lake. We loved it. It's part of me, and I'm part of that ——— mountain. And if it took my place, and I got out of here, I wouldn't live a day, not a ——— day. By God, my wife went down that ——— road ——— feet first, and that's the way I'm gonna go or I'm not gonna go."

On May 18, 1980, Mount St. Helens buried Harry and his lodge under hundreds of feet of ash and debris.

measured because they destroyed the measuring instruments. Equipment at an unmanned station at Fowey Rocks reported sustained winds of 142 miles an hour and gusts up to 169 miles an hour. Andrew's storm surge near landfall on Florida was 17 feet. The storm killed 23 in the U.S. and three more in the Bahamas and caused $26.5 billion damage in the U.S. alone.

The next year brought severe flooding to the Midwest. Stalled weather patterns in the early and middle parts of the year produced long-term heavy rains over much of the region. From the 1st of June through August more than 12 inches of rain fell across the region, amounts that were 200 to 350 percent higher than normal. And the rain seemingly never stopped. Usually rain falls here on 8 or 9 days in July, but in 1993 it rained on 20 of July's days.

Flooding from May through September became one of the most significant and damaging natural disasters ever to hit the U.S. Some 150 major rivers and their tributaries flooded. For two months barge traffic on the Missouri and Mississippi Rivers came to a stop. Seventy-five towns were flooded and 10,000 homes destroyed. Tens of thousands of people were evacuated, and some were never able to return to their homes. Levees failed by the hundreds, 50 people were killed, and damage estimates rose to $15 billion. It was without question the largest flood event to occur in the U.S.

The so-called Great Flood of 1993 affected nine states and 400,000 square miles. It demonstrated again that levees prevent floodplains from controlling floods, and the U.S. Army Corps of Engineers was directed to evaluate alternatives to levees for flood control in future planning. As Mark Twain once wrote, the Mississippi River "cannot be tamed, curbed or confined...you cannot bar its path with an obstruction which it will not tear down, dance over and laugh at."

LEFT: *Triggered by a magnitude 5.0 earthquake, Mount St. Helens in Washington erupts in a massive cloud of dust and ash, May 18, 1980.*

# MISBEHAVING *in* AMERICA

## Scandals and Shame

Early in the morning of October 7, 1974, a noisy disturbance occurred at the Tidal Basin in Washington, D.C., when local stripper Fanne Foxe jumped out of a car and into the waters of the Potomac. With her in the car was the chairman of the powerful House Ways and Means Committee, Wilbur Mills, Democrat from Arkansas. The resulting publicity boosted Fanne's weekly earnings from $600 to $3,000 a week, but cost Mills his leadership. Another congressman, John Jenrette of South Carolina, gained fame in Washington for making love to his wife while standing on the steps of the U.S. Capitol while other congressmen passed.

One-time presidential hopeful Gary W. Hart ran afoul of the press when he seemingly defied them to prove allegations of womanizing, despite the fact that he had been photographed with attractive Donna Rice—not his wife—on his lap aboard a yacht named *Monkey Business*. Though he had been the leading Democratic contender for the 1988 presidential nomination, he withdrew from the race after the *Washington Post* presented evidence of another extramarital relationship. He admitted that he had made "big mistakes, but not bad mistakes."

Senator Bob Packwood, Republican from Oregon, faced a unanimous bipartisan vote in the Senate for his expulsion after allegations of sexual harassment that spanned a 20-year period and involved a string of ten women campaign workers, lobbyists, and Senate staffers alleging that he had made unwelcome advances, kissing and fondling them. Rather than face expulsion from the Senate, Packwood resigned on October 1, 1995, in the midst of his fifth term.

It's been called "the most scandalous constitutional crisis in American history," and it began with "a third-rate burglary attempt." When five men were arrested early on the morning of June 17, 1972, inside the Democratic Party's national headquarters in the Watergate office complex in Washington, they had cameras and electronic surveillance gear and clearly were

attempting to bug the offices. Documents found on the burglars led investigators to G. Gordon Liddy and E. Howard Hunt in the White House of Richard Nixon. They were tried, along with the original five, and convicted early in 1973 of conspiracy, burglary, and eavesdropping. President Nixon vehemently denied any knowledge of the burglary.

While in prison one of the convicted men alleged that he and others had been pressured by high Republican Party officials to keep quiet and plead guilty. His most startling claim was that John N. Mitchell, former U.S. Attorney General in the Nixon administration, had sanctioned the Watergate break-in. As incriminating disclosures piled one atop

another, the White House defense began to crumble.

A Senate committee headed by Senator Samuel J. Ervin, Jr., began televised hearings on the matter on May 17, 1973, and more revelations came tumbling out of criminal activities in the White House that was scrambling to cover up the scandal. A former aide testified that Nixon had taped conversations in the White House since 1971, and legal maneuvering began to acquire the tapes.

In the end, several high-up White House officials served time in prison on various convictions, and Nixon, on the verge of impeachment, announced his resignation on August 8, 1974. By increasing distrust of the federal government, the Watergate matter generated the Independent Counsel law in 1978, which would torment a later president.

In a tangled web of deceit and secret deals, President Ronald Reagan, beloved for his strong stance against fanatical terrorism, found himself on the defensive for the Iran-Contra scandal.

At the heart of the matter was a 38-year-old Marine Corps lieutenant colonel named Oliver Laurence North, who was brought into the White House in 1981 to compile military reports for the National Security Council. Within three years the young Marine was running The Enterprise, a secret military junta with millions of dollars in Swiss bank accounts, dummy companies, and its own airplanes, pilots, airfield, and ship.

One of President Reagan's top priorities was finding ways to aid the Contras, the rebel army trying to overthrow the leftist Sandinista government of Nicaragua. The CIA had been giving aid, but Congress was about to put a stop to it. President Reagan ordered that "the resistance must be held together body and soul." CIA Director Bill Casey persuaded National Security Adviser Robert McFarlane to let North find a way—though evidently the entire scheme was Casey's idea.

It involved selling arms to Iran—a nation Reagan said was "run by the strangest collection of misfits, Looney Tunes and squalid criminals since the advent of the Third Reich"—in exchange for Iran's releasing American hostages.

Profits from the arms sales would be funneled to the Contras, and everyone would gain. Reagan first authorized a shipment of 96 U.S. antitank missiles, routed through Israel; in return, four of the seven Americans being held by pro-Iranian Shi'ites in Beirut would be released. On August 20, 1985, the missiles were sent, but no hostages were returned.

This pattern repeated itself over the next 15 months—Americans steadfastly handing over weapons for hostages, Iranians consistently failing to come through. In the end, the Iranians released only three hostages.

The affair came to light in an obscure Lebanese magazine, *Al Shiraa*, on November 4, 1986, and unleashed a storm of outrage. Reagan, in what writer Garry Wills called "constantly expanding areas of forgetfulness," called the charges "utterly false." U.S. Attorney General Edwin Meese III conducted a probe into the scandal. His report revealed that the U.S. government had supplied $12 million in weapons and spare parts to Israeli representatives, who then sold them to Iran for a profit. The money paid for the arms—apparently between $10 and $30 million—was deposited in Swiss bank accounts where it was under the control of agents of the Nicaraguan Contras.

North admitted to misleading Congress. McFarlane called the arms transfer a "mistake" and tried to commit suicide. Reagan, still confused but sorry, said, "I told the American people I did not trade arms for hostages. My heart and my best intentions tell me that is true, but the facts and the evidence tell me that it is not."

In 1998 President Bill Clinton became the second president in U.S. history to be impeached. Several scandals led to the impeachment: Clinton's sexual misconduct, which led to charges of perjury and obstruction of justice; independent counsel Kenneth Starr's relentless investigations into Clinton's financial dealings and personal life; and the Republicans' obsession with repaying the Democrats for the shame of Nixon's trial.

In 1995 Clinton began having an affair with Monica S. Lewinsky, a 21-year-old White House intern. Kenneth Starr, who was investigating the Whitewater affair, a real estate development company which the Clintons had been involved with in Arkansas, broadened his inquiries to investigate the allegations of Paula Corbin Jones, a former Arkansas state employee. Jones alleged that Clinton had violated her civil rights by sexually harassing her and caused her to be discriminated against at work. Clinton famously lied about the affair with Lewinsky—"I did not have sex with that woman, Ms. Lewinsky"—and on December 19, 1998, the House of Representatives narrowly impeached Clinton for perjury and obstruction of justice. The nation was riveted by nearly four months of sometimes salacious impeachment hearings, but in February 1999 the Senate acquitted Clinton on both charges.

ABOVE: *Departing in disgrace, President Richard M. Nixon boards a helicopter to begin the journey to his new home in California on August 10, 1974, having resigned the presidency over the Watergate scandal. His was the first presidential resignation in American history.*
OPPOSITE: *USMC Lt. Col. Oliver North swears to tell the truth to a House committee investigating the Iran-Contra "arms for hostages" affair.*

# The GULF WAR

## Operation Desert Storm

Fight them with your faith in God, fight them in defense of every free honorable woman and every innocent child, and in defense of the values of manhood and the military honor…Fight them because with their defeat you will be at the last entrance of the conquest of all conquests. The war will end with…dignity, glory, and triumph for your people, army, and nation." Saddam Hussein, addressing his people on the radio on January 19, 1991, rallied them to oppose the coming invasion by America. The Gulf War, fought during 1990 and 1991, began when Iraq invaded Kuwait on August 2, 1990. Iraq was attempting to expand its power in the Gulf region, to void a large

debt that Iraq owed Kuwait, and to control Kuwait's huge oil reserves.

The UN Security Council called for Iraq to withdraw and imposed a worldwide ban on trade. The invasion was a threat to Saudi Arabia, the world's largest oil producer and exporter; the U.S. and its Western European NATO allies rushed troops to deter a possible attack. The military buildup was called Operation Desert Shield.

British Prime Minister Margaret Thatcher told President George Bush, "Remember, George, this is not time to go wobbly." He issued an ultimatum to Saddam Hussein. "A line has been drawn in the sand….Withdraw from Kuwait

unconditionally and immediately, or face the terrible consequences."

On November 29, 1990, the UN Security Council authorized the use of force against Iraq. An allied coalition responded, and by January 1991, 700,000 troops, including 550,000 from the U.S. and lesser numbers from Britain, France, Egypt, Saudi Arabia, Syria, and several other countries, were assembled there.

The fighting began on January 16, 1991. General Norman Schwarzkopf addressed his troops: "I have seen in your eyes a fire of determination to get this war job done quickly. My confidence in you is total, our cause is just. Now you must be the thunder and lightning of Desert Storm."

President Bush spoke to the nation that night: "As I report to you, air attacks are under way against military targets in Iraq…. Our troops will have the best possible support in the entire world, and they will not be asked to fight with one hand tied behind their back." Called Operation Desert Storm, the attack on Iraq began with sustained aerial bombardment, which smashed bridges, roads, refineries, munitions plants, buildings, and communica-

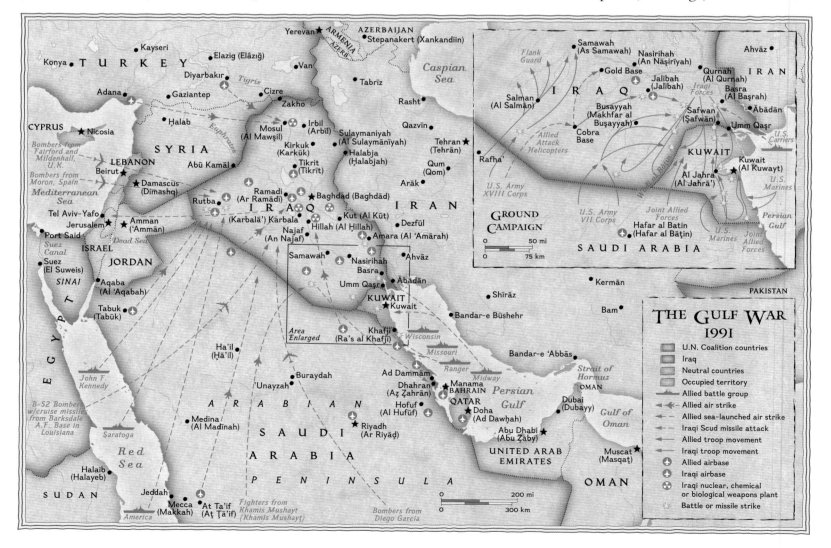

## COLIN POWELL

The son of Jamaican immigrants who settled in New York City, Colin Powell found his calling in the Reserve Officers Training Corps in college. He served with distinction in several posts around the world, including two tours in Vietnam, where he was wounded, and rose quickly through the Army's ranks. When President George H. W. Bush named him to lead the Joint Chiefs of Staff in 1989, he was, at 52, the youngest man and the first African American ever to attain the country's highest military office. Just months into his tenure he led the intervention that ousted Panama dictator Manuel Noriega. When U.S. officials called for interventions, or shows of force, around the world, Powell urged caution: such movement of troops as a signal was too often an attempt "to give the appearance of clarity to mud."

In his autobiography, *My American Journey,* he writes: "Many of my generation,...seasoned in that war [Vietnam] vowed that when our turn came to call the shots, we would not quietly acquiesce in half-hearted warfare for half-baked reasons that the American people could not understand or support."

tions networks. Several weeks before Baghdad was bombed, U.S. intelligence had successfully inserted a virus into Iraq's military computers, disabling much of the air-defense system; bombing destroyed the rest. By mid-February Iraq's forward troops in Kuwait and southern Iraq were the target of bombers.

On February 24, Operation Desert Sabre, a ground offensive, moved out of Saudi Arabia into Kuwait and southern Iraq, and within three days retook Kuwait City. In the meantime, 120 miles west of Kuwait, Saddam's armored reserves were being attacked from the rear by U.S. tanks. By February 27, most of Iraq's elite Republican Guard units had been destroyed, and by February 28 Iraqi resistance had collapsed and President Bush declared a cease-fire.

Iraqi forces had extensive experience in warfare—they had recently ended an eight-year war with Iran—but it was the wrong kind of experience: a stolid, positional war, wearing down Iranian forces, instead of a fast-moving mobile campaign.

An attempt was made on Saddam Hussein's life on the final night of the war. Just before the cease-fire, two U.S. Air Force bombers attacked a bunker 15 miles northwest of Baghdad where Saddam was

thought to be. Two specially designed 5,000-pound bombs destroyed the bunker, but Saddam was not killed.

The U.S. and its allies lost 300 troops in the conflict, but an estimated 60,000 Iraqi soldiers were killed. Lieutenant General Tom Kelly said, "Iraq went from the fourth-largest army in the world to the second-largest army in Iraq in 100 hours." As many as a quarter of the Americans who were killed died from so-called friendly fire.

The defeated Hussein agreed to destroy his weapons of mass destruction—nuclear, biological, and chemical—and recognized Kuwait's sovereignty. Economic sanctions against Iraq continued until compliance was assured. When Iraq failed to cooperate with UN weapons inspectors in 1998, Operation Desert Fox caused a resumption of fighting.

With Saddam defeated, northern Kurds and southern Shi'ites rose up in rebellion but were suppressed. "No-fly" zones were created over their regions to provide some protection.

ABOVE: *Like creatures from another world, environmentalists in protective suits examine the tar-encrusted ground amid raging oil fires in Kuwait. Iraq's 1990 invasion of its neighbor led to widespread damage to the country's oilfields.*

# *The* INTERNET TAKES OFF

## *The Dot-Com Bubble*

The Internet, say computer experts, is "a system architecture" that allows various computer networks around the world to interconnect. It was first developed in the 1970s but didn't become a part of the average American's life until the early 1990s. By the beginning of the 21st century approximately 6 percent of the world's population—360 million people—had access to the Internet. By 2010 half the world's people will. The Internet has revolutionized the handling of information, both for people seeking it and those sharing it. The ubiquitous e-mails, "chat rooms," newsgroups, and audio and video transmission let people work together from many different locations. It supports the World Wide Web and a growing number of "e-businesses." It may transform society in ways as yet undreamed of.

The first computer networks were built in the late 1950s and early 1960s, one, called SABRE, to handle airline reservations, and another, AUTODIN 1, a defense command and control system. Early applications connected research universities and government agencies. Control of the Internet steadily devolved from government stewardship to private sector participation and finally to private custody with the government merely providing oversight.

In the early 1980s, the personal computer and the workstation came upon the scene, developments that were fueled by great progress in integrated circuit technology and the rapid decline in computer prices. Suddenly, everyone could have a computer at home. By the late 1980s the Internet was doubling in size every year. The University of Illinois made its use much easier in 1993 when it introduced the "browser," new software called Mosaic

that used a "mouse" to let users point and click their way through their files and along the information highway.

By the late 1990s so many Internet Service Providers (ISPs) had sprung up—10,000 of them, all over the world—that consolidation was inevitable. America

Online became one of the largest: In the late 1990s it was the leading provider of Internet services in the world and by 2000 had more than 25 million subscribers.

In the future, wireless access to the Internet will grow and enable applications not previously possible. For example, a coupling of wireless Internet access and a global positioning system will make it difficult for anyone to get lost. Such a combination would also make it easier to locate accident sites and improve the flow of traffic. Everything will be faster. Data rates of a trillion bits per second will become commercially feasible soon.

The World Wide Web—the familiar "www" of Internet addresses—is the leading information retrieval service of the

Internet. It was developed at CERN, an international scientific organization in Geneva, Switzerland, and it introduced the HyperText Transfer Protocol—the equally familiar "http"—in 1992.

Most people experience the Internet today through e-commerce, the selling of information, services, and goods by means of computer telecommunications networks. The beginnings of e-commerce can be traced to the 1948-49 Berlin airlift, when the U.S. Army discovered the traditional manner of doing business, accompanied by paper order, was too slow to keep up with the flow of goods into Berlin. Edward A. Guilbert, a logistics officer in the army, invented a system for ordering via telex, radio-teletype, and telephone. Various industries built on this system in the next few decades. When the first browser software appeared in 1993, e-commerce took off, with some companies, such as Amazon.com, springing up practically overnight. Even established companies turned to their Web sites for sales: In 1999, for instance, the Intel Corporation sold nearly half of its $30 billion in computer chips directly through its Web site. From its founding in 1995, the auction site eBay grew to more than 42 million members by 2001.

Much of the Internet technology was conceived in the so-called Silicon Valley, the industrial region around the southern shores of San Francisco Bay, with its intellectual center at Stanford University in Palo Alto. The Stanford Research Park, established in 1951, became America's premier high-tech manufacturing region. In symbiotic relationships, professors consulted with rent-paying tenants, industrial researchers taught courses on campus, and companies recruited the best students. In the 1980s and 1990s, the Silicon Valley manufacturers switched from producing semiconductors to making computers, then switched again to concentrate on producing computer software. During those years Stanford students established roughly 100 new companies a year. In the 90s, more than 230,000 jobs were created in the Valley, an increase of nearly 25 percent.

It couldn't last. During the late 1990s arose a speculative frenzy in the stocks of

dot-com companies in the Valley. Companies with little more to their name than an idea raised millions of dollars from venture capitalists and investors, even though they had never sold a product or made a profit. Securities and Exchange Chairman Alan Greenspan spoke of "irrational exuberance."

The bubble began to burst on March 10, 2000, when the Nasdaq stock market index peaked at 5048.62, more than double its value a year earlier. By 2001 it was in freefall. Companies failed left and right. Wags spoke of "dot-compost." For the broadcast of the 2000 Super Bowl 17 dot-com companies had paid more than $2 million for 30-second spots; for the next year's Super Bowl, only three dot-coms bought advertising time. A few of the established companies, such as Amazon.com and eBay, managed to survive and even thrive.

It helped to be nimble and quick-thinking. A company called Intrnets.com changed its name twice and its business plan twice before finally succeeding. It was born in 1997 as Intranetics, offering software to help businesses manage their daily activities. When sales of the software lagged in mid-1999, it changed its name to Intranets.com to call attention to its core service, the setting up and running of company intranet sites. It also gave away its online services and relied solely on Internet advertising for revenue. This strategy, too, did not work. The dot-com crash forced the company to change strategies again, this time becoming a paid online service. By early 2004 the company had tens of thousands of customers and was generating burgeoning revenues, which rose from $1 million in 2001 to $3.7 million in 2002 to $6 million in 2003.

"Google is not a conventional company," its founders, Larry Page and Sergey Brin, have written. "We do not intend to become one." The two founded the secretive company, which emerged as the most popular method for searching the Internet for information, while still graduate students at Stanford.

When they started the company they had no clear idea how they would make money from it, but stumbled onto one of the most potent business concepts in history: directing people searching for information directly to advertisements. Unlike most advertising, which tries to interrupt and distract people, advertising on Google often gives them exactly what they are looking for. And since the ads on Google are simply a few lines of text linked to Web sites, a company that could never afford the services of a large advertising agency can reach a worldwide audience. Google claimed in 2004 to have more than 150,000 individual advertisers.

The company planned to begin selling stock later in 2004, which is expected to give Google a market value on Wall Street of between $30 and $50 billion.

In addition to everything else, Google's success is once again bringing optimism to battered Silicon Valley.

---

ABOVE: *Youthful entrepreneurs Larry Page (left) and Sergey Brin pose inside the server room of Google, the internet search company they founded in 1998.*

OPPOSITE: *eBay is an incredibly successful Internet auction site.*

# The 2000 PRESIDENTIAL ELECTION

## A Nation Divided

Al Gore, vice-president of William Jefferson Clinton, faced off against the son of George Herbert Walker Bush, Republican George W. Bush, in perhaps the most controversial presidential election in American history. It was also the closest.

Results were not finalized until more than a month after election day, as various recounts, court challenges, and debates dragged on and on.

In the popular vote, Vice President Gore received 539,947 more votes than

Bush, but Bush tallied 271 electoral votes, one more than he needed for a majority and five more than Gore. The election in 2000 was the first in 112 years in which the leader in the popular vote lost the White House because his opponent prevailed in the Electoral College.

The race all came down to Florida, whose 25 electoral votes ultimately

decided the election by a razor-thin margin of actual votes.

For a few days after the November 7 election, confusion reigned. The TV networks were announcing the results of their exit polls as the polls closed in each state. In Florida, they first announced that Gore had won, then backed off and declared the race "too close to call." Later they awarded Florida to Bush, but later still returned to their earlier verdict. Gore called Bush and

conceded defeat, but soon called back to retract his concession.

Florida law dictates a recount if the margin of victory is small, and the final—and disputed—official Florida count gave the victory to Bush by 537 votes. Gore's campaign kept an eye on three issues: the legal imperative of capturing every Democratic vote possible in

Florida; the mission of presenting Gore as reasonable and dignified; and the political goal of keeping his supporters on board while buying time for the lawyers to do their battling.

Once the machine recounts were concluded—which reduced Mr. Bush's lead to a mere 327—the Gore campaign quickly sought manual recounts in four counties where Gore had polled well and where the Democrats contended there had been signs of trouble: Broward, Miami-Dade, Palm Beach, and Volusia.

### CHAD

Americans learned a new word during the 2000 presidential election: chad. Further, they learned about hanging chads, bulging chads, pregnant chads, and dimpled chads.

A chad is the part of a paper ballot that gets punched out when a voter casts a vote. In the 2000 presidential election, various Florida recounts got bogged down in the careful—indeed, obsessive—examination of chads.

The problem was not new. A 1996 Democratic primary for a house seat in Massachusetts hinged on 956 disputed ballots. The state's supreme court inspected the ballots and counted as valid votes even chads that were merely dimpled. "If the intent of the voter can be determined with reasonable certainty from an inspection of the ballot...effect must be given to that intent and the vote counted," the court ruled. It added, a voter who failed to push out the chad completely "could have done a better job expressing his or her intent. [But] such a voter should not automatically be disqualified."

An Alaska court in 1987 counted as valid punch-card votes that had been marked with a pen instead of being punched. In Indiana in 1981 a court ruled that "hanging chads" indicated the intent of a voter, so allowed them to be counted. In a South Dakota county election, a judge found it necessary to examine two ballots under a microscope; he found a single bulge in a pregnant chad. The South Dakota Supreme Court, ruling that a vote "shall be counted if the voter's intent is sufficiently plain," declared the ballot valid. But that caused the race to end in a tie. The two candidates played a game of poker to choose a winner. The Republican, with a pair of tens, won.

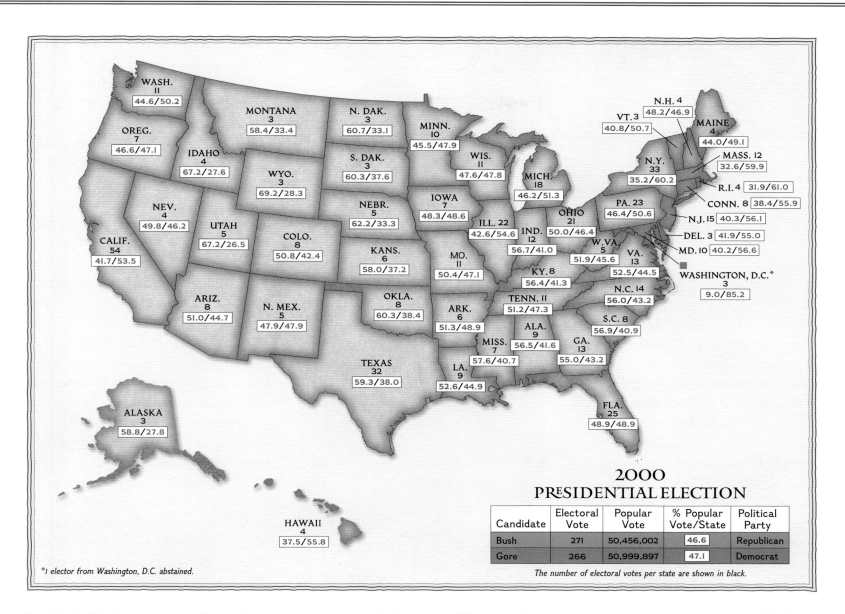

WASH. 11
44.6/50.2

OREG. 7
46.6/47.1

IDAHO 4
67.2/27.6

MONTANA 3
58.4/33.4

N. DAK. 3
60.7/33.1

MINN. 10
45.5/47.9

WYO. 3
69.2/28.3

S. DAK. 3
60.3/37.6

WIS. 11
47.6/47.8

NEV. 4
49.8/46.2

UTAH 5
67.2/26.5

COLO. 8
50.8/42.4

NEBR. 5
62.2/33.3

IOWA 7
48.3/48.6

MICH. 18
46.2/51.3

CALIF. 54
41.7/53.5

ARIZ. 8
51.0/44.7

N. MEX. 5
47.9/47.9

KANS. 6
58.0/37.2

ILL. 22
42.6/54.6

IND. 12
56.7/41.0

OHIO 21
50.0/46.4

MO. 11
50.4/47.1

OKLA. 8
60.3/38.4

ARK. 6
51.3/48.9

KY. 8
56.4/41.3

TENN. 11
51.2/47.3

W. VA. 5
51.9/45.6

VA. 13
52.5/44.5

N.C. 14
56.0/43.2

TEXAS 32
59.3/38.0

LA. 9
52.6/44.9

MISS. 7
57.6/40.7

ALA. 9
56.5/41.6

GA. 13
55.0/43.2

S.C. 8
56.9/40.9

FLA. 25
48.9/48.9

ALASKA 3
58.8/27.8

HAWAII 4
37.5/55.8

N.H. 4
48.2/46.9

VT. 3
40.8/50.7

MAINE 4
44.0/49.1

N.Y. 33
35.2/60.2

MASS. 12
32.6/59.9

R.I. 4
31.9/61.0

CONN. 8
38.4/55.9

N.J. 15
40.3/56.1

PA. 23
46.4/50.6

DEL. 3
41.9/55.0

MD. 10
40.2/56.6

WASHINGTON, D.C.*
3
9.0/85.2

## 2000 PRESIDENTIAL ELECTION

| Candidate | Electoral Vote | Popular Vote | % Popular Vote/State | Political Party |
|---|---|---|---|---|
| Bush | 271 | 50,456,002 | 46.6 | Republican |
| Gore | 266 | 50,999,897 | 47.1 | Democrat |

*1 elector from Washington, D.C. abstained.

The number of electoral votes per state are shown in black.

But Bush filed a preemptive federal lawsuit on November 11, challenging the constitutionality of manual recounts. Numerous local court rulings went both ways, some ordering recounts and others declaring that a selective manual recount in only a few counties would be unfair. Gore appealed to the Florida Supreme Court, which ordered that the recounting proceed. But Bush appealed to the U.S. Supreme Court, which took up *Bush* v. *Gore* on December 1. On December 12, all lower court rulings became moot when the Supreme Court handed down two decisions in favor of Bush: One, voted 7-2, declared the recount procedure then under way unconstitutional because it was not being done over the entire state; and the other, voted 5-4, banned further recounts using other procedures. The matter was settled when the U.S. Congress accepted Florida's electoral delegation.

Gore disagreed, but, "for the sake of our unity of the people and the strength of our democracy, I offer my concession."

Bush responded, saying, "The President of the United States is the President of every single American, of every race and every background."

Several factors may have favored Bush in Florida.

- The notorious Palm Beach "butterfly ballot" produced an unexpectedly large number of votes for third-party candidate Patrick Buchanan.
- A purge of 50,000 alleged felons from the Florida voting rolls included many voters who actually were eligible to vote under Florida law. A disproportionate number of them were African-Americans or Hispanics, largely Democrats.
- Television news declared Gore the winner around 9:00 p.m., Florida time, while voters in the western panhandle of the state were still voting, perhaps depressing voter turnout.
- Bush's brother Jeb was governor of Florida at the time, leading to various allegations of impropriety, though nothing was ever proved.
- A number of overseas ballots were

either missing postmarks or filled out improperly. This led the Democrats to move to have all overseas ballots thrown out, but they included many military ballots, which the Republicans argued to have accepted.

Embarrassment about the imbroglio in Florida led to widespread calls for electoral reform in the U.S. and ultimately to the passage of the Help America Vote Act. The act authorizes the federal government to provide funds to the states for replacing their mechanical voting equipment with electronic voting machines. This has led to new controversies because of the security weaknesses of the computers and the lack of paper-based methods providing backup for verification and recounts.

OPPOSITE: *Vice President Al Gore, at left, manages to summon a smile as he escorts President-elect George W. Bush into his home on December 19, 2000. Bush had just won the closest presidential election in American history—a victory filled with controversy.*

# FANATICS *and* ZEALOTS

~~~~~~~~~~~~~~~~~~

## *Terror Comes to America*

Isolated by surrounding oceans and insulated by complacency, America long felt secure from terrorist violence. That changed with a massive, smoky explosion on April 19, 1995, when the entire front of the Alfred P. Murrah Federal Building in Oklahoma City was blown off. The blast was the worst terrorist attack in U.S. history; it killed 169 men, women, and children and injured 850 more. On June 11, 2001, Timothy McVeigh, convicted of planting the bomb, was put to death in Terre Haute, Indiana, the first federal prisoner to be executed since 1963.

McVeigh and his partner Terry Nichols used a mixture of ammonium nitrate fertilizer and diesel fuel to make their explosive and rented a Ryder truck with which to deliver it. Their target, the Federal Building, housed mostly beneficent federal offices—welfare and social security, for instance—but it also housed the regional offices of the federal Bureau of Alcohol, Tobacco, and Firearms, from which agents

had been sent to Waco, Texas, to take part in the standoff at the Branch Davidian headquarters that had ended so violently. As such, it was a suitable tar-

get for antigovernment, right-wing militias. McVeigh had been linked to one, the Michigan Militia, a survivalist organiza-

tion that believed the U.S. government was behind a program to completely control the life of every American. They believed the government would use UN forces armed with cast-off Soviet military equipment, hordes of communist Chinese troops, and Latino and black inner-city American street gangs to crush opposition. Unemployed and drifting, McVeigh feared social marginality in the future and, though a white Protestant male, perceived American society to be moving in a direction that would make him and his class increasingly peripheral. The date he chose for the attack—April 19—was important to him, an anniversary of several events: Patriot's Day in New England, the day the American Revolution had begun in 1775; the day in 1943 that the Nazis had moved on the Warsaw ghetto to destroy the city's Jewish population; and the day in 1993 when the Branch Davidian compound in Waco, Texas, burned to the ground.

McVeigh went to his execution unrepentant. In an interview with the *Sunday Times* of London, he said, "When they [the government] govern by the sword, they must reckon with protest by the sword."

On September 11, 2001, hijackers operating under the direction of the wealthy son of a Saudi Arabian businessman, Osama bin Laden, commandeered commercial jetliners and flew them into targets in New York and Washington, D.C.

The first plane, a Boeing 767, struck the North Tower of the World Trade

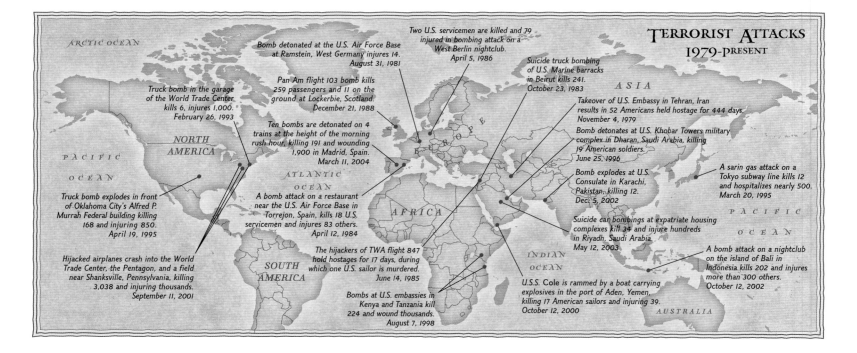

**TERRORIST ATTACKS**
**1979-PRESENT**

ARCTIC OCEAN

*Bomb detonated at the U.S. Air Force Base at Ramstein, West Germany injures 14. August 31, 1981*

*Two U.S. servicemen are killed and 79 injured in bombing attack on a West Berlin nightclub. April 5, 1986*

*Suicide truck bombing of U.S. Marine barracks in Beirut kills 241. October 23, 1983*

ASIA

*Truck bomb in the garage of the World Trade Center kills 6, injures 1,000. February 26, 1993*

*Pan Am flight 103 bomb kills 259 passengers and 11 on the ground at Lockerbie, Scotland. December 21, 1988*

*Takeover of U.S. Embassy in Tehran, Iran results in 52 Americans held hostage for 444 days. November 4, 1979*

*Ten bombs are detonated on 4 trains at the height of the morning rush hour, killing 191 and wounding 1,900 in Madrid, Spain. March 11, 2004*

*Bomb detonates at U.S. Khobar Towers military complex in Dharan, Saudi Arabia, killing 19 American soldiers. June 25, 1996*

NORTH AMERICA

PACIFIC OCEAN

EUROPE

ATLANTIC OCEAN

*Bomb explodes at U.S. Consulate in Karachi, Pakistan, killing 12. Dec. 5, 2002*

*A sarin gas attack on a Tokyo subway line kills 12 and hospitalizes nearly 500. March 20, 1995*

*Truck bomb explodes in front of Oklahoma City's Alfred P. Murrah Federal building killing 168 and injuring 850. April 19, 1995*

*A bomb attack on a restaurant near the U.S. Air Force Base in Torrejon, Spain, kills 18 U.S. servicemen and injures 83 others. April 12, 1984*

AFRICA

*Suicide car bombings at expatriate housing complexes kill 34 and injure hundreds in Riyadh, Saudi Arabia. May 12, 2003*

PACIFIC OCEAN

*Hijacked airplanes crash into the World Trade Center, the Pentagon, and a field near Shanksville, Pennsylvania, killing 3,038 and injuring thousands. September 11, 2001*

SOUTH AMERICA

*The hijackers of TWA flight 847 hold hostages for 17 days, during which one U.S. sailor is murdered. June 14, 1985*

INDIAN OCEAN

*A bomb attack on a nightclub on the island of Bali in Indonesia kills 202 and injures more than 300 others. October 12, 2002*

*Bombs at U.S. embassies in Kenya and Tanzania kill 224 and wound thousands. August 7, 1998*

*U.S.S. Cole is rammed by a boat carrying explosives in the port of Aden, Yemen, killing 17 American sailors and injuring 39. October 12, 2000*

AUSTRALIA

Center in New York a little before 9:00 a.m., just as the city was beginning a work day. A few minutes later a second plane struck the South Tower. Both planes, recently filled with highly volatile jet fuel, exploded into fireballs that ignited the top floors of the two towers. Then, as America watched transfixed, the horror grew worse: Within a mushrooming cloud of gray dust and smoke, the South Tower collapsed upon itself. A billowing cloud of dust, smoke, and debris spread through the canyon-like streets of lower Manhattan. Half an hour later, the North Tower also collapsed. Fires, fueled by the 10,000 gallons of jet fuel that each plane carried, had heated steel girders up to 2,000°F, softening them to the point where they could no longer support their great weight.

Meanwhile, the horror continued elsewhere. At 9:40 a.m., a third hijacked plane en route from Washington, D.C., to Los Angeles dove like a missile into one side of the Pentagon in Arlington, Virginia, across the Potomac from Washington. In rural Pennsylvania, another hijacked plane, whose passengers had learned from conversations on their cell phones what was happening,

fought back against the hijackers. Their plane crashed into an empty field. Its intended target had evidently been either the White House or the U.S. Capitol.

The attackers, most of whom were soon identified, were filled with religious conviction, hatred of secular society, and the determination to demonstrate power through acts of violence. America is often a trading partner and political ally of regimes around the world that are regarded by their religious opponents as primary foes. In an increasingly small world, the cultural image that America projects, through MTV, Hollywood movies, and the Internet, is seen as a threat in fundamentalist Islamic cultures. Even multinational corporations are thought to be primarily American in attitude. Ayatollah Khomeini once identified the "satanic" forces out to destroy Islam as corporate leaders with "no religious belief" who saw Islam as "the major obstacle in the path of the materialistic ambitions and the chief threat to their political power." Self-destructive violence, they devoutly believed, assured them of an immediate martyrdom and eternal bliss in heaven. With the finger of blame pointing to bin

Laden, American and British warplanes on October 7, 2001, attacked Afghanistan, bringing down the Taliban regime that had protected and supported him. The Taliban were soon defeated and bin Laden and his Al Qaeda cohorts went into hiding in the desolate mountains along the Afghanistan border with Pakistan.

After the attacks, Americans returned to normal life very slowly. By the weekend, closed airports were once again open for business and planes were flying. On Monday, Wall Street resumed trading. A week later, the major league football and baseball teams resumed their schedules. And a newly formed Department of Homeland Security would go to work trying to prevent such attacks in the future.

ABOVE: *Still smoldering 15 days after the attack, ground zero presents a huge void in lower Manhattan. The twin towers of the World Trade Center were destroyed by Islamic zealots, who flew hijacked airliners into the structures on September 11, 2001.*

OPPOSITE: *The Pentagon in Arlington, Virginia, suffered a similar attack on the same day, though the casualty toll was far less.*

# A SECOND WAR *in the* GULF

## *Operation Iraqi Freedom*

Saddam Hussein emerged onto the world's front pages again in 2003. Suspicions that he was developing weapons of mass destruction—chemical, biological, and nuclear—that could be used against enemies in the Gulf or traded to terrorists prompted President George W. Bush to issue an ultimatum to the Iraqi dictator: Allow UN weapons inspectors back into your country or suffer the consequences.

Years of economic sanctions, imposed on Iraq by the United Nations at the close of the first Gulf War in 1991, had taken a toll. The hope was to weaken Hussein's

government by imposing the sanctions, which prevented all trade with Iraq. Only medical supplies and food could be imported to Iraq. No-fly zones were also set up to keep Iraq's military in check.

Thirty-five years of misrule by Saddam Hussein's Ba'ath Party had left Iraq broken. Iraq's infrastructure was crumbling and people were suffering severe hardships, including malnutrition. Rivalries between ethnic groups and religious splits between the two main branches of Islam, the Sunnis and the Shi'ites, caused deep divisions within the country.

Hussein's troops had invaded neigh-

boring Kuwait in 1990, hoping to control its immense oil wealth. Operation Desert Storm drove the Iraqi troops out of Kuwait in less than two months, but Saddam Hussein stayed in power.

In December 1998 UN inspectors complained that Iraq was blocking their work and began departing from the country. In January 2002 President George W. Bush labeled the country a part of an "axis of evil." He insisted that the world must confront the "grave and gathering danger" of Iraq.

In February 2003 protests against a possible war with Iraq took place in more than 350 cities worldwide. Some of America's allies, including France, Germany, and Russia, opposed an attack on Iraq without an authorizing resolution from the United Nations. French President Jacques Chirac said, "We are no longer in an era where one or two countries can control the fate of another country." But more than 40 countries around the world announced their support for the use of force against Iraq.

On November 27, 2002, a weapons inspection team from the United Nations

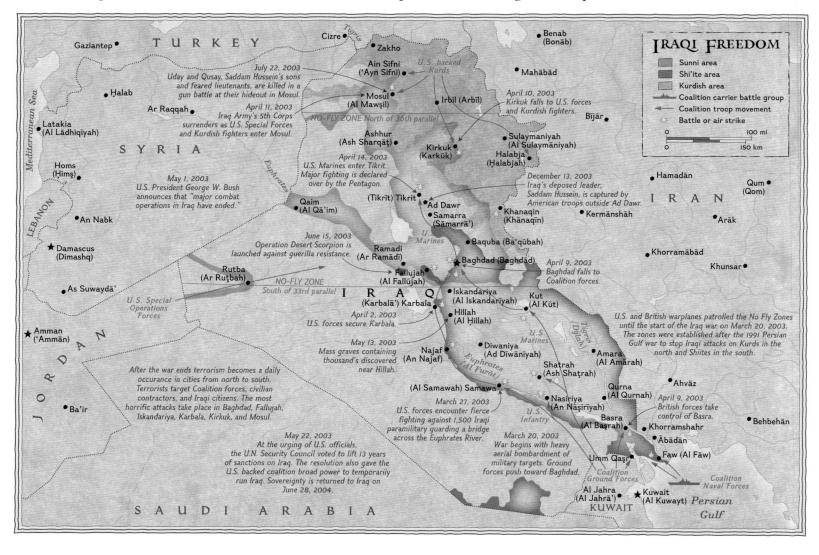

returned to Iraq. U.S. Secretary of State Colin Powell went before the UN Security Council several times in February 2003 to convince the 15-member group that only military action could stop Saddam Hussein from hiding weapons of mass destruction. President Bush gave Hussein 48 hours to leave Iraq.

Two hours after the expiration of the deadline, the U.S. and its allies launched Operation Iraqi Freedom. On March 19, 2003, forces consisting of 40 cruise missiles and strikes by two F-117s from the 8th Fighter Squadron and other aircraft attacked. President Bush addressed the American public, announcing that coalition forces were in the "early stages of military operations to disarm Iraq, to free its people, and to defend the world from grave danger."

There were several justifications offered for the war and a number of objectives. The primary object was to eliminate Saddam Hussein from the world's stage once and for all and to destroy his weapons of mass destruction. A suspected link to terrorists was to be pursued and terrorist networks sought out and destroyed. A more benign objective was to end the economic sanctions imposed on Iraq so aid could be given to the many impoverished citizens and refugees in the coun-

## SADDAM HUSSEIN

The son of poor farmers, Saddam Hussein grew up in a village of mud-brick huts called *Al-ouja*. An uncle who was an army officer and crusader for Arab unity inspired him to go into politics.

He joined the socialist Ba'ath party at 19 and made his mark three years later by participating in a 1959 assassination attempt against Iraq's Prime Minister, Abdul Karim Qasim. Saddam was wounded in the leg during the failed effort and fled the country.

In 1963 he returned to Iraq and helped lead the revolt in 1986, under Gen. Ahmed Hassan al-Bakr, that brought the Ba'ath Party to power. He was made vice president of the country and built an elaborate network of secret police to suppress dissidents. Eleven years later he deposed Bakr and made himself president.

He allowed no dissenting voices to be raised and killed dozens of government officials he suspected of disloyalty. In the 1980s he resorted to chemical weapons to crush a Kurdish rebellion, brutally killing thousands.

In 1980 he invaded Iran, starting an eight-year war that ended in stalemate. And in August 1990 he invaded Kuwait, defying UN directives to withdraw and provoking what he called "the mother of all battles."

try. And finally, coalition forces expected to secure Iraq's oil fields, allowing oil production to resume, and to install a representative form of self-government.

Operation Iraqi Freedom was the biggest military operation mounted since the Vietnam War. Most of the forces were American, but the United Kingdom and Australia also provided troops.

On December 13, 2003, forces from the 4th Infantry Division, coalition forces, and special operations forces captured the Iraqi dictator in a remote farmhouse near Tikrit. Operation "Red Dawn" consisted of some 600 soldiers, including cavalry, artillery, aviation, engineering, and special operation forces. Hussein was found in a small, walled mud-hut compound with a metal lean-to. An orange and white taxi was parked nearby. The former dictator was found within a "spider hole," its entrance camouflaged with bricks and dirt. He gave little or no resistance, though he had two AK-47 rifles, a pistol—and about $750,000 in U.S. dollars.

ABOVE: *U.S. Marines in Tikrit battle sand and Iraqi troops in April 2003. The Gulf War, Round Two, deposed Iraqi leader Saddam Hussein but found no weapons of mass destruction, the chief rationale for the war.*

# HIGHER, DEEPER, FARTHER

## *The Final Frontier*

D r. Sylvia Earle allowed herself to be bolted into Jim, a cumbersome pressurized diving suit. A small submarine descended with her to a depth of 1,250 feet off the island of Oahu. Once on the ocean bottom, she unhooked herself from the sub and set off to explore. With no connection to the surface, and only a thin communications line attaching her to the sub, she wandered alone for two and a half hours.

Her solo expedition to the seafloor in 1979 would help change the space explorer profile forever: It led to one of the first class of women entering the U.S. astronaut

training program (in 1978) being chosen for a mission. She had proven that women had the physical endurance necessary for space exploration. And with Sally Ride women began to explore the universe in a new NASA brainchild: the space shuttle.

In January 1972 the Apollo moon program was coming to an end, even though there were two lunar landings yet to come. NASA looked around for new projects and settled upon a space shuttle, a reusable craft that would lift off like a rocket, carry people and cargo into Earth orbit, then land on a runway like an airplane. After servicing, it would be ready to fly again.

President Nixon said, "I have decided today that the United States should proceed at once with the development of an entirely new type of space transportation system designed to help transform the space frontier of the 1970s into familiar territory, easily accessible for human endeavor in the 1980s and 1990s." The space shuttle was meant to make space flight routine, all the while carrying 65,000 pounds of cargo and seven people.

In the early 1980s, haste and carelessness led to an early disaster, the *Challenger* accident, which cost a shuttle and its entire crew. The shuttle disaster *Columbia*, on February 1, 2003, has further weakened NASA's rationale for the shuttle.

Between 1995 and 1998, the shuttle cooperated in an endeavor to service *Mir,* the Russian modular space station. The first piece of *Mir* was sent into orbit in 1986, and it grew during the next decade as five more pieces were added to it: two science modules that contained remote-sensing instruments to help with studies of the ecology and the environments of Earth; a laboratory for investigating the science of materials; a module for storing extra life support equipment;

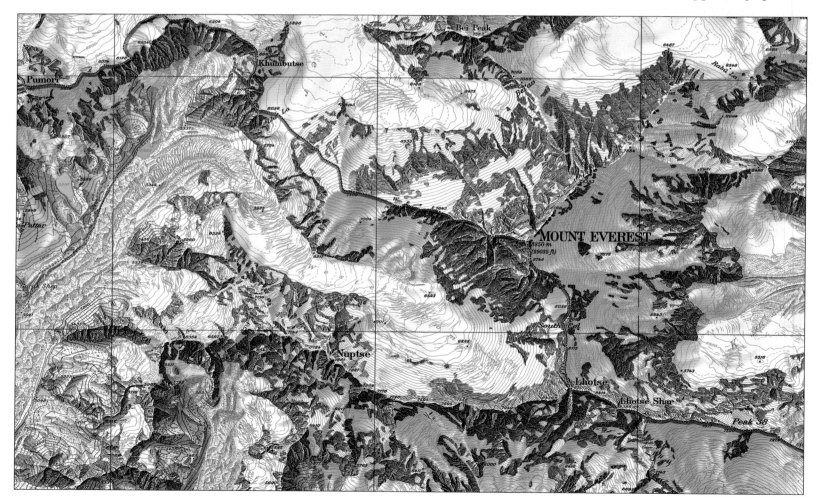

experienced crew of seven astronauts set off on December 2, 1993, to fix Hubble. They would install a package to correct the flaw in the mirror, as well as replace two gyroscopes that had worn out, remove Hubble's damaged solar arrays and replace them with new ones, and install a new wide-field camera. Working with delicate tools and techniques in the weightlessness of space, the astronauts did their job, and four weeks later NASA pronounced Hubble fixed. By 1993 Hubble had looked deeper into the universe than ever had been done before, revealing thousands of galaxies and allowing astronomers to trace the evolution of the universe.

In its first ten years, Hubble snapped 330,000 exposures and focused on 14,000 targets in space. Today its future is in some doubt as NASA funds may be shifted toward President Bush's manned missions to Mars.

Twenty-first-century exploration has incorporated robotic technology to augment human voyages. Latest in a long line of robotic explorers in space, NASA's *Opportunity* and *Spirit* were scuttling around on the surface of Mars in early 2004, photographing and gathering readings on the Martian minerals. Their primary mission is to look for evidence that Mars was once warmer and wetter than it is today. In February, *Spirit,* using a diamond-tipped abrasion tool spinning 3,000 times a minute, ground into a rock termed Adirondack, allowing scientists to get their first look at pristine Martian minerals. New generations of robotic explorers are planned.

---

ABOVE: *Dangling beneath a minisub, Dr. Sylvia Earle ascends to the surface following a solo stroll on the seafloor in 1979. At a depth of 1,250 feet she performed a two-and-a-half-hour exploration. Earle's walk proved the dexterity of women and was a precursor to women being selected for space shuttle flights.*

OPPOSITE: *Stereo photographs from the space shuttle* Columbia *and aerials taken from a Learjet helped create the most detailed map ever drawn of Mount Everest, the highest point on the planet, famously first ascended by Hillary and Tenzing in 1953. The project converted and digitized the photographs into contour lines.*

and an astrophysics observatory. For more than 14 years *Mir* was a versatile laboratory parked far out in space, even though its original design called for it to be serviceable for only five years. Seven American astronauts, ferried by the space shuttle, served tours on *Mir* as part of a merged space station program. Language and cultural barriers proved difficult, and two onboard mishaps—a fire during an astronaut's stay in 1997 and a collision with a supply craft four months later—strained relations.

On March 23, 2001, after suffering a series of equipment failures and accidents, *Mir* was abandoned and fell into the Pacific.

One of the shuttle's most important accomplishments was the launching and repair of the Hubble Space Telescope. On April 24, 1990, the NASA announ-cer intoned, "…and liftoff of the space shuttle *Discovery* with the Hubble Space Telescope—our window on the universe."

But it was a foggy window.

NASA scientists discovered that the telescope's vision was flawed—its primary mirror was 2.5 millionths of a meter too flat at the edge. Images sent back to earth had a smudge or blur in the center of each image. The telescope couldn't be brought back to earth and repaired, so it would have to be done in space. A highly

# The AMERICAN PRESIDENTS
## *1789-Present*

| PRESIDENT | VICE PRESIDENT | POLITICAL PARTY | YEARS OF TERM |
|---|---|---|---|
| George Washington | John Adams | Federalist | 1789–1797 |
| John Adams | Thomas Jefferson | Federalist | 1797–1801 |
| Thomas Jefferson | Aaron Burr (1801-1805) | Democratic-Republican | 1801–1809 |
| James Madison | George Clinton (1805–1813) | Democratic-Republican | 1809–1817 |
| | Elbridge Getty (1813–1817) | | |
| James Monroe | Daniel D. Tompkins | Democratic-Republican | 1817–1825 |
| John Quincy Adams | John C. Calhoun | Democratic-Republican | 1825–1829 |
| Andrew Jackson | John C. Calhoun (1829–1833) | Democratic | 1829–1837 |
| | Martin Van Buren (1833-1837) | | |
| Martin Van Buren | Richard M. Johnson | Democratic | 1837–1841 |
| William Henry Harrison | John Tyler | Whig | 1841 |
| John Tyler | None—Became President after Harrison's death. | Whig | 1841–1845 |
| James K. Polk | George M. Dallas | Democrat | 1845-1849 |
| Zachary Taylor | Millard Fillmore | Whig | 1849–1850 |
| Millard Fillmore | None—Became President after Taylor's death. | Whig | 1850–1853 |
| Franklin Pierce | William R. D. King | Democrat | 1853–1857 |
| James Buchanan | John C. Breckinridge | Democrat | 1857–1861 |
| Abraham Lincoln | Hannibal Hamlin(1861–1865) Andrew Johnson (1865) | Republican | 1861–1865 |
| Andrew Johnson | None—Became President after Lincoln's asassination. | Democrat | 1865–1869 |
| Ulysses S. Grant | Schuyler Colfax (1869–1873) Henry Wilson (1873–1877) | Republican | 1869–1877 |
| Rutherford B. Hayes | William A. Wheeler | Republican | 1877–1881 |
| James A. Garfield | Chester A. Arthur | Republican | 1881 |
| Chester A. Arthur | None—Became President after Garfield's asassination. | Republican | 1881–1885 |
| Grover Cleveland | Thomas A. Hendricks | Democrat | 1885–1889 |
| Benjamin Harrison | Levi P. Morton | Republican | 1889–1893 |
| Grover Cleveland | Adlai E. Stevenson | Democrat | 1893–1897 |
| William McKinley | Garret A. Hobart (1897–1901) Theodore Roosevelt (1901) | Republican | 1897–1901 |
| Theodore Roosevelt | Became President after McKinley's assassination. Charles Fairbanks (1905–1909) | Republican | 1901–1909 |
| William Howard Taft | James S. Sherman | Republican | 1909–1913 |

| PRESIDENT | VICE PRESIDENT | POLITICAL PARTY | YEARS OF TERM |
|---|---|---|---|
| Woodrow Wilson | Thomas R. Marshall | Democrat | 1913–1921 |
| Warren G. Harding | Calvin Coolidge | Republican | 1921–1923 |
| Calvin Coolidge | Became President after Harding's death. Charles G. Dawes (1925–1929) | Republican | 1923–1929 |
| Herbert Hoover | Charles Curtis | Republican | 1929–1933 |
| Franklin D. Roosevelt | John N. Garner (1933–1941) Henry A. Wallace (1941–1945) Harry S. Truman (1945) | Democrat | 1933–1945 |
| Harry S. Truman | Became President after Roosevelt's death. Alben W. Barkley (1949–1953) | Democrat | 1945–1953 |
| Dwight D. Eisenhower | Richard M. Nixon | Republican | 1953–1961 |
| John F. Kennedy | Lyndon B. Johnson | Democrat | 1961–1963 |
| Lyndon B. Johnson | Became President after Kennedy's assassination. Hubert Humphrey (1965-1969) | Democrat | 1963–1969 |
| Richard M. Nixon | Spiro T. Agnew (1969–1973) Gerald R. Ford (1973–1974) | Republican | 1969–1974 |
| Gerald R. Ford | Became President after Nixon's resignation. Nelson Rockefeller (1974–1977) | Republican | 1974–1977 |
| Jimmy Carter | Walter F. Mondale | Democrat | 1977–1981 |
| Ronald Regan | George H. W. Bush | Republican | 1981–1989 |
| George H. W. Bush | Dan Quayle | Republican | 1989–1993 |
| William Jefferson Clinton | Al Gore | Democrat | 1993–2001 |
| George W. Bush | Richard B. Cheney | Republican | 2001–Present |

# The ELECTORAL COLLEGE
## States' Number of Votes

| STATE | VOTES | STATE | VOTES | STATE | VOTES | STATE | VOTES |
|---|---|---|---|---|---|---|---|
| Alabama | 9 | Indiana | 11 | Nebraska | 5 | South Carolina | 8 |
| Alaska | 3 | Iowa | 7 | Nevada | 5 | South Dakota | 3 |
| Arizona | 10 | Kansas | 6 | New Hampshire | 4 | Tennessee | 11 |
| Arkansas | 6 | Kentucky | 8 | New Jersey | 15 | Texas | 34 |
| California | 55 | Louisiana | 9 | New Mexico | 5 | Utah | 5 |
| Colorado | 9 | Maine | 4 | New York | 31 | Vermont | 3 |
| Connecticut | 7 | Maryland | 10 | North Carolina | 15 | Virginia | 13 |
| Delaware | 3 | Massachusetts | 12 | North Dakota | 3 | Washington | 11 |
| Florida | 27 | Michigan | 17 | Ohio | 20 | West Virginia | 5 |
| Georgia | 15 | Minnesota | 17 | Oklahoma | 7 | Wisconsin | 10 |
| Hawaii | 4 | Mississippi | 6 | Oregon | 7 | Wyoming | 3 |
| Idaho | 4 | Missouri | 11 | Pennsylvania | 21 | District of Columbia | 3 |
| Illinois | 21 | Montana | 3 | Rhode Island | 4 | | |

# STATE FLAGS *and* FACTS

| STATE | ABBR. | CAPITAL | YEAR SETTLED | ENTERED UNION | FLAG | APPENDIX MAP PAGE |
|-------|-------|---------|--------------|---------------|------|-------------------|
| Alabama | ALA. | Montgomery | 1702 | 12/14/1819 | | 228–229 |
| Alaska | ALAS. | Juneau | 1784 | 1/3/1959 | | 236 |
| Arizona | ARIZ. | Phoenix | 1776 | 2/14/1912 | | 234 |
| Arkansas | ARK. | Little Rock | 1686 | 6/15/1836 | | 228 |
| California | CALIF. | Sacramento | 1769 | 9/9/1850 | | 236–237 |
| Colorado | COLO. | Denver | 1858 | 8/1/1876 | | 232–233 |
| Connecticut | CONN. | Hartford | 1634 | 1/9/1788 | | 224–225 |
| Delaware | DEL. | Dover | 1638 | 12/7/1787 | | 227 |
| Florida | FLA. | Tallahassee | 1565 | 3/3/1845 | | 228–229 |
| Georgia | GA. | Atlanta | 1733 | 1/2/1788 | | 229 |
| Hawaii | HI. | Honolulu | 1820 | 8/21/1959 | | 234 |
| Idaho | ID. | Boise | 1842 | 7/3/1890 | | 232 |
| Illinois | ILL. | Springfield | 1720 | 12/3/1818 | | 230 |
| Indiana | IND. | Indianapolis | 1733 | 12/11/1816 | | 230 |
| Iowa | IOWA | Des Moines | 1788 | 12/28/1846 | | 230–231 |
| Kansas | KANS. | Topeka | 1727 | 1/29/1861 | | 233 |
| Kentucky | KY. | Frankfort | 1774 | 6/1/1792 | | 230 |
| Louisiana | LA. | Baton Rouge | 1699 | 4/30/1812 | | 228 |
| Maine | ME. | Augusta | 1624 | 3/15/1820 | | 225 |
| Maryland | MD. | Annapolis | 1634 | 4/28/1788 | | 227 |
| Massachusetts | MASS. | Boston | 1620 | 2/6/1788 | | 225 |
| Michigan | MICH. | Lansing | 1668 | 1/26/1837 | | 230–231 |
| Minnesota | MINN. | St. Paul | 1805 | 5/11/1858 | | 231 |
| Mississippi | MISS. | Jackson | 1699 | 12/10/1817 | | 228 |

| STATE | ABBR. | CAPITAL | YEAR SETTLED | ENTERED UNION | FLAG | APPENDIX MAP PAGE |
|-------|-------|---------|--------------|---------------|------|-------------------|
| Missouri | MO. | Jefferson City | 1735 | 8/10/1821 | | 230 |
| Montana | MONT. | Helena | 1809 | 11/8/1889 | | 232–233 |
| Nebraska | NEBR. | Lincoln | 1823 | 3/1/1867 | | 233 |
| Nevada | NEV. | Carson City | 1849 | 10/31/1864 | | 236–237 |
| New Hampshire | N.H. | Concord | 1623 | 6/21/1788 | | 225 |
| New Jersey | N.J. | Trenton | 1660 | 12/18/1787 | | 227 |
| New Mexico | N.MEX. | Santa Fe | 1610 | 1/6/1912 | | 234–235 |
| New York | N.Y. | Albany | 1614 | 7/26/1788 | | 224–225 |
| North Carolina | N.C. | Raleigh | 1660 | 11/21/1789 | | 229 |
| North Dakota | N.DAK. | Bismarck | 1812 | 11/2/1889 | | 233 |
| Ohio | OHIO | Columbus | 1788 | 3/1/1803 | | 226 |
| Oklahoma | OKLA. | Oklahoma City | 1889 | 11/16/1907 | | 235 |
| Oregon | OREG. | Salem | 1811 | 2/14/1859 | | 237 |
| Pennsylvania | PA. | Harrisburg | 1682 | 12/12/1787 | | 226–227 |
| Rhode Island | R.I. | Providence | 1636 | 5/29/1790 | | 224–225 |
| South Carolina | S.C. | Columbia | 1670 | 5/23/1788 | | 229 |
| South Dakota | S.DAK. | Pierre | 1859 | 11/2/1889 | | 233 |
| Tennessee | TENN. | Nashville | 1769 | 6/1/1796 | | 228–229 |
| Texas | TEX. | Austin | 1682 | 12/29/1845 | | 234–235 |
| Utah | UTAH | Salt Lake City | 1847 | 1/4/1896 | | 232 |
| Vermont | VT. | Montpelier | 1724 | 3/4/1791 | | 225 |
| Virginia | VA. | Richmond | 1607 | 6/25/1788 | | 226–227 |
| Washington | WASH. | Olympia | 1811 | 11/11/1889 | | 237 |
| West Virginia | W.VA. | Charleston | 1727 | 6/20/1863 | | 226–227 |
| Wisconsin | WIS. | Madison | 1766 | 5/29/1848 | | 230–231 |
| Wyoming | WYO. | Cheyenne | 1834 | 7/10/1890 | | 232–233 |
| Washington, D.C. | D.C. | Nation's Capital | | 12/1/1800 | | 227 |

# NORTHEAST

National park system
Indian reservation
Explorer route or trail
Historic road
★ National capital
◉ State capital
• Other town
✕ Battlefield
■ Site

miles 0 — 50
kilometers 0 — 75

KEY TO LARGE SCALE MAPS

GREAT PLAINS AND ROCKIES PP. 232-233
NORTHEAST PP. 224-225
FAR WEST PP. 236-237
MIDWEST PP. 230-231
MID-ATLANTIC PP. 226-227
SOUTHWEST PP. 234-235
SOUTHEAST PP. 228-229

C A N A D A

Champlain 1615

Georgian Bay

Ottawa

Champlain 1615

★ Ottawa

Montréal

Champlain 1615

Lake Simcoe

Lake Scugog

Rice Lake

Long-debated navigation and power project begun in 1954. In 1959 deep-draft oceangoing ships entered Lake Ontario, while hydoelectricity powered factories and homes.

St. Lawrence

ST. REGIS MOHAWK

In 1885 conservation-conscious legislators established the Adirondack Forest Preserve. The wilderness lured hunters, fishermen, and health seekers. Many of today's visitors—an estimated ten to twelve million annually—come with the same goals.

Site of the 1932 and 1980 winter Olympics, known as the winter sports capital of the world. Year-round tourist destination nestled in the Adirondack Mountains.

Falls of the Black River powered pulp- and paper-making industry in the 1800s.

ST. LAWRENCE SEAWAY

• Lake Placid

Mt. Marcy 5,344 ft + 1,629 m

Vital completing link in the water route connecting the Atlantic Ocean and the interior. Impetus for the early 19th-century burst of canal building, which was ended by the railroad era. Still carries freight.

In the 1800s the Oswego and Welland Canals spurred industrial growth. Became a major flour-milling center.

• Watertown

Black

ADIRONDACK MOUNTAINS

• Toronto

LAKE ONTARIO

The English built Fort Stanwix in 1758 to protect the strategic portage between the Great Lakes and the Mohawk-Hudson Rivers.

Hudson

Lake George

Prime tourist attraction first harnessed for hydroelectricity in the late 1800s, the falls now power homes and industries.

Oswego

FORT STANWIX NAT. MONUMENT

Exclusive social and sporting center in the 1800s; still popular as spa and horse-racing resort.

Great Sacandaga Lake

• Hamilton

Erie Canal

By 1800 the first road west from Utica to Geneva followed an Indian trail; it became part of a turnpike extending to the Great Lakes in the in the early 1800s.

Oneida L.

Erie Canal

Rome

Oriskany ✕ Aug. 6, 1777

Saratoga Springs

In 1803 Joseph Ellicott, an agent of the Holland Land Company, laid out a city modeled on Washington, D.C. As western terminus of the Erie Canal, Buffalo channeled farm produce east and manufactured goods west. Railroads converged on this "break-bulk" point where goods were transferred from one form of transportation to another, and in the late 1800s manufacturers profited by converting grains into flour and iron ore into steel.

Niagara Falls
TUSCARORA
Niagara Falls
TONAWANDA
Niagara
THEODORE ROOSEVELT INAUGURAL NATIONAL HISTORIC SITE
Buffalo

Rochester

Opening of the Erie Canal stimulated exploitation of salt deposits; later the railroads promoted industrial diversification.

Genesee Road

Syracuse

ONONDAGA

Utica

Great Western Turnpike

SARATOGA NAT. HISTORICAL PARK

Laid out by New Englanders after the Revolutionary War. Competed with Albany for Hudson River trade. Became a major iron and steel center in the 1800s.

Troy

LAKE ERIE

CATTARAUGUS

Location on the Erie Canal and falls of the Genesee River made it a flour-milling boomtown in the 1820s: technical pioneering, as by Xerox and Eastman Kodak, and research make the modern city.

Finger Lakes

Seneca Lake

Cayuga Lake

As a more direct, but hillier road west than the Mohawk Valley route, the turnpike reinforced Albany's gateway position.

NEW YORK

Cooperstown

Albany ◉

Only non-Indian U.S. city built on tribal land. Its 99-year lease was scheduled to expire in 1991; however, after a lengthy legal battle the lease was extended for 40 years.

ALLEGANY
Salamanca

OIL SPRING

Ithaca

Founded in 1786 by Judge William Cooper, early land speculator and father of novelist James Fenimore Cooper. Birthplace of modern baseball and home to the National Baseball Hall of Fame.

MARTIN VAN BUREN NATIONAL HISTORIC SITE

• Erie

Jamestown

Elmira

Newtown ✕ Aug. 29, 1779

Binghamton

In 1783 Nantucket Quakers and other New Englanders moved to the heart of Dutch North America because their whaling activities had been curtailed by the Revolutionary War. By 1790 Hudson was home port to a substantial fleet engaged in whaling, sealing, and trade with the West Indies.

Hudson

CATSKILL

MOUNTAINS

**PROVIDENCE, RHODE ISLAND**
"Having a sense of God's merciful providence unto me," Puritan rebel Roger Williams founded a farming colony on this spacious harbor in 1636. During the American Revolution, Providence served as a gateway to Boston, and in the late 1700s sailed ahead of its maritime rival, Newport. Tool and textile manufacturing and the making of fine jewelry became important in the early 1800s.

**WOONSOCKET, RHODE ISLAND**
By the mid-1800s the swiftly flowing Blackstone River and its tributaries powered the most heavily industrialized region in the U.S. The Blackstone Canal, a financially unsuccessful bid by Providence to enlarge its orbit, opened in 1828 to Worcester, Massachusetts, stimulating textile towns such as Woonsocket, Rhode Island.

Susquehanna

PENNSYLVANIA

APPALACHIAN

UPPER DELAWARE SCENIC AND RECREATIONAL RIVER

VANDERBILT MANSION NAT. HISTORIC SITE

HOME OF FRANKLIN D. ROOSEVELT NAT. HISTORIC SITE

Poughkeepsie

For more than 150 years New Yorkers have vacationed at resorts both grand and rustic. Spectacular scenes inspired painters of the Hudson River school, and legendary Rip Van Winkle slept here for 20 years.

Hudson

• Williamsport

Scranton

Wilkes-Barre

Strategic redoubt in the Revolution: Congress in 1802 established on the site an academy to train the nation's Army officers.

U.S. MILITARY ACADEMY

NEW JERSEY

Stamford

**HARTFORD, CONNECTICUT**
Although the Dutch built a post at the head of the Connecticut River navigation in 1633, permanent settlement awaited Puritans from Massachusetts in 1635–36. Connecticut's first constitution, a then radical document embracing authority by popular vote, was framed in Hartford. The nation's insurance capital is also home to leading financial services companies, and several manufacturers of aircraft engines and space equipment.

**NEWPORT, RHODE ISLAND**
Puritan dissidents from Boston, led by William Coddington and John Clarke, a Baptist, founded Newport in 1639. A hub of shipbuilding and maritime commerce, the town grew opulent from the slave trade. Its days as a summer resort began in the mid-1800s.

Best known example of planned suburbia; begun in 1947 to house World War II veterans and their families.

September 11, 2001, terrorists hijacked four passenger planes, crashing two into the Twin Towers of the World Trade Center, and one into the Pentagon; a fourth crashed into a field in Shanksville, Pennsylvania. Almost 3,000 were killed.

• State College

Delaware

Yonkers

SAGAMORE HILL NAT. HISTORIC SITE

New York

Levittown

U.S. entry port for 12 million immigrants between 1892 and 1954. Peak: one million in 1907.

Ellis I.
STATUE OF LIBERTY NAT. MON.

First settled by the Dutch, remained a city unto itself until incorporated into New York City in 1898.

BROOKLYN

GATEWAY NAT. REC. AREA

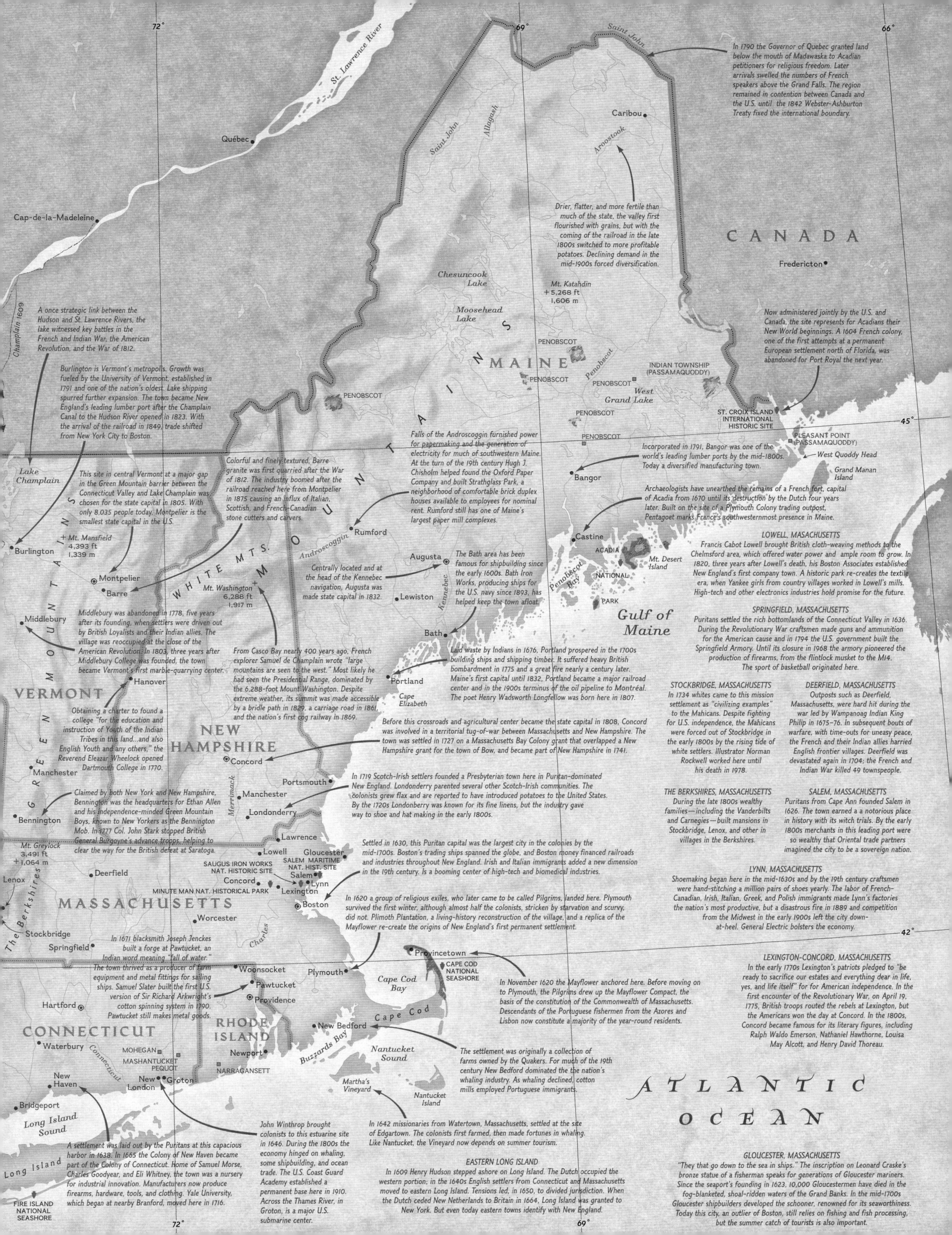

72°
69°
66°
45°
42°
St. Lawrence River
Saint John
Québec
Cap-de-la-Madeleine
Champlain 1609
Caribou
Saint John
Allagash
Aroostook
CANADA
Fredericton
Chesuncook Lake
Moosehead Lake
Mt. Katahdin +5,268 ft 1,606 m
MAINE
PENOBSCOT
Penobscot
INDIAN TOWNSHIP (PASSAMAQUODDY)
West Grand Lake
ST. CROIX ISLAND INTERNATIONAL HISTORIC SITE
PLEASANT POINT (PASSAMAQUODDY)
West Quoddy Head
Grand Manan Island
Bangor
Castine
ACADIA NATIONAL PARK
Mt. Desert Island
Penobscot Bay
Gulf of Maine
Rumford
Androscoggin
Augusta
Lewiston
Kennebec
Bath
Portland
Cape Elizabeth
MOUNTAINS
WHITE MTS.
Mt. Washington + 6,288 ft 1,917 m
Lake Champlain
Burlington
+ Mt. Mansfield 4,393 ft 1,339 m
Montpelier
Barre
Middlebury
GREEN MOUNTAINS
VERMONT
Hanover
Manchester
Bennington
NEW HAMPSHIRE
Concord
Merrimack
Manchester
Londonderry
Portsmouth
Lawrence
Lowell
Gloucester
SALEM MARITIME NAT. HIST. SITE
SAUGUS IRON WORKS NAT. HISTORIC SITE
Salem
Lynn
Concord
MINUTE MAN NAT. HISTORICAL PARK
Lexington
Boston
Mt. Greylock 3,491 ft + 1,064 m
Lenox
Deerfield
MASSACHUSETTS
The Berkshires
Worcester
Stockbridge
Springfield
Charles
Provincetown
CAPE COD NATIONAL SEASHORE
Cape Cod Bay
Plymouth
Woonsocket
Pawtucket
Providence
Hartford
CONNECTICUT
RHODE ISLAND
Waterbury
MOHEGAN
MASHANTUCKET PEQUOT
Connecticut
New Bedford
Cape Cod
Buzzards Bay
Newport
NARRAGANSETT
Nantucket Sound
Martha's Vineyard
Nantucket Island
New Haven
New London
Groton
Bridgeport
Long Island Sound
Long Island
FIRE ISLAND NATIONAL SEASHORE
ATLANTIC OCEAN
In 1790 the Governor of Quebec granted land below the mouth of Madawaska to Acadian petitioners for religious freedom. Later arrivals swelled the numbers of French speakers above the Grand Falls. The region remained in contention between Canada and the U.S. until the 1842 Webster-Ashburton Treaty fixed the international boundary.
Drier, flatter, and more fertile than much of the state, the valley first flourished with grains, but with the coming of the railroad in the late 1800s switched to more profitable potatoes. Declining demand in the mid-1900s forced diversification.
Now administered jointly by the U.S. and Canada, the site represents for Acadians their New World beginnings. A 1604 French colony, one of the first attempts at a permanent European settlement north of Florida, was abandoned for Port Royal the next year.
A once strategic link between the Hudson and St. Lawrence Rivers, the lake witnessed key battles in the French and Indian War, the American Revolution, and the War of 1812.
Burlington is Vermont's metropolis. Growth was fueled by the University of Vermont, established in 1791 and one of the nation's oldest. Lake shipping spurred further expansion. The town became New England's leading lumber port after the Champlain Canal to the Hudson River opened in 1823. With the arrival of the railroad in 1849, trade shifted from New York City to Boston.
Falls of the Androscoggin furnished power for papermaking and the generation of electricity for much of southwestern Maine. At the turn of the 19th century Hugh J. Chisholm helped found the Oxford Paper Company and built Strathglass Park, a neighborhood of comfortable brick duplex houses available to employees for nominal rent. Rumford still has one of Maine's largest paper mill complexes.
Incorporated in 1791, Bangor was one of the world's leading lumber ports by the mid-1800s. Today a diversified manufacturing town.
Archaeologists have unearthed the remains of a French fort, capital of Acadia from 1670 until its destruction by the Dutch four years later. Built on the site of a Plymouth Colony trading outpost, Pentagoet marks France's southwesternmost presence in Maine.
This site in central Vermont at a major gap in the Green Mountain barrier between the Connecticut Valley and Lake Champlain was chosen for the state capital in 1805. With only 8,035 people today, Montpelier is the smallest state capital in the U.S.
Colorful and finely-textured, Barre granite was first quarried after the War of 1812. The industry boomed after the railroad reached here from Montpelier in 1875 causing an influx of Italian, Scottish, and French-Canadian stone cutters and carvers.
Centrally located and at the head of the Kennebec navigation, Augusta was made state capital in 1832.
The Bath area has been famous for shipbuilding since the early 1600s. Bath Iron Works, producing ships for the U.S. navy since 1893, has helped keep the town afloat.
LOWELL, MASSACHUSETTS
Francis Cabot Lowell brought British cloth-weaving methods to the Chelmsford area, which offered water power and ample room to grow. In 1820, three years after Lowell's death, his Boston Associates established New England's first company town. A historic park re-creates the textile era, when Yankee girls from country villages worked in Lowell's mills. High-tech and other electronics industries hold promise for the future.
SPRINGFIELD, MASSACHUSETTS
Puritans settled the rich bottomlands of the Connecticut Valley in 1636. During the Revolutionary War craftsmen made guns and ammunition for the American cause and in 1794 the U.S. government built the Springfield Armory. Until its closure in 1968 the armory pioneered the production of firearms, from the flintlock musket to the M14. The sport of basketball originated here.
Middlebury was abandoned in 1778, five years after its founding, when settlers were driven out by British Loyalists and their Indian allies. The village was reoccupied at the close of the American Revolution. In 1803, three years after Middlebury College was founded, the town became Vermont's first marble-quarrying center.
From Casco Bay nearly 400 years ago, French explorer Samuel de Champlain wrote "large mountains are seen to the west." Most likely he had seen the Presidential Range, dominated by the 6,288-foot Mount Washington. Despite extreme weather, its summit was made accessible by a bridle path in 1829, a carriage road in 1861, and the nation's first cog railway in 1869.
Laid waste by Indians in 1676, Portland prospered in the 1700s building ships and shipping timber. It suffered heavy British bombardment in 1775 and a great fire nearly a century later. Maine's first capital until 1832, Portland became a major railroad center and in the 1900s terminus of the oil pipeline to Montréal. The poet Henry Wadsworth Longfellow was born here in 1807.
Obtaining a charter to found a college "for the education and instruction of Youth of the Indian Tribes in this land...and also English Youth and any others," the Reverend Eleazar Wheelock opened Dartmouth College in 1770.
STOCKBRIDGE, MASSACHUSETTS
In 1734 whites came to this mission settlement as "civilizing examples" to the Mahicans. Despite fighting for U.S. independence, the Mahicans were forced out of Stockbridge in the early 1800s by the rising tide of white settlers. Illustrator Norman Rockwell worked here until his death in 1978.
DEERFIELD, MASSACHUSETTS
Outposts such as Deerfield, Massachusetts, were hard hit during the war led by Wampanoag Indian King Philip in 1675–76. In subsequent bouts of warfare, with time-outs for uneasy peace, the French and their Indian allies harried English frontier villages. Deerfield was devastated again in 1704; the French and Indian War killed 49 townspeople.
Before this crossroads and agricultural center became the state capital in 1808, Concord was involved in a territorial tug-of-war between Massachusetts and New Hampshire. The town was settled in 1727 on a Massachusetts Bay Colony grant that overlapped a New Hampshire grant for the town of Bow, and became part of New Hampshire in 1741.
In 1719 Scotch-Irish settlers founded a Presbyterian town here in Puritan-dominated New England. Londonderry parented several other Scotch-Irish communities. The colonists grew flax and are reported to have introduced potatoes to the United States. By the 1720s Londonderry was known for its fine linens, but the industry gave way to shoe and hat making in the early 1800s.
Claimed by both New York and New Hampshire, Bennington was the headquarters for Ethan Allen and his independence-minded Green Mountain Boys, known to New Yorkers as the Bennington Mob. In 1777 Col. John Stark stopped British General Burgoyne's advance troops, helping to clear the way for the British defeat at Saratoga.
THE BERKSHIRES, MASSACHUSETTS
During the late 1800s wealthy families—including the Vanderbilts and Carnegies—built mansions in Stockbridge, Lenox, and other in villages in the Berkshires.
SALEM, MASSACHUSETTS
Puritans from Cape Ann founded Salem in 1626. The town earned a a notorious place in history with its witch trials. By the early 1800s merchants in this leading port were so wealthy that Oriental trade partners imagined the city to be a sovereign nation.
Settled in 1630, this Puritan capital was the largest city in the colonies by the mid-1700s. Boston's trading ships spanned the globe, and Boston money financed railroads and industries throughout New England. Irish and Italian immigrants added a new dimension in the 19th century. Is a booming center of high-tech and biomedical industries.
LYNN, MASSACHUSETTS
Shoemaking began here in the mid-1630s and by the 19th century craftsmen were hand-stitching a million pairs of shoes yearly. The labor of French-Canadian, Irish, Italian, Greek, and Polish immigrants made Lynn's factories the nation's most productive, but a disastrous fire in 1889 and competition from the Midwest in the early 1900s left the city down-at-heel. General Electric bolsters the economy.
In 1620 a group of religious exiles, who later came to be called Pilgrims, landed here. Plymouth survived the first winter, although almost half the colonists, stricken by starvation and scurvy, did not. Plimoth Plantation, a living-history reconstruction of the village, and a replica of the Mayflower re-create the origins of New England's first permanent settlement.
In 1671 blacksmith Joseph Jenckes built a forge at Pawtucket, an Indian word meaning "fall of water." The town thrived as a producer of farm equipment and metal fittings for sailing ships. Samuel Slater built the first U.S. version of Sir Richard Arkwright's cotton spinning system in 1790. Pawtucket still makes metal goods.
In November 1620 the Mayflower anchored here. Before moving on to Plymouth, the Pilgrims drew up the Mayflower Compact, the basis of the constitution of the Commonwealth of Massachusetts. Descendants of the Portuguese fishermen from the Azores and Lisbon now constitute a majority of the year-round residents.
LEXINGTON-CONCORD, MASSACHUSETTS
In the early 1770s Lexington's patriots pledged to "be ready to sacrifice our estates and everything dear in life, yes, and life itself" for for American independence. In the first encounter of the Revolutionary War, on April 19, 1775, British troops routed the rebels at Lexington, but the Americans won the day at Concord. In the 1800s, Concord became famous for its literary figures, including Ralph Waldo Emerson, Nathaniel Hawthorne, Louisa May Alcott, and Henry David Thoreau.
The settlement was originally a collection of farms owned by the Quakers. For much of the 19th century New Bedford dominated the the nation's whaling industry. As whaling declined, cotton mills employed Portuguese immigrants.
John Winthrop brought colonists to this estuarine site in 1646. During the 1800s the economy hinged on whaling, some shipbuilding, and ocean trade. The U.S. Coast Guard Academy established a permanent base here in 1910. Across the Thames River, in Groton, is a major U.S. submarine center.
In 1642 missionaries from Watertown, Massachusetts, settled at the site of Edgartown. The colonists first farmed, then made fortunes in whaling. Like Nantucket, the Vineyard now depends on summer tourism.
A settlement was laid out by the Puritans at this capacious harbor in 1638. In 1665 the Colony of New Haven became part of the Colony of Connecticut. Home of Samuel Morse, Charles Goodyear, and Eli Whitney, the town was a nursery for industrial innovation. Manufacturers now produce firearms, hardware, tools, and clothing. Yale University, which began at nearby Branford, moved here in 1716.
EASTERN LONG ISLAND
In 1609 Henry Hudson stepped ashore on Long Island. The Dutch occupied the western portion; in the 1640s English settlers from Connecticut and Massachusetts moved to eastern Long Island. Tensions led, in 1650, to divided jurisdiction. When the Dutch ceded New Netherlands to Britain in 1664, Long Island was granted to New York. But even today eastern towns identify with New England.
GLOUCESTER, MASSACHUSETTS
"They that go down to the sea in ships." The inscription on Leonard Craske's bronze statue of a fisherman speaks for generations of Gloucester mariners. Since the seaport's founding in 1623, 10,000 Gloucestermen have died in the fog-blanketed, shoal-ridden waters of the Grand Banks. In the mid-1700s Gloucester shipbuilders developed the schooner, renowned for its seaworthiness. Today this city, an outlier of Boston, still relies on fishing and fish processing, but the summer catch of tourists is also important.

MICHIGAN

Livonia
Ann Arbor
Detroit
Windsor

Lake
St. Clair

CANADA

LAKE ERIE

Pelee Island

A garrison at Presque Isle in 1753 completed a cordon of French forts
from the Great Lakes to the mouth of the Mississippi. By the end of the
decade, however, the British had seized control of the strategic Ohio
Valley. In 1792 Pennsylvania, which for years had lobbied for territory
fronting on Lake Erie, acquired a lakeshore track near former Presque Isle
for 75 cents an acre. Erie was laid out in 1795 and was a coveted strategic
point in the War of 1812. It burgeoned in the mid-1800s with the opening
of the Erie and Pittsburgh Canal and the building of railroads.

Erie

Toledo

Mentor

Meadville
Titusville

Cleveland

Sandusky

Became a major oil
center after nearby
Titusville strike—the
world's first—in 1859.

Oil City

Permanent settlement began in 1817. Toledo was
incorporated in 1837, a year after the conclusion of the
bitter "Toledo War" boundary dispute between Michigan and
Ohio. Famed for its glass factories, the industrial city today
ships more bituminous coal than any other U.S. port. It also
handles grain, iron ore, potash, military cargo, and road-
building equipment. The Toledo Shipyard and the
redeveloped waterfront herald a renaissance.

Maumee

In 1796 Gen. Moses Cleaveland of the Connecticut Land Company platted a town at the mouth of
the Cuyahoga River to serve as the headquarters of the Connecticut's Western Reserve. Canals
fueled phenomenal growth after the mid-1820s. Steel milling and the shipping of iron ore and
coal were mainstays in the late 1800s, when Cleveland was briefly the nation's petroleum capital.
Ohio's second largest city, with almost half a million people, it is a diversified industrial complex.

Kent

Akron

Youngstown

New
Castle

In 1754 the French seized an
unfinished British garrison at the
strategic forks of the Ohio, the first
of successive forts located at the
confluence of the Monongahela and
Allegheny Rivers. The British gained
control of the site in 1758, and
Pittsburgh sprouted as a gateway for
pioneers transferring from roads to
riverboats. Later a canal terminus
and railroad hub, it grew into a
steel-industry giant.

Fort
Wayne

Van Wert

Lima

Akron grew up in the 1820s at an Indian portage between the Cuyahoga and Tuscarawas Rivers.
Dr. Benjamin F. Goodrich opened the first rubber factory in 1871, and rubber propelled a surge in
the economy between 1910 and 1920. Soon Akron was processing nearly half the world's rubber.
Today one of the world's premier liquid crystal and polymer research and development centers.

Canton

Ushered in an era of interstate
highways. The first section of
the 470-mile (756 km) limited-
access road opened in 1940.

Pittsburgh

Bethel Park

Bushy Run
Aug. 5-6, 1763

Route 30

Celina

Marion

Early Quaker meeting place.
Published the nation's first
abolitionist newspaper in 1817
and later was a stop for slaves
on the Underground Railroad.

Wagon trail called Forbes' Road carried English troops to
Fort Duquesne (Pittsburgh) in 1758. Became an early
central Appalachian route for westward-bound settlers.

Bellefontaine

In 1816 the state government was moved from
Chillicothe to more central Columbus. A feeder
to the Ohio and Erie Canal, the National Road,
and—after 1850—railroads spurred farm trade
and manufacturing. The land-grant Ohio
State University opened in the 1870s.

While surveying the road from Wheeling,
West Virginia, to northern Kentucky in 1797,
Ebenezer Zane founded Zanesville. It was one of
several towns he established at river crossings
of Zane's Trace, a major land route through
Ohio. State capital from 1810 to 1812.

Mt. Pleasant

Wheeling

Brownsville

In 1811 the first long-distance federal road
started westward from Cumberland,
Maryland, eventually reaching Vandalia,
Illinois. Revived during the early 1900s.

Richmond

National Road

Columbus

Route 40

Zanesville

Moundsville

Flatboat and later steamboat building boomed at
Brownsville, the easternmost embarkation point for
Pennsylvania pioneers using the Ohio River.

Dayton

OHIO

In 1818 the National Road reached this
major embarkation point and trading
center. Site of the secessionist
Wheeling conventions in 1861 and
twice West Virginia's capital.

FORT NECESSITY
NATIONAL BATTLEFIELD

Lancaster

Morgantown

Settled in 1796, despite warnings by Indians about flooding.
Farm-machinery and railroad-car manufacturing expanded
Dayton by the mid-1800s; the mass production of cash registers
began in the 1880s. In 1910 Orville and Wilbur Wright opened an
experimental airplane factory and aviation remains important.

HOPEWELL
CULTURE
NATIONAL MONUMENT

Chillicothe

Ohio's oldest permanent
settlement was staked out as
capital of Northwest Territory in
1788 by New Englanders of the
Ohio Company of Associates.
Governor Arthur St. Clair's
opposition helped delay Ohio's
statehood until 1803. Ropemaking
and shipbuilding flourished in
the 19th century, exploitation of
petroleum in the early 20th.

Big Bottom
Jan. 2, 1791

Marietta

Named for the Grave Creek Mound, one of the
largest prehistoric Indian earthworks east of the
Mississippi. Burial chambers contained skeletons,
copper bracelets, shell beads, and mica, probably
traded from present-day North Carolina.

Providing access to rivers flowing into the
Ohio country, this southern terminus of a road
to Pittsburgh channeled migrants westward in
the early 1800s. The first railroad arrived in
1886. Glass manufacturing boosted
Morgantown in the early 1900s.

Cincinnati

The trading center for the Scioto Valley
region, Chillicothe became capital of the
eastern division of the Northwest Territory
in 1800 and was twice state capital before
1820. Boomed with the Ohio and Erie
Canal in 1832. The paper industry, which
emerged around 1810, is still important.

Scioto

Parkersburg

Clarksburg

Explorer Christopher Gist passed through
the area in 1751, but settlers did not arrive
for another three decades. The steamboat
port and railroad junction grew rapidly
with the opening of oil fields after 1860
and with gas finds in the 1880s.

In 1842 representatives of northwestern Virginia
counties met in Clarksburg to discuss secession, and in
1861 the city hosted the first meeting of the movement
that spawned West Virginia. Confederate hero Thomas J.
"Stonewall" Jackson was born here in 1824.

SPRUCE KNOB-
SENECA ROCKS NAT.
RECREATION AREA

Construction of a "substantial fortress" began in
1789. By the 1820s steamboats had made centrally
positioned Cincinnati the Ohio Valley's hub,
soon boosted by the Miami-Erie Canal. By 1860
Porkopolis, as the meat-packing center was
called, had 160,000 people, many of them Irish
and German immigrants. A commercial bridge
between the industrial North and the rural South.

Ohio

Gallipolis

In the late 1780s Scioto Company speculators issued
false titles to French buyers of acreage in proposed
Gallipolis (City of Gauls). land actually owned by
the Ohio Company. Congress offered them tracts
elsewhere, but many chose to repurchase their lots.

HARPERS FERRY, WEST VIRGINIA
Robert Harper established a ferry service across the Potomac in 1747 in this strategic gap in
the Blue Ridge Mountains where the Shenandoah joins the Potomac River. In 1796 George
Washington persuaded Congress to authorize the building of a federal arsenal here. By 1850
the B & O Railroad and the C & O Canal had passed through en route to Cumberland. John
Brown, self-proclaimed "instrument of God sent to liberate all slaves," seized the arsenal in
1859. He was later hanged for treason. The restored town is a popular resort.

In 1736 William Beverley was granted a tract "in
consideration for inducing a large number of settlers to
the community." The area lured many Scotch-Irish
settlers, and Staunton was founded in 1749. The Museum
of American Frontier Culture recreates pioneer days.

Frankfort

Lexington

In 1826 the region's first charcoal furnace began
producing pig iron, soon known for its strength
and purity. Founded in 1849, Ironton prospered in
the Civil War. Depletion of ore and competition
from the Pittsburgh-Youngstown complex
led to its decline in the late 1800s.

Ironton

Charleston

Founded in the late 1780s, it was a major producer
of salt. In 1885 this rail center for the mineral-rich
Kanawha Valley was chosen over Wheeling as
permanent state capital. Chemical plants and glass
factories attracted southern blacks in the early 1900s.

WEST
VIRGINIA

New

Carnifex Ferry
Sept. 1861

Droop Mountain
Nov. 6, 1863

MTS.

Staunton

Danville

Kentucky

Licking

Founded in 1777, Lexington was one of a string of county seats and market
towns in the Shenandoah Valley. Washington and Lee University was
established as Augusta Academy in 1749; the Virginia Military Institute dates
from 1839. Robert E. Lee and Stonewall Jackson are both buried here.

KENTUCKY

Tug Fork

NEW RIVER GORGE
NATIONAL RIVER

In 1755 a fort was built at this strategic intersection of the Seneca and Kanawha
Trails. Lewisburg was incorporated in 1782. In 1833 the Virginia Supreme Court of
Appeals began holding sessions as a service to Virginians living west of the
mountains; Lewisburg was the "western capital of Virginia" until the Civil War.

Lewisburg

White Sulphur
Springs

Lexington

Socially and politically ambitious Southerners
gathered in this summer resort, also favored
by Presidents courting the southern vote.
Presidents Cottage, built in 1835 and now
a museum, was the summer White House
of five pre-Civil War Presidents.

ALLEGHENY

BLUE RIDGE

Elkhorn City

Grundy

Bluefield

Lynchburg

Somerset

Took shape in 1888 as the Norfolk and Western
Railway's shipping point for the Pocahontas
coalfield, opened five years before.

New

Roanoke

BOOKER T.
WASHINGTON
NAT. MONUMENT

A hamlet called Big Lick grew up
after 1852, when the Virginia and
Tennessee Railroad built a depot in a
bowl-shaped depression between the
Allegheny Mountains and the Blue
Ridge. The settlement was renamed
Roanoke in 1882, when two
additional railroad lines came in.

John Lynch was 17 when he
began a ferry service here in 1757. He later
built the town's first tobacco warehouse, and by the
1800s this hub of the western Piedmont was a leading
market for dark tobacco. Fleets of riverboats carried the
tobacco to Richmond for transshipment to Europe. In 1840
the James River and Kanawha Canal reached Lynchburg from
Jamestown, followed soon after by a railroad.

CUMBERLAND PLATEAU

APPALACHIAN

MT. ROGERS NAT.
RECREATION AREA

Mt. Rogers
+5,729 ft
1,746 m

CUMBERLAND GAP
NATIONAL HISTORICAL
PARK

Danville

TENNESSEE

Danville arose in the late 1700s as a tobacco inspection
station. The town boomed after tobacco auctioning was
introduced in the early 1850s and is still one of the
largest markets for flue-cured Virginia tobacco.

84°

81°

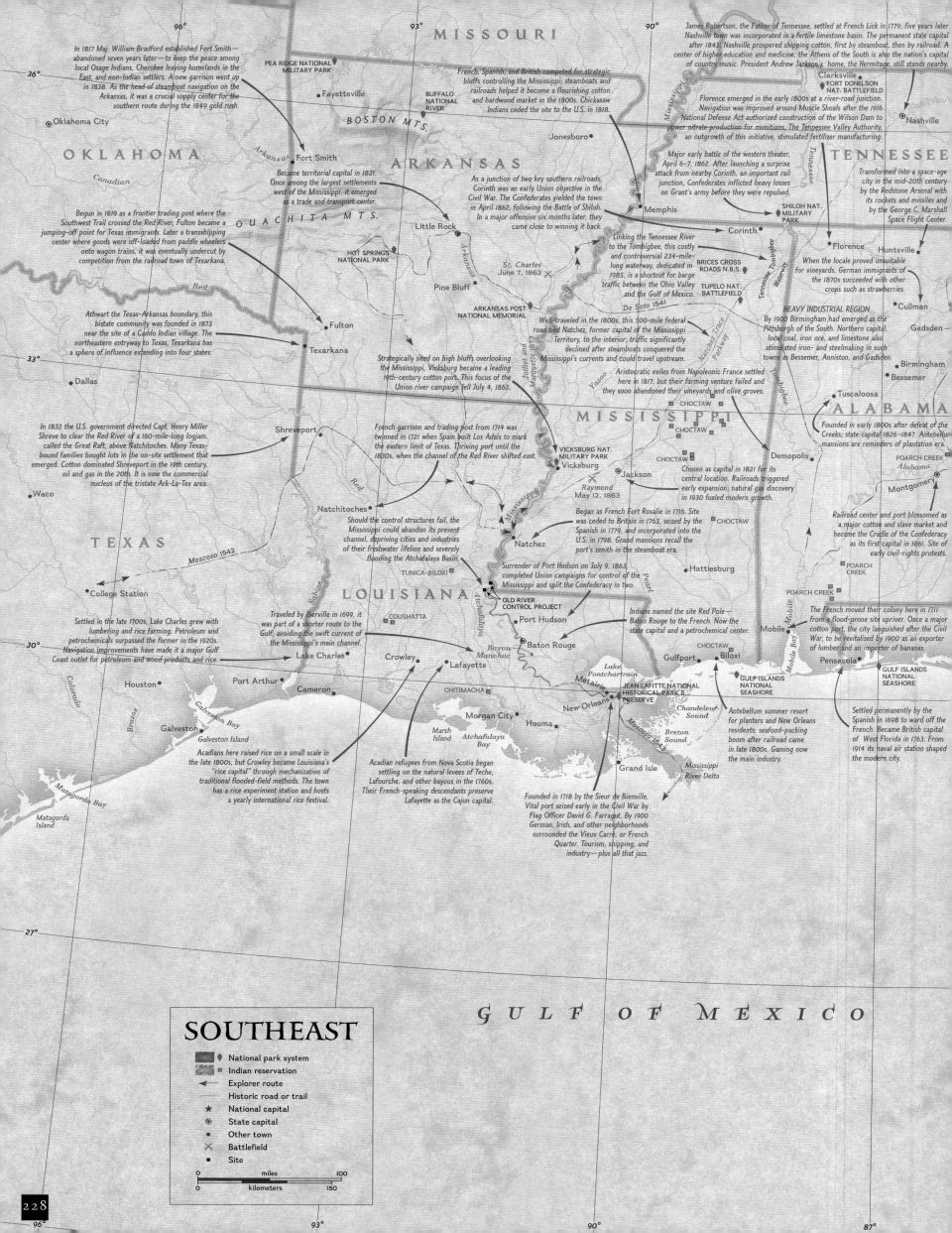

MISSOURI

TENNESSEE

James Robertson, the Father of Tennessee, settled at French Lick in 1779; five years later Nashville town was incorporated in a fertile limestone basin. The permanent state capital after 1843, Nashville prospered shipping cotton, first by steamboat, then by railroad. A center of higher education and medicine, the Athens of the South is also the nation's capital of country music. President Andrew Jackson's home, the Hermitage, still stands nearby.

In 1817 Maj. William Bradford established Fort Smith—abandoned seven years later—to keep the peace among local Osage Indians, Cherokee leaving homelands in the East, and non-Indian settlers. A new garrison went up in 1838. As the head of steamboat navigation on the Arkansas, it was a crucial supply center for the southern route during the 1849 gold rush.

French, Spanish, and British competed for strategic bluffs controlling the Mississippi; steamboats and railroads helped it become a flourishing cotton and hardwood market in the 1800s. Chickasaw Indians ceded the site to the U.S. in 1818.

Florence emerged in the early 1800s at a river-road junction. Navigation was improved around Muscle Shoals after the 1916 National Defense Act authorized construction of the Wilson Dam to power nitrate production for munitions. The Tennessee Valley Authority, an outgrowth of this initiative, stimulated fertilizer manufacturing.

Became territorial capital in 1821. Once among the largest settlements west of the Mississippi, it emerged as a trade and transport center.

As a junction of two key southern railroads, Corinth was an early Union objective in the Civil War. The Confederates yielded the town in April 1862, following the Battle of Shiloh. In a major offensive six months later, they came close to winning it back.

Major early battle of the western theater, April 6–7, 1862. After launching a surprise attack from nearby Corinth, an important rail junction, Confederates inflicted heavy losses on Grant's army before they were repulsed.

Transformed into a space-age city in the mid-20th century by the Redstone Arsenal with its rockets and missiles and by the George C. Marshall Space Flight Center.

Begun in 1819 as a frontier trading post where the Southwest Trail crossed the Red River, Fulton became a jumping-off point for Texas immigrants. Later a transshipping center where goods were off-loaded from paddle wheelers onto wagon trains, it was eventually undercut by competition from the railroad town of Texarkana.

Linking the Tennessee River to the Tombigbee, this costly and controversial 234-mile-long waterway, dedicated in 1985, is a shortcut for barge traffic between the Ohio Valley and the Gulf of Mexico.

When the locale proved unsuitable for vineyards, German immigrants of the 1870s succeeded with other crops such as strawberries.

HEAVY INDUSTRIAL REGION
By 1900 Birmingham had emerged as the Pittsburgh of the South. Northern capital, local coal, iron ore, and limestone also stimulated iron- and steelmaking in such towns as Bessemer, Anniston, and Gadsden.

Athwart the Texas-Arkansas boundary, this bistate community was founded in 1873 near the site of a Caddo Indian village. The northeastern entryway to Texas, Texarkana has a sphere of influence extending into four states.

Well-traveled in the 1800s, this 500-mile federal road tied Natchez, former capital of the Mississippi Territory, to the interior; traffic significantly declined after steamboats conquered the Mississippi's currents and could travel upstream.

Strategically sited on high bluffs overlooking the Mississippi, Vicksburg became a leading 19th-century cotton port. This focus of the Union river campaign fell July 4, 1863.

Aristocratic exiles from Napoleonic France settled here in 1817, but their farming venture failed and they soon abandoned their vineyards and olive groves.

In 1832 the U.S. government directed Capt. Henry Miller Shreve to clear the Red River of a 160-mile-long logjam, called the Great Raft, above Natchitoches. Many Texas-bound families bought lots in the on-site settlement that emerged. Cotton dominated Shreveport in the 19th century, oil and gas in the 20th. It is now the commercial nucleus of the tristate Ark-La-Tex area.

French garrison and trading post from 1714 was twinned in 1721 when Spain built Los Adais to mark the eastern limit of Texas. Thriving port until the 1830s, when the channel of the Red River shifted east.

Founded in early 1800s after defeat of the Creeks; state capital 1826–1847. Antebellum mansions are reminders of plantation era.

Chosen as capital in 1821 for its central location. Railroads triggered early expansion; natural gas discovery in 1930 fueled modern growth.

Railroad center and port blossomed as a major cotton and slave market and became the Cradle of the Confederacy as its first capital in 1861. Site of early civil-rights protests.

Should the control structures fail, the Mississippi could abandon its present channel, depriving cities and industries of their freshwater lifeline and severely flooding the Atchafalaya Basin.

Began as French Fort Rosalie in 1716. Site was ceded to Britain in 1763, seized by the Spanish in 1779, and incorporated into the U.S. in 1798. Grand mansions recall the port's zenith in the steamboat era.

Surrender of Port Hudson on July 9, 1863, completed Union campaigns for control of the Mississippi and split the Confederacy in two.

The French moved their colony here in 1711 from a flood-prone site upriver. Once a major cotton port, the city languished after the Civil War, to be revitalized by 1900 as an exporter of lumber and an importer of bananas.

Settled in the late 1700s, Lake Charles grew with lumbering and rice farming. Petroleum and petrochemicals surpassed the former in the 1920s. Navigation improvements have made it a major Gulf Coast outlet for petroleum and wood products and rice.

Traveled by Iberville in 1699, it was part of a shorter route to the Gulf, avoiding the swift current of the Mississippi's main channel.

Indians named the site Red Pole—Baton Rouge to the French. Now the state capital and a petrochemical center.

OLD RIVER CONTROL PROJECT

Galveston Island
Acadians here raised rice on a small scale in the late 1800s, but Crowley became Louisiana's "rice capital" through mechanization of traditional flooded-field methods. The town has a rice experiment station and hosts a yearly international rice festival.

Acadian refugees from Nova Scotia began settling on the natural levees of Teche, Lafourche, and other bayous in the 1760s. Their French-speaking descendants preserve Lafayette as the Cajun capital.

Founded in 1718 by the Sieur de Bienville. Vital port seized early in the Civil War by Flag Officer David G. Farragut. By 1900 German, Irish, and other neighborhoods surrounded the Vieux Carré, or French Quarter. Tourism, shipping, and industry—plus all that jazz.

Antebellum summer resort for planters and New Orleans residents; seafood-packing boom after railroad came in late 1800s. Gaming now the main industry.

Settled permanently by the Spanish in 1698 to ward off the French. Became British capital of West Florida in 1763. From 1914 its naval air station shaped the modern city.

GULF OF MEXICO

SOUTHEAST

🏞 National park system
▪ Indian reservation
← Explorer route
— Historic road or trail
★ National capital
◉ State capital
● Other town
✕ Battlefield
▪ Site

0 miles 100
0 kilometers 150

229

# MIDWEST

**Legend**
- National park system
- Indian reservation
- Explorer route
- Historic road or trail
- State capital
- Other town
- Battlefield
- Site

miles 100 150
kilometers 100 150

**CANADA**

**NORTH DAKOTA** — Fargo · Grand Forks

**SOUTH DAKOTA** — Sioux Falls · PIPESTONE NATIONAL MONUMENT · UPPER SIOUX · LOWER SIOUX

**MINNESOTA** — RED LAKE · WHITE EARTH · LEECH LAKE · Mille Lacs · St. Paul · Minneapolis · Mankato · Rochester · Sauk Centre · Duluth · Superior

**WISCONSIN** — HO-CHUNK NATION · Madison · Milwaukee · Oshkosh · Green Bay · Peshtigo · Portage · Sault Ste. Marie · Marquette · St. Ignace

**MICHIGAN** — Grand Rapids · Flint · Saginaw Bay · Isabella · Little River Ottawa Indians of Michigan

**Lakes:** Lake Winnipeg · L. Manitoba · Lake of the Woods · Rainy Lake · LAKE SUPERIOR · LAKE MICHIGAN · LAKE HURON · Lake Winnebago · Green Bay · Saginaw Bay

---

**MINNESOTA WILD RICE**
Staple foodstuff of Indians and an early trade item with the French, wild rice grows along streams and shallow lakes in Manitoba, Saskatchewan, northern Minnesota, northern Wisconsin, and southern Ontario. In the first half of the 1900s, Minnesota became the center of a wild-rice trade. Commercial cultivation of wild rice in paddies began in the 1960s. Although overshadowed by cultivated varieties grown in Minnesota and California, natural stands of wild rice in lakes continue to be hand harvested. Minnesota now produces half the world's lake rice, mostly from the White Earth, Leech Lake, and Bois Forte reservations.

Minnesota's northern boundary owes its jutting alignment to a cartographic blunder. Under the Treaty of Paris ending the American Revolution, the international boundary was described as extending from Lake of the Woods to the Mississippi, which the maps mistakenly showed west of the lake. After a series of boundary conventions Canada and the U.S. finally resolved the dilemma in 1925, agreeing on a line known as the Northwest Angle.

**PORTAGE, WISCONSIN**
A marshy strip between the Fox and Wisconsin Rivers—the only interruption in a water route connecting the Great Lakes to the Mississippi and the Gulf of Mexico—was pivotal to the French fur trade, British military occupation, and finally U.S. settlement. In 1836, a year after the French took root, a company was formed to build a canal, but the waterway proved useless. The Wisconsin River was unnavigable for barges, and railroads soon put canals out of business.

**MADISON, WISCONSIN**
Pioneers called the area "beautiful but uninhabitable," yet in 1836 this isthmus between lakes was chosen to be the capital of Wisconsin Territory. Today Madison is a food-processing center for the rich agricultural area of south-central Wisconsin.

In 1890 Leonidas Merritt and his brothers discovered that the Mesabi Range held a mother lode of iron ore. Open-pit mining used steam shovels to gouge out ore from the Mesabi's soft, shallow deposits. Towns such as Hibbing and Virginia boomed during the early 1900s, and European immigrants—notably Finns, Scandinavians, Poles, and Slovenes—provided labor for the mines.

Laid out in the 1850s, these cities at the tip of Lake Superior grew with lumbering and shipbuilding. French explorer Daniel Greysolon, Sieur du Luth, lent his name to Duluth, which was made the eastern terminus of a transcontinental railroad in 1870 and became a grain transshipping point. But as a rail center it could not compete with Chicago.

**OSHKOSH, WISCONSIN**
By 1870 steam-driven mills in Oshkosh were sawing huge volumes of lumber floated into surrounding lakes. "Sawdust City," as Oshkosh came to be known, was a leading lumber center. By the early 1900s local forests had been cut down, and the city turned from raw lumber production to the making of finished wood products based on imported lumber.

**GREEN BAY, WISCONSIN**
Jean Nicolet claimed the Green Bay region for France in 1634, but the nation showed little interest in "La Baye" until the second half of the 1600s, when Jesuit fathers built a mission and fur traders began combing the area around the Fox and Wisconsin Rivers. The settlement was platted in 1829 when the American Fur Company dominated the lower Fox. Lumbering soon overtook the fur trade, and by the turn of the 20th century Green Bay had become a significant port and industrial center.

Native Americans mined copper on Keweenaw Peninsula for centuries before the French explorers noted the resource. The U.S. government acquired title to the region in 1842, and the rush to "Copper country" began in 1843. The Portage Lake Ship Canal opened, and just over a decade later a railroad reached Chicago. Copper production fell after World War I.

French explorer Étienne Brûlé skirted St. Mary's Rapids while seeking the Northwest Passage about 1620. French Jesuits set up a mission in 1668. For more than a century traders portaging furs around the rapids sustained settlement. Today two canals and four huge locks raise boats 21 feet from the level of Lake Huron to Lake Superior.

**MILWAUKEE, WISCONSIN**
Indians ceded their lands by 1835, and settlement began in earnest around what had once been the world's biggest swamp. The North West Company fur post by 1831. Milwaukee was a mineral-rich tract. By 1857 Milwaukee had 46,000 people. Nearly half were German immigrants. The Civil War spurred manufacturing, and during the late 19th century Milwaukee was North West. Intense competition with American brewers. Intense beer made the city famous.

Michigan's statehood in 1837 ended years of territorial wrangling with Ohio. The former gave up its claim to the 468-square-mile "Toledo strip," including the mouth of the Maumee River. At the same time Wisconsin relinquished its portion of the Upper Peninsula, a mineral-rich tract between Lake Michigan and Lake Superior acquired on the Upper.

**DETROIT, MICHIGAN**
This political and commercial hinge for the Great Lakes began taking shape in the 1700s when the French built Fort Pontchartrain, northern link in a chain of fur posts in Illinois country. Few Americans settled in the area until traffic began flowing on the Erie Canal in 1825. As a result of a sagging motor industry, first automobiles rolled out in "Motor City" in 1899. As a result of race riots in 1967, roughly one-third of its residents today subsist below the poverty line.

Nomadic Indians used this location as a rendezvous long before the French made the Straits of Mackinac, later described as "the bottleneck of the Great Lakes," the gateway to their interior empire. In 1781 the British built a stronghold on Mackinac Island. Intense competition with American brewers focused on this strategic conduit in the War of 1812.

With the rise of the lumber industry in the mid-1800s, Grand Rapids made rapid strides. Local cabinetmakers carved fine furniture, and the city's craftwork achieved nationwide recognition at the Philadelphia Centennial Exposition in 1876.

Farmers and fishermen from northwest Europe, among them Belgians and Icelanders, settled here after the mid-1800s. It forms the westernmost part of the limestone Niagara Escarpment.

The economy of Flint and other cities in Detroit's orbit, such as Pontiac and Dearborn, is kept running by automobile manufacturing. Flint boomed in the early 1900s when the Buick Motor Company started up.

In 1820 Col. Josiah Snelling began building a fort near the confluence of the Mississippi and Minnesota Rivers. As railroads tapped wheatlands in the 1870s, Minneapolis became the flour-milling hub of the Northern Plains. By 1880 the sprawling city next to St. Paul counted more people than compact St. Paul. Both places grew rapidly with Scandinavian, German, and Irish immigration.

By the 1840s St. Paul, known as Pig's Eye and described as a "mixture of forests, hills, running brooks, whisky, mosquitoes, snakes, and Indians," contained a handful of fur traders, farmers, and lumbermen. Voted territorial capital in 1849, the town became the state seat when Minnesota joined the Union in 1858.

Hometown of Nobel Prize-winning novelist Sinclair Lewis (1885-1951), Sauk Centre took center stage in the literary world as the setting for Main Street, a chronicle about life in a small town.

During the drought-stricken summer of 1871, numerous fires broke out in the cutover lands of northeastern Wisconsin. On October 8, coincidentally the same night as Chicago's great conflagration, Peshtigo and several other lumber settlements burned to the ground as flames swept the woods in Wisconsin's Great Fire. More than 1,000 people died in the holocaust.

Rochester is a famous medical center, thanks to the dedication of Dr. William Worrall Mayo, who emigrated from England in 1845, and his two sons. St. Mary's hospital was opened in 1889, and the first office tower of the modern Mayo Clinic went up in the 1920s.

Sioux Indians resisted settlers who laid out a town on a great bend of the Minnesota River in 1852. As a result of a general Sioux uprising a decade later, 38 Indians were hanged in Mankato in the largest official execution in U.S. history.

A fur-trading rendezvous for Indians and French coureurs de bois (runners of the woods) developed soon after explorers Louis Jolliet and Father Marquette reached the Mississippi in the early 1780s. Frenchmen founded a permanent settlement in 1673. During the War of 1812 the U.S. built a fort, which was captured by British troops.

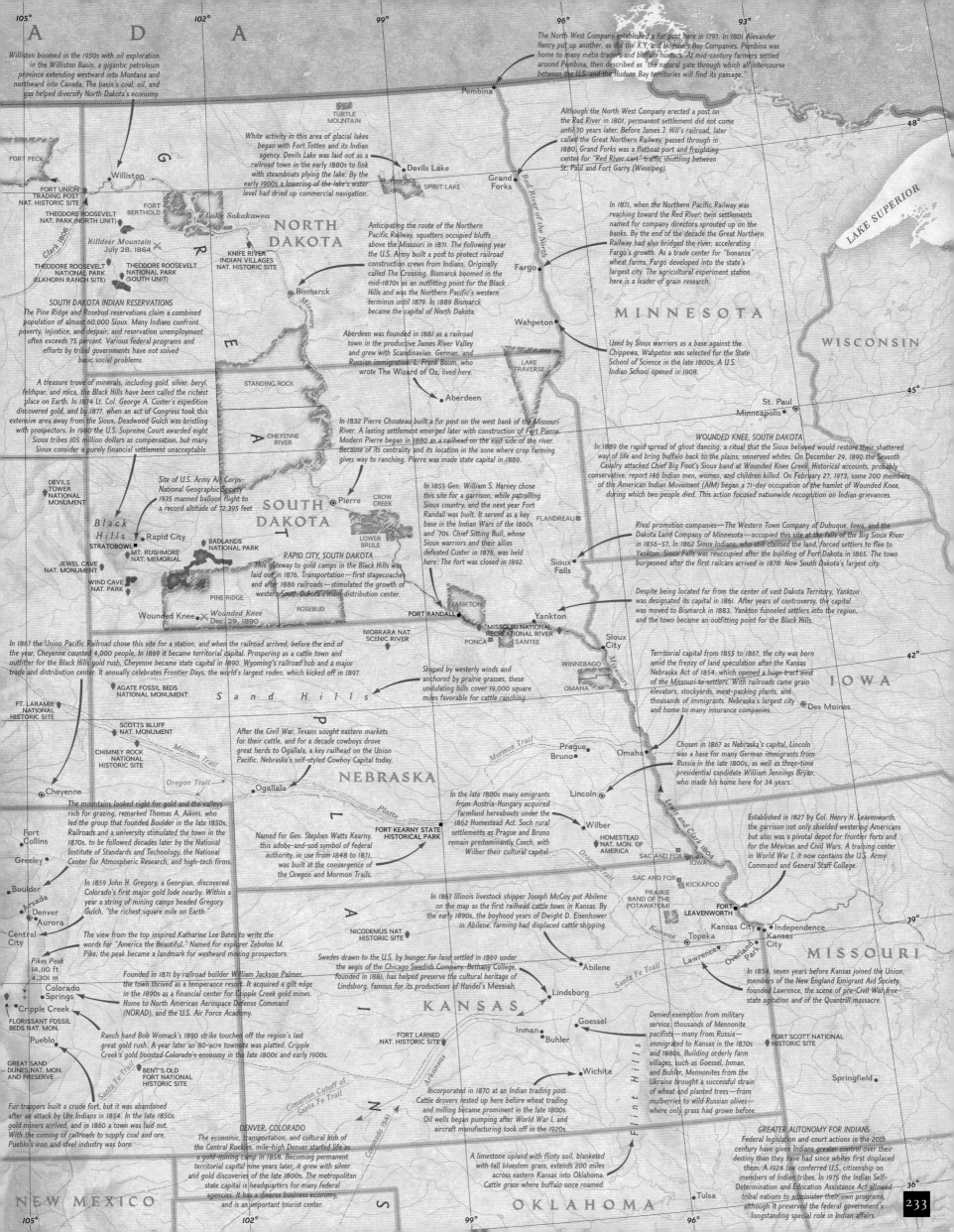

Williston boomed in the 1950s with oil exploration in the Williston Basin, a gigantic petroleum province extending westward into Montana and northward into Canada. The basin's coal, oil, and gas helped diversify North Dakota's economy.

The North West Company established a fur post here in 1797. In 1801 Alexander Henry put up another, as did the X.Y. and Hudson's Bay Companies. Pembina was home to many métis traders and buffalo hunters. At mid-century farmers settled around Pembina, then described as "the natural gate through which all intercourse between the U.S. and the Hudson Bay territories will find its passage."

Although the North West Company erected a post on the Red River in 1801, permanent settlement did not come until 70 years later. Before James J. Hill's railroad, later called the Great Northern Railway, passed through in 1880, Grand Forks was a flatboat port and freighting center for "Red River cart" traffic shuttling between St. Paul and Fort Garry (Winnipeg).

White activity in this area of glacial lakes began with Fort Totten and its Indian agency. Devils Lake was laid out as a railroad town in the early 1880s to link with steamboats plying the lake. By the early 1900s a lowering of the lake's water level had dried up commercial navigation.

In 1871, when the Northern Pacific Railway was reaching toward the Red River, twin settlements named for company directors sprouted up on the banks. By the end of the decade the Great Northern Railway had also bridged the river, accelerating Fargo's growth. As a trade center for "bonanza" wheat farms, Fargo developed into the state's largest city. The agricultural experiment station here is a leader of grain research.

Anticipating the route of the Northern Pacific Railway, squatters occupied bluffs above the Missouri in 1871. The following year the U.S. Army built a post to protect railroad construction crews from Indians. Originally called The Crossing, Bismarck boomed in the mid-1870s as an outfitting point for the Black Hills and was the Northern Pacific's western terminus until 1879. In 1889 Bismarck became the capital of North Dakota.

Aberdeen was founded in 1881 as a railroad town in the productive James River Valley and grew with Scandinavian, German, and Russian immigration. L. Frank Baum, who wrote The Wizard of Oz, lived here.

Used by Sioux warriors as a base against the Chippewa, Wahpeton was selected for the State School of Science in the late 1800s. A U.S. Indian School opened in 1908.

**SOUTH DAKOTA INDIAN RESERVATIONS**
The Pine Ridge and Rosebud reservations claim a combined population of almost 60,000 Sioux. Many Indians confront poverty, injustice, and despair, and reservation unemployment often exceeds 75 percent. Various federal programs and efforts by tribal governments have not solved basic social problems.

A treasure trove of minerals, including gold, silver, beryl, feldspar, and mica, the Black Hills have been called the richest place on Earth. In 1874 Lt. Col. George A. Custer's expedition discovered gold, and by 1877, when an act of Congress took this extensive area away from the Sioux, Deadwood Gulch was bristling with prospectors. In 1980 the U.S. Supreme Court awarded eight Sioux tribes 105 million dollars as compensation, but many Sioux consider a purely financial settlement unacceptable.

In 1832 Pierre Chouteau built a fur post on the west bank of the Missouri River. A lasting settlement emerged later with construction of Fort Pierre. Modern Pierre began in 1880 as a railhead on the east side of the river. Because of its centrality and its location in the zone where crop farming gives way to ranching, Pierre was made state capital in 1889.

Site of U.S. Army Air Corps-National Geographic Society 1935 manned balloon flight to a record altitude of 72,395 feet

**WOUNDED KNEE, SOUTH DAKOTA**
In 1889 the rapid spread of ghost dancing, a ritual that the Sioux believed would restore their shattered way of life and bring buffalo back to the plains, unnerved whites. On December 29, 1890 the Seventh Cavalry attacked Chief Big Foot's Sioux band at Wounded Knee Creek. Historical accounts, probably conservative, report 146 Indian men, women, and children killed. On February 27, 1973, some 200 members of the American Indian Movement (AIM) began a 71-day occupation of the hamlet of Wounded Knee, during which two people died. This action focused nationwide recognition on Indian grievances.

In 1855 Gen. William S. Harney chose this site for a garrison, while patrolling Sioux country, and the next year Fort Randall was built. It served as a key base in the Indian Wars of the 1860s and '70s. Chief Sitting Bull, whose Sioux warriors and their allies defeated Custer in 1876, was held here. The fort was closed in 1892.

Rival promotion companies—The Western Town Company of Dubuque, Iowa, and the Dakota Land Company of Minnesota—occupied this site at the falls of the Big Sioux River in 1856–57. In 1862 Sioux Indians, who still claimed the land, forced settlers to flee to Yankton. Sioux Falls was reoccupied after the building of Fort Dakota in 1865. The town burgeoned after the first railcars arrived in 1878. Now South Dakota's largest city.

**RAPID CITY, SOUTH DAKOTA**
This gateway to gold camps in the Black Hills was laid out in 1876. Transportation—first stagecoaches and after 1886 railroads—stimulated the growth of western South Dakota's main distribution center.

Despite being located far from the center of vast Dakota Territory, Yankton was designated its capital in 1861. After years of controversy, the capital was moved to Bismarck in 1883. Yankton funneled settlers into the region, and the town became an outfitting point for the Black Hills.

In 1867 the Union Pacific Railroad chose this site for a station, and when the railroad arrived, before the end of the year, Cheyenne counted 4,000 people. In 1869 it became territorial capital. Prospering as a cattle town and outfitter for the Black Hills gold rush, Cheyenne became state capital in 1890. Wyoming's railroad hub and a major trade and distribution center. It annually celebrates Frontier Days, the world's largest rodeo, which kicked off in 1897.

Territorial capital from 1855 to 1867, the city was born amid the frenzy of land speculation after the Kansas-Nebraska Act of 1854, which opened a huge tract west of the Missouri to settlers. With railroads came grain elevators, stockyards, meat-packing plants, and thousands of immigrants. Nebraska's largest city and home to many insurance companies.

Shaped by westerly winds and anchored by prairie grasses, these undulating hills cover 19,000 square miles favorable for cattle ranching.

After the Civil War, Texans sought eastern markets for their cattle, and for a decade cowboys drove great herds to Ogallala, a key railhead on the Union Pacific. Nebraska's self-styled Cowboy Capital today.

Chosen in 1867 as Nebraska's capital, Lincoln was a base for many German immigrants from Russia in the late 1800s, as well as three-time presidential candidate William Jennings Bryan, who made his home here for 34 years.

The mountains looked right for gold and the valleys rich for grazing, remarked Thomas A. Aikins, who led the group that founded Boulder in the late 1850s. Railroads and a university stimulated the town in the 1870s, to be followed decades later by the National Institute of Standards and Technology, the National Center for Atmospheric Research, and high-tech firms.

Named for Gen. Stephen Watts Kearny, this adobe-and-sod symbol of federal authority, in use from 1848 to 1871, was built at the convergence of the Oregon and Mormon Trails.

In the late 1800s many emigrants from Austria-Hungary acquired farmland hereabouts under the 1862 Homestead Act. Such rural settlements as Prague and Bruno remain predominantly Czech, with Wilber their cultural capital.

Established in 1827 by Col. Henry H. Leavenworth, the garrison not only shielded westering Americans but also was a pivotal depot for frontier forts and for the Mexican and Civil Wars. A training center in World War I, it now contains the U.S. Army Command and General Staff College.

In 1859 John H. Gregory, a Georgian, discovered Colorado's first major gold lode nearby. Within a year a string of mining camps beaded Gregory Gulch, "the richest square mile on Earth."

In 1867 Illinois livestock shipper Joseph McCoy put Abilene on the map as the first railhead cattle town in Kansas. By the early 1890s, the boyhood years of Dwight D. Eisenhower in Abilene, farming had displaced cattle shipping.

The view from the top inspired Katharine Lee Bates to write the words for "America the Beautiful." Named for explorer Zebulon M. Pike, the peak became a landmark for westward moving prospectors.

In 1854, seven years before Kansas joined the Union, members of the New England Emigrant Aid Society founded Lawrence, the scene of pre-Civil War free-state agitation and of the Quantrill massacre.

Founded in 1871 by railroad builder William Jackson Palmer, the town thrived as a temperance resort. It acquired a gilt edge in the 1890s as a financial center for Cripple Creek gold mines. Home to North American Aerospace Defense Command (NORAD), and the U.S. Air Force Academy.

Swedes drawn to the U.S. by hunger for land settled in 1869 under the aegis of the Chicago Swedish Company. Bethany College, founded in 1881, has helped preserve the cultural heritage of Lindsborg, famous for its productions of Handel's Messiah.

Ranch hand Bob Womack's 1890 strike touched off the region's last great gold rush. A year later an 80-acre townsite was platted. Cripple Creek's gold boosted Colorado's economy in the late 1800s and early 1900s.

Denied exemption from military service, thousands of Mennonite pacifists—many from Russia—immigrated to Kansas in the 1870s and 1880s. Building orderly farm villages, such as Goessel, Inman, and Buhler, Mennonites from the Ukraine brought a successful strain of wheat and planted trees—from mulberries to wild Russian olives—where only grass had grown before.

Fur trappers built a crude fort, but it was abandoned after an attack by Ute Indians in 1854. In the late 1850s gold miners arrived, and in 1860 a town was laid out. With the coming of railroads to supply coal and ore, Pueblo's iron and steel industry was born.

Incorporated in 1870 at an Indian trading post, cattle drovers rested up here before wheat trading and milling became prominent in the late 1800s. Oil wells began pumping after World War I, and aircraft manufacturing took off in the 1920s.

**DENVER, COLORADO**
The economic, transportation, and cultural hub of the Central Rockies, mile-high Denver started life as a gold-mining camp in 1858. Becoming permanent territorial capital nine years later, it grew with silver and gold discoveries of the late 1800s. The metropolitan state capital is headquarters for many federal agencies. It has a diverse business economy, and is an important tourist center.

A limestone upland with flinty soil, blanketed with tall bluestem grass, extends 200 miles across eastern Kansas into Oklahoma. Cattle graze where buffalo once roamed.

**GREATER AUTONOMY FOR INDIANS**
Federal legislation and court actions in the 20th century have given Indians greater control over their destiny than they have had since whites first displaced them. A 1924 law conferred U.S. citizenship on members of Indian tribes. In 1975 the Indian Self-Determination and Education Assistance Act allowed tribal nations to administer their own programs, although it preserved the federal government's longstanding special role in Indian affairs.

LAKE SUPERIOR

MINNESOTA

WISCONSIN

NORTH DAKOTA

SOUTH DAKOTA

NEBRASKA

KANSAS

IOWA

MISSOURI

OKLAHOMA

NEW MEXICO

233

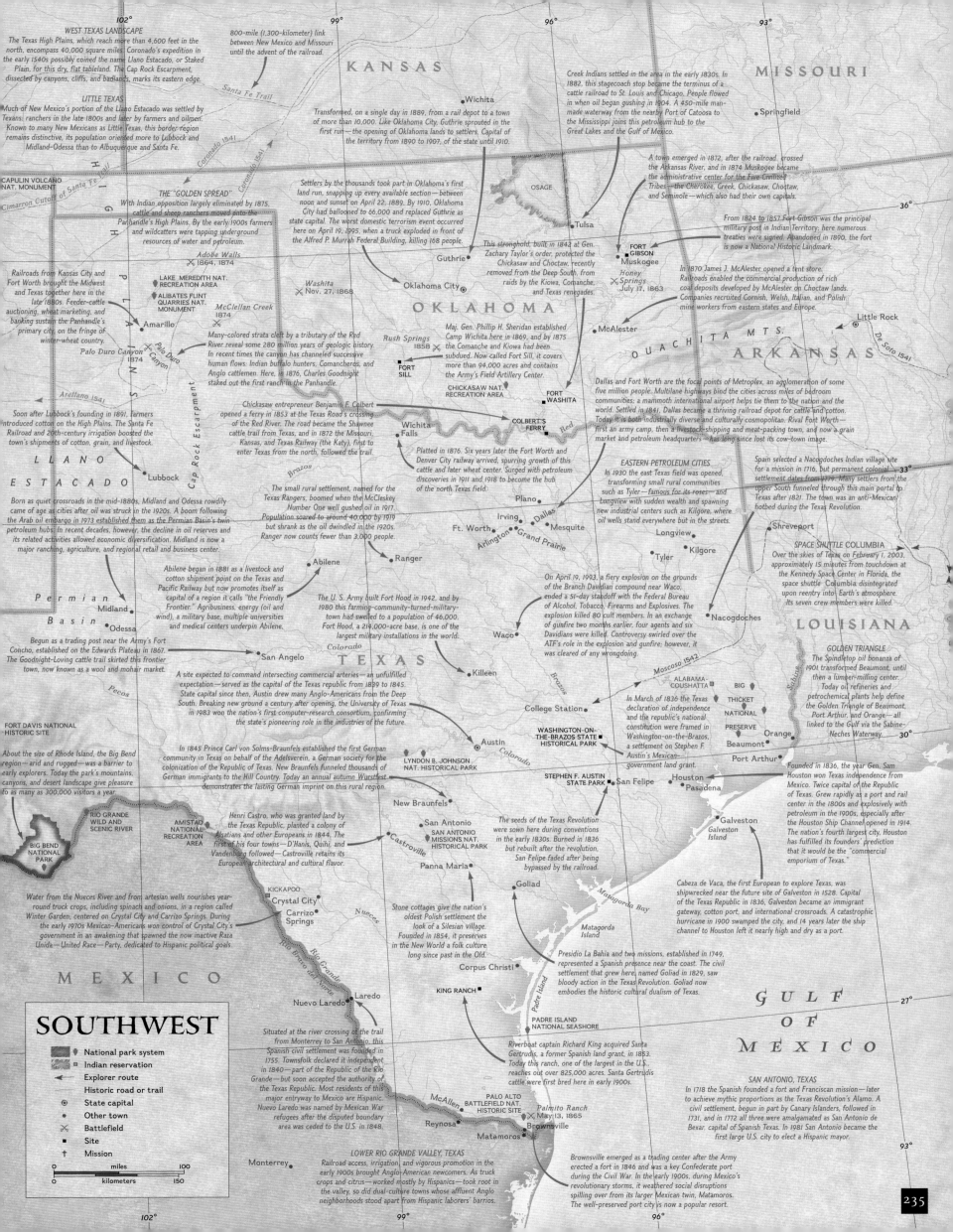

# INDEX

**Boldface** indicates illustration


Aaron, Henry 173, 176
Abernathy, Ralph 188
Abolition 26, 47, 78, 80–81, 90–91
Adams, Henry 49, 124
Adams, John 27, 34, 35, 36, **36**, 38, 44
Adams, Samuel 37
Addams, Jane 138
African Americans **80**, **96**; athletes 172–173, 176; education 83, 185, 186–187; NAACP 118, 184, 185; organized labor 105; population map 184; Reconstruction 97; riots 166, 187; soldiers 90, 136–137, 184, 186, 209; voting rights 78, 184, 185, 186; *see also* Slavery
Agriculture 11, 40, 155, 162–165; maps 163, 165
Ahern, Michael 146
Airplanes **121**, 123, **123**, 136, 166–167, **195**
Alamo, San Antonio, Texas 66–67; Santa Anna's map 66
Alaska 13, 78, 109, 177
Aldrich, Thomas Bailey 148
Aldrin, Edwin E., Jr. 176, **196**
Ali, Muhammad 173
Allen, Eliza 65
American Red Cross 104
Anders, William 196
Anthony, Susan B. 138, 139
Appleton, Nathan 58
Archer, William 177
Armour, Philip 75
Armstrong, Louis **151**
Armstrong, Neil A. 176, 195, 196
Arnaz, Desi **178**
Arthur, Chester A. 180
Ashley, William 60
Astronauts **194**, 194–197, 218–219
Atomic bombs 169, 170–171, 183
Audubon, John James 57, 71
Austin, Stephen F. 64
Automobiles 118, **126–131**
Autry, Micajah 67
Aviation 85, 120–123; map of pioneers 120
Baker, Newton 136
Bakr, Ahmed Hassan 217
Ball, Lucille **178**
Baltimore & Ohio Railroad 44, 98, 104
Barnard, Christiaan 198
Barton, Clara 104
Baseball 172, 173, 176, 177, **180**, 180–181
Beachey, Lincoln 122
Bean, Phantly "Roy" 107
Bell, Alexander Graham 110, **110**
Bennett, Harry 131
Bennett, James Gordon 47
Berle, Milton 178
Bessemer, Henry 102
bin Laden, Osama 214–215
Birkbeck, Morris 61
Bison 97, 109
Blacks *see* African Americans
Block, Martin 151
Bonaparte, Napoleon **48**, 48–49
Bonds, Barry 173
Bonney, William H. 79, 106
Borman, Frank 196
Boston, Massachusetts 11, 26, 104, 111
Bow, Clara 144, **144**
Bowie, James 66
Boycotts 26, 139, 186, 187
Brady, James 189
Brady, Matthew 95
Brannan, Sam 74
Bridger, Jim 44, 108
Bridges 99, 152
Brin, Sergey 211, **211**
Browaski, Hulda 154
Brown, Henry "Box" 80
Brown, Jim 173
Brown, John 80
Brown, Louise Joy 198
Brown, Moses 58
Bucroft, John 75
Bureau of Indian Affairs 158–159
Burnett, John G. 63
Burr, Aaron 38
Burr, Raymond 157
Bush, George H. W. 208, 209, 212
Bush, George W. 177, 197, **212**, 212–213, 216, 217, 219
Bush, Jeb 213
Bushnell, David 32
Cabot, John 17, 20
Caesar, Sid 178–179
California: agriculture 163, 165; Civil War loyalty 85; gold rush 74–75, **75**; Great Depression 163; immigrants 148; Mexico ceding to United States 65; missions 22–23, 26; parks 108; railroads 98–99; statehood 86
Calvert, Leonard 30
Campbell, John 46
Canals 54, 57
Capone, Al 141
Carnegie, Andrew 102, 103
Carr, William **107**
Carranza, Venustiano 132–133
Carson, Kit 60, 101
Carter, Jimmy 176, 202, 203
Carter, Rosalynn 203
Casey, Bill 206
Cather, Willa 69
Catholics 11, 23, 73, 147, 185
Catlin, George 108
Cattle ranches 100–101; map 100
Chaffee, Roger 195
Chaplin, Charlie 118, 137, 144–145; films **145**
Charleston, South Carolina 28, 29, 47
Chayefsky, Paddy 179
Cherokee Indians 18, 44, **62**, 62–63, 65, 71
Chesnut, Mary Boykin 96
Chicago, Illinois: fires 78, 146; gangs 141; immigrants 149; railroads 98, 104; riots 104; skyscrapers 153; slums 138, 139; stockyards 100, 124
Child labor 112, **124**, 124–125; map of legislation 125
Chirac, Jacques 216
Chrysler, Walter P. 127
Chrysler Building, New York, New York 153
Chrysler Corporation 127
Churchill, Winston 119, 122, 154
Civil rights 172, 177, 184–187; map 184
Civil Rights Acts 83, 96, 97, 186
Civil War 31, 78, 79, 86–89, 106; battlefields **76–77**; fife and drum corps **86**; maps 40, 87, 88, 97; medicine 104; photography 95, **95**; Reconstruction 96–97, 184
Civilian Conservation Corps (CCC) 156–157
Clark, Edward 112
Clark, Jane Forbes 180
Clark, William 50–53; map of trek 50–51
Clay, Cassius 173
Clay, Henry 38, 65, 68
Clemens, Samuel *see* Twain, Mark
Clinton, DeWitt 54
Clinton, William J. 177, 207, 212
Cloning 199
Coal 59, 92, 93, 102, 118, 124, **124**; map 103
Coffin, Levi 80, 81, 90
Coleridge, Samuel Taylor 79
Collier, John 159
Colonies: currency 26, 31; map 30, 31; taxes 26, 27, 32
Colorado 75, 139
Colorado River 114, 115, 165
Columbus, Christopher 10, 16, **16**, 17
Comic books **160**, 160–161
Communism 182, 190, 201; map 201
Como, Perry 179
Concord, Massachusetts 34–35
Connecticut 30
Constitution *see* U.S. Constitution
Continental Congress 35, 36–37
Coolidge, Calvin 150
Cooper, James Fenimore 44, 47, 61
Corps of Discovery 50–53; map 50–51
Cotton 40–41, 58, 90; maps 40
Cowboys 100–101
Crazy Horse, Chief (Sioux) **94**
Crocket, Davy 66–67
Cuba 10, 79; missiles **200**
Currency 26, 31, 35
Currier, Charles 99
Curtis, Edward S. 95
D-Day 119, 168
Daguerre, Louis-Jacques-Mandé 94–95
Dams 114–115, 165
Daniels, Jonathan 167
Davis, Elmer **150**
Davis, Jefferson 78, 86, 89
Davis, Rennie 193
Davy, Sir Humphry 143
Day, Benjamin 47
De Forest, Lee 150
de Soto, Hernando 10, 20
de Tocqueville, Alexis 45, 79, 108
Declaration of Independence 35, 36–37, 44
Delany, Martin 91
Delaware 30, 44
Democratic Party 38, 184, 206
Depressions: economic 68, 71, 79, 112, 118, 154–157
Detroit, Michigan 126, 127, 166, 187
Dever, William E. 141
Dickinson, John 37
Dies, Martin 157
DiMaggio, Joe 181, **181**
Dinwiddie, Robert 34
Doolittle, Jimmy 122
Doubleday, Abner 180
Douglas, Stephen 86, 90
Douglass, Frederick 80
Draft (military) 136, 173, 192, 193
Drake, Edwin 92
Du Bois, W. E. B. 118, 136–137
Dulles, John Foster 190
Dunlap, John 36
Dunne, Peter Finley 124
Dust Bowl 155
Earhart, Amelia 122, **122**
Earle, Sylvia 218, **219**
Earp, Morgan 106
Earp, Virgil 106, 107
Earp, Wyatt 106
Eaton, Fred 164, **164**
eBay 210, **210**, 211
Edison, Mina 144
Edison, Thomas 130, 142–143, **144**, 180
Education 27, 45, 82–83, 118; segregation 185, 186–187
Edward, Bob 198
Einstein, Izzy 141
Eisenhower, Dwight David 128, 183, 186–187, 190
Elections, presidential 38–39, 65, 86, 89, 95, 97, 179, 186, 188, 206, 212–213; map 213
Electricity 115, 143; nighttime photo of United States **143**
Elizabeth I, Queen (England) 20
Ellis Island, New York, New York 79, 146–147, 148
Emancipation Proclamation 88, 90–91
Embree, Elihu 47, 90
Empire State Building, New York, New York 153, **153**
Energy 102; hydroelectric 114–115; oil 92–93
England: colonies 20–21, 26, 27, 32; land claims 48, 65, 70; policies toward Indians 11; surrender at Yorktown **24–25**; war with France 10, 26, 27, 32
Entertainment 151, 155, 160–161, 178–179, 185
Erie Canal 54
Erik the Red 14, 15; map of voyages 14
Eriksson, Leif 14–15; map of voyages 14
Ervin, Samuel J., Jr. 206
Eskimos 13, 18
Evans, Harold 139, 141, 190
Everest, Mount, China-Nepal: map 218
Exploration: maps 21, 50–51, 52; New World 10, 17, 20, 64; space 176, 194–197, 218–219; underwater 218, **218**; West (region) 50–53
Factories 112–113; automobile 118, 126–131, **131**; child labor 112, 124–125; firearms 44, 58; fires 118; steel 102–103; textile mills 58–59, **59**; women workers 58, **112**; World War II 169
Fairbanks, Douglas 145
Fairfield, John 80
Fargo, William 75
Farms *see* Agriculture
Faulkner, William 119, 144
Federalist Party 38, 49
Ferdinand, Francis 134
Fermi, Enrico 170, 171
Film *see* Motion pictures
Firearms 58, 189
Firestone, Harvey 130, 143
Fitzgerald, F. Scott 140, 144
Flight *see* Aviation
Flint, Timothy 57
Floods 177, 205
Florida 12, 20, 22, 129, 212–213
Floyd, Charles 51
Ford, Edsel 131
Ford, Gerald 189
Ford, Henry 126, 127, 130, 131, 143; patents **131**
Fowler, Rhonda 172
Foxe, Fanne 206
France: colonies 20; land claims 48; policies toward Indians 11; war with England 10, 26
Franklin, Benjamin 11, 26, 27, 36, **36**, 46, 82
Franklin, James 46
Frémont, John C. 38, 73
French and Indian War 32, 34
Fromme, Lynette 189
Fulton, Robert 41, 44, 54, 57
Gagarin, Yuri 194
Gage, Thomas 34–35
Galbraith, John Kenneth 154
Gardner, Alexander 95
Garrett, Thomas 90
General Motors 126–127
George III, King (England) 30, 34, 36
Georgia 12, 30, 37, 40, 62
Gettysburg, Pennsylvania **76–77**, 88
Gibbon, John 198
Giscard d'Estaing, Valéry 177
Glenn, John 176, 194–195
Glidden, Joseph F. 101
Goddard, Robert 194
Godkin, E. L. 47
Gold rush 74–75, **75**, 84; map 74
Golden Gate Bridge, San Francisco, California 152
Gompers, Samuel 104
Gorbachev, Mikhail S. 201, **201**
Gore, Al **212**, 212–213
Gorgas, Josiah 88
Grant, George 172
Grant, Ulysses S. 88–89, 96, 97, 152; memorial 108–109
Great Awakening 23, 73
Great Depression 85, 118, 126, 127, **154**, 154–157, 162, 163
Greeley, Horace 45, 47, 61, 74, 104
Greene, Catherine 41
Greene, Nathaniel 35, 41
Greenland 10, 14–15
Gregory, Dick 185
Griffith, D. W. 145
Grimké, Sarah 90
Grissom, Virgil "Gus" 195
Guilbert, Edward A. 210
Gulf War 208–209; map 208
Gulf War (second) 216–217
Gunther, Madison 172
Hadlin, Oscar 104
Hall, John H. 58
Hamel, Gustav 122
Hamilton, Alexander 38
Hancock, John 37
Harris, Benjamin 46
Hart, Gary W. 206
Hart, Liddell 136
Hawaii 12, 79, 129, 149, 177
Hayes, Rutherford B. 97, 143
Hearst, William Randolph 47, 79, 119
Heart transplants 198, **198**, **199**
Henson, Josiah 29
Hinckley, John 189
Hiroshima, Japan 169, 170, 171, **171**
Hitler, Adolf 119, 130, 167, 169, 172–173
Hoffman, Abbie 193
Holley, Alexander 102
Holliday, Doc 106
Hollywood, California 144, 145
Homesteading **2–3**, **68**, 68–69, 78, 79; map 69
Hoover, Herbert 118, 155, 156
Hoover Dam 114, **115**, 165
Hopkins, Harry 156
Hornaday, William Temple 109
Hough, Franklin B. 109
Housing: discrimination 185, 186, 187
Houston, Sam 64, **64**, 65
Howells, William Dean 104
Hubble Space Telescope 219
Hudson, Henry 21
Huerta, Victoriano 132
Hughes, Howard 123
Hunt, E. Howard 206
Hurricane Andrew 204–205
Hussein, Saddam 208, 209, 216–217
Hydroelectric power 114–115; map 114
Illinois 112, 113
Immigration 41, 45, 79, 146–149; living conditions **148**; map of ethnicity 146, 149
Impeachment 96, 206, 207
Independence, Missouri 61
Indian Removal Act 11, 62
Indian Reorganization Act 159
Indians *see* Native Americans
Indians of All Tribes 159
Industrial Revolution 58–59
Ingstad, Anne Stine 15
Ingstad, Helge 15
Integration 172–173, 181, 186–187, **187**
Internet 210–211
Interstate Highway System 126, 128–129
Inuit 13, 18
Iran: hostages **202**, 202–203, 206–207
Iran-Contra scandal 206–207
Iraq 177, 208–209, 216–217
Iron Curtain 119, 200–201
Iron manufacturing 102
Irrigation 78, 164–165; map 165
Islam 23, 215, 216
Jackson, Andrew 38, 62, 65, 68
Jackson, Jesse 186
Jackson, Maynard 186
Jackson, Reggie 173
James, Duke of York 30
James, Frank 106
James, Jesse 106
Jamestown, Virginia 21, 28, 31
Japanese Americans 166
Jefferson, Thomas 35, 36, **36**, 82; cartoon **48**; death 44; Declaration of Independence 37; Lewis and Clark Expedition 50, 51, 52, 53; Louisiana Purchase 48–49; political party 38
Jenkins, John H. 67
Jenrette, John 206
Jews 23, 73, 185
Jim Crow laws 184
Johnson, Andrew 89, 96
Johnson, E. W. 96
Johnson, Lyndon B. 176, 190, 192
Jones, Paula Corbin 207
Jordan, Michael 173
Journalism 46–47
Kahn, Albert 130
Kamehameha, King (Hawaii) 12
Kansas 38, 69, 86
Keller, K. T. 127
Kelley, Florence 138–139
Kelly, Tom 209
Kelly, William 102
Kennedy, Jackie 189
Kennedy, John F. **188**; assassination 176, 179, 188, 189, **189**; Cuban missile crisis 200; space program 194, 195; Vietnam War 190
Kennedy, John F., Jr. 189
Kennedy, Robert F. 176, 188
Kent State University, Kent, Ohio 192, **193**
Kentucky 26, 40, 80
Key, Francis Scott 44
Khan, Yahya 200
Khomeini, Ayatollah Ruhollah 202, 215
Khrushchev, Nikita 201
Kilpatrick, James R. 131
King, Martin Luther, Jr. 176, **186**, 187, 188
Kissinger, Henry 200
Korean War 119, 181, 182–183, **183**, 200; map 182, 183
Koufax, Sandy **180**
Ku Klux Klan 97, 137, 184, 185
Kuwait 208–209; oil fires **209**
Labor unions 104–105, 125, 131, 157; strikes 79, 104, 105, **105**, 118
Lamb, William 153
Lawrence, Ernest Orlando 170
Lazarus, Emma 149
League of Nations 118, 137
Lee, Robert E. 88, 89
Lefebvre, Eugène 122
Lenin, V. I. 136
Lewinsky, Monica S. 177, 207
Lewis, Jane 80
Lewis, John L. 104
Lewis, Meriwether 50–53
Lewis, Sinclair 157
Lewis and Clark Expedition 50–53; drawings **53**; map 50–51
Lexington, Massachusetts 34–35
Liddy, G. Gordon 206
Lincoln, Abraham 80, 86, 88, 89, **89**; Emancipation Proclamation 78, 90–91; presidential race 38, 95; railroads 98
Lindbergh, Charles A. 121–122
Lindbergh, Reeve 121
Lippincott, J. B. **164**
Little Rock, Arkansas 186–187, **187**
Livingston, Robert R. 36, 37, 48, 49, 57
Longfellow, Henry: "Paul Revere's Ride" 35
Los Angeles, California 164, 187
Louisiana Purchase 48–49; cartoon **48**; map 49
Lovejoy, Elijah 47
Lovell, James 196
Lowell, Francis 58
Lowell, Massachusetts 58, 59
Lucas, Anthony 92
Lynchings 185, **185**
MacArthur, Douglas 119, 182, 183
Macaulay, David 152
Mail service 84–85, 121, 122, 177
Mailer, Norman 192
Manchester, New Hampshire 58
Mandan Indians 18, 52, **158**
Manhattan Island 11, 21, 30
Manhattan Project 170–171; map 170
Manifest Destiny 61, 65, 70–71, **71**, 79, 145; map 70
Mann, Horace 82, 83
Mannes, Marya 179
Manufacturing *see* Factories
Mao Zedong 200
Markel, Howard 198
Markham, Edwin 124
Marshall, George C. 200
Marshall, James 74
Marshall, John 38, 62
Marshall Plan 200
Marx, Groucho 154
Maryland 11, 23, 26, 27, 30, 129
Massachusetts 23, 27, 30, 112
Massachusetts Bay Colony 23, 30
Masterson, Bat 106–107
*Mayflower* (ship) 30
Mays, Willie 173
McCarthy, Joseph 178
McClellan, George 89
McCormick, Cyrus 130
McCoy, Joseph G. 100
McCullough, David 114, 120
McFarlane, Robert 206, 207
McGwire, Mark 173
McLaury brothers 106
McVeigh, Timothy 177, 214
Medicine and health 45, 176, 177, 198–199
Meese, Edwin, III 207
Menlo Park, New Jersey 142, 144
Meredith, James 187
Mexican War 70, 85, 86
Mexico: governing Texas 64–65; Revolution 132–133
Michaux, F. A. 55
Midwest (region): floods 177, 205
Miller, Jeffrey **193**
Mills, Wilbur 206
Mir space station 218–219
Missionaries 10, 22–23, 26, 66–67; map 23
Mississippi 29, 40
Mississippi River 10, **54**, 54–57, 88, 205; map 56
Missouri Compromise 86
Missouri River 51, 52, 54, 57, 205
Mitchell, Charles 154
Mitchell, John N. 206
Monroe, James 44, 49
Monroe, Lincoln Perry 185
Montgomery, Alabama 186, 187
Moon **197**
Moon landing 176, 179, 194, 196–197
Moore, Annie 146
Morgan, J. P. 103
Mormons 23, 45, 69, 73, 78, 148
Morrill, Justin 83
Morse, Samuel F. B. 45, 85, 110
Motion pictures 118, 132, 144–145, 155, 166; poster **161**

Mott, Lucretia 45, 80
Mountbattan, Louis 145
Movies *see* Motion pictures
Muir, John 109, **109**
Mulholland, William 164, **164**
Murphy, Isaac Burns 172
Murrow, Edward R. 150, 178, **183**
Nagasaki, Japan 169, 170, 171
Napoleon 48–49; cartoon **48**
Nashua, New Hampshire 58
National Aeronautics and Space Administration (NASA) 194–195, 218
National anthem 44, 181
National Association for the Advancement of Colored People (NAACP) 118, 184, 185
National Guard **187**, 192, 193
National parks 108–109; map 108
Native Americans **94**, 140, **158**; athletes 173; and Europeans 11, 17, 18; government policies 11, 97, 118, 158–159, 159; Lewis and Clark Expedition 50–53; map of cultures 19; map of reservations 159; and missionaries 22–23; photographs 95; pre-European settlement 11, 12–13, 18; reservations 11, 97, 158–159; Trail of Tears 62–63; treaties 27, 62; and westward expansion 45, 71, 75, 78; written languages 44
Natural disasters 204–205
Nebraska 38, 69, 86, **101**
Nesterov, Petr 122
New Deal 156–157, 162
New Hampshire 30, 37
New Mexico 10, 12, 61, 65
New Orleans, Louisiana 11, 29, **42–43**, 45, 48, 57
New York, New York **123**, **155**; diseases 45; factories **112**, 118; immigrants 148, **148**, 149; labor strikes **105**; newspapers 47; skyscrapers 153; slums 104; terrorist attack 214–215, **215**; trains 99, 118; utilities 111, **111**, 143
New York Stock Exchange 27, 154
Newell, Frederick H. 164
Newfoundland, Canada 14, 17
Newspapers 45, 79, 85, 90, 91, 110
Nez Percé Indians 53, 158
Nixon, Richard M. 179, 186, **207**; relations with China 200; resignation 207; space program 218; Vietnam War 190, 191, 192, 193; Watergate 206
North, Oliver Laurence 206, **206**, 207
North, Simeon 58
North America: maps 8–9, 20
North Atlantic Treaty Organization (NATO) 200, 208
North Carolina 30, 120
Northwest Coast Indians 12, 18
Nuclear weapons 169, 170–171, 183, 200, 201
Ochs, Adolph 47
Ode, Robert C. 203
Ohio 27, 91, 100, 112
Ohio River 54–55
Oil 92–93; fires **209**; map 92
Oklahoma City, Oklahoma: bombing 177, 214
Olds, Ransom Eli 129, 130
O'Leary, Kate 146
Oliver, Aaron 46
Olympic Games 172–173
Operation Desert Shield 208
Operation Desert Storm 208–209, 216
Operation Iraqi Freedom 216–217, **217**; map 216
Oppenheimer, Robert 170, 171
Oregon 23, 61, 65, 70
Oregon Trail 61; map 60
O'Sullivan, John 61, 65, 70
O'Sullivan, Timothy 95
Oswald, Lee Harvey 189
Ott, John 142
Owens, Jesse **172**, 172–173
Owens Valley, California 164
Packwood, Bob 206
Page, Larry 211, **211**
Paige, Satchel 172
Paine, Thomas 35, 72
Painter, Nell Irvin 139
Paleo-Indians 12–13
Panama Canal 118, 153, 176; map 152–153
Parker, Dorothy 144
Parks, Rosa 186, 187
Paul, Alice 138
Pearl Harbor, Hawaii 167, 169; Japanese chart 168; Japanese preparing to attack **168**
Pearson, Benjamin 80
Penn, William 30
Pennsylvania 23, 26, 27, 30, 91, 93, 128, 215
Pentagon, Arlington, Virginia: terrorist attack **214**, 215
Pershing, John J. "Black Jack" 133, 136
Petroleum *see* Oil
Philadelphia, Pennsylvania: Centennial Exposition 78, 104, 110; Continental Congress 26, 36; immigrants 148, 149; newspapers 46, 47
Phonograph 142–143
Photography 94–95
Pickford, Mary 145
Pierpoint, Robert 189
Pilgrims 30
Pittsburgh, Pennsylvania 102, 104, 149
Plantations 40; map 55
Pletcher, David M. 71
Plymouth, Massachusetts 10, 11, 21, 30
Political parties 38–39, 138
Polk, James K. 65, 74
Ponce de León, Juan 10, 17, 20
Pony Express **84**, 84–85; map 84–85
Postal service *see* Mail service
Powell, Colin 209, 217
Presidents: elections 38–39, 65, 86, 89, 95, 97, 179, 186, 188, 206, 212–213; number from Virginia 31
Presley, Elvis 177, 179
Prohibition 118, 119, **140**, 140–141; map 141
Protestants 23, 73
Public Works Administration (PWA) 156, **156**; map 157
Pulitzer, Joseph 47
Puritans 11, 23, 72
Quakers 11, 23, 90
Quiroga, Miguel Angel González 71
Radio 150–151, 166, 180–181, 196
Railroads 44, 79, 85, 86, **98**, 98–99, 104; map 99
Raleigh, Sir Walter 20, 21
Ranches 100–101, **101**; map 100
Randolph, A. Philip 105
Rankin, Jeannette 138
Rankin, John 81
Ray, James Earl 188
Reagan, Ronald 177, 189, **201**, 203, 206–207
Reconstruction 78, 96–97, 184; map 97
Reisner, Marc 165
Religions 11, 22–23, 72–73, 90, 147, 159; map 72
Republican Party 38, 91, 96, 184, 206
Reuther, Walter 131
Revere, Paul 34, 35
Revolutionary War 26, 27, **32**, 32–35, 36; British surrender **24–25**; maps 33, 37
Rhee, Syngman 182
Rhode Island 23, 27, 31, 35, 58
Rhodes, James 192
Rhodes, Theodore 172
Rice, Donna 206
Rice, Thomas D. 184
Richmond, Virginia 88; tobacco factory **41**
Rickey, Branch 172
Ride, Sally 197, 218
Riis, Jacob 95
Riots 104, 166, 187
Roads 126, 128, **128**; map 127
Roanoke Island, Virginia 21; Secotan Indian village **18**
Robinson, Harriet 58
Robinson, Jackie 172, 173, **173**
Rockefeller, John D. 92–93; cartoon **102**
Rockefeller family 154
Rockwell, Norman 118, 168
Roebling, Emily 152
Roebling, John 152
Roebling, Washington 152
Rolfe, John 21, 28
Roosevelt, Eleanor 138
Roosevelt, Franklin Delano 105, 122, 156, 159, 162, 171; fireside chats 150–151; Tennessee Valley Authority Act 115; World War II 166
Roosevelt, Theodore **7**, 109, **109**, 118, 124, 138, 153
Rubin, Jerry 193
Ruby, Jack 189
Rusk, Dean 182
Ruth, Babe 173, 176, 181
Sacagawea 50–51, 53
San Antonio, Texas 64, 66–67
San Francisco, California: bridges 152; earthquakes 118, 177; gold rush 75; immigrants 148, 149
*San Francisco Examiner:* editorial 47
San Jacinto, Battle of **64**, 65, 67
Santa Anna, Antonio Lopez de **64**, 64–65, 66, 67
Santa Fe Trail 61; map 60
Santo Domingo, Dominican Republic, West Indies 10, 48–49
Scandals 118, 206–207
Schneiderman, Rose 105
Schools 27, 45, 82–83, **83**, 118, 185–187, **187**
Schroeder, William **199**
Schubert, Franz 61
Schwarzkopf, Norman 208
Schwitzgebel, John 154
Scott, Winfield 65, 88
Scovell, Bessie Laythe 140
Seaman (dog) 50, 51
Sears, Roebuck & Co.: catalog 113, **113**
Secotan Indians: village **18**
Seeger, Alan 134
Segregation 79, 83, 172–173, 184–185
Sennett, Mack 144
Sequoyah, Chief (Cherokee) 44, 62
Sewing machines 112
Shah of Iran 202–203
Shakers: village **73**
Sheep raising 101
Shepard, Alan 194, 196
Sherman, William Tecumseh 69, 78, 86, 88, 89, 97
Sidey, Hugh 189
Simms, Willie 172
Sinclair, Upton 124, 125
Singer, Isaac 112, 130
Sioux Indians 51, 158
Sirhan, Sirhan 188
Skyscrapers 152–153
Slater, Samuel 58
Slavery 27, 28–29, 65, 78, 86, 88; abolition 26, 47, 78, 80–81, 90–91; of Indians 17; Kansas-Nebraska Bill 38; map 29, 90; population 41; Underground Railroad 80–81
Slaves: ban on importation 44; freedom 96; introduction into New World 10; rebellions 28, 45; religion 23, 73; resettlement in Liberia 44; scarred back **28**
Sloan, Alfred 126–127
Smith, Joseph 73
Smith, Oliver 182
Social Security 156
South Carolina 12, 28, 31, 35, 86, 98
South (region) 97; African American women **96**; Reconstruction 78, 96–97, 184; Reconstruction map 184; religion 72–73
Soviet Union 157, 200
Space exploration 176, 179, 194–197, 218–219
Space shuttles 218
Spain: colonies 10, 20; exploration 17, 64; horses 18; land claims 48; missionaries 10, 22; policies toward Indians 11, 17
Spiller, Bill 172
Spindletop, Texas 92, 93, **93**
Sports 172, 173, 176, 177, 180–181; integration 172–173
St. Helens, Mount, Washington: eruption 204, **205**
St. John de Crèvecour, J. Hector 35, 79
St. Louis, Missouri 47, 55, 57, 99
Stalin, Joseph 157, 169, 182
Stamp Act 46
"The Star-Spangled Banner" 44, 181
Starr, Henry 106
Starr, Kenneth 177, 207
Statue of Liberty, New York, New York 149
Steamboats 44, 54–57
Steel industry 102–103
Steffens, Lincoln 125
Steiger, Rod 179
Steinbeck, John 126, 156
Steptoe, Patrick 198
Stevens,Thaddeus 89, 96
Stock market 27, 118, 154–155, 210–211
Stowe, Harriet Beecher 78, 80, 81
Strauss, Levi 75
Studebaker, John 75
Submarines 32
Suffrage 138–139, 139, **139**
Sullivan, Ed 179
Sung, Kim Il 182
Sutter, John 74
Taliban 215
Tallyrand-Périgord, Charles Maurice 49
Tarbell, Ida 125
Taxes 26, 27, 32, 169, 186
Telegraphs 45, 84, 85, 110
Telephones 85, 110–111
Television **178**, 178–179, **179**, 181
Tennessee 40, 62, 65, 97
Tennessee Valley Authority 115, 156
Terrorism **214**, 214–215, **215**
Texas 45, 70, 93, 100; map of Revolution 65; Revolution 64–67
Textile industry 41, 58–59
Thatcher, Margaret 208
Thorpe, Jim 173
Tobacco 10, 21, 40, 177; factory **41**
Tombstone, Arizona 79, 106, 107
Torrio, John 141
Toscanini, Arturo 151
Toussaint-L'Ouverture 48
Toynbee, Arnold 177
Trail of Tears **62**, 62–63; map 63
Travis, William Barret 66
Trenton, New Jersey 26, 35
Triangle Shirtwaist Company: fire 118, 148
Trippe, Juan 122
Troup, Robert William, Jr. 126
Truman, Edna 204
Truman, Harry 204
Truman, Harry S. 162, 171, 178, 182, 183, 200
Truth, Sojourner 91, **91**
Tubman, Harriet 80, **80**
Twain, Mark 55, 57, 61, 74, 75, 79, 205
*Uncle Tom's Cabin* (Stowe) 78, 80, 81, 185
Underground Railroad 80–81; map 81
Underwater exploration 218, **219**
Union Pacific Railroad 98–99
United Nations 182, 208, 216–217
United States: digital mosaic image **174–175**; flag 26; national debt 45; nighttime photo **143**
U.S. Air Force 187, 194
U.S. Army 58, 118
U.S. Army Corps of Engineers 205
U.S. Constitution: 13th Amendment 78; 14th Amendment 97, 184, 187; 15th Amendment 78, 97, 184; 18th Amendment 141; 19th Amendment 118, 139; 21st Amendment 141; 24th Amendment 186; interpretation by Supreme Court 44
U.S. Department of Homeland Security 177, 215
U.S. Mail service *see* Mail service
U.S. Marine Corps 119, 177, **217**
U.S. Military Academy, West Point, New York 133
U.S. Navy 150, 152, 169
U.S. Postal Service *see* Mail service
U.S. Steel Corporation 154; map of properties 103
U.S. Supreme Court 62; *Brown* v. *Board of Education, Topeka, Kansas* 185, 187; Dred Scott case 78, 86; first woman Justice 176; interpretation of Consitution 44; *Marbury* v. *Madison* 44; Miranda Case 176; *Plessy* v. *Ferguson* 83, 184–185, 187; *Shelley* v. *Kramer* 185; *Smith* v. *Allwright* 185
Utah 23, 139, 148
Vail, Alfred 110
Valentino, Rudolph 145
Van Buren, Martin 65
Van Doren, Charles 179
Vance, Cyrus 203
Vecchio, Mary Ann **193**
Vespucci, Amerigo 10, 16
Vietnam War 176, 179, 186, **190**, 190–193, 201, 209; maps 191; protests **192**, 192–193
Vikings 10, 13, 14–15, **15**; map of voyages 14
Villa, Francisco "Pancho" **132**, 132–133; map of raids 133
Virginia 10; Civil War 88, 89; French and Indian War 34; interstate highways 129; land claims 45; origin of name 21; public schools 82; public whippings 11; Revolutionary War 35; settlement 30, 31; slavery 28, 29, 45
Volta, Alessandro 110
von Braun, Wernher 196, 197
Voting rights: African Americans 184, 185, 186; map 138; women 118, 138–139
Wallace, Harry 162
Warsaw Pact 200
Washington, Booker T. 184
Washington, D.C.: burning of buildings by British 44; civil rights marches 177, **186**, 187; interstate highways 129; land 27; map, 1792 39; Vietnam War protests **192**, 192–193
Washington, George 26, 27, **32**, 34, 35, 38
Water rights 164–165
Watergate 176, 206
Watts area, Los Angeles, California 187
Webner, Frank E. **84**
Webster, Daniel 38
Welch, Joseph 178
Weld, Angelina 90
Weld, Theodore Dwight 90
Welles, Orson 150
Wells, Henry 75
Wertham, Frederic 161
West (region), U.S. 78, 106–107, 115, 145
Westward expansion **2–3**, 48–49, 60–61, **61**, 68–69; maps 52, 60
Wheeler-Nicholson, Malcolm 160–161
Whig party 38
White, Ed 195
Whitewater 177, 207
Whitman, Marcus 61
Whitman, Walt 11, 71, 78
Whitney, Eli 40–41, 58
Whitney, Richard 154
Wilcox, Horace 144
Williams, Roger 23
Williams, Ted 181
Wilson, Edith 137
Wilson, Woodrow 109, 118, 125, 132–133; Fourteen Points 136, 137; voting rights for women 138; World War I 135–136, 137
Women: astronauts 197; factory workers **112**; organized labor 105; rights 45, 139; telephone operators 111; voting rights 118, 138–139; voting rights demonstration **139**; wages 104, 105; World War II workforce 168, 169
Woodland Indians 12, 13
Works Progress Administration (WPA) 156, 157
World Trade Center, New York, New York: terrorist attack 214–215, **215**
World War I **134–137**; African Americans 184; airplanes 122, 136; baseball games 181; maps 134, 136; Treaty of Versailles 118; veterans 119; women's roles 139
World War II 119, 128, 166–171, **167**, 200; bombing raids 122; comic books 161; criticism 121–122; immigration to U.S. 149; map of European Theater 166; map of Pacific Theater 169; radio broadcasts 150, **150**; soldiers **116–117**, 181; war with Japan 178
World Wide Web 210–211
Wright, Frank Lloyd 153
Wright, Wilkinson 121
Wright Brothers 120–121, **121**, 122
Yeager, Chuck 194, 195
Yellowstone National Park, U.S. 108
Yorktown, Virginia 35; British surrender **24–25**; map 34
Young, Brigham 23, 73, 78
Zapata, Emiliano **132**
Zhou Enlai 200


# ILLUSTRATIONS

2-3, Hulton Archive/Getty Images; 4,Hulton Archive/Getty Images; 7, Hulton Archive/ Getty Images; 8-9, Bettmann/CORBIS; 13, George H.H. Huey/CORBIS; 15, Bibliotheque Nationale (Paris); 16, Archivo Iconographica S.A./CORBIS; 17, CORBIS; 18, The British Museum; 20, Victor R. Boswell, Jr.; 22, The British Library; 24-5, Hulton Archive/Getty Images; 28, CORBIS; 30, The Library Company of Philadelphia; 32, Yale University Art Gallery; 34, unique per image, courtesy Clements Library, University of Michigan; 36, courtesy The Library of Congress; 37, CORBIS; 39, courtesy The Library of Congress; 40, CORBIS; 41, Memphis and Shelby County Room, Memphis/Shelby County Public Library and Information Center; 42-3, courtesy The Library of Congress; 46, Chicago Architectural Photographing Company; 48, Hulton Archive/Getty Images; 50-1, courtesy The Library of Congress; 53 (UP), American Philosophical Society; 53 (LO), Ewell Sale Stewart Library, The Academy of Natural Sciences of Philadelphia; 54, CORBIS; 55, The Historic New Orleans Collection; 59, George Eastman House; 61, Association of American Railroads; 62, Woolaroc Museum, Bartlesville Oklahoma; 64, Texas State Capitol; 66, Eugene C. Barker Texas History Center (Austin); 67, National Archives; 68, Western History Collections, University of Oklahoma Libraries; 71, CORBIS; 73, CORBIS; 75, California State Library; 76-7, courtesy The Library of Congress; 80, Hulton Archive/Getty Images; 83, Western Reserve Historical Society, Cleveland; 84, CORBIS; 86, Bettmann/CORBIS; 88, Hulton Archive/Getty Images; 89, courtesy The Library of Congress; 91, THE GRANGER COLLECTION, New York; 93, American Petroleum Institute; 94, Edward S. Curtis; 95, courtesy The Library of Congress; 96, Collection of The New-York Historical Society, Neg. #; 98, Special Collections Division University of Washington Libraries, Neg. ; 101, Hulton Archive/Getty Images; 102, courtesy The Library of Congress; 103, courtesy The Library of Congress; 105, Brown Brothers; 107, Bettmann/CORBIS; 109, Hulton Archive/Getty Images; 110, Hulton Archive/ Getty Images; 111, courtesy The Library of Congress; 112, THE GRANGER COLLECTION, New York; 113, Chicago Historical Society; 115, Brown Brothers; 116-7, CORBIS; 121, Hulton Archive/Getty Images; 122, THE GRANGER COLLECTION, New York; 123, Bettmann/CORBIS; 124, CORBIS; 126, Chicago Architectural Photographing Company; 128, Hulton Archive/Getty Images; 129, Smithsonian Institution; 130, US Patent Office; 132, Hulton Archive/Getty Images; 134, Packard Motor Co.; 135, courtesy National Archives; 137 (LO), courtesy The Library of Congress; 137 (UP), CORBIS; 139, THE GRANGER COLLECTION, New York; 140, Hulton Archive/ Getty Images; 142, NOAA/NGDC, DMSP Digital Archive; 143, Science & Society Picture Library; 144, Hulton Archive/Getty Images; 145, Hulton Archive/Getty Images; 147, Museum of the City of New York; 148, Museum of the City of New York; 150, Hulton Archive/Getty Images; 151, Hulton Archive/ Getty Images; 152-3, courtesy The Library of Congress; 153, Library of Congress; 154, Hulton Archive/ Getty Images; 155, Hulton Archive/Getty Images; 156, Bettmann/CORBIS; 157, Joseph H. Bailey; 158 (UP), Hulton Archive/Getty Images; 158 (LO), Bettmann/ CORBIS; 160, Ted Streshinsky/ CORBIS; 161, Swim Ink/CORBIS; 162, Wisconsin Historical Society; 164, National Geographic Image Collection; 167, Hulton Deutsch/CORBIS; 168 (UP), M. Nakamura; 168 (LO), courtesy National Archives; 171, Bettmann/ CORBIS; 172, Hulton Archive/Getty Images; 173, Bettmann/CORBIS; 174-5, M-SAT, at Eurimage, Space Imaging-Landsat; 178, Hulton Archive/Getty Images; 179, Hulton Archive/Getty Images; 180, Bettmann/CORBIS; 181, Bettmann/CORBIS; 182, Marine Corps Historical Center; 183, Hulton Archive/Getty Images; 185, Bettmann/CORBIS; 186, Bettmann/CORBIS; 187, CORBIS; 188, CORBIS; 189, Bettmann/CORBIS; 190, Tim Page/CORBIS; 191, Stone LesCORBIS SYGMA; 192, Leif Skoogfors/CORBIS; 193, Hulton Archive/ Getty Images; 194, Hulton Archive/Getty Images; 195, Hulton Archive/ Getty Images; 196, BETTMANN/ CORBIS; 197, BETTMANN/CORBIS; 198, TIME LIFE PICTURES/ GETTY IMAGES; 199, BLACK STAR; 200, CORBIS; 201, Larry Downing/ Woodfin Camp & Associates; 202, Bettmann/ CORBIS; 205, Roger Werth/Woodfin Camp & Associates; 206, CORBIS; 207, Bettmann/ CORBIS; 209, Steve MCCurry; 210, Getty Images; 211, Kim Kulish/CORBIS; 212, Reuters/CORBIS; 214, Time Life Pictures/ Getty Images; 215, Reuters/CORBIS; 217, CORBIS; 218, NG Maps; 219, Flip Nicklin

# NATIONAL GEOGRAPHIC
## HISTORICAL
## ATLAS *of the*
## UNITED STATES

### PUBLISHED BY THE
### NATIONAL GEOGRAPHIC SOCIETY

| | |
|---|---|
| John M. Fahey, Jr. | *President and Chief Executive Officer* |
| Gilbert M. Grosvenor | *Chairman of the Board* |
| Nina D. Hoffman | *Executive Vice President* |

### PREPARED BY THE BOOK DIVISION

| | |
|---|---|
| Kevin Mulroy | *Vice President and Editor-in-Chief* |
| Charles Kogod | *Illustrations Director* |
| Marianne R. Koszorus | *Design Director* |
| Barbara Brownell Grogan | *Executive Editor* |

### STAFF FOR THIS ATLAS

| | |
|---|---|
| Johnna Rizzo | *Project Editor* |
| Melissa Farris | *Art Director* |
| Marilyn Moffort Gibbons | *Illustrations Editor* |
| Carl Mehler | *Director of Maps* |
| Matt Chwastyk | *Map Production Manager* |
| Nicholas P. Rosenbach, *Principal* | *Map Editors* |
| Tim Carter, Sven M. Dolling, | |
| Maureen Flynn, Victoria Garrett-Jones, | |
| Joseph F. Ochlak | |
| Jerome Cookson, | *Map Research and Production* |
| M. Brody Dittemore, | |
| Nathaniel Vaughn Kelso, | |
| Gregory Ugiansky, Martin S. Walz, | |
| National Geographic Maps, | |
| and XNR Productions | |
| Julian Smith, Laura Fravel, | *Researchers* |
| Dan O'Toole | |
| Rick Wain | *Production Project Manager* |
| John Paine | *Contributing Editor* |
| Sharon Kocsis Berry | *Illustrations Assistant* |
| Cameron Zotter | *Production Assistant* |
| Connie Binder | *Indexer* |

### MANUFACTURING AND QUALITY CONTROL

| | |
|---|---|
| Christopher A. Liedel | *Chief Financial Officer* |
| Phillip L. Schlosser | *Managing Director* |
| John T. Dunn | *Technical Director* |
| Clifton M. Brown | *Manager* |

Color separations by NEC, Nashville, TN.

Printed and bound by Mondadori Printing, Verona, Italy.

One of the world's largest nonprofit scientific and educational organizations, the National Geographic Society was founded in 1888 "for the increase and diffusion of geographic knowledge." Fulfilling this mission, the Society educates and inspires millions every day through its magazines, books, television programs, videos, maps and atlases, research grants, the National Geographic Bee, teacher workshops, and innovative classroom materials. The Society is supported through membership dues, charitable gifts, and income from the sale of its educational products. This support is vital to National Geographic's mission to increase global understanding and promote conservation of our planet through exploration, research, and education.

For more information, please call 1-800-NGS LINE (647-5463) or write to the following address:

National Geographic Society
1145 17th Street N.W.
Washington, D.C. 20036-4688 U.S.A.

Visit the Society's Web site at
www.nationalgeographic.com.

Library of Congress Cataloging-in-Publication Data

Fisher, Ronald M.
  National Geographic historical atlas of the United States / adapted by Ron Fisher.
   p. cm.
  Includes index.
  Contents: 1400 through 1750. New people in a new world 1750 through 1799. Forming a more perfect union -- 1800 through 1849. A nation comes of age -- 1850 through 1899. A nation at war -- 1900 through 1949. Decades of change -- 1950 through present.
   ISBN 0-7922-6131-3
   1. United States--Historical geography--Maps. I. Title: Historical atlas of the United States. II. National Geographic Society (U.S.) III. Title.

G1201.S1F5 2004
911'.73--dc22

                                    2004050421

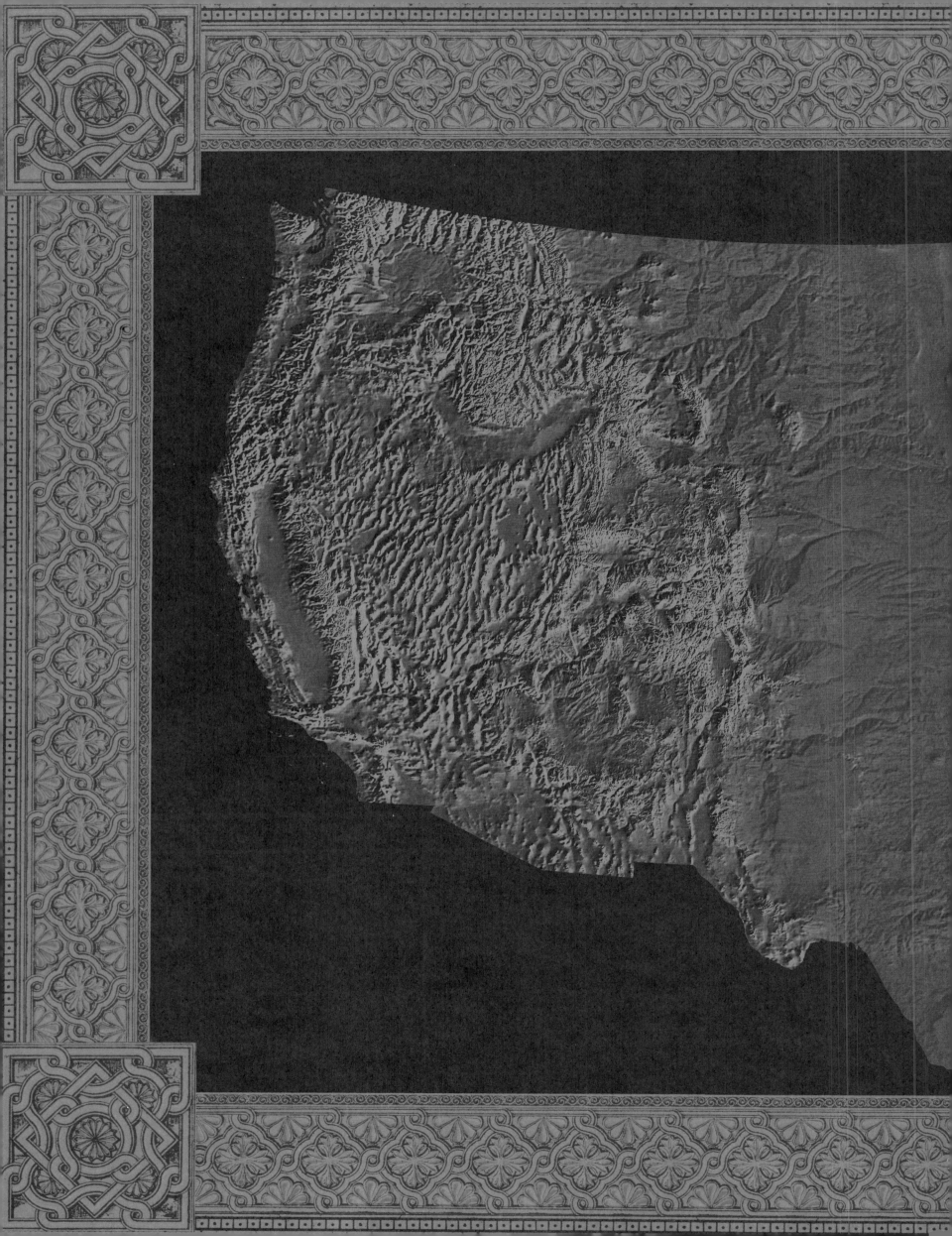